Memory and New Ways of Knowing

STUDIES IN KNOWLEDGE PRODUCTION AND PARTICIPATION

Series Editors: **Mary Jane Curry,** *University of Rochester, USA* and **Theresa Lillis,** *The Open University, UK*

Full details of all the books in this series and of all our other publications can be found on http://www.multilingual-matters.com, or by writing to Multilingual Matters, St Nicholas House, 31–34 High Street, Bristol, BS1 2AW, UK.

All books in this series are externally peer-reviewed.

Other books in the series

Global Academic Publishing – Policies, Perspectives and Pedagogies
Mary Jane Curry and Theresa Lillis (eds)
Grassroots Literacy and the Written Record – A Textual History of Asbestos Activism in South Africa
John Trimbur
Decoloniality, Language and Literacy – Conversations with Teacher Educators
Carolyn McKinney and Pam Christie (eds)
Digital Genres in Academic Knowledge Production and Communication – Perspectives and Practices
María José Luzón and Carmen Pérez-Llantada
From Southern Theory to Decolonizing Sociolinguistics – Voices, Questions, Alternatives
Ana Deumert and Sinfree Makoni (eds)
Knowledge-Making from a Postgraduate Writers' Circle: A Southern Reflectory
Lucia Thesen

Front cover image: Permission given by Diosa Caren García who created the textile and by Isabel Arango who produced the digital image.

STUDIES IN KNOWLEDGE PRODUCTION AND PARTICIPATION: 7

Memory and New Ways of Knowing

Narratives of the Armed Conflict in Colombia

Edited by
Blanca Yaneth González Pinzón and Theresa Lillis

MULTILINGUAL MATTERS
Bristol • Jackson

DOI https://doi.org/10.21832/GONZAL6307
Library of Congress Cataloging in Publication Data
A catalog record for this book is available from the Library of Congress.
Names: González Pinzón, Blanca Yaneth, editor. | Lillis, Theresa M., editor.
Title: Memory and New Ways of Knowing: Narratives of the Armed Conflict in Colombia/
    Edited by Blanca Yaneth González Pinzón and Theresa Lillis.
Description: Bristol, UK; Jackson, TN: Multilingual Matters, 2025. | Series: Studies in
    Knowledge Production and Participation: 7 | Includes bibliographical references and index.
    | Summary: "This book is an interdisciplinary project centering on the testimonios of
    survivors in order to understand experiences of violence arising from the armed conflict in
    Colombia. The concepts of Testimony, Narrative and Memory are mobilized across the
    chapters to explore how survivors reconstruct experiences and imagine new ways of
    knowing and being"—Provided by publisher.
Identifiers: LCCN 2024059436 (print) | LCCN 2024059437 (ebook) | ISBN 9781800416291
    (paperback) | ISBN 9781800416307 (hardback) | ISBN 9781800416314 (pdf) | ISBN
    9781800416321 (epub)
Subjects: LCSH: Political violence—Colombia—History—20th century. | Political violence—
    Colombia—History—21stcentury.|Collectivememory—Colombia.|Colombia—History—1974-
Classification: LCC HN310.Z9 V545 2025 (print) | LCC HN310.Z9 (ebook) | DDC
    303.609861—dc23/eng/20250202
LC record available at https://lccn.loc.gov/2024059436
LC ebook record available at https://lccn.loc.gov/2024059437

British Library Cataloguing in Publication Data
A catalogue entry for this book is available from the British Library.

ISBN-13: 978-1-80041-630-7 (hbk)
ISBN-13: 978-1-80041-629-1 (pbk)
ISBN-13: 978-1-80014-631-4 (pdf)
ISBN-13: 978-1-80041-632-1 (epub)

Open Access

Except where otherwise noted, this work is licensed under the Creative Commons Attribution-NoDerivatives 4.0 International License. To view a copy of this license, visit http://creativecommons.org/licenses/by-nd/4.0/ or send a letter to Creative Commons, PO Box 1866, Mountain View, CA 94042, USA.

Multilingual Matters
UK: St Nicholas House, 31–34 High Street, Bristol, BS1 2AW, UK.
USA: Ingram, Jackson, TN, USA.
Authorised Representative: Easy Access System Europe – Mustamäe tee 50, 10621 Tallinn, Estonia, gpsr.requests@easproject.com.

Website: https://www.multilingual-matters.com
Bluesky: https://bsky.app/profile/multi-ling-mat.bsky.social
X: Multi_Ling_Mat
Facebook: https://www.facebook.com/multilingualmatters
Blog: https://www.channelviewpublications.wordpress.com

Copyright © 2025 Blanca Yaneth González Pinzón, Theresa Lillis and the authors of individual chapters.

All rights reserved. No part of this work may be reproduced in any form or by any means without permission in writing from the publisher.

The policy of Multilingual Matters/Channel View Publications is to use papers that are natural, renewable and recyclable products, made from wood grown in sustainable forests. In the manufacturing process of our books, and to further support our policy, preference is given to printers that have FSC and PEFC Chain of Custody certification. The FSC and/or PEFC logos will appear on those books where full certification has been granted to the printer concerned.

Typeset by Techset Composition India(P) Ltd, Bangalore and Chennai, India.

Contents

Map	vii
Contributors	ix
Acknowledgements	xiii
About the Production of this Book	xv
Acronyms	xvii
Introduction	xxi

Part 1: Historical Context of the Colombian Armed Conflict and Theoretical Approaches to Analysing its Narratives

1 Colombia, Eight Decades in Search of Peace and Democracy   3
   Luis Eduardo Celis

2 Theoretical Approaches to Analysing Conflict Narratives   15
   Blanca Yaneth González Pinzón and Claudia Bungard

Part 2: Narratives of the Colombian Armed Conflict

3 Narrative as an Emotional Resource for the Empowerment of the Survivors of the Colombian Armed Conflict   43
   Blanca Yaneth González Pinzón

4 'Walking the Word' with the Nasa People: A Perspective from the Narrative of *The Strength of the Umbilical Cord* (*La Fuerza del Ombligo*)   80
   José Navia Lame

5 Narratives to Transform War Imaginaries in Colombia: An Animation Workshop with Ex-Guerrilla Children   108
   Cecilia Traslaviña González

6 *Testimonios* of Armed Conflict Survivors: Participants in Narrative Workshops in Medellín   134
   Claudia Bungard

7 The Memory of the Future: Voices of FARC-EP Reincorporated Combatants in the Construction of Peace Imaginaries   158
   Mario Ramírez-Orozco

| 8 | Weaving Memory and Unweaving Trauma: Textile Narratives on the Conflict in Colombia
Emilia Perassi | 179 |

Part 3: Reflections

9	Voicing Experiences of Conflict and Violence: Placed, Dis-placed and Re-placed Resources *Theresa Lillis*	207
10	*Chronos* and *Kairos*: A Time to Resist and a Time to Speak Out *José Vicente Arizmendi Correa*	214
11	Closing Thoughts *Blanca Yaneth González Pinzón*	222
	Index	228

Map

Typology of municipalities and departments affected by Colombia's armed conflict before the 2016 Peace Agreements (1986–2015). The gray scale represents the level of impact of the conflict; the darkest one indicates very high and the lighter one, very low.

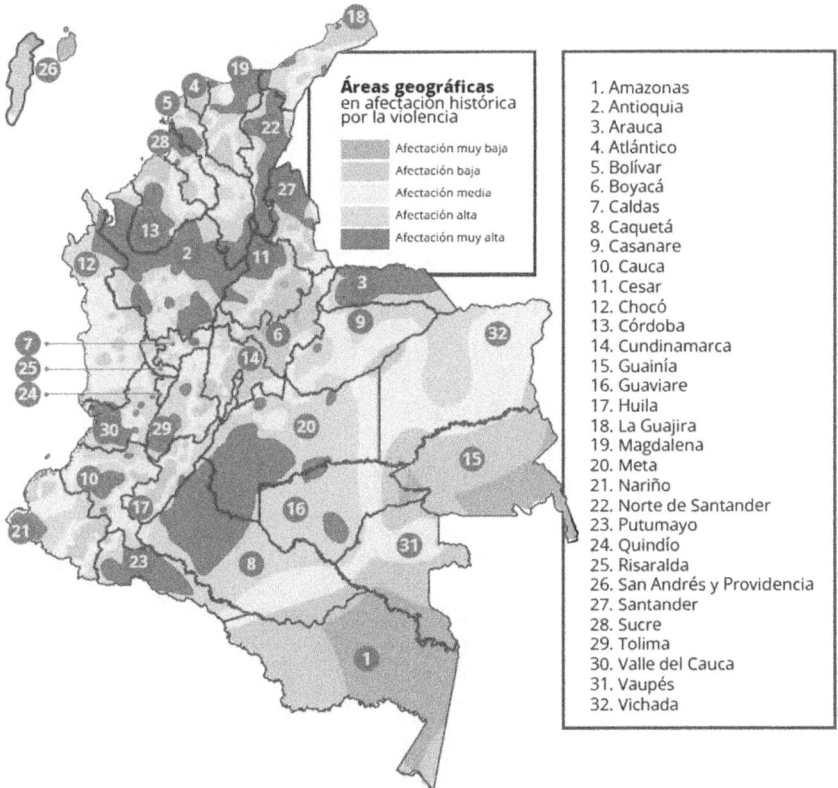

Source: Salas-Salazar, L.G. (2016) Conflicto armado y configuración territorial: Elementos para la consolidación de la paz en Colombia. [Armed conflict and territorial configuration: Elements for peacebuilding in Colombia]. *Bitácora Urbano Territorial* 26 (2), 45–57.

Contributors

José Vicente Arizmendi is a journalist from the Universidad de La Sabana. He has a master's degree in Business Administration with a dual degree from Temple University, USA, and Pontificia Universidad Javeriana, Colombia. He also has diplomas in Television Drama from the University of London, UK, and Journalism from the Universidad de Navarra, Spain. He has over 30 years of experience in audiovisual production and journalism in television, print media and radio. He has worked at the Pontificia Universidad Javeriana in Cali and Bogotá since 2002, where he has served as a program director, department director, academic dean and assistant professor. His main research interest is the history of media outlets in Colombia.

Claudia Bungard is a journalist, writer and editor with a master's degree in Latin American Studies from the University of Arizona. She has published three books under the pen name 'Claudia Arroyave': *Mientras Dios descansa* (Editorial Eafit, 2005, short stories), *El pueblo de las tres efes* (Hombre Nuevo Editores, 2008, reportage) and *La ruta del tren dormido* (Sílaba Editores, 2020, travel chronicle). She is the founder and main editor of *Diario de Paz Colombia* (www.diariodepaz.com), a non-profit organization focusing on the collective study of the country's history, peacebuilding and the promotion of reading and writing with different functions. Her academic interest revolves around producing testimonial narratives in the context of the Colombian armed conflict. Over the last few years, she has supported dozens of beginner and professional authors in coming up with, creating and editing literary projects. Claudia has lived in Arizona, USA, since 2012.

Luis Eduardo Celis studied Sociology at the Universidad Nacional de Colombia and has worked as an analyst of armed conflict, organized violence and the prospects for overcoming these. He is a researcher on peace and conflict issues at the Fundación Paz y Reconciliación and was an advisor to Redprodepaz. Luis Eduardo regularly writes for the newspaper *El Espectador* and the news portal *Lasillavacia*, two significant media outlets in Colombia. He has a weekly column on the Fundación Paz y Reconciliación website. In 2019, he wrote the book *Una paz sin dolientes*.

Diálogos y negociaciones con el ELN 1982–2019 (Cooperativa multiactiva de producciones y comunicaciones, 2019).

Cecilia Traslaviña González is an animator and visual artist with a master's degree in Literature. She has a teaching and research position in the Department of Visual Arts at the Pontificia Universidad Javeriana, Bogota. Her artwork has been selected in numerous national and international film festivals, and she has been a juror in the Annecy International Animation Film Festival, France; Animafest, Zagreb; Vienna Independent Short Film Festival; Etiuda&Anima, Krakow; CineAutopsia, Bogota Experimental Film Festival; and Animateka, Ljubljana. She has also collaborated with multiple artists and audiovisual schools to create collective productions. She has curated several academic programmes on Colombian and Latin American experimental animation for different institutions. Part of her work focuses on exploring memories and the unconscious from non-linear narratives, consistent with visual arts techniques. She is an active member of the Moebius Animación website (www.moebiusanimacion.com), which aims to amplify the voices of Latin American animation.

Blanca Yaneth González Pinzón has a degree in Philology and Languages with an emphasis on classical languages and a master's degree in Social and Educational Development. She directed the Writing Center at Pontificia Universidad Javeriana, Bogota, between 2011 and 2015 and has advised university reading and writing programmes in different universities in the country and abroad. Blanca has been developing national educational projects with the Colombian Association of Universities for 14 years. She has developed her research work in educational contexts to analyse, understand and solve problems in teaching and learning systems to improve teaching quality and to transform curricula. Her most recent co-authored publications are *Exploring Professional Writing in Colombian Cases: Lessons Across Boundaries* (The WAC Clearinghouse, 2021) and *De la educación superior a los entornos profesionales: Aprendizajes emergentes del estudio de las prácticas y pasantías* (Universidad Nacional de Colombia – Tecnológico de Monterrey, 2024).

José Navia Lame is a journalist specializing in urban journalism from the Universidad Pontificia Bolivariana. He was considered one of the 'Nuevos Cronistas de Indias' (New Chroniclers of the Indies) by the Foundation for New Ibero-American Journalism (FNPI). He has been a reporter and editor for the newspaper *El Tiempo* and a contributor to various national media outlets. Most of his work has been carried out in areas affected by the armed conflict, especially in indigenous territories located in Northern Cauca (number 10 on the map). His chronicles have received awards such as the King of Spain Prize, the Inter-American Press Association Prize and the Simón Bolívar Prize. He has been a professor of journalism at multiple universities. He is the author of the books: *El lado oscuro de las ciudades* (Intermedio editores, 2000), *Confesiones de un delincuente* (Intermedio editores, 2000), *Historias nuevas para la ropa vieja* (Editorial Universidad de Antioquia, 2001) and *La fuerza del ombligo, crónicas del conflicto en territorio nasa* (Editorial Universidad del Cauca, 2015).

Theresa Lillis is an Emeritus Professor of English Language and Applied Linguistics at the Open University, UK. She has researched writing for over 30 years, focusing on the politics of access, production and participation. Theresa has also taught at secondary school, adult (community education) and university levels. She has published widely in academic journals and has authored, co-authored and edited books and special journal volumes. Her key works include *Student Writing: Access, Regulation, Desire* (2001, Routledge); *Academic Writing in a Global Context*, with Mary Jane Curry (2010, Routledge); *The Sociolinguistics of Writing* (2013, Edinburgh); *The Politics of Language and Creativity in a Globalised World*, with David Hann (2016, The Open University); *Gender and Academic Writing*, with Jenny McMullan and Jackie Tuck (2018). Her publications in Spanish include articles in *Signo y Pensamiento, Enunciación* and *Cuadernos del Sur*. Her current research focuses on writing by social workers about which she has published in *Social Work Education* (2024), *Applied Linguistics Review* (2023), *Applied Corpus Linguistics* (2021), *Written Communication* (2020), *Journal of Applied Linguistics and Professional Practice* (2017), *Text and Talk* (2017).

Emilia Perassi holds a PhD in Latin American Literature from the University of Bologna. She is currently a Senior Lecturer in Latin American Literature at the University of Turin. She coordinates the 'Literature and Human Rights' project with 19 universities in Latin America and the USA. Her research interests focus on testimonial and post-testimonial narratives, migration literature and transatlantic relationships. She has co-edited *Letteratura testimoniale in América Latina* with Laura Scarabelli; the monographic issue *Poesía y violencia* of the journal *Tintas* with Sandra Lorenzano; and *Donde no habite el olvido. Herencia y trasmisión del testimonio en América Latina in Argentina* with Giuliana Calabrese. Among her publications dedicated to the narratives of trauma are: *Testimonio y genealogía: Marta Dillon, Julián López, Sebastián Hacher and Mariana Corral* (Alter/Nativas-Université Lyon2, 2018); *En el pecho encerrada una tormenta. Apropiaciones dantescas en la literatura latinoamericana contemporánea* (Letteratura & Letterature, 2019); *Teatro latinoamericano y testimonio. Una breve introducción* (Orillas, Rivista di Ispanistica, 2019); *Objetos-testigo. Fracturas y reconstrucciones del relato identitario* (Kamchatka, Revista de análisis cultural, 2020); and *Narrative latinoamericane del confine. Dalla traversata oceanica alla Frontera Norte* (Milano University Press, 2022).

Mario Ramírez-Orozco holds a BA and MA in Spanish and Latin American Studies from the University of Bergen, Norway, and a PhD in Latin American Studies from the Universidad Nacional Autónoma de México. He did a postdoctoral stay in Education at the Instituto de Educação, Universidade de Lisboa. He has been a lecturer and researcher in Norwegian institutions in the field of Latin American political, educational and cultural studies. He was Full Professor I (Doctor III) at Universidad de La Salle in the Education and Society doctorate. He was a visiting professor and tutor in doctoral programs in education and political science at universities in Latin America and Europe. His most recent publications include: *Comunicación y lenguajes de paz*; *Nonviolent Resistance in the Struggle for Housing in Urban Areas of Brazil: The Direct Action of the Roofless Workers Movement* (Palgrave Macmillan, 2019) and *Dos momentos de resistencia no violenta en Brasil: Acción de los movimientos sociales durante la dictadura militar y el golpe a Dilma Rousseff* (FLACSO Ecuador y Ediciones Universidad de La Salle, 2019).

Acknowledgements

The authors dedicate this work to:

- All the survivors of the Colombian armed conflict. Through these pages, we seek to honour their stories and their lives and to contribute to the Collective Memory, in the hope that the horrors they endured will never be repeated and that peace will always prevail. Their lives inspire us deeply.
- Each of our families in which there is either a survivor of a violent event or someone tragically affected.
- The Kiwe Tegnas, walkers of the word, thought and territory.
- The boys and girls of Benposta for their trust in the team of mediators in the animation production workshop.

We want to thank:

- Theresa Lillis, who believed in this project from the very first conversation we had in Santiago de Chile in 2018. This book would not have been possible without her trust, sensitivity and dedication.
- The book series editors Mary Jane Curry and Theresa Lillis for supporting the publication of this book with Multilingual Matters.
- Eloisa Lamilla Guerrero for her participation in the initial mapping of writing experiences for symbolic reparation in the country.
- Mathew Charles, who extended the invitation to participate in the project *Mi historia: La niñez que peleó la guerra en Colombia* [*My Story: The Children that Fought the War in Colombia*] and supported, with his knowledge and sensitivity, the writing and production of the animations of the boys and girls of Benposta.
- Tatiana Vaca, Diego Cortés, Carolina Lucio y Julián Arias, who accompanied Cecilia, Mathew and the boys and girls of Benposta in the production of animations.
- Patricia Nieto creator and director of *De su puño y letra* [*In their own handwriting*].
- Feminist movement La Ruta Pacifica de la Mujeres for facilitating the use of texts from *La verdad de las mujeres* [*The truth of women*].
- Alcaldía Mayor de Bogotá [Mayor of Bogotá] for facilitating the use and translation to English language of fragments from *Almas que escriben memorias y esperanza* [*Souls writing memories and hope*].

- Centro Nacional de Memoria Histórica [National Centre of Historical Memory] for accepting in its repository for public access, a Spanish-medium version of the book, for facilitating the use of fragments from ¡Basta ya! [*Enough already!*] report in English, and for facilitating the use and translation to English language of fragments from *Exilio Colombiano: Huellas del conflicto armado más allá de las fronteras* [*Colombian exile: Traces of the armed conflict beyond borders*].
- Medellín's Casa de la Memoria Museum for facilitating the use and translation to English language of fragments from *Narrativas del desplazamiento como construcción de identidad* [*Narratives of displacement for the construction of identity*] and *Escritura viva para la paz* [*Live writing for peace*].
- Luis Gabriel Salas Salazar for facilitating the use of the map *Typology of municipalities and departments affected by Colombia's armed conflict before the 2016 Peace Agreements (1986-2015)*.
- Review Dissolve for facilitating the image of *The Blanca Nieves Meneses quilt*.
- Vice-rector's Office for Research and Editorial Development of the Universidad del Cauca for facilitating the use of fragments from the book *La fuerza del Ombligo, crónicas del conflicto en territorio Nasa* [*The strength of the umbilical cord, chronicles of the conflict in the Nasa Territory*].
- Isabel González Arango from Archivo Digital de Textiles Testimoniales [Digital Archive of Testimonials Textiles] for facilitating the use of images and texts.
- Artesanal Tecnológica for facilitating the use of images and texts.
- Diosa Caren García, from Memoria Tejido and Salud Mental de Medellín [Sewing Workshop Fabric, Memory and Mental Health of Medellín] for authorizing the use of the cover image: *Recomenzar* [*Begin again*] tapestry.
- Simone Ferrari, an Italian researcher, who contributed to discussions with Emilia Perassi about the Colombian conflict.

About the Production of this Book

This book has been three years in the making underpinned by many years of lived experience of the conflict in Colombia.

Blanca was the originator of the idea for an edited collection aimed at a non-Colombian audience that would gather together interdisciplinary studies and experiences, highlighting the multiple forms of resistance by hundreds of survivors from different regions of the country. The goal was to contribute to their dignification, add to the historical memory of the country, and, above all, amplify our voices to defend against the repetition of tortuous events – a necessary condition for rebuilding a country that is slowly and arduously advancing towards peace.

Theresa worked with Blanca on the original proposal and on all drafts of the versions in Spanish and English, acting as a critical outsider-reader and commentator on all aspects of expression and content. A key challenge was to think through what kind of contextual, discoursal and disciplinary assumptions might be made by readers less familiar with the Colombian conflict and to work hard in the text at responding to, and at times challenging, taken-for-granted assumptions. No doubt some chapters will raise more questions than answers for some readers, but we hope all readers will be able to engage with people's lived narratives.

This book has been produced in Spanish and English and has involved many iterations in the process of moving between the two languages. Authors wrote their texts in Spanish which were revised following critical reading from Blanca and Theresa. Authors then worked with Blanca and a group of professional translators of the 'Polífona' team to develop an English-medium version which involved Mary Jane Curry as critical reader. This English-medium version was then revised and developed by Blanca and Theresa and further sharpened in response to comments by Mary Jane Curry and two (anonymous at the time of their reading) reviewers: Nora Solari from Argentina, an expert in Language, Literature and Latin, reading a Spanish medium version, and Bronwyn Williams, an expert in literacy studies and community writing at the University of Louisville, USA, reading an English medium version. Final versions in Spanish and English represent revisions made in both languages based on considerations of content and expression, as well as many discussions and decisions based on our assumptions about readers' understandings about the conflict in Colombia from different parts of the world and readers' expectations premised on specific disciplinary frameworks. The Spanish medium version of the book *Memoria y nuevas formas de saber: Narrativas del conflicto armado colombiano* is also published open access by the Centro Nacional de Memoria Histórica [National Centre of Historical Memory].

The value of this work rests on the fragments of *testimonios* from more than a hundred people, bringing us closer, from different places of understanding and representation, to a great narrative called Colombia. Survivors have *bled with words* following the poet Blas de Otero; and in this spirit, their direct testimonies are preserved in their original language as well as in translation in English.

Acronyms

ACIN	Asociación de Cabildos Indígenas del Norte del Cauca
	Association of Indigenous *Cabildos* of Northern Cauca
ACNUR	Oficina del Alto Comisionado de Naciones Unidas para los Refugiados
	Office of the United Nations High Commissioner for Refugees
ACR	Alta Consejería para la Reintegración Social y Económica de Personas y Grupos Alzados en Armas
	High Council for Social and Economic Reintegration of Armed Groups and Individuals
ADM-19	Alianza Democrática M-19
	M-19 Democratic Alliance
ADTTC	Archivo Digital de Textiles Testimoniales
	Digital Archive of Testimonial Textiles
AICMA	Acción Integral Contra Minas Antipersonal
	Integrated Action Against Antipersonnel Mines
AMARÚ	Asociación de Mujeres Defensoras del Agua y de la Vida
	Association of Women Defenders of Water and Life
ANAPO	Alianza Nacional Popular
	National Popular Alliance
ANUC	Asociación Nacional de Usuarios Campesinos
	National Association of Peasant Users
ARN	Agencia Gubernamental para la Reincorporación y la Normalización
	Governmental Agency for Reincorporation and Normalisation
ASVIMARIN	Asociación de Mujeres Víctimas, Artesanas e Innovadoras de Hoy para el Mañana
	Association of Women Victims, Craftswomen and Innovators of Today for Tomorrow
AUC	Autodefensas Unidas de Colombia
	United Self-Defence Forces of Colombia
CEDHUL	Centro de Derechos Humanos y Litigio Internacional
	Center for Human Rights and International Litigation
CERLALC	Centro Regional para el Fomento del Libro en América Latina y el Caribe
	Regional Center for the Promotion of Books in Latin America and Caribbean
CEV	Comisión para el Esclarecimiento de la Verdad, la Convivencia y la No repetición
	Commission for the Clarification of Truth, Coexistence and Non-Repetition

CIDH	Comisión Interamericana de Derechos Humanos
	Inter-American Commission on Human Rights
CILESG	Congreso Internacional de Lectura y Escritura en la Sociedad Global
	International Congress on Reading and Writing in the Global Society
CIRC	Comité Internacional de la Cruz Roja
	International Committee of the Red Cross
CMPR	Centro de Memoria Paz y Reconciliación
	Centre of Memory, Peace and Reconciliation
CNMH	Centro Nacional de Memoria Histórica
	National Centre of Historical Memory
CNTI	Comisión Nacional de Territorios Indígenas
	National Commission of Indigenous Territories
CONADEP	Comisión Nacional Sobre la Desaparición de Personas (Argentina)
	National Commission for the Disappearance of Persons (Argentina)
CRIC	Consejo Regional Indígena del Cauca
	Regional Indigenous Council of Cauca
DAICMA	Dirección para la Acción Integral Contra Minas Antipersonal
	Directorate for Integral Action against Antipersonnel Mines
DIH	Derecho Internacional Humanitario
	International Humanitarian Law
ELN	Ejército de Liberación Nacional
	National Liberation Army
EPL	Ejército Popular de Liberación
	People's Liberation Army
ESAP	Escuela Superior de Administración Pública
	Graduate School of Public Administration
ESMAD	Escuadrón Móvil Antidisturbios
	Mobile Anti-Disturbances Squadron
ETCR	Espacio Territorial de Capacitación y Reincorporación
	Territorial Space for Training and Reincorporation
FARC-EP	Fuerzas Armadas Revolucionarias de Colombia – Ejército del Pueblo
	Revolutionary Armed Forces of Colombia – People's Army
FEDES	Federación Colombiana de Deporte Especial
	Colombian Federation of Special Sports
FESCOL	Fundación Friedrich-Ebert-Stiftung en Colombia
	Friedrich-Ebert-Stiftung Foundation in Colombia
FIV	Foro Internacional de Víctimas
	International Victims Forum
FNPI	Fundación para el Nuevo Periodismo Iberoamericano
	Foundation for the New Ibero-American Journalism

GMH	Grupo de Memoria Histórica
	Historical Memory Group
ICANH	Instituto Colombiano de Antropología e Historia
	Colombian Institute of Anthropology and History
INDEPAZ	Instituto de Estudios para el Desarrollo y la Paz
	Institute of Studies for Development and Peace
JEP	Jurisdicción Especial para la Paz
	Special Jurisdiction for Peace
LGBTIQ+	Lesbiana, Gay, Bisexual, Trans, Intersexual, Queer y otras identidades
	Lesbian, Gay, Bisexual, Trans, Intersex, Queer and Other Identities
MAFAPO	Asociación de Madres de Falsos Positivos de Soacha y Bogotá
	Mothers of 'False Positive' Victims in Bogotá and Soacha
MAQL	Movimiento Armado Quintín Lame
	Quintín Lame Armed Movement
MINCIENCIAS	Ministerio de Ciencias y Tecnología
	Ministry of Science and Technology
M-19	Movimiento 19 de Abril
	April 19 Movement
ODTPI	Observatorio de Derechos Territoriales de los Pueblos Indígenas
	Observatory of Territorial Rights of Indigenous Peoples
OEI	Organización de Estado Iberoamericanos
	Organization of Ibero-American States
OIM	Organización Internacional para las Migraciones
	International Organisation for Migration
OMC	Observatorio de Memoria y Conflicto
	Observatory on Memory and Conflict
ONG	Organizaciónes no Gubernamentales
	Non-Governmental Organisations
ONIC	Organización Nacional Indígena de Colombia
	National Indigenous Organisation of Colombia
ONU	Organización de las Naciones Unidas
	United Nations
REDLEES	Red de Lectura y Escritura en Educación Superior
	Network on Reading and Writing in Higher Education
REDPRODEPAZ	Red Nacional de Programas Regionales de Desarrollo y Paz
	National Network of Regional Programmes for Development and Peace
SENA	Servicio Nacional de Aprendizaje
	National Apprenticeship Service
SIVJRNR	Sistema Integral de Verdad, Justicia, Reparación y no Repetición
	Integral System of Truth, Justice, Reparation and Non-Repetition

SIVOSPI	Sistema de Información de Violencia Sociopolítica de los Pueblos Indígenas
	Information System on Sociopolitical Violence Against Indigenous Peoples
UAIIN	Universidad Autónoma Indígena Intercultural
	Autonomous Indigenous Intercultural University
UBPD	Unidad de Búsqueda de Personas Dadas por Desaparecidas
	Missing Persons Search Unit
UNAD	Universidad Nacional Abierta y a Distancia
	National Open and Distance University
UP	Unión Patriótica
	Patriotic Union
ZIDRES	Zonas de Interés de Desarrollo Rural Económico y Social
	Rural Economic and Social Development Interest Areas

Introduction

The writer Patricia Lara says that if we were to collect the stories of the more than seven million survivors[1] in Colombia and give each one just one page to tell their story, we would need about 13,000 volumes of 300 pages each: a lifetime would not be enough to read them. Expressing this same idea but in terms of time, Francisco de Roux, president of the Commission for the Clarification of the Truth (CEV),[2] stated, 'If we were to observe a minute of silence for each of the victims of the armed conflict, the country would have to be silent for 17 years'. Undoubtedly, these are appeals to the communal reconstruction of ruptures, silences and losses. They are a call to a society anaesthetised by everyday life, recurrence of violence and the weight of tragedies, to remove its deeply-rooted amnesia. This book attempts to respond to this call by foregrounding the voices of Colombian survivors, extracting from their voices the ways in which they re-signify their lives, their relationship with the territory and their local knowledge, because, as will be seen in their *testimonios*,[3] the process of managing paralysing pain is the engine that animates their lives once again.

The Colombian armed conflict has overlapping layers of horror and survival. Owing to this complexity, it must be analysed from multiple perspectives. The book's first part consists of two chapters: the first contextualises the social and political scenario in which survivor *testimonios* emerge and the second frames the positions chosen by the authors to analyse these *testimonios* and reflect on their meanings and contributions to the building of a collective Memory. Memory is understood as the set of remembrances shared by a group or community that are fundamental to its identity, not as a simple accumulation of individual remembrances, but a social construct that is articulated through symbols, rituals, monuments and other elements that act as anchors of collective identity (Nora, 2008). The second part has six chapters (Chapters 3 to 8), in which each author proposes a path to interpret the different ways of producing, dealing with and understanding the *testimonios* in the context of the Colombian armed conflict. The authors (who participated in the conflict as citizens) attempt to recover meanings, raise questions about injustice and call on others to understand what has happened, through the protagonists' oral, written, or pictorial narratives. The third and final part contains reflections and conclusions from authors who have engaged with the book from different positionalities.

In Chapter 1, political scientist and conflict expert Luis Eduardo Celis traces the multiple forms of violence the country has experienced, decade by decade. By doing so, he contributes to understandings about the burdens of horror that have given rise to the fragments of *testimonios*[4] collected in this book. The author begins with the 1940s, presenting the decade as a series of overlapping conflicts that contribute to the most regrettable embedding of war in society, and from which it will be challenging to recover in subsequent years. He then covers the 1950s, presenting a resurgence of the conflicts that triggered horrendous crimes and, consequently, new wars. Covering the 1960s, he mentions the historical exclusions that led to the emergence of new rebel identities. Writing about the 1970s, he focuses on the lack of credibility offered by the State, which led to an increasing public mistrust and rebellion by new armed groups. For Celis, the 1980s were characterised by the intertwining of various fronts, the magnitude of which led to multiple attempts to achieve peace and to the beginning of the contemporary political peace process in the 1990s, but which, paradoxically, promoted a broader geography of violence.

In his description of the first two decades of the 21st century, Luis Eduardo Celis shows how the first decade was characterised by attempts to dismantle powerful structures without reducing the number of armed groups or the horrifying consequences of their actions and how the second decade brings glimpses of an illusion of peace, tarnished by the residual groups that did not participate in the 2016 Agreement, as well as criminal groups of all kinds who unleashed a new cycle of violence.[5] Concluding the chapter and reflecting on the first quarter of the 21st century, the author risks making a proposal for 'total peace' based on the actions of a government radically different from those that preceded it.

In Chapter 2, philologist and social educator Blanca Yaneth González Pinzón and journalist Claudia Bungard offer a possible framework for exploring the experiences narrated in the chapters in this book by using interdisciplinary contributions, aware that the *testimonios*, the conflict and experiences of surviving can be analysed from multiple theoretical perspectives. By means of four analytical concepts – Narrative, Testimony, Memory, Knowledge – they provide critical reflections on what happened, to go beyond specific events themselves and frame them in the history of a nation. These four essential elements are intended to enable us – citizens and readers – to understand the meaning of what is narrated from individual perspectives, and above all from the perspective of the conditions of their making and their effects on the collective, which is vital for a country moving towards peace and striving for 'non-repetition'. The concept of 'non-repetition' is understood as the obligation to stop, throughout the entire territory and by all legal and illegal armed actors, the enactment of crimes that violate fundamental rights.

The second part of the book opens with Chapter 3, where philologist and researcher in social studies and education, Blanca Yaneth González

Pinzón, presents the results of an exploratory investigation into collective actions[6] for 'Symbolic Reparation', which incorporate oral, pictorial and written *testimonios*, developed in different regions of the country. The author selects fragments of *testimonios* compiled in 12 open access documents (resulting from 10 actions) produced for research, workshop and community meetings, in which men and women who experienced the conflict from different positions (ex-guerrillas, ex-paramilitaries, hired killers [*sicarios*], civilians) recount their experiences. In addition to offering details about how these actions were carried out, González discusses three axes that emerge from the analyses: the emotional mechanisms for healing that underlie the act of narrating tortuous events; the individual and collective contributions of *testimonios* to the recovery of Memory in the country; and the transformations and perspectives for the future that the great majority of the subjects who experienced the war head-on have embraced. One of the essential contributions of this chapter for future proposals for workshops and collective reparation meetings, mediated by narratives, is the need to find ways to avoid the re-victimisation of subjects.

In Chapter 4, Nasa-descendant[7] journalist José Navia Lame, in recognition of the indigenous peoples who were mistreated throughout the conflict and made invisible by hegemonic history, makes an essential contribution to the recovery of Memory through reflective analysis of a particular genre of narrative, 'chronicles'.[8] In these works, the author focuses on aspects related to resistance, coexistence with war, the relationship between the cosmogonic[9] and the political, and the contributions of the indigenous people of Cauca to other social processes in the country. José Navia Lame's reflections combine what he produces as a journalist with the voices of interviewees, an example of what is often known as writing from the perspective of the 'subaltern' subject, a theme discussed in Chapter 2. Interviewees include members of the indigenous guard or *Kiwe Thegnas,* demobilised indigenous guerrillas, indigenous community members, indigenous mayors and governors or *Thê Walas*,[10] indigenous leaders and, recently, *Neehnwee'sx* or members of the *Kueke neehnwee'sx*. The latter is a governing council created in the last five years in some Nasa communities to replace the *cabildos* (local council organisations of Spanish heritage). Thus, José Navia Lame brings us closer to an understanding of the cosmogony of this ancient people who survive even while, in the 21st century, they continue to be shaken by residual forces in the war in Colombia and by the inequality to which they have been subjected for centuries.

In Chapter 5, visual arts professor Cecilia Traslaviña González, combines *testimonio* and animation to describe the experiences, methodological processes and products of several workshops conducted with minors who were forcibly recruited by illegal armed groups. These youth (five women and two men) recount and reconstruct some of their experiences as former combatants. They also create new knowledge, not only as a form of expression with artistic and procedural processes to create animations, but also as a personal recognition of what was transformed in them.[11] Given the expressive possibilities of animation, the procedural and methodological aspects occupy a central place in this chapter. The chapter provokes reflections on the trampled innocence and the mistreatment of young people just as they were beginning their adult development.

In Chapter 6, journalist, creator and director of the virtual newspaper *Diario de Paz,* Claudia Bungard, describes the impact of the writing project *De su puño y letra* [*In their own handwriting*], which resulted in three books. These publications demonstrate that, despite various cultural barriers, people can write *testimonios* without the mediation of the questions of a journalist, facilitator, or researcher. The workshops for this project were carried out at three different times, with three groups of survivors living in Medellín, Department of Antioquia (number 2 on the map). This chapter focuses on the perceptions of several of the survivors, whom the author contacted seven years after the publication of the last book from the project, to talk about victimisation and the effects of writing to alleviate trauma. Several sections allow a parallel reading of what survivors expressed in the 2017 interviews with what they had produced as *testimonios* in the workshops seven years earlier.

In Chapter 7, Mario Ramírez Orozco, a specialist in Latin American Studies, identifies the peace imaginaries of ex-guerrilla men and women, residents of the Tierra Grata Territorial Training and Reincorporation Space (ETCR) in the Department of Cesar (number 11 on the map), based on critical participant observation and *testimonios*. He considers the different ways in which they are moving forward with their new lives through individual and collective action. The reflections generated through his interviewees' voices demand that society take a considered look at how a large group of men and women abandoned their weapons and submitted themselves, with uncertainty, to a process of 'reincorporation', in a transcendent experience. These survivors question society's understanding of the new subjectivities that they are building in this transition. They also question a discourse that is no longer one of 'confrontation' but of 'integration', which means not necessarily abandoning an identity or a political desire but incorporating new representations and actions with different mechanisms. The *testimonios* and reflections presented by Ramírez Orozco place us in a terrain of complexity for which society has probably not received sufficient preparation, and which labels *reincorporados* not with different and reworked imaginaries but with the same burden with which they were marked, particularly by the mass media, when they were active combatants.

In Chapter 8, Emilia Perassi, a specialist in literature and human rights, looks at the construction of active and collective Memory, relational aesthetics and ontologies, and the creation of objects as the production and reinstallation of identities. The author analyses several 'narr'actions' based on a study of the 'textimonial' productions (including weaving) of diverse collectives organised in different regions of the country. Interviews with the weavers involved in these projects are also included. Her objective is to look for cases of *textimonio* as artefact and heritage; colonial narrative practices; non-normative use of narrative practices; non-disciplinary aesthetics and sensographic writings. She explores artistic and narrative forms that function in the construction of social bonds of affectation and empathy, the production of desire and the invention of ways of doing and living that contribute to a radical transformation of the present.

The third part of the book opens in Chapter 9 with reflections by a scholar in literacy studies and social linguistics. Theresa Lillis joins the multidisciplinary viewpoints presented in the book by advocating for, above all, 'non-repetition' of violence. Through her reading, Lillis unravels aspects of the dialogue between the chapters and the insights they offer to the specific field of social linguistics. Bringing together her two research orientations – social linguistics and literacy studies – she outlines four key dimensions: (a) the notion of voice and the conditions of 'decibilidad/sayability' and listening in *testimonios*; (b) the body and symbolic violence; (c) placed, dis-placed and re-placed resources and subjectivities; and (d) the semiotic resources directed towards 'non-repetition' and transformation. The author underlines the fundamental value of *testimonios* in transitional justice and the clarification of the truth.

In Chapter 10, the journalist and director of a university radio station José Vicente Arizmendi Correa, using the Greek figures of *Chronos* and *Kairos*, reflects on the historical moment in which the majority of the *testimonios* selected for the book's chapters were produced, as well as on the 'right moment' to produce a story or *testimonio*. Furthermore, he emphasises certain ethical and methodological elements that emerge from the discussions in the chapters, with the aim of highlighting their importance in the recovery of Memory. To complete the map of fragments of *testimonios* located before, during and after the Peace Agreement, he contributes other narratives collected in 2022 and 2023 for a documentary series broadcast on the university radio station he directs. The addition of these *testimonios* completes a linear, albeit unplanned trajectory in the book, which goes from 1985 to 2022.

The book concludes with closing thoughts by the lead editor, Blanca Yaneth González Pinzón, that summarise the central discussions on which the chapters are based, echoing the call made throughout for solidarity, 'non-repetition', dignity and healing as a nation.

Throughout the book, survivors are referred to in different ways based on careful ethical considerations. The use of anonymity, initials, first names or the mention of a position to refer to the interviewees or authors of the fragments of *testimonios* reflect prior agreements with the individuals involved. Permissions to include different types of data extracts were secured by the authors of chapters. In Chapters 4, 5, 6, 7 and 10, where the authors worked with interviews and fragments of *testimonios*, verbal or written authorisations and informed consent were given by interviewees and authors of *testimonios*. Several of the fragments of the actions mapped in Chapter 3 are taken verbatim from the publications that documented them, in their original Spanish language, and are duly referenced. We have kept the fragments of narratives in Spanish to preserve the direct *testimonio* of the survivors, as well as providing translations in English. Permission to provide translated versions was sought in all cases and several organisations provided explicit authorisation to translate the fragments into English. In cases where such authorisations for translation were sought but not obtained for different reasons (among them the difficulty of locating the relevant persons responsible), we took the decision to include translated versions, on the grounds that providing the original wordings and close translations in English would constitute a fair and ethical representation of survivors' words. For Chapter 8, which works with photographs collected in various repositories that include weaving, permission was obtained to use the images from Isabel González Arango, the manager and leading person in charge of the *Archivo Digital de Textiles Testimoniales* (ADTTC) [*Digital Archive of Testimonials Textiles*] of the Colombian armed conflict, a project carried out as part of the ongoing research of Artesanal Tecnológica.

Translations into English of other cited texts and sources were carried out in different ways: in Chapter 8, the textual quotes from Italian to Spanish were made by Emilia Perassi and were translated from Spanish to English by the book's translators. The *¡Basta Ya!* [*Enough already!*] *Report* referred to in several chapters has been officially translated into English and these published translated versions of extracts were used, for example in Chapter 3. Quotes from Spanish medium academic texts were translated by authors in collaboration with the book's translators and editors. The source references are provided in the original language in the references list.

We hope this book will be of value to readers with many different interests, experiences and backgrounds and we would encourage readers to take different routes through the book. One route is to read each chapter from beginning to end, engaging with theory, history and academic analysis. Another route through is to read only the fragments of *testimonios* to listen directly to the voices of survivors. We think both routes – and any others that readers choose – are valid.

Blanca Yaneth González Pinzón and Theresa Lillis

Notes

(1) This book differentiates survivor from victim, the latter of which is used in a specific legal sense. Survivors are understood as people who are capable of influencing the transformation of their life story. This condition of self-recognition allows them to take responsibility and actively commit themselves to the processes that the State provides for their reparation. This implies going beyond being empowered to request assistance and attention from the institutions that represent them by virtue of their constitutional responsibility (Bustamante, 2017; Jarque, 2008).

(2) The peace dialogues were a series of conversations held in Havana, Cuba and Norway between the State, represented by the government of Juan Manuel Santos, and the FARC guerrilla group (2012–2016). The result was the *Final Agreement for the termination of the conflict and the construction of a stable and lasting peace*, ratified on 24 November 2016, a triumph for which the President was awarded the Nobel Peace Prize in the same year. See https://www.jep.gov.co/Documents/Acuerdo%20Final/Acuerdo%20Final.pdf. Under this Agreement, the *Commission for the Clarification of Truth, Coexistence, and Non-Repetition* was created (through Legislative Act 01 of 2017 and Decree 588 of 2017) as a temporary and extrajudicial mechanism of the Integral System of Truth, Justice, Reparation, and Non-Repetition – SIVJRNR. (OACP, 2017: para. 143).

(3) In Latin America, 'testimonio' has acquired a particular meaning associated with denouncing injustice and fighting oppression. It refers to the life stories of people who have suffered repression, violence or marginalisation, and who seek to give voice to their experiences of resistance. George Gugelberger (1996), Susan Chase (2005) and John Beverley (1989, 1993, 2005) use the word 'testimonio' rather than 'testimony' because they are working in the context of Latin American literature and critical theory, where the term 'testimonio' has specific and relevant connotations.

(4) We use 'fragment' to signal that extracts included in the book are just a part of extensive *testimonios* produced orally, in writing, or pictorially by survivors of the Colombian armed conflict.

(5) As a result of the transition towards the search for peace, the Congress of the Republic enacted Law 1448 of 2011, known as the *Ley de víctimas y restitución de tierras* [*Law of victims and land restitution*], which established mechanisms of attention, assistance and comprehensive reparation for the victims of the internal armed conflict. The National Centre for Historical Memory (CNMH) was also founded in 2011 and became very important after the signing of the 2016 Peace Agreement, as well as the creation of the CEV and the establishment of a Special Jurisdiction for Peace (JEP). See https://centrodememoriahistorica.gov.co/.

(6) In the Law 975, 2005, the diverse forms of reparation are called 'actions' ('actions that promote restitution, compensation, rehabilitation, satisfaction; and guarantees of non-repetition of the conduct'). Specifically concerning rehabilitation, it is proposed to 'take actions aimed at the recovery of victims who suffer physical and psychological trauma as a consequence of the crime'. (Article 8, Law 975, 2005)

(7) The Nasa indigenous people are located in the Department of Cauca, in the southwest of the country (number 10 on the map). The name Nasa is part of the evolution of the resistance process. Until the mid-2000s, this people were known as *Paeces* (the name by which they were known to the Spanish conquistadors owing to their geographical location near the Paez River canyon).

(8) To produce a chronicle, the journalist first carries out ethnographic work, from which he collects, through interviews, information and *testimonios* from the people. One of its characteristics as a narrative genre is that the chronicle combines information with a certain degree of subjectivity and literary elements.

(9) **Cosmovision** is the set of beliefs through which a general concept of the world is elaborated. It is the basis for interpreting culture and the nature of everything that exists. On the other hand, **Cosmogony** refers to the explanation of the origin of everything that exists. The Nasa People explain their origins as follows: 'Nasa People, in our cosmovision [...] we descend from the star and the water. That is why they call him *Yu' luuçx*, son of the water and the star; that is how the first Nasa was created. The star impregnated the lagoon, and the lagoon gave birth.' (Interview with Major Wilder Güegia of the Nasa Yuwe people – Rueda, 2022: 76–77).

(10) Throughout the book we use capital T but also lower case t if t was used in the original source.

(11) Because it is difficult for the justice system to receive the *testimonios* of minors, the evocation of these young people through art is a way of showing society the events they faced when they were minors. Because of this knowledge value, the *testimonios* collected and produced in these workshops were recognised by the CEV as valid testimonios for clarifying the explanatory causes of the armed conflict and to promote the recognition of what happened. See https://comisiondelaverdad.co/actualidad/noticias/operacion-berlin-la-ninez-que-peleo-la-guerra-en-colombia.

References

Beverley, J. (1989) *Testimonio: Sobre la política de la verdad*. Bonilla Artigas Editores.

Beverley, J. (1993) *Against Literature*. University of Minnesota Press.

Beverley, J. (2005) Testimonio, subalternity, and narrative authority. In N.K. Denzin and Y.S. Lincoln (eds) *The Sage Handbook Of Qualitative Research* (3rd edn, pp. 547–558) Sage Publications.

Bustamante, V. (2017) De víctimas a sobrevivientes: Implicaciones para la construcción de paces en Colombia. *Revista de Sociología y Antropología: Virajes* 19 (1), 147–163. https://doi.org/10.17151/rasv.2017.19.1.8 (accessed March 2018).

Chase, S. (2005) Narrative inquiry: Multiple lenses, approaches, voices. In N.K. Denzin and Y.S. Lincoln (eds) *The Sage Handbook of Qualitative Research* (3rd edn, pp. 651–679). Sage Publications.

Gugelberger, G.M. (1996) Introduction: Institutionalization of transgression: Testimonial discourse and beyond. In G.M. Gugelberger (ed.) *The Real Thing: Testimonial Discourse and Latin American* (pp. 1–23). Duke University Press.

Jarque, L. (2008) *Curso Victimología – Parte de psicología*. Universidad de Alicante.

Nora, P. (2008) Entre memoria e historia. La problemática de los lugares. In *Los lugares de la memoria*. Trilce.

Rueda, E. (2022) Orígenes y trayectorias de la humanidad: Narraciones originarias y emancipación. In E. Rueda, A. Larrea, A. Castro, O. Bonilla, N. Rueda and C. Guzmán (eds) *Retornar al origen. Narrativas ancestrales sobre humanidad, tiempo y mundo*. CLACSO- UNESCO.

Part 1

Historical Context of the Colombian Armed Conflict and Theoretical Approaches to Analysing its Narratives

1 Colombia, Eight Decades in Search of Peace and Democracy

Luis Eduardo Celis

This journey through the last eight decades of Colombia's history has three main objectives: firstly, to outline the sequence of events that has profoundly marked our history, until violence became an integral part of the daily lives of Colombians; secondly, to promote a common, inclusive national project that contributes to the construction of a great pact of coexistence and quality democracy; and thirdly, to characterise the context that serves as a backdrop to the *testimonios* collected in the second part of the book. It is not my intention to validate the horrors that continue to plague the country, but rather to honour the Memory of the victims and the disappeared, and to highlight the dignity of the survivors: men, women, boys and girls from all regions of the country.[1]

This account will begin in the 1940s and end (with an open-ended conclusion) in the third decade of the 21st century. I will focus on the most significant events of each period, which form the grand narrative of a society grappling with unresolved historical issues and problems. I will reiterate that instances of control over wealth and territory, and the denial of rights and exclusion based on skin colour, gender or sexual orientation are manifestations of an authoritarian culture that ignores and violates the social order of fundamental rights.[2] If it were not for the fact that atrocious acts have led to massacres, expulsions, torture, kidnappings and many other victimising events, it could be said that these are the problems that every society has had to face throughout history. However, the repetition of these reprehensible acts, the scale of cruelty and the atypical nature of their mission explain why they have caused so much pain and how they have become normal and natural as almost irreparable events.

The 1940s: A Violence that Takes Root

By the early 1940s, Colombia was facing two major challenges inherited from the colonial order: a highly concentrated rural property structure – with a significant amount of land in a few hands and many landless peasants – and a highly competitive political landscape that led to numerous instances of violence and disappearances to eliminate the political opposition (Archila, 1992, 2001).

The 19th century saw the emergence of a two-party political system, with liberal and conservative sectors vying for power (González, 2014). These parties engaged in a contentious political struggle, often resulting in violence, such as the 22 civil wars that took place in the rural areas of Colombia. As the century drew to a close, another war broke out: the so-called Thousand Days' War, which the Conservative Party won, maintaining its hegemony for three more decades.[3]

The Conservative Party's period of dominance was followed by the Liberal Party's *'Revolución en Marcha'* [*Revolution in Progress*] government (1934–1938), which sought to establish the foundations of a social state based on fundamental rights. This aim was achieved through an interventionist model that proposed reformist policies, including the creation of industry; the transformation of the unequal rural order; and the advancement of the rights of the nascent working class. Jorge Eliécer Gaitán, a leader with a humble background and leftist tendencies, added to this liberal reformism and became the voice of the people demanding change. Nevertheless, upon the return of the conservatives to power, the country was subjected to a severe authoritarian order, which reached Dantesque proportions following the assassination of Jorge Eliécer Gaitán on 9 April 1948.

The 1950s: A Decade of Horror and Deep Wounds

The civil war intensified, and the events of 1948 aroused the people's emotions. In the 1950s, a reduced Communist Party, in the process of consolidation, promoted the idea of peasant self-defence in the face of massacres. Concurrently, the Liberal Party endorsed the use of weapons in political action. In certain regions, there were instances of coordinated action between these two political groups. These were years of intense confrontation. Millions of peasant families in rural areas were compelled to flee the pervasive horror and poverty that had become common (Archila, 2003). Colombia underwent a significant demographic shift, moving from a predominantly rural country to a country with a significant network of cities. Simultaneously, industrialisation began, facilitated by the 'import substitution policy', whereby domestic products are prioritised over foreign goods (Rovner, 2002). Coffee, the country's principal export commodity, was in high demand in post-war Europe, serving as a gateway for Colombia's integration into the global economy.

In the context of the bipartisan struggle, General Rojas Pinilla, a military *caudillo*, staged a coup d'etat in 1953. The leaders of the two political parties negotiated an agreement to end the dictatorship, supported by several of the country's most influential figures. The presidency of Alberto Lleras Camargo, representing the Liberal Party, marked the beginning of this period. The agreement led to the establishment of the '*Frente Nacional*' [National Front], a mechanism by which, from 1958 onwards, the two traditional parties attempted to pacify the rural areas. Many scholars have posited that the National Front was an optimal method for distributing power and alternating control of the government. This approach has led many to conclude that the violence between liberals and conservatives came to an end at the cost of excluding from political competition anyone who did not belong to these political groups. This division furthered exclusion, the concentration of wealth and the formalisation of the use of the State apparatus by private and elite interest groups.

The 1960s: Exclusions and New Rebel Identities

In the 1960s, left-wing guerrillas emerged in opposition to the political tradition perpetuated by the government. Once more, there was a recurrence of violence between siblings. As urban areas expanded, the countryside continued to be overlooked, leading to a growing sense of frustration, non-conformity and distrust by rural residents. The Revolutionary Armed Forces of Colombia (FARC) were established in 1964 as a response to peasant discontent and were linked from the outset to the Communist Party. In 1964, the National Liberation Army (ELN) was also established, followed by the Popular Liberation Army (EPL) in 1967. The recent triumph of the Cuban Revolution facilitated these developments. Camilo Torres Restrepo (1929–1966), a middle-class priest who studied sociology in Louvain and died fighting in the ranks of the nascent ELN, is well known in Colombian history.

In the context of these insurgencies, the doctrine of national security, taught by colonels and generals, led to the persecution of leftist leaders and university students who questioned the current state of affairs and, in particular, the education they were receiving. This doctrine provided a rationale for the military to be present and intervene in several State and social organisation arenas. In his final years in office (1966–1970), President Carlos Lleras Restrepo legalised the National Association of Peasant Users (ANUC), which had emerged and expanded in rural areas. Meanwhile, there was a growing desire for the recognition of fundamental rights and for these to be respected.

The 1970s: Growing Mistrust and Rebellion

Another presidential election was held in 1970. This was the final period of the National Front, during which a conservative candidate, Misael Pastrana Borrero, stood against General Gustavo Rojas Pinilla, who had formed the National Popular Alliance (ANAPO). This movement sought to challenge the concentration of power created by the liberal-conservative two-party system. The elections were held on 19 April. The vote count left a sense of uncertainty, because on election night, early reports indicated that Gustavo Rojas Pinilla was winning with a significant lead. However, the final vote count declared Misael Pastrana Borrero the winner. The peasantry's struggle intensified, accompanied by their growing desire for land. An aspiration for a life with dignity was gaining ground among students, workers and the middle classes. In urban working-class neighbourhoods, demands for water, healthcare and educational facilities persisted. There were two distinct Colombias at the same time: one trying to access basic necessities and opportunities, and another encountering a power that impeded the struggle.

Hundreds of thousands of dispossessed families were forced to move to the Orinoquia (departments marked with numbers 3, 9, 20 and 32 on the map) and Amazonia (departments marked with numbers 1, 8, 15, 16 and 23) (Palacios & Safford, 2002), owing to exclusion and land concentration – the control of land by a small number of owners. These territories needed roads, schools and hospitals. In these challenging circumstances, coca became a source of income to support families. Small guerrilla groups grew and spread throughout the rural areas, and the perception of fraud in the presidential elections gave rise to the Movimiento 19 de Abril (M-19). The new guerrilla movement had an urban vocation and a desire to break out of the leftist niche and reach out to social groups beyond the peasantry.

In September 1977 urban protest was growing amongst trade unions, student organisations, peasant movements and left-wing political parties. While the elites perceived discontent in these protests, the guerrillas read the moment as a prelude to a final insurrection. Leftist insurgent violence grew in several areas far from the urban centres where the economy was concentrated and economic and political power was based (Sánchez, 1991; Sánchez et al., 2003). The situation took a turn when, on 31 December 1978, the M-19 stole 5000 weapons from the main military garrison in Bogotá. This offence was met with brutality against those involved as well as innocent citizens. Critical intellectuals were treated with suspicion; many had their homes searched and were tortured. Fearing for his safety, Gabriel García Márquez, the Nobel prize-winning author, emigrated to Mexico to protect his life and dignity.

The 1980s: Early Peace Dialogues and Intersecting Violence

In the early 1980s, an event known as the 'embassy takeover' was a response to a situation that arose when the military, with the tacit approval of the civilian government, carried out barbaric acts. The M-19 took hostage the US ambassador, the apostolic nuncio, eight other ambassadors and 14 diplomats in the Dominican Republic embassy. They demanded the release of nearly 500 political prisoners, including guerrilla members and social leaders. This difficult impasse was eventually resolved peacefully. Julio César Turbay Ayala, the liberal president in power, agreed to allow the guerrilla group to leave for Cuba. Although M-19 were unable to free their fellow rebels, they succeeded in drawing the world's attention to Colombia and to the torture and other human rights abuses that were taking place.

Two years later, two representatives of different ideological camps raised the banner of dialogue and began negotiations to achieve peace. In 1982, the newly elected president, Belisario Betancur, and the founder of the M-19, Jaime Bateman Cayón, began peace negotiations, arguing that dialogue would be more fruitful than armed struggle. The government, the M-19, the FARC and the EPL supported this dream. The initiative was greeted with great enthusiasm and a spirit of citizen mobilisation; many people were eager to contribute to overcoming the ever-growing violence.

In November, 1985, however, hopes for peace were dashed in Bogotá. In an erratic move, the M-19 stormed the Palace of Justice, which housed the High Courts. These courts had been trying members of the military for torture in the late 1970s and early 1980s. The takeover was an attempt to highlight the government's failure to fulfil its duties: it talked about peace but showed little willingness to achieve it. The guerrilla action was met with a military response, and there were chilling scenes of tanks bursting through the front doors of the Palace of Justice. After 36 hours, the death toll was enormous. Many members of the Supreme Court of Justice were killed in the military operation, along with a large number of civilians and a group of 36 guerrilla members.

That same year, the Patriotic Union (UP) was formed amid a ceasefire with the FARC, which was growing in strength. The FARC promoted this political movement under the leadership of the Communist Party. It gained considerable strength, presence and organisation: 50,000 men and women participated in social and political activities. Under this leadership, the UP took part in the elections and won a small parliamentary mandate of less than 10%. It took part in the 1986 presidential elections, with Jaime Pardo Leal winning less than 7% of the vote against the liberal Virgilio Barco, who won the presidency. This small minority of communists faced severe challenges from the day it was formed. Its members were killed, disappeared or forced into exile, and in October 1987, its former presidential candidate was assassinated. The total number of deaths of UP members is estimated at over 5000. The State has been condemned for these atrocities on numerous occasions by both the Inter-American Commission on Human Rights (IACHR) and its Court (IDH Court).[4]

During these years, left-wing rebellions were met with violent right-wing armed actions, a dynamic known as paramilitarism. Violence spread to new areas of the country, consolidating in the Andes and increasing in the Caribbean, the Amazon and the Orinoco (the Pacific was the least affected region). At the heart of the right-wing groups were, and remain, the drug-trafficking mafias. Those mafias were the result of the doctrine of national security emanating from the military headquarters, a retrograde alliance of armed interests to defend the privileges, exclusions and dispossessions that have prevailed in the country.

After the violence against the UP, the Communist Party and its allies, the FARC returned to the war with renewed vigour. The decade ended with an increase in violence perpetrated simultaneously by multiple groups, including mafias, guerrillas and illegal armed groups in alliance with paramilitary groups and the army.

The 1990s: Political Peace and the Expansion of Violence

The 1990s were the cruellest and most intense decade of the Colombian armed conflict. Despite various efforts at sociopolitical transformation, this period was characterised by multiple forms of violence.[5] In March 1990, five years after the tragedy at the Palace of Justice, the M-19 and President Barco signed the first peace agreement of the contemporary period. Led by Carlos Pizarro Leongómez, the M-19 renounced armed rebellion on political principle.

This year 1990 was crucial for Colombia's precarious democracy, because a youth movement promoted the drafting of a new political constitution. Citizens took to the streets, peace with the M-19 was accepted, and a courageous stand was taken against both the mafias running rampant throughout the country and against State authoritarianism. The youth pushed for a seventh round to be added to the forthcoming presidential elections, with a mandate to form a National Constituent Assembly. Once again, however, the interests of war overshadowed these efforts to transform institutions and sign a new democratic pact; as the assembly was being elected, the army attacked the headquarters of the FARC secretariat and moved in to end the armed rebellion by force.

The composition of the National Constituent Assembly was consolidated, and the M-19 was transformed into a legal political force (Alianza Democrática M-19) and won an important seat in the Assembly. This triumph of the M-19 was encouraging for peace, as three forces organised a collective leadership between the conservative Álvaro Gómez Hurtado, who had been kidnapped by the guerrillas years earlier, Antonio Navarro Wolff, a member of the M-19 leadership, and the liberal leader Horacio Serpa. The composition of this Assembly better reflected the diversity of Colombian society. A constitution articulating many rights was drafted; it modernised the State with an institutional design of checks and balances and three powers: executive, legislative and judicial, to which were added control bodies and a constitutional court to safeguard what was enshrined in the constitution. Indigenous peoples, peasants, workers and trade unionists participated in drafting the constitution, and made significant contributions, though they were in the minority. It was a significant step forward in respecting and exercising fundamental rights and improving institutions' design and functioning. However, the reality on the ground differed: while other guerrilla groups were invited to participate in the constitutional process, the FARC and ELN, which had not ceased their insurgency, were excluded.

During these years, the drug trafficking mafias were divided into two major cartels: the Medellín cartel (the capital of the department marked number 2 on the map), led by Pablo Escobar, and the Cali cartel (the capital of the department marked number 30 on the map), led by the Rodríguez Orejuela brothers. Despite carrying out distinct actions, the former fighting against the established power and the latter imitating it, in the end both were defeated after a wave of macabre acts condoned by the traditional parties, who always benefited from their immense resources and later repudiated the actions. As a result, drug trafficking and society continued to coexist in multiple spaces. The defeat of these two cartels was not the end of the mafias; they adopted new strategies and maintained, and still maintain, complex alliances with the traditional political and economic powers.

During these years the ELN was weakened, but the FARC grew, and a new wave of paramilitarism began to operate in full force. Together with the United Self-Defence Forces of Colombia (AUC) – hand in hand with drug trafficking and supported by corrupt military commanders steeped in the doctrine of the 'internal enemy' – these forces ravaged much of the national territory with blood and fire.

The millennium ended with hopes of a peace agreement between the government of President Andrés Pastrana, son of former President Misael Pastrana, and a euphoric and emboldened FARC. The country was increasingly affected by the conflict but not powerless, as the strong civil mobilisation for peace that followed showed. The FARC grew from 48 peasants in 1964 to a guerrilla army of tens of thousands of disciplined, trained and armed fighters ready for confrontation on the ground, with a significant territorial presence. They relied on the resources of a coca tax and a desire to emerge triumphant. Peace was a distant, perhaps impossible dream in a society that did not believe in dreams of change through armed action.

The New Millennium: War and the Dismantling of Powerful Military Structures

At the beginning of the new millennium, by mutual agreement between government and guerillas, a large area in the municipality of Caguán (in the department marked 20 on the map) was cleared of military and police forces: 44,000 square kilometres. The FARC's forces doubled in size, with recruits who may not have been entirely motivated or ideologically convinced of the need for armed struggle. During the talks, 10,000 rifles bought from traffickers and mercenaries entered the country from the Middle East, via Peru. These weapons were parachuted into the Colombian Amazon. After four years of talks and negotiations with little progress, the government decided to end them in February 2002, following the kidnapping of an influential politician. A few days later, in an event of international importance, presidential candidate Ingrid Betancourt Pulecio, also a French citizen, was kidnapped and held in the remote Amazon.

The new presidential campaign saw a shift in emphasis between the search for peace (led by Liberal candidate Horacio Serpa Uribe) and the promise of a firm stance and military defeat of the guerrillas (promised by Álvaro Uribe Vélez). Because of its opposition to the FARC, a significant part of Colombian society supported the authoritarian solution. Álvaro Uribe Vélez governed for two four-year terms (2002–2010) and received the support of some mafia and paramilitary groups, consolidating an essential link with regional powers. This pragmatic alliance between the AUC and politicians from a large part of the rural world led to the control of large productive areas, dispossession of lands, the emergence of large agro-industrial projects and a problematic strengthening of the coca business and drug trafficking. Uribe's presidency was marked by numerous corruption scandals that attempted to legalise the mafias, overlooking their crimes and their links to political spaces. However, these attempts to guarantee impunity and legalise the massive, unaccountable expropriations of paramilitary groups met with opposition from the left and sectors of traditional power. As a result, criminal investigations and trials were launched against politicians who were in alliance with the paramilitaries. These trials are known in Colombia as the 'parapolitics trials'.

On the insurgency side, the president was committed to the military defeat of the FARC. He received extensive support from the US, UK, Israel and France in training army and police units in counter-insurgency and intelligence techniques. With the help of external forces and air supremacy (which the FARC tried in vain to counter by finding surface-to-air missiles on the illegal market), the guerrilla group gradually diminished and was driven out of the urban centres it had surrounded. They retreated into the jungles and mountains, where they remained until they were convinced that their goal of seizing power by force was no longer viable. During these two periods of government, the policy of 'democratic security' was diligently applied to finally destroy the old insurgency and those who supported real change. In pursuit of the results the government wanted, it encouraged the killing of innocent people, many of them young and vulnerable. This deplorable situation is known as the 'false positives'[6] phenomenon. According to the investigations carried out by the institutions responsible for establishing the truth about the number of victims, there are more than 6402 cases, most of them from 2002 to 2008.

The Second Decade of the 21st Century: Illusions of Peace and a New Cycle of Violence

In the second decade of the millennium, President Juan Manuel Santos (2010–2018) was elected for two terms.[7] Having served as defence minister in the previous government, he knew that the FARC had not yet been defeated and that its destruction was not feasible. With this in mind, he reopened the dialogue and negotiations for a peace agreement. The FARC, weakened, accepted the offer. This negotiation took place in the context of immense rural inequality, with thousands of landless peasant families being displaced and forced into colonised territories, whether in the Amazon, Orinoquia or other less populated areas of the Andes. These territories were not overseen by the State and had weak or non-existent infrastructures.

In this scenario, between 2010 and 2016, the Peace Agreement[8] was negotiated in Havana, Cuba, to generate political and economic changes and the recognition of the rights of the survivors of violence. The Agreement established a Comprehensive System of Truth, Justice, Reparation and Non-Repetition, integrated into the structure of the State.[9] It comprises several key elements, including the Special Jurisdiction for Peace (JEP), which plays a vital role in the pursuit of justice; the Commission for the Clarification of Truth, Coexistence and Non-Repetition, which delivered its comprehensive report in 2022; and the Unit for the Search for Persons Reported Missing (UBPD) in the Framework and Due to the Armed Conflict. With the ratification of the *Final Agreement for the Termination of the Conflict and the Construction of a Stable and Lasting Peace* on 24 November 2016, there was a sense that peace could be achieved in Colombian society.

Although the Agreement was an essential step in the right direction and was signed by the majority of FARC commanders, a minority of FARC leaders did not fully embrace it owing to various factors, including the influence of external pressures such as legal traps and deceptions orchestrated by the ultra-right. The enthusiasm that brought the hope of peace to large sectors of society, especially in the areas that had suffered multiple acts of violence, was met with severe opposition, led by a current senator, Álvaro Uribe Vélez, who was and still is the subject of several investigations.

After the Santos presidency, Iván Duque (2018–2022) was elected on the ticket of a far-right party that promised to 'tear the peace to pieces' under the auspices of Uribe Vélez. Duque was an unknown senator who would be at the centre of numerous corruption cases and would shatter the illusions of peace by obstructing the implementation of the agreements to the utmost. This attitude has encouraged a new cycle of violence involving drug trafficking mafias, FARC dissidents and an ELN that continues its armed resistance. This government represented the eternal return to the defence of the interests of the traditional elites. By insisting on the failed war on drugs imposed by the United States, it refused to propose solutions to historical inequalities. This scenario was aggravated when Duque's finance minister tried to impose a third tax reform, with high exemptions for significant national and transnational capital and increasing the tax burden on struggling sectors. In response, countless citizen demonstrations took place between 2019 and 2021, demanding rights and actions for change, including challenging the restrictions on mobility justified by the global COVID-19 pandemic. These expressions of discontent have been met with violent actions by the national police's mobile anti-riot squads (ESMAD), resulting in deaths and many injuries, eyes shot out and teenagers raped.

The Third Decade of the 21st Century: Transformation and 'Total Peace', with Democratic Transition

For the first time in the history of the Colombian republic, the 2022 elections were won on the political platform of a left-wing coalition, the 'Historic Pact', led by Gustavo Petro, a former M-19 guerrilla and signatory of the first modern peace agreement (March 1990), and Vice-President Francia Márquez, an Afro-descendant from one of the most marginalised sectors of Colombian society. The president's record includes a courageous and tenacious political career as a parliamentarian – denouncing abuses through his investigations into parapolitics and paramilitarism – and as mayor of Bogotá. With this election and the strong support for this coalition in the Senate and Chamber of Deputies elections, Colombia has expressed its hope for real change, the reduction of structural inequalities, the desire to promote fundamental rights and the path of transition towards a legitimate and quality democracy, summed up in the values of freedom, equality and solidarity.

*****

At the beginning of my journey in this chapter, I talked of an open-ended conclusion. There is hope to break out of the spiral of illegality, violence and bloodshed that has consumed us for more than half a century and for which Colombia is known throughout the world. The current political proposals for change are crucial to reverse the long and useless war on drugs, to get rid of the mafias that have operated throughout the powers of the State. Colombia is beginning to discuss these issues as a matter of international concern, an area in which strategies need to be rethought and reformulated. Colombia continues to work towards a democratic order with fundamental rights and committed citizenship. This maturing of our society is enabling us to move towards overcoming the many injustices that have been experienced since the establishment of the colonial order and which remain present.

Notes

(1) Colombia has six regions, administratively divided into 32 departments (see map). They comprise a total of 1103 municipalities. In 200 of them, the conflict has had a particularly negative impact. According to the CEV's interviews with survivors, family members and witnesses, the departments with the highest number of violent incidents are Antioquia (number 2 on the map), Valle del Cauca (number 30), Cauca (number 10), Nariño (number 21), Meta (number 20), Putumayo (number 23), Bogotá (number 14), Caquetá (number 8), Cesar (number 11), Santander (number 27) and Tolima (number 29) (La Comisión para el Esclarecimiento de la Verdad, la Convivencia y la No Repetición, 2022).

(2) I refer to the set of rights inherent to all people, recognised and protected by the country's political constitution. These rights are considered essential for human dignity and the integral development of individuals. Fundamental rights include civil, political, economic, social, cultural and collective rights. These rights are based on the Universal Declaration of Human Rights, the International Covenants on Civil and Political Rights, and on Economic, Social and Cultural Rights of the UN, as well as the constitutions of member countries.

(3) In order to achieve a more comprehensive understanding of the various issues discussed in this text and their typification, including social movements, periods of violence and armed actors, it may be beneficial to consult the works of Archila, M. (1992, 2001, 2003), Vega, R. (2002), González, F. (2014), Villamizar, D. (2020), Gutiérrez, F. (2007), Sánchez, G. (1991) and Guillén, F. (2008). Furthermore, CNMH and CEV publications are accessible online, for example: *Análisis cuantitativo del paramilitarismo en Colombia* [Quantitative Analysis of Paramilitarism in Colombia](CNMH, 2019), *Tomas y ataques guerrilleros* [Takeovers and Guerrilla Attacks](1965–2013) (CNMH, 2016), and *Hay futuro si hay verdad: Informe Final de la Comisión para el Esclarecimiento de la Verdad, la Convivencia y la No Repetición* [There is a Future if there is Truth: Final Report of the Commission for the Clarification of Truth, Coexistence, and Non-Repetition] (Comisión para el Esclarecimiento de la Verdad, 2022), which are available in 11 tomes and 24 volumes.

(4) The ruling was issued on 27 July 2022 and 30 January 2023. The IACHR condemned the Colombian State for the disappearance of more than 6000 UP militants since 1984. The persecution and extermination involved judges, the military, businessmen and agents of multiple governments, as well as other institutions. See https://centrodememoriahistorica.gov.co/la-cidh-declaro-responsable-al-estado-colombiano-por-el-exterminio-de-la-union-patriotica/.

(5) According to the 2019 database of the National Centre for Historical Memory (CNMH), 262,197 Colombians have been killed in recent decades (approximately 95,000 deaths are attributed to paramilitaries, 35,683 to guerrillas and 9804 to State agents. The vast majority were civilians: 215,005 civilians versus 46,813 combatants), more than 7 million internally displaced, 80,514 disappeared and 37,094 kidnapped. During this period, almost 20% of the country's population was directly affected, physically and/or psychologically.

(6) This is one of the most despicable and abhorrent events in Colombia's recent history. The JEP determined in February 2021 that in Colombia, between 2002 and 2008, at least 6402 people, mostly minors and young adults, were presented by the State as combat victims, when in fact they were killed by the army in order to obtain benefits and show results.

(7) Juan Manuel Santos is part of the traditional republican power (Eduardo Santos Montejo, his great-uncle, was president of Colombia between 1938 and 1942), a power always reluctant to solve the agrarian issues that are at the root of the armed uprising and also explained the consolidation of drug-trafficking and paramilitarism. The Zidres Law, Zones of Interest for Rural Economic and Social Development, are

illustrative of the problems caused by the country's extremely unequal distribution of land and its hoarding by the landowning and political elites. Santos signed this law while negotiating the first point of the Peace Accords: 'Towards a new Colombian countryside: Integral rural reform'. With this law, the government further opened the door for large investors to acquire vacant land from the nation, which should be destined to fulfil the social and ecological function of the land. See Arias (2017).

(8) *Acuerdo final para la terminación del conflicto y la construcción de una paz estable y duradera* [*Final agreement for the termination of the conflict and the construction of a stable and lasting peace*], ratified on 24 November 2016. See https://www.jep.gov.co/Documents/Acuerdo%20Final/Acuerdo%20Final.pdf.

(9) See Función Pública. 'Manual de Estructura del Estado colombiano' [Colombian State Structure Manual] (n.d.). See https://www.*funcionpublica.gov.co/eva/gestor-normativo/manual-estado/sistema-verdad.php*

References

Archila, M. (1992) *Cultura e identidad obrera. Colombia 1910–1945*. Cinep.

Archila, M. (2001) *Movimientos sociales, Estado y democracia en Colombia*. CES – Universidad Nacional de Colombia. Icanh.

Archila, M. (2003) *Idas y venidas, vueltas y revueltas. Protestas sociales en Colombia, 1958–1990*. Icanh, Cinep.

Arias, B. (2018) Subjects suffering in resistance: An approach to the subjectivities of the Colombian armed conflict. *Social Medicine* 12 (12), 1–7.

CNMH (2016) *Tomas y ataques guerrilleros (1965–2013)*. CNMH, Iepri.

CNMH (2019) *Análisis cuantitativo del paramilitarismo en Colombia*. CNMH.

Comisión Nacional de Territorios Indígenas (2022) *El eterno retorno de la violencia contra los pueblos indígenas en Colombia*. Informe del Observatorio de Derechos Territoriales de los Pueblos Indígenas. CNTI.

González, F. (2014) *Poder y violencia en Colombia*. Cinep, Odecofi y Colciencias.

Guillén, F. (2008) *El poder político en Colombia*. Planeta.

Gutiérrez, F. (2007) *Lo que el viento se llevó. Los partidos políticos y la democracia en Colombia, 1948–2002*. Norma.

Palacios, M. and Safford, F. (2002) *Colombia: País fragmentado, sociedad dividida*. Norma.

Rovner, E.S. (2002) *Colombia años 50: Industriales, política y diplomacia* (vol. 4). Universidad Nacional de Colombia.

Sánchez, F., Díaz, A. and Formisano, M. (2003) *Conflicto, violencia y actividad criminal en Colombia: Un análisis espacial*. Universidad de los Andes, Facultad de Economía, CEDE.

Sánchez, G. (1991) *Guerra y política en la sociedad colombiana*. El áncora.

Vega, R. (2002) *Gente muy rebelde: Enclaves, transportes y protestas obreras*. Pensamiento Crítico.

Villamizar, D. (2020) *Las guerrillas en Colombia. Una historia desde los orígenes hasta los confines*. Debate.

2 Theoretical Approaches to Analysing Conflict Narratives

Blanca Yaneth González Pinzón and
Claudia Bungard

> Show a people as one thing, only one thing,
> over and over again, and that is what they become.
> Chimamanda Ngozi Adichie, 2018

Introduction

The enforced recruitment of a child to a military group, the death of a family member and the forced displacement of people are just a few of the most common events in Colombia's history. These events have a significant impact on survivors, who are forced to make substantial changes in their personal lives and changes in their communities. All aspects of life are affected by war, as the ¡Basta Ya![1] [*Enough Already*!] *Report* correctly states: 'Violence deconstructs the spatial, social, spiritual and natural references that organize the worlds of families and social groups' (CNMH, 2013a: 331). However, the paralysing experience of war, paradoxically, also provides fertile ground for resistance and review of hegemonic history.

Beyond painful events, what matters are the forms of resistance, and empowerment, alongside expectations for the future, and the adoption of new ways of knowing that we can glimpse in the *testimonios* of many young people, and adult men and women. The aim of including the *testimonios*, creations and interviews in the second part of the book is to help society to recognise the survivors and their role in rebuilding a country. To make this a true contribution to the country's Memory and 'non-repetition' of tortuous events, it is important to understand what has been studied in terms of Narrative, Testimony, Memory and the forms of resistance, survival and knowing that emerge in all the existential disruptions present in the fragments of *testimonios*. Without exhausting any of the concepts, but rather inviting us to study them in depth, this chapter presents an overview of just a few of the many possible perspectives for understanding the narrative fragments.

Topics of Convergence between Narrative and Testimony

It is difficult to talk about Testimony without also talking about Narrative, as Testimony is one of the many forms in which Narrative can be developed. Therefore, in this chapter, we discuss both concepts and their interrelationship in terms of the characteristics and functions of each.

To begin with, let's observe the basic aspects of Narrative. Ricoeur (2000) argues that everything can be narrated because it happens over time. This possibility – that time is conceivable because it allows us to be aware of its passage through what happens and can be told – is very powerful. In some way, time is humanly determined through narrative.

Along the same theoretical lines, Chase (2005: 652) says that a Narrative 'may be oral or written and maybe elicited or heard during fieldwork, an interview or a naturally occurring conversation'. For these reasons, Narrative can be:

a) a short, topical story about a particular event and specific people, such as an encounter with a friend, boss, or doctor; b) a longer story about a significant aspect of one's life, such as schooling, work, marriage, divorce, childbirth, illness, trauma, or participation in war or social movements; or c) a narrative of one's entire life, from birth to the present (Chase, 2005: 652).

Accordingly, the author posits that narratives can serve a variety of functions, including the ability to 'explain, entertain, inform, defend, complain, and confirm or challenge the *status quo*' (2005: 657). This, and the sum of other imaginative and creative conditions, is why narratives can take the form of a story, a novel, an epic, a film, a comic strip, a song, a diary, a soap opera, a drama essay or – as is illustrated in the chapters in this book – a chronicle, a *testimonio*, a weaving.

In the fragments of *testimonios* used in the chapters in this book, the authors zoom in on specific episodes that serve to exemplify the specific topics they focus on in their discussions. However, all of these episodes are part of *testimonios* that are complete narratives (oral, pictorial and written) produced in a specific time and place. Each of them, in their entirety, has a narrative structure which, according to Labov (2010), has three main components: temporal organisation, orientation and coda. Temporal organisation defines how the events are organised, orientation defines the desired tone and the coda defines the resolution of the conflict. The narrative needs to be structured so that it is clear and coherent. This involves defining the tone, the facts, the conflict and the resolution. It is obvious that the narrative becomes a coherent and deliberate chain of events with a purpose and an end. It is not a random composition. On a second level Labov's proposal presents seven components. The primary element is the central idea or framework of the composition, which is delineated by six orbitals: (1) the general idea (a recognition of the starting point and the intended destination), (2) the orientation (the identification of temporal, spatial, character, activity and situational elements), (3) the complexifying action (the resolution of the identified issues), (4) the appraisal (the reasons why the information is valuable to the audience, a point on which he agrees with Chase (2005), (5) the denouement or resolution and (6) the coda or conclusion (the moment when everything is clear and justifies the attention paid to the narrative). The length of the narrative is irrelevant as long as these elements guarantee its comprehensibility and meaningfulness.

This sequence of elements is what Ricoeur (2000) calls the intelligibility of the Narrative. This intelligibility is what distinguishes the Narrative from a mere enumeration or sequence of facts. Narratives are textual productions that configure meanings from which we read how people experience the world and configure their identities: in the case of the conflict in Colombia, how people have suffered an event, how they interpret it, how they attempt to heal by sharing it with society and projecting themselves into the future and how their narratives contribute to Memory and social justice, which turns their stories into complex structures.

Narrative, according to Muñoz-González (2012), is a structured quality of experience, understood and seen as a story; that is, a particular reconstruction of experience, which can be represented in multiple forms. From this perspective, every narrative matters because it represents what is possible and intelligible within a particular social context at a particular time (Chase, 2005; Arizmendi in this book, Chapter 10).

In addition to the different forms that Narrative takes, researchers have classified corpora of narratives according to their purpose. For example, Garzón (2014) speaks of 'narratives of return' to refer to the narratives of people who return to their places of origin after being displaced. Similarly, Jelin (2001) speaks of 'narrative memories,' when past events are recalled to construct meaning from them. Reyes-Aparicio (2013) refers to 'narratives of violence', while Figueroa (2004: 98) describes them as a form that 'reworks facts, fictionalising or reinventing them to create literary spaces where the transfigured reality allows a greater and better understanding of hidden motives, triggering effects or unresolved aftereffects of violence'. For Yúdice (1996), 'truth is invoked to denounce a current situation of exploitation and oppression, or to exorcise and correct official history' (quoted in Gugelberger, 1996: 9). Jara and Vidal (1986) and Beverley (1989) refer to 'narratives of emergence', encompassing issues such as oppression, poverty, marginality, exclusion, pain, displacement or even survival and the demand for rights. In Colombia, following the implementation of Law 1448 of 2011, many of the workshops with communities focused on 'narrative for symbolic reparations'. This practice is discussed in Chapters 3 and 6 of this book.

Bruner (2003) suggests that a compelling story and a well-structured argument have the same capacity to persuade, but differ in the specific content they seek to convey. Narratives aim to persuade through their verisimilitude and similarity to real-world scenarios, whereas arguments aim to persuade about a particular truth.

In short, the malleability of narrative allows it to be situated in different spheres of life and for purposes defined either by those who produce and enact them or by those who study them. As aesthetic systems of representation, as Figueroa (2004: 98) notes, they 'encompass the subjective and the objective, the personal and the collective, the psychological and the sociological, the visible and the invisible, the documentary and the fictional'.

Specific orientations towards Narrative are influenced by specific fields of social and human knowledge and include psychological, historical, communicational, sociological, anthropological, linguistic and sociolinguistic approaches. Terms such as autoethnography, narrative ethnography, autobiography, *testimonio*, oral history, life story, interview, group interview, personal narrative, diary and letters are provided by different disciplinary fields (Acedo, 2017; Blanco, 2012; Connerton, 1989; Chase, 2005; Gaitán, 2000; Grosfoguel, 2011; Hernández, 2011; Madison, 2003; Muñoz-González, 2012; Salazar-Henao & López-Moreno, 2016; Thompson, 2000). The specific techniques and positioning of the researcher also determine whether the Narrative is presented in the first or third person. As noted, this is particularly relevant in the case of the 'subaltern' subject (Beverley, 1989; Henderson, 2001; Rivara-Kamaji, 2007), discussed in the next section *Modalities for collecting testimonies*, and also discussed in Chapters 4 and 7.

With regard to Testimony, the various methods of producing it, as an act of narration, have led to multiple approaches to defining its characteristics as a genre (Acedo, 2017; Sklodovska, 1996). We can distinguish between Testimony as a legal resource (Grandin, 2005; Krog, 2013; Ross, 2003; Stover, 2005), which in Colombia has contributed to the specific processes of transition to peace after periods of war, and as a broader classification, which includes multiple forms involving a range of linguistic and aesthetic resources. Here the fields of literature and social sciences have contributed frameworks for identifying and analysing Testimony. Consequently, we can identify a number of different types of *testimonio* text, including oral history, memory, autobiography, chronicle, confession, life story, life narrative, testimonial novel, or non-fiction story (Castillejo, 2013).

Acedo (2017) has identified various ways of understanding Testimony, depending on the discipline that deals with it. The philosophical field, for example, includes the debate on the duality of subjectivity and truth; this includes the truth told and the way it is reinterpreted and remembered. The place of the witness in cultural history is also analysed. In contrast, in historiography it is the status of remembrance[2] and the role of Memory, which establishes boundaries between the value of the individual, and what it represents for the collective as Memory (Ricoeur, 2004).

More recently, Testimony has become especially associated with the (usually oral) narratives of Latin American activists in revolutionary movements (Chase, 2005). It is an explicitly political type of oral history, life narrative, or life story that describes situations of oppression and resistance to it (Beverley, 2005; Chase, 2005; Tierney, 2000).

Specific *testimonios* entail a condition of story 'told in the first person by a narrator who is also a real protagonist or witness of the events she or he recounts. Its unit of narration is usually a "life" or a significant life experience' (Beverley, 1989: 128). Moraña (cited in Acedo, 2017) states that the first characteristic is that all *testimonio* is written or produced on the basis of information given by a witness who either experienced what is recounted or is knowledgeable about what is being recounted as an observer. This core principle of personal experience-knowledge characterises all the *testimonio* fragments included in this book.

Jara and Vidal (1986: 45) argue that a *testimonio* is almost always a 'narrativised image' arising from different atmospheres of repression, anxiety, anguish, or heroic exaltation and that it is produced out of the need to leave a record. The production of *testimonio* can also be motivated by the specific desire to leave a historical record that can be used as evidence in future cases, to seek justice and to preserve the remembrance of past events (Huyssen, 2007).

In the chapters in this book, the selected fragments from *testimonios* challenge society and call for an understanding of the history of others (Violi, 2014). These *testimonios* reflect the diversity and elasticity of the notion of Narrative. In these fragments, the Narrative enters territories of disdain, contempt, insult and cruelty, and then, offers glimpses a horizon of understanding and forgiveness (Montoya, 2022). It is therefore essential that listeners, readers and observers possess a narrative imagination that enables them to empathise with the experiences of others, which can be achieved by adopting an intelligent reading of another's story, as Nussbaum (2015) suggests.

Modalities for collecting *testimonios* and contributions to social justice in post-conflict contexts

Being aware of the key aspects of the different modalities for requesting and collecting *testimonios* allows them to be valued in different ways. The first modality is a classic method of the collection of *testimonios*. In most cases, this takes the form, of a mediator collecting the *testimonio* of a 'subaltern' subject through interviews (Sommer, 1991; Yúdice, 1996). Here 'subaltern' refers to the condition of depending on a third party to offer a testimony and not producing it directly. This method is illustrated in Chapters 3, 6 and 7 of this book. The *testimonio* material is analysed, processed and reconstructed for dissemination by a journalist, a professional (e.g. a social worker, psychologist), or a researcher.

The second modality pertains to experiences that are designed to facilitate recovery from trauma, with the objective of externalisation and cathartic release. It may have therapeutic effects and collective (usually) or individual healing of pain (Adorna, 2013; Caruth, 1996; De Salvo, 1999; Di Meglio, 2022; Henke, 1998; Orfaley et al., 2019; Pennebaker, 1990; Vélez-Rendón, 2003; Zerillo, 2006, 2008, 2014), as evidenced in Chapters 3, 5 and 8. Depending on the purpose, the focus may be on different dimensions: the victimising event; the revelation of fundamental human aspects such as changes in identity; the effects on relationships with others; changes in ideology and cosmogony; transformations in the relationship with the territory and the family.

The third modality emphasises the generation of *testimonios* for the preservation of Historical Memory in Latin America, as directed by governmental and non-governmental agents to reconstruct the individualised experiences of the victims of human rights violations. Chapter 3 includes eight of this type of *testimonios*. These are memories which Todorov (2008) would characterise as being of particular value because of their subsequent use, distinguishing these from memories as the mere recovery of the past as a goal in themselves. As Dupláa (1996: 28) states, 'Testimonio or discourse-testimonio is a message, mostly verbal, aimed at verifying events that occurred and were experienced by an actor or actor-witness who, for ideological reasons, have not been recorded in the Collective History of humanity'. In other words, it is a means of giving visibility to those who are not present in official History.

The fourth modality, related to the previous, is that of the *testimonios* collected as a mechanism to achieve social justice or political transformation (Beverley, 1989; Bungard, 2019; Housková, 1989; Maldonado, 2008; Nance, 2006; Yúdice, 2002). Throughout this book, there are references to reports such as ¡Basta ya! [*Enough Already!*] *Report, La verdad de las mujeres* [*The truth of women*] and *Hay futuro si hay verdad*[3] [*There is future if there is truth*] with an emphasis on this collective purpose.

In concluding this brief section on Testimony and its interrelationship with Narrative, it should be stressed that Testimony acts as a form of resistance and a project for the future (Jara & Vidal 1986). This possibility for the future is represented in how survivors self-manage knowledge to transform it into forms of perseverance and, in many cases, to overcome the victimising event (Jara & Vidal, 1986; Navia-Lame, 2015; Rueda, 2022). Testimony is of significance as a record, but also as a form of liberation for the individuals concerned, enabling them to make a reasoned recognition of their history.

Development of Testimony in Colombia

The fertile ground for war in Colombia, and the multiple ways that violent acts have been perpetrated, have produced varied forms of narratives (oral, written and pictorial), and, therefore, of producing *testimonios*. The largest number of testimonial documents of which we are aware was produced after the second decade of the 21st century. From different governmental organisations and NGOs, a clear will has emerged not only to collect *testimonios*, but also to disseminate them. The intention of reparation inscribed in the Ley de Víctimas [Law on Victims] (2011) has contributed significantly to this purpose, as the narratives become vehicles for recognising the *testimonios* of those who have lived through the war and for defending their rights to legal protection.

In the academic literature, three distinct trends emerge when classifying Colombian *testimonios*: (1) as experiential accounts, or stories written or told by the protagonists of the events; (2) as partisan accounts, in which citizens of one party or another defend their positions and hold each other responsible for the confrontation (in the second half of the 20th century, the period of 'La Violencia', see Celis in Chapter 1); (3) as studies in interdisciplinary fields (scientific-social), with multiple interpretations, which transcend the political framework as the sole source of explanation of the violence (Vivas, 2007).

There is also a temporal classification, which is explained by the type of historical circumstance experienced at each point in time, as discussed in Chapter 1: *testimonios* written before the 1960s and those written from then until the 1990s (Ortiz, 1994). It is only after this second period that the *testimonios* of the survivors begin to gain social importance, not as a result of laws or governmental or legal regulations, but because of the interest of social scientists, thanks to the consolidation of Social Sciences as an academic discipline in Colombia. During this period, *testimonios* most commonly took the form of people telling the story of their lives during the *guerrilla*. From the 1960s onwards, sociologists and political scientists began to play an active role in the generation and analysis *testimonios* imbuing their analysis with much of their disciplinary discourses, techniques and themes (Suárez, 2011).

In the 1980s, the expansion of drug trafficking and the emergence of paramilitary groups, as well as the intensification of violence by guerrilla groups, led to the expansion of testimonial narratives (Carmona, 2023; Celis, in Chapter 1; Vivas, 2007). This provided the context for the profound sociopolitical changes that thematically affected the products of the *testimonios* in Colombia. A number of the published works can be considered to fall between journalism and literature, occupying a position on the borders of historiography (Ortiz, 1994). However, they can also be considered as falling within the broad spectrum of Testimony.

In the 1980s and 1990s, there was a surge in what some scholars refer to as 'direct *testimonio*', based on the experience of the individual (Ortiz, 1997), as opposed to that provided by a 'subaltern subject'. In these latter cases the narratives are not authored by the victims themselves, but by journalists who have listened to and then written about them (for example, Gabriel García Márquez's *Noticia de un secuestro* [*News of a kidnapping*], 1996). The narratives encompass accounts of hired killings, youth gangs and drug trafficking. The Nasa Indians' *testimonios* in Chapter 4 are an example of *testimonios* produced from within this subaltern subject positioning.

Towards the end of the 20th century and the beginning of the 21st century, *testimonios* were characterised by the narratives of well-known figures from the country's social and political landscape. In contrast to the thousands of victims, these individuals were extensively covered in the news owing to events such as their kidnapping or attacks against them. Additionally, autobiographical books were produced, which were part of a global literature known as 'instant books'. In Colombia, several books were produced and published rapidly to meet market demands. Best sellers such as Leslie Kalli's 1999 account, which began as a kidnapping diary and was later bought by a publisher, illustrate this phenomenon.

In the 21st century, the testimonial literature has continued to expand. The Historical Memory construction groups and the CEV have played an important role in making visible the experience of entire communities affected by victimising events, such as massacres and forced displacements, revealing difficult truths about the experiences of children, young people and women (López, 2012). The *testimonios* relate to organised crime, violence against the State and the civilian population perpetrated by residual guerrilla groups that did not sign the 2016 Peace Agreement. *Testimonios* also encompass instances of violence perpetrated by State authorities on children, known as 'false positives', (Chapter 1) and violence resulting from the defence of the interests of companies or landowners who exceed the legal frameworks, giving rise to paramilitarism. In some of the selected fragments in the book, accounts involve paramilitarism and guerrillas simultaneously.

The tragic atypical nature of the scenario in which the Colombian armed conflict unfolded – and still unfolds – has resulted in testimonial narratives in this country diverging from those produced elsewhere on the continent, such as in Chile, El Salvador, Guatemala and Argentina. While in other countries the role of the State in enforced disappearances is clear, almost as a single perpetrator, in Colombia such perpetrations are not from a single entity such as the State, but from many legal and illegal actors, simultaneously, all acting on the same populations.

The *testimonios* in this book have been drawn from three key types of resources:

(a) from existing published resources as the CNMH and the CEV: *Basta Ya* [*Enough Already!*] Report, *La verdad de las mujeres* [*The truth of women*]as discussed in Chapter 3 and the project *Mi historia: La niñez que peleó la guerra en Colombia* [*My story: Children who fought in the war in Colombia*] as presented in Chapter 5;

(b) from projects in which the authors have been directly involved (producing oral stories, autobiographies, chronicles, life histories, life stories, etc.) that have been promoted by different governmental, non-governmental and community organisations to give a voice to those made invisible by the hegemonic discourses of violence (Acedo, 2017; Beverley, 1989; Housková, 1989; Strejilevich, 2006), as presented in Chapters 4, 5, 6 and 8;

(c) from workshops and interviews conducted by chroniclers, journalists or researchers, as presented in Chapters 3 and 7.

Memory

Contributions of *testimonios* to Historical Memory

It is crucial to acknowledge that Memory is a correlate of History, despite also being a form of resignification. Memory with a capital 'M' can be seen to emerge from the actions forgotten and left behind by hegemonic or official History. Recently, the subject of Memory has become a pervasive concern (Calveiro, 2006; Carmona, 2023; Fuentes, 2007; Nora, 2008) attributed by Nora (2008: 19) to the impact of 'globalisation, democratisation, massification, mediatisation', which has led to rapid and continuous change.

Memory, and Historical Memory in particular, is a relatively recent concept, attributed to Pierre Nora. He refers to the fact that in French there was only one word to designate both lived history and the intellectual operation to make it intelligible (History). Nora (1989) makes clear the differences between these phenomena:

> Memory and history, far from being synonymous, appear now to be in fundamental opposition. **Memory** is life, borne by living societies founded in its name. It remains in permanent evolution, open to the dialectic of remembering and forgetting, unconscious of its successive deformations, vulnerable to manipulation and appropriation, susceptible to being long dormant and periodically revived. **History**, on the other hand, is the reconstruction, always problematic and incomplete, of what is no longer. **Memory** is a perpetually actual phenomenon, a bond tying us to the eternal present; history is a representation of the past. **Memory**, insofar as it is affective and magical, only accommodates those facts that suit it; it nourishes recollections that may be out of focus or telescopic, global or detached, particular or symbolic-responsive to each avenue of conveyance or phenomenal screen, to every censorship or projection. **History**, because it is an intellectual and secular production, calls for analysis and criticism. **Memory** installs remembrance within the sacred; history, always prosaic, releases it again. **Memory** is blind to all but the group it binds-which is to say, as Maurice Halbwachs has said, that there are as many memories as there are groups, that memory is by nature multiple and yet specific; collective, plural, and yet individual. **History**, on the other hand, belongs to

everyone and to no one, whence its claim to universal authority. **Memory** takes root in the concrete, in spaces, gestures, images, and objects; history binds itself strictly to temporal continuities, to progressions and to relations between things. **Memory** is absolute, while history can only conceive the relative. (Nora, 1989: 8–9, taken from the French translation in *Representations* by the University of California; emphasis ours)

In short, for Nora, Memory is constantly evolving, which does not prevent it from being reinterpreted and misinterpreted. In our case, as we will see in the next section, what has been collected to recover Memory has allowed us to learn about events that, in official History, are never addressed.

González and Pagés (2014) provide an analysis of the insertion of the concept of Memory in the different spheres of social, cultural and intellectual life since the 1980s. They identify three key turning points: the turn towards the past, the linguistic turn and the subjective turn. In summary, the first is produced by the general violence that exacerbates exterminations and massacres; an aspect that calls into question the notion of human progress, in which the future is secondary to the need to recover and to preserve traditions and the restoration of existence. The linguistic turn questions hegemonic History, that is, the grand narratives and global approaches (an idea shared by Muñoz-González, 2012). The authors note that 'we have moved from a History of great interpretive models to a History that is more sensitive to detail, more responsive to political events, and more attentive to historiographical craft' (González & Pagés, 2014: 278). The subjective turn foregrounds the voices of subjects as witnesses and protagonists of experience. Oral history plays a pivotal role in this process, providing a valuable methodological tool through interviews, which enables a more subjective approach to historical recovery. Much of this book illustrates the subjective turn.

Throughout the 1980s and into the 1990s, the concept of Historical Memory was defined by a clear distinction between those who violated human rights and the victims of such violations. In Colombia, the credibility of the recently established National Centre for Historical Memory (CNMH) and the Commission for the Clarification of the Truth (CEV) was challenged,[4] as has happened with commissions in other parts of the world (Grandin, 2005; Hayner, 2011). The discomfort of survivors in the face of impunity for perpetrators has made it difficult to establish the truth. However, the sheer volume of individual *testimonios* generated has made it possible to identify different ways of clarifying the truth about historical violence.

As in the case of Testimony, the concept of Historical Memory becomes more complex and broadens its possibilities for study according to the various forms in which it is offered and presented. Castillejo (2013) refers to the public sphere, where the concept of Memory can be divided into several categories: Historical Memory, Collective Memory, Social

Memory, cultural Memory, oral Memory, traumatic Memory, History and Memory, Memory archives, Memory documents, Memory construction, Memory reconstruction, Memory recovery and truth. The vast majority of the *testimonios* in this book respond to Memory recovery and truth. At their heart, the multifaceted dimensions of violence are explored to uncover the truth in a multitude of ways aimed at facilitating 'non-repetition' and, most importantly, the dignity of those who have been abused.

Arroyave (2013: 4) expresses the principle of the permanent updating of Memory:

> There are long-lasting memories of tradition and brief or disruptive events; individual, group, collective and social memories. In other words, memory allows us to dwell in a distant memory, in a past that is longed for. In short, we would say that memory collects what imagination, experience, emotion, and reason accumulate, which is why we refer to it as 'the present of the past': a support for the collection (or reserve) and resignification of the meanings of interior spaces that are constantly reconstructed and reinvented with the passing of the days. (Translated from Spanish by the authors)

To discuss Memory and Historical Memory, it is essential to examine the relationship between the individual and the collective subject (Arendt, 2015; Bergalli & Rivera, 2010; Calveiro, 2006; Chartier, 2001; Díaz, 2010; Errl, 2012; Herrera, 2008; Villa-Gómez, 2016). In all the experiences included in this book, the individual account is of great importance, not least because it gives the narrator a sense of dignity. At the same time, the co-presence of interlocutors who can hear or read the account and are aware of the narrator's story is an essential aspect of this process of offering a *testimonio* to recovering Memory. However, as we discuss below, the collective account is of paramount importance in countering denial and confirming that the event in question has indeed happened and should not be repeated.

The role of subjectivity in Historical Memory

The functions and forms of Memory converge in a central aim in this book: 'non-repetition'. This was a responsibility mentioned in Chapter I, of Legislative Act 1 of 2017, which established comprehensive reparation measures for peacebuilding and guarantees for the 'non-repetition' of the victimising acts. For this reason, several chapters emphasise that, to achieve reparation, the 'non-repetition' of torturous acts must also be considered (Chapters 3, 6 and 8). In the *testimonios*, we focus on the interpretation of the event, rather than on the event itself. The more spheres of life that can be reflected and conveyed in the *testimonios*, the greater the possibility of identifying the specific nature of a conflict.

Colombia's history has been narrated predominantly through its most epic episodes, encompassing the period of conquest and subsequent liberation processes. In his work, Nora (2008: 20) includes official history in this type of evocation when he states that it 'refers from the ancestral past to the undifferentiated time of the heroes of origin and myth'. Furthermore, the official narrative has been shaped by the two-party system, whereby the veracity of historical accounts is contingent upon the perspective from which they are presented (Celis, Chapter 1). This official representation of History foregrounds the event and the perpetrator, with the survivor being a rare exception. Testimony and Memory are generated in parallel, influencing and reinforcing each other.

On the basis of the role of subjectivity, Historical Memory opens up a range of possibilities for interpretation, because, beyond the effects on the country's territories and production, the conflict has permeated the emotions and mental health of an entire people (Arias, 2018). The *testimonios* reveal countless aspects that official History does not want to tell. The CEV report *Hay futuro si hay verdad* [*There is future if there is truth*] (2022) looks at three macro aspects: the impact on people's lives; the impact on the economy, culture and nature, and the political impact on democracy. Within these, issues emerge that have never been touched upon in official History, at least not in the history told in schools: these include forced disappearances, mourning, massacres, torture, sexual violence, landmines, mental health, discrimination, violation of freedom and autonomy, kidnapping, violence against territory, places of tradition and sacred sites, persecution of ideas, impunity, attacks on the justice system, false positives, among others. *La verdad de las mujeres* [*The truth of women*], one of the most comprehensive reports on women's narratives in the context of the conflict, was developed from more than 200 subcategories of almost 50 problematic themes. The extensive report *¡Basta ya! Colombia: Memorias de guerra y dignidad* [*Enough Already! Colombia: memories of war and dignity*] also addresses the issues from the perspective of the survivors' voices, recovering not only the best-known facts, but also those that the survivors want to tell.

It is important to recognise the role of technology as a disseminator of information, contributing to the visibility of communicative, informative and artistic manifestations that include photography, video, chronicles, documentaries and music (Vélez-Rendón, 2003) and, as we see in Chapter 8, weaving. The reasons behind this drive for such visibility are multiple and include the exposure of crimes, abuses or violations of human rights. The use of old media (e.g. weaving) and the advent of newer media (e.g. social media) have made it increasingly challenging to conceal instances of abuse and their perpetrators.

The discussion of Memory, as with Testimony, oscillates between the validity of individual (subjective) trauma and its value as truth for historiography. Some argue that distinctions between the value of individual *testimonios* vs the collective, are not important. What is important is that the collective is valued to give the past a recognisable face (Arendt, 2015; Bergalli & Rivera, 2010; Errl, 2012; Herrera, 2008; Villa-Gómez, 2016; Vinyes, 2009). The fine details may fail any individual memory, especially when it comes to tortuous events, but the what, the where, the impact on who or whom, and the how in the remembrances of an entire community provide traces of an ascertainable truth (Muñoz-González, 2012). 'This [the failings of any individual memory] is undoubtedly attributable to the fact that we are dealing with representations that are too coarse and that our memory is a relatively too precise instrument, and that it normally controls only what is located in its field, that is, only what can be located' (Halbwachs, 2004a: 24).

Halbwachs (2004b) also problematises any straightforward concerns about form, since it does not matter how narratives are told or remembered (written, oral, pictorial; with forgetfulness, with intervals, in sequence, etc.), because it is not the form of the *testimonios* themselves that is important, but the sum of the plural contents. In the same vein, García Márquez, in *Vivir para contarla* [*Living to tell the tale*] (2014), says that life is not as it happened, but as each person remembers it. Individual *testimonios* contribute to the configuration of a Collective Memory, which García Márquez understands as the sum of individual remembrances nourished by the remembrances of others and inscribed in public affairs to foster the possibility of recognition.

Moreover, when reparation and justice are added in, as they are in several of the *testimonios* analysed in this book, the issue becomes more complex. Many of the witnesses who could have remembered certain events are disappearing, but the vestiges of what happened cannot disappear with them. 'Memory is life, always embodied by living communities' (Nora, 2008: 20); hence the vital role of the witness, especially in the case of Colombia, where entire populations were victims of the bloodiest fighting. Not just one, but many survivors can contribute their voices, however fragmented, to this reconstruction (Piña, 1986).

A final reflection in this section is that just as Memory diversifies and expands according to participants, conditions and purposes (e.g. oral Memory, plural Memory, Collective Memory, Historical Memory), it also correlates to 'forgetting', from three points of view. The first relates to elimination of remembrances, as presented by Rieff (2012), who notes cases in the history of societies where it is necessary not to remember a traumatic past, but to practise a healing process through forgetting. A second perspective is that of selective memory, as discussed by Reyes-Aparicio (2013: 253), who states: 'Forgetting plays an important role in that it contributes or subtracts elements to what is evoked and, in turn, constitutes it'. Forgetting can be perceived as a means of negating past events that are deemed undesirable. A third, and arguably the most important perspective is that of reconciliation, which encompasses the process of overcoming past injustices and silenced memories, but does not negate the need to address issues surrounding the past. 'The questions surrounding the recovery of official Memory must be directed towards the silences and forgetfulness that are generated in the context of national reconciliation' (Muñoz, 2013: 385–386).

The need to remember in order to understand is underlined by the poignant questions raised by Francisco de Roux at the presentation of the CEV's final report, and by Patricia Lara in a newspaper column:

> What have religious leaders done in the face of this crisis of the spirit? [...][5] What have educators done? What have judges and prosecutors who allow impunity to accumulate said? What role have opinion formers and the media played? How did we dare to let it happen and to let it continue? (De Roux, 2022)

> What happened to us as human beings, for God's sake? Why didn't we react to this barbarity? How could we sleep peacefully for so many decades? In just 33 years of conflict, between 1985 and 2018, we killed more than 450,000 of our people, 80% of them civilians. There is no justification for this horror! Let's stop it now! (Lara, 2022, para. 5)

The fragments of *testimonios* collected in this book are all preceded or followed by analyses or reflections by the authors who call on society not only to listen and understand their meanings but also to remain silent no longer in the face of justice and impunity.

Resistance, Survival and Knowledge

Survivor empowerment

Rueda (2022) says that History is usually taught from a defeated perspective, not by the people who can resist. A mantle of irredeemable shame and defeat is imposed on entire peoples because this contributes to the dominance of a single version of events. One of the most serious consequences of the Colombian conflict has been the rupture of social ties, understood as 'relationships with other members of the community or reference groups that provide social support, information, material support or a shared sense of life' (CNMH, 2013b: 101). In Colombia, in many cases, one of the ways in which the population has been deliberately weakened is by affecting collective and community dynamics, which are real possibilities for transforming living conditions.

That is why it is so valuable to recover the *testimonios* of the hundreds of thousands of men, women, children and young people who participated in that other side of History, in which the conflict, with its injustices and impunity, is recognised. In countries where the violation of human rights is concealed by the official narrative, with the press and mass media at its service contributing to the lack of concern and invisibility of the humble and defenceless subject, it is essential to have narratives that oppose the annulment of the victims and neutralise the relevance that the press gives to the perpetrators (Javlonka, 2017).

'When we realise that there is never a single story about any place, we regain a kind of paradise', says Chimamanda Ngozi-Adichie (2018). All the people behind the fragments of *testimonios* collected in this book have moved from obscurity to self-recognition and self-determination, as a sign of survival and dignity; that is, in Adichie's words, the tiny slice of the paradise of peace and well-being that they deserve and can reclaim, with the same right that they should be granted to participate in the reshaping of a country's history. This is what Strejilevich (2006) calls participation in counter-history.

Undertaking an intellectual operation to organise and produce a narrative is in itself a form of reinterpretation and transformation, not only of discourse but also of identity. It is the emancipatory and transformative power of elaborating a narrative about what has happened, rethinking and reorienting one's life (Carmona, 2023; Chase, 2005; Jara & Vidal, 1986; Strejilevich, 2006); it is an act that positions subjects as conscious citizens who are social actors from different sites of representation (Ferry, 2001; Ricoeur, 1996). In the same way that we recover remembrances that seemed to have disappeared and discover others when we visit houses, neighbourhoods and cities of the past, as Halbwachs (2004a) says, in narrating we are constantly going back and forth between what happened. Only after many displacements are we able to order the remembrances into a more coherent arrangement that resembles what happened.

War may be an obstacle to the future lives of those who survive it, but many of the *testimonios* in this book show that, despite everything, they can also offer alternatives for the reorganisation of existence. Despite the debilitating effects of loss, the need to survive challenges those affected to find new ways, new defences and even new forms of production. Chapter 4 shows the cultural reinventions and multiple forms of resistance that the Nasa Indians of Cauca (number 10 on the map) have adopted to maintain themselves as a people. Their struggle has contributed and continues to contribute to other social processes in the country.

Some authors of *testimonios*, in Chapters 3 and 6, are not 'subaltern'; they create direct *testimonios* whose value lies in their contribution to the country's Historical Memory. Their protagonism is highlighted by the CEV and the CNMH. The same applies to the children and young people who created the animations (Chapter 5) that served as a testimonial document for the CEV. Chapter 7 examines how FARC reincorporated combatants passing through the Territorial Training and Reinsertion Spaces (ETCR), in San José de Oriente, Tierra Grata, Cesar Department (number 11 on the map), are open to recovering the knowledge abandoned by the dynamics of war, as well as the new knowledge offered by the spaces for reinsertion into civil society, which is essential for them to continue their lives after the conflict. The fact that weaving, a central activity in Chapter

8, is practised by women from Chocó (number 12 on the map), Antioquia (2), Cauca (10) and Cundinamarca (14) is evidence of their resilience, their commitment to peace in the country, their contribution to the visibility and recognition of the conflict and its victims. The weaving illustrates the protagonism of survivors in transitional justice processes, and new forms of adaptation to economic alternatives as a means of subsistence. No one who has not suffered extreme situations can carry out such acts of conscience.

For Connerton (1989: 130),[6] recording with writing or any other symbolic system, as a vehicle of 'inscription', is a form of fixity that favours remembrance, when it is mediated by the will to retain something. Such inscription allows society 'an exponential development of its capacity to remember'. In the desire to do so consciously, there is already an emancipatory exercise that drives the subject, for example, not to remain static in the face of injustice; in other words, mechanisms of resistance are created (Beverley, 2005; Chase, 2005; Jara & Vidal, 1986; Tierney, 2000). This shift from one idea to another, from one situation to another, from silence to the spoken word, is an assumption of meaning that affects the symbolic. It is the creation of 'something different, something new and unrecognisable, a new field of negotiation of meaning' (Bhabha, 1994, cited in Vives-Riera, 2011: 73). It is not, as can be seen, a simple act of remembering and telling; they are internal and external mobilisations of the utmost importance and significance on a personal and social level.

Future expectations

What happens in the mind, spirit and other spheres of life of someone who tells a *testimonio* to free themselves from it? 'When people make memory, through our discourse we sustain, reproduce, extend, engender, alter and transform our relationships. That is to say, each person's memory changes in the relationship and changes [also] the relationships' (Vásquez, 2001, as cited in Mendoza, 2004: 75). It is no longer a defeated person who enunciates, but a transformed subject. Identity is thus confronted with a kind of reinvention of the self, with an ethical project that puts into tension what this life has been and what it will be (Muñoz-González, 2012).

The fact that survivors explore writing, weaving, orality, film or painting also opens up the possibility of approaching different ways of navigating remembrances, dealing with pain, managing hopes and, above all, understanding themselves, even recognising themselves in the *testimonios* of others to see a different future (Chase, 2005; CNMH, 2013b; Muñoz-González, 2012; Violi, 2014). As subjects with identities, sometimes recovered, sometimes re-signified – but never static – other forms of knowledge emerge in the *testimonios* of survivors, as we see in all the chapters of this book. Here, remembrances function as a thread that weaves the narrative, giving it meaning and providing arguments to explain what happened, why one lives as one does in the present, and what one's desires are for the future (Cervantes, 2020; Garzón, 2014; Muñoz-González, 2012).

In studies of narratives of violence, Testimony and Memory coincide in the diachronic thread that integrates past, present and future (Acedo, 2017; Muñoz, 2013; Muñoz-González, 2012; Nora, 2008; Riaño, 2006). Acedo (2017) posits that the process of transforming these remembrances into *testimonio* serves not only to repair lives but also to confront horror to provide meaning and hope. This meaning is sought not in a return to the past, but rather in engaging with the past from the present and hopes for the future. Garzón (2014) argues that these narratives convey the present, encompassing one's current circumstances and aspirations for the future. Furthermore, following Riaño (2006), it can be posited that a bridging memory is constructed which links the past, present and future.

Emphasis is placed on the configuration of a person across time, someone who, with this past self, has to live in a present that necessarily also draws him or her towards the future, towards something different. In the same vein, Garzón (2014: 71), referring to the construction of narratives of return, mentions four common points: '1. Life before forced displacement. 2. When 'what happened' happened. 3. The return itself and, finally, 4. The present and expectations for the future'. This corresponds to what Lopera (2011), drawing on an idea of Sousa Santos, distinguishes when he speaks of that which removes the veil and reveals the diversity of experiences that occur in infinite social practices (sociology of absences) and that which leads us to traverse the fields of possible future experiences (sociology of emergencies). In Chapter 3, the author reveals the explicit and implicit structures of the organisation of the workshops in the ten selected actions, which follow a sequence of past, present and future.

Transforming knowledge and adopting new ways of knowing

The Colombian conflict developed mainly in rural areas, as discussed in the opening chapter. In this field of constant adaptation and learning, it is worth discussing the issues of lost, transmitted and learned local and indigenous knowledge, and the social bonds created by these and other traditions. It is also important to consider what a society loses when whole populations are culturally affected by the loss of a tradition or a form of production. In several of the fragments, survivors' actions and knowledge emerge spontaneously in the narratives as essential to their identity and lives. With displacement, irreparable transformations and effects occurred: on the one hand, some local knowledge remained with the displaced and could be shared in other territories of displacement, generating hybridisation. In many other cases, local knowledge was lost when those who could not recover their territories had to face other forms of survival in their places of arrival.[7]

Survivors have a stock of experiential knowledge. They have been exposed to modes of production throughout their lives that have built mental structures that are conducive to different kinds of learning and knowledge. People are always capable of learning, especially when they are confronted with non-routine experiences that take them out of habitual practices (Engeström & Sannino, 2010).

Rajasekaran *et al.* (1991), Inglis (1993) and Kolawole (2001) define 'local knowledge' as the knowledge that rural people have developed about their land and crops through direct contact with nature, which is almost always considered marginal and peripheral. This issue is closely related to the tension between the ignorance of traditional, indigenous and local knowledge and the colonising imposition of official knowledge. Experience can also be learned through the body (incorporation) (Connerton, 1989; Vives-Riera, 2011), not necessarily through instruction. Hence, from the end of the 20th century, according to Feliu (2007), the emphasis has been on acknowledging local knowledge as legitimate, at the same time making visible the effects of race, class, gender, social position and other socially configured determinants in the recognition of knowledge as possible.

All the dislocations of the *status quo* suffered by subjects necessarily configure other ways of knowing (Aranguren, 2010; Muñoz-González, 2012; Stetsenko, 2023; Todorov, 2002). It is in these operations of reinterpretation that transformations are made in knowledge (Muñoz-González, 2012), since, as Feliu (2007: 267) states, 'knowledge is intertwined with concrete lives and personal experiences'. What is known or learned as new in the world of a person's life? When experiences and knowledge shift and move from one place to another, one becomes aware of beginning a new existence with openness, in the vast majority of cases, to different knowledge, even when confronted with negative emotions such as hostility, hatred, or anger (as reflected in some fragments in Chapters 3, 5 and 6).

Fals-Borda (1981), a prominent author in the early days of the consolidation of Social Sciences in Colombia, points out how the knowledge produced in Latin America and other colonised regions has historically been subordinated and persistently recolonised by the knowledge produced in the Western world, especially in Europe and the United States. It is precisely this intellectual colonialism (Said, 2023) that has prevented the recognition of the creative capacity of people's knowledge making, as Western paradigms and theories have been imposed as the standards for evaluating what is learned and what is produced as knowledge. Fals Borda (1981) advocates the need to develop a 'home-grown science' that would be based on valuing and strengthening local knowledge and perspectives, incorporating the experiences of local communities and seeking solutions to the specific problems of these regions from their own cultural and social contexts. His work is an important contribution to the debate on promoting more inclusive and contextualised approaches to knowledge.

He argues that 'scientific and intellectual colonialism' ignores popular knowledge as a contribution towards the transformation of society.

When certain knowledges are delegitimised, the production of new knowledge, which is possible through the interrelation of knowledges, is hindered. This creates a contradiction: while the subjects of narratives produce knowledge which address local and global issues, those engaged in academic pursuits produce knowledge to solve problems within their respective disciplines (Grosfoguel, 2011; Rueda, 2022; Said, 2023). It is this condition of marginality that has also allowed little attention to be paid to those knowledges and traditions that are insignificant for States and their policies when they are in danger of disappearing owing to the effects of war; they are considered 'handicaps', (Feliu, 2007) or 'peripheral wisdoms' (Fernández, 2000). Nevertheless, the difficult social and cultural transitions of marginalised peoples have strengthened the fields of research in the social and human sciences; both subjects and scholars are the architects of what is produced as theory. Without the contribution of subjects, the spaces of ignorance that exist in all knowledge would not be filled (García-González, 2011).

With the existence of narratives, the articulation between those who have the information, because they are social actors, and those who systematise it to produce knowledge, becomes crucial. The subjects in these conditions contribute with their narratives to scientific work; where 'theory and practice are not presented as separate and dichotomous elements, they are constituted as theoretical practices in the search for an articulation between knowledge and action' (García-González, 2011: 113).

Rueda (2022) warns of two aspects of analysis that are not necessarily contradictory, but can be uncomfortable when it comes to valuing and legitimising what ancestral peoples have contributed to culture, with regard to their knowledge and original narratives: the first has to do with epistemic hierarchies that ignore authorised, local and indigenous knowledge, because of the use of highly institutionalised disciplinary frameworks based on Western knowledge; and the second centres on the vertical nature of studies that do not ask about the realities and needs of the territory and its inhabitants, but centre on the researcher's need to understand them. This stance reduces peoples to mere sources, with little recognition of their contribution to social research, for which they receive little in return. The result: responses that are politically detached from their realities and which, according to Rueda (2022: 20) 'can rarely be appropriated to feed emancipatory processes'.

In recent works in Colombia, developed by Memory recovery groups, the subjects are the protagonists, and their narratives are consciously produced to contribute to the methodological procedures that will lead to understandings and theory for History and Memory; the experiences of making such contributions, in turn, are part of the symbolic reparation of the survivors. In the words of García-González (2011: 114): 'Social movements, among other non-academic actors, become one of the main agents of epistemological transformation'. He urges scholars to transcend disciplinary boundaries to research 'alongside' and 'with' social movements rather than 'about' them: the overturning of the divisive duality of researcher/researcher as a producer of knowledge versus social movement as an object of knowledge (2011: 116). This would eliminate the subalternation of subjects, their reification and depolitization, as Vives-Riera (2011: 67) notes: 'The inequality generated translates into the symbolic subordination of some subjects compared to others'.

In order for the contributions of survivors, systematised by the Memory groups, not to become simply a circumstantial and episodic matter of concern of transitional justice, we are morally obliged to expand the understandings that these essential actors of history reveal. Contrary to 'cosmopolitan reason', this way of recognising knowledge in any field expands the horizons of understanding, 'achieving with this expansion the condition of possibility for the emergence of existing possible worlds' (Almanza, 2011: 81). Nothing less than a commitment to the future of individuals and peoples is at stake in the recognition or non-recognition of who survivors are, what they are capable of producing and what they know, regardless of the circumstances in which their experiences and knowledge are lost or reinvented.

The knowledge produced in these kind of narratives also becomes a great narrative (Feliu, 2007), which this book exemplifies. However particular the fragments of *testimonios* collected here may be, all of them, taken as a whole, allow us to unravel the political reasons, actors, places, consequences, perceptions and effects of the conflict as a social and collective product. A context can be understood through the events experienced by a person (Blanco 2012; Ferraroti, 1988; Muñoz-González, 2012). For this reason, several factors have contributed to the growing use of positional narratives as a research tool: the growing interest in Native American cultures and the threat of their extinction, and the demands of feminist groups and liberation and civil rights movements (Chase, 2005; Muñoz-González, 2012; Tappan, 1997). In addition to serving to make minorities visible, narratives have also acted as direct sources for rescuing subjectivities, which makes stories transcendental for social studies.

In this book, survivors are not only authors and co-authors of *testimonios* but also contributors to studies that have built new knowledge. This new knowledge acts as a record of Memory to document how the conflict in Colombia has been (and is being) experienced. Without the *testimonios* of survivors, governmental and non-governmental researchers and mediators would not have been able to compile documents which reveal the many factors of personal and social life that have been affected during the conflict. This book aims to recognise the value of survivors' lives and stories, in uncovering what History will not know if it relies only on legitimised sources, such as the accounts of the media and the perpetrators.

Notes

(1) This report can be read in English. See https://babel.banrepcultural.org/digital/collection/p17054coll2/id/114.
(2) Owing to the fact that the concepts of Memory and Historical Memory are used in the chapter to refer to collective acts aimed at recovering events that contribute to the dignification of peoples who have suffered torturous acts in conflict contexts and to social justice actions, we use 'remembrance' to refer to individual and specific acts of recollection.
(3) This report can be read in English. See https://www.comisiondelaverdad.co/etiquetas/there-future-if-there-truth
(4) During the term of the previous government (2018–2022), there was a major controversy over the appointment of the director of this Centre. The government that appointed him did not acknowledge the conflict or prioritise victims in the decision-making process. These ambiguities contributed to the exclusion of the Centre from the Colombian Network of Sites of Memory and the Network of Latin American and Caribbean Sites of Memory (Reslac). Similarly, the CEV's report was criticised by members of the same governing party, given the revelations about the State's co-responsibility for the atrocities.
(5) Throughout the book, in the fragments of *testimonios* ... are used to indicate that the witness made a pause. [...] are used to indicate that quotations or *testimonios* were intervened by the authors of the chapters to shorten part of the content.
(6) Connerton (1989), in *How Societies Remember*, contrasts 'inscribing practices' and 'incorporating practices' to differentiate the ways in which cultural learning is retained: 'inscribing' relates to 'devices for storing and retrieving information, print, encyclopedias, indexes, photographs, sound tapes, computers, all require us to do something that captures and retains information'(1989: 96) and 'incorporating', to the way the body retains culturally learned ways of acting.
(7) These are just a few examples of authors and books that address the loss of traditions and productive systems in the context of the armed conflict in Colombia. The titles offer a deeper insight into the complex dynamics surrounding such losses: *Resistencia en la Sierra: El pueblo Kankwy y el conflicto armado contemporáneo* 1980–2004 [*Resistence in La Sierra: the Kankwy People and the Contemporary Armed Conflict 1980–2004*] by Natalia Isabel Ramírez Manjarrés; *Guerreros y campesinos: El despojo de la tierra en Colombia* [*Warriors and Peasants: Land Dispossession in Colombia*] by Alejandro Reyes Posada; and *Reflexiones sobre el sentido y génesis del desplazamiento forzado en Colombia* [*Reflections About the Sentiment and Genesis of Forced Displacement in Colombia*] by Nelson Jair Cuchumbé-Holguín and Julio Cesar Vargas-Bejarano.

References

Acedo, N. (2017) El género testimonio en Latinoamérica. Aproximaciones críticas en busca de su definición, genealogías, y taxonomía. Mirador Latinoamericano. *Latinoamérica* (64), 39–69.
Adorna, R. (2013) *Practicando la escritura terapéutica*. Editorial Desclée de Brouwer.
Almanza, R. (2011) Ausencias y presencias para una interculturalidad crítica postabismal desde el sur global. En VVAA (2011) *Formas-Otras: Saber, nombrar, narrar, hacer. IV Training Seminar de Jóvenes Investigadores en Dinámicas Interculturales* (pp. 79–87). CIDOB.
Aranguren, J. (2010) De un dolor a un saber: Cuerpo, sufrimiento y memoria en los límites de la escritura. *Papeles del CEIC* 2 (63), 1–27.
Arendt, H. (1997) *¿Qué es la política?* Paidós.
Arendt, H. (2015) *Vita activa. La condizione umana*. Bompiani.

Arroyave, M. (2013) *Objetos de la memoria en el destierro: El presente del pasado*. Tesis de maestría inédita, Universidad Nacional de Colombia, Sede Medellín.

Bergalli, R. and Rivera, I. (coords.) (2010) *Memoria colectiva como deber social*. Anthropos.

Beverley, J. (1989) *Testimonio: Sobre la política de la verdad*. Bonilla Artigas Editores.

Beverley, J. (2005) Testimonio, subalternity, and narrative authority. In N.K. Denzin and Y.S. Lincoln (eds) *The Sage Handbook Of Qualitative Research* (3rd edn, pp. 547–558). Sage Publications.

Blanco, M. (2012) Autoetnografía: Una forma narrativa de generación de conocimientos. *Andamios* 9 (19), 49–74.

Bruner, J. (2003) *La fábrica de historias. Derecho, literatura, vida*. Fondo de Cultura Económica.

Bungard, C. (2019) Writing by Heart. Victims of the Colombian armed conflict write their testimonies. Electronic thesis, University of Arizona.

Calveiro, P. (2006) Testimonio y memoria en el relato histórico. *Acta poética* 27 (2), 65–86.

Carmona, O. (2023) Narrativas y testimonios de la verdad en Colombia El testimonio y su emergencia en tiempos difíciles. In AA.VV *Perspectivas y retos en la construcción de verdad: Miradas desde lo narrativo, educativo y metodológico* (pp 109–133). Universidad Tecnológica de Pereira.

Caruth, C. (1996) *Unclaimed Experience: Trauma, Narrative, and History*. Johns Hopkins University Press.

Castillejo, A. (2013) La ilusión de la palabra que libera: Hacia una política del testimonio en Colombia. In A. Castillejo and F. Reyes (eds) *Violencia, memoria y sociedad: Debates y agendas en la Colombia actual* (pp. 21–40). Universidad Santo Tomás.

Cervantes, A. (2020) *Testimonios*. In L. Comas-Díaz and E. Torres Rivera (eds) *Liberation Psychology: Theory, Method, Practice, and Social Justice* (pp. 133–147). American Psychological Association.

Chartier, R. (2001) La historia, entre relato y conocimiento. *Historia y espacio* 17, 185–206.

Chase, S. (2005) Narrative inquiry: Multiple lenses, approaches, voices. In N.K. Denzin and Y.S. Lincoln (eds) *The Sage Handbook of Qualitative Research* (3rd edn, pp. 651–679). Sage Publications.

Comisión Nacional de Territorios Indígenas (2022) *El eterno retorno de la violencia contra los pueblos indígenas en Colombia*. Informe del Observatorio de Derechos Territoriales de los Pueblos Indígenas. CNTI.

Cuchumbé-Holguín, N. and Vargas-Bejarano, J. (2007) Reflexiones sobre el sentido y génesis del desplazamiento forzado en Colombia. *Universitas humanística* (65), 173–196.

CNMH (2013a) *Informe ¡Basta ya! Colombia. Memorias de guerra y dignidad*. CNMH.

CNMH (2013b) *La verdad de las mujeres. Víctimas del conflicto armado en Colombia*. CNMH.

Connerton, P. (1989) *How Societies Remember*. Cambridge University Press.

De Roux, F. (2022) *Discurso de presentación del informe final de la Comisión para el Esclarecimiento de la Verdad*. 28 de junio de 2022. See https://www.youtube.com/watch?v=SNtTe9c-mj4 (accessed January 2024).

De Salvo, L. (1999) *Writing as a Way of Healing. How Telling Our Stories Transform Our Lives*. HarperCollins.

Díaz, N. (2020) *Postcolonial Love Poem*. Faber and Faber.

Díaz, P. (2010) La memoria histórica. *Sociedad de la información*, 19. Cefalea.

Di Meglio, E. (2022) Hablar desde el silencio: La escritura autoficcional como elaboración discursiva de lo traumático. *Revista del Centro de Letras Hispanoamericanas* 44, 118–133.

Dupláa, C. (1996) *La voz testimonial en Montserrat Roig: Estudio cultural de los textos*. Icaria.

Engeström, Y. and Sannino, A. (2010) Studies of expansive learning: Foundations, findings and future challenges. *Educational Research Review* 5 (1), 1–24.
Errl, A. (2012) *Memoria colectiva y culturas del recuerdo*. Estudio introductorio. Universidad de los Andes.
Fals-Borda, O. (1981) *Ciencia propia y colonialismo intelectual*. Carlos Valencia Editores.
Feliu, J. (2007) Nuevas formas literarias para las ciencias sociales: El caso de la autoetnografía. *Athenea Digital* 12, 262–271. See http://psicologiasocial.uab.es/athenea/index.php/atheneaDigital/article/view/447 (accessed October 2020).
Fernández, J.W. (2000) Peripheral wisdom. In A. Cohen (ed.) *Signifying Identities. Anthropological Perspectives on Boundaries and Contested Values* (pp. 117–135). Routledge.
Ferraroti, F. (1988) Biografía y ciencias sociales. Historia oral e historias de vida. *Cuadernos de Ciencias Sociales* 18, 81–96.
Ferry, J.M. (2001) *La ética reconstructiva*. Biblioteca Francesa de Filosofía. Universidad Nacional de Colombia y Siglo del Hombre.
Figueroa, C. (2004) Gramática-violencia: Una relación significativa para la narrativa colombiana de segunda mitad del siglo XX. *Tabula Rasa* 2, 93–110.
Fuentes, M. (2007) Enzo Traverso: Els usos del passat. Història, memòria, política. *Recerques: Història, economia, cultura*, 155–159.
Gaitán, A. (2000) Exploring alternative forms of writing ethnography. Review essay. In C. Ellis and A. Bochner (eds) *Composing Ethnography: Alternative Forms of Qualitative Writing. Forum: Qualitative Social Research* 1 (3), Art. 42. See http://nbn-resolving.de/urn:nbn:de:0114-fqs (accessed September 2023).
García-González, N. (2011) Movimientos sociales y producción de conocimientos: La relevancia de las experiencias de autoformación. En VVAA (2011) *Formas-Otras: Saber, nombrar, narrar, hacer* (pp. 109–121). Barcelona Centre for International Affairs.
García-Márquez, G. (1996) *Noticia de un secuestro*. Norma.
García-Márquez, G. (2014) *Vivir para contarla*. Vintage español.
Garzón, M.A. (2014) Las narrativas del retorno. *Revista Encuentros* 12 (2), 67–77. Universidad Autónoma del Caribe.
González, M.P. and Pagés, J. (2014) Historia, memoria y enseñanza de la historia: Conceptos, debates y perspectivas europeas y latinoamericanas. *Historia y memoria* 9, 275–311. See http://www.scielo.org.co/scielo.php?pid=S2027-51372014000200010&script=sci_arttext (accessed July 2023).
Grandin, G. (2005) The instruction of great catastrophe: Truth commissions, national history, and state formation in Argentina, Chile, and Guatemala. *American Historical Review* 110 (1), 46–67.
Grosfoguel, R. (2011) La descolonización del conocimiento: Diálogo crítico entre la visión descolonial de Frantz Fanon y la sociología descolonial de Boaventura de Sousa Santos. En VVAA (2011) *Formas-Otras: Saber, nombrar, narrar, hacer* (pp. 97–108). Barcelona Centre for International Affairs.
Gugelberger, G.M. (1996) Introduction: Institutionalization of transgression: Testimonial discourse and beyond. In G.M. Gugelberger (ed.) *The Real Thing: Testimonial Discourse and Latin American* (pp. 1–23). Duke University Press.
Halbwachs, M. (2004a) *La memoria colectiva*. Prensas Universitarias de Zaragoza.
Halbwachs, M. (2004b) El sueño y las imágenes-recuerdos. *Los marcos sociales de la memoria* 39, 13–56.
Hayner, P. (2011) *Unspeakable Truths: Transitional Justice and the Challenge of Truth Commissions*. Routledge.
Henke, S. (1998) *Shattered Subjects: Trauma and Testimony in Women's Life-Writing*. St. Martin's Press.
Henderson, S. (2001) Latin American testimonio: Uncovering the subaltern's gender, race, and class. *The History Journal* 10, 83–84. San Francisco State University.

Hernández, F. (2011) Las historias de vida en el marco del giro narrativo en la investigación en Ciencias Sociales: Los desafíos de poner biografías en contexto. In F. Hernández, J.M. Sancho and J.I. Rivas (Coord.) *Historias de vida en educación: Biografías en contexto* (4th edn, pp. 13–22). Esbrina.

Herrera, A. (2008) Memoria colectiva y procesos de identidad en el Movimiento Nacional de Víctimas de Crímenes de Estado. Tesis de maestría inédita, Universidad Nacional de Colombia.

Housková, A. (1989) El testimonio como género literario. *Iberoamericana Pragensia* 22, 11–20.

Huyssen, A. (2007) *En busca del futuro perdido. Cultura y memoria en tiempos de globalización*. Fondo de Cultura Económica.

Inglis, J.T. (1993) *Traditional Ecological Knowledge: Concepts and Cases*. Museo Canadiense de la Naturaleza.

Jara, R. and Vidal, H. (1986) *Testimonio y literatura*. Sociedad para el Estudio de las Literaturas Revolucionarias Hispánicas y Lusófonas Contemporáneas.

Javlonka, I. (2017) *Laëtitia o el fin de los hombres*. Anagrama.

Jelin, E. (2001) *Los trabajos de la memoria*. Siglo XXI Editores.

Kalli, L. (1999) *Secuestrada: Una historia de la vida real*. Simon and Schuster.

Kolawole, O.D. (2001) Utilización de los conocimientos locales y desarrollo rural sostenible en el siglo XXI. *Monitor* 9 (3), 13–15.

Krog, A. (2013) *Conditional Tense: Memory and Vocabulary after the South African Truth and Reconciliation Commission*. Seagull Books.

Labov, W. (2010) Oral narratives of personal experience. *Cambridge Encyclopedia of the Language Sciences*, 546–548.

Lara, P. (2022) *Un informe final para leer muchas veces*. El Espectador. See https://www.elespectador.com/opinion/columnistas/patricia-lara-salive/un-informe-final-para-leer-muchas-veces/ (accessed January 2024).

Lopera, G. (2011) Sociología de las ausencias y de la emergencias. En VVAA (2011) *Formas-Otras: Saber, nombrar, narrar, hacer* (pp. 91–96). IV Training Seminar de jóvenes investigadores en Dinámicas Interculturales. CIDOB.

López, C. (2012) *Trauma, memoria y cuerpo: El testimonio femenino en Colombia (1985–2000)*. Asociación Internacional de Literatura y Cultura Femenina Hispánica.

Madison, D. (2003) Performance, personal narratives, and the politics of possibility. In N. Denzin and Y. Lincoln (eds) *The Future of Performance Studies: Visions and Revision* (pp. 469–486). Rowman & Littlefield Publishers.

Maldonado, J. (2008) *El intelectual y el sujeto testimonial en la literatura latinoamericana*. Editorial Pliegos.

Mendoza, J. (2004) Las formas del recuerdo. La memoria narrativa. *Athenea digital: Revista de pensamiento e investigación social* 6, 153–168.

Montoya, P. (2022) Paz y reconciliación, la casa común. *Revista Arcadia*. Número especial para la comisión de la Verdad. See https://www.semana.com/periodismo-cultural—-revista-arcadia/articulo/la-casa-comun/72021/ (accessed March 2022).

Muñoz, C.A. (2013) Acercamiento al concepto de memoria desde la visión crítica de la democracia. In A. Castillejo and F. Reyes (eds) *Violencia, memoria y sociedad: Debates y agendas en la Colombia actual* (pp. 375–387). Universidad Santo Tomás.

Muñoz-González, G. (2012) El alcance metodológico de las narrativas. In S. Soler Castillo (Comp.) *Lenguaje y Educación: Perspectivas metodológicas y teóricas para su estudio* (pp. 161–182). Universidad Distrital Francisco José de Caldas.

Nance, K.A. (2006) *Can Literature Promote Justice? Trauma Narrative and Social Action in Latin American Testimonio*. Vanderbilt University Press.

Navia-Lame, J. (2015) *La fuerza del ombligo, crónicas del conflicto en territorio Nasa*. Universidad del Cauca.

Ngozi-Adichie, C. (2018) *El peligro de la historia única*. Random House.

Nora, P. (1989) Between Memory and History: Les Lieux de Mémoire. *Representations [Special Issue: Memory and Counter Memory]* 26, 7–24. See https://eclass.uoa.gr/modules/document/file.php/ARCH230/PierreNora.pdf (accessed August, 2024).
Nora, P. (2008) Entre memoria e historia. La problemática de los lugares. In *Los lugares de la memoria*. Trilce.
Nussbaum, M. (2015) Discurso de recibimiento del doctorado honoris causa de la Universidad de Antioquia. See https://redfilosofia.es/atheneblog/2015/12/25/discurso-de-martha-nussbaum-en-antioquia-con-ocasion-de-su-honoris-causa/ (accessed November 2023).
Orfaley, M., Bedoya, M. and Díaz, V. (2019) *Escribir para reinventarse*. Universidad de Antioquia.
Ortiz, C. (1994) Historiografía de la violencia. *La historia al final del milenio: Ensayos de historiografía colombiana y latinoamericana* 1, 390–92.
Ortiz, L. (1997) La novela colombiana hacia finales del siglo veinte: Una aproximación desde la historia. *Wor(l)d of Words*, 27.
Pennebaker, J. (1990) *Opening Up: The Healing Power of Expressing Emotions*. University of Texas.
Piña, C. (1986) Sobre las historias de vida y su campo de validez en las ciencias sociales. *Revista Paraguaya de Sociología* 23 (67), 143–162.
Rajasekaran, B., Warren, D.M. and Babu, S.C. (1991) Indigenous natural-resource management systems for sustainable agricultural development – A global perspective. *Journal of International Development* 3 (3), 387–401.
Reyes-Aparicio, P. (2013) Narrativa, violencia y memoria: Rupturas y secuencias. In A. Castillejo and F. Reyes (eds) *Violencia, memoria y sociedad: Debates y agendas en la Colombia actual* (pp. 237–256). Ediciones USTA.
Reys-Posada, A. (2009) *Guerreros y campesinos: El despojo de la tierra en Colombia*. Norma.
Riaño, P. (2006) *Jóvenes, memoria y violencia en Medellín: Una antropología del recuerdo y el olvido*. Universidad de Antioquia. Icahn.
Ricoeur, P. (1996) *Sí mismo como otro*. Siglo XXI.
Ricoeur, P. (2000) Narratividad, fenomenología y hermenéutica. *Anàlisi: Quaderns de comunicació i cultura* 25, 189–207.
Ricoeur, P. (2004) *La memoria, la historia, el olvido*. Fondo de Cultura Económica.
Rieff, D. (2012) *Contra la memoria*. Random House Mondadori.
Rivara-Kamaji, G. (2007) El testimonio: Una forma de relato. *Revista Bajo Palabra* 2, 111–118.
Ross, F.C. (2003) *Bearing Witness: Women and the Truth and Reconciliation Commission in South Africa*. Pluto Press.
Rueda, E. (2022) Orígenes y trayectorias de la humanidad: Narraciones originarias y emancipación. In E. Rueda, A. Larrea, A. Castro, O. Bonilla, N. Rueda and C. Guzmán (eds) *Retornar al origen. Narrativas ancestrales sobre humanidad, tiempo y mundo*. CLACSO-UNESCO.
Said, E.W. (2023) Intellectuals in the post-colonial world. In D. Bridon (ed.) *Postcolonlsm* (pp. 29–46). Routledge.
Salazar-Henao, M. and López-Moreno, L. (2016) Las narrativas como método de investigación en las ciencias sociales: Una mirada a la investigación transformadora. *V Encuentro Latinoamericano de Metodología de las Ciencias Sociales. Memoria Académica*. See http://www.memoria.fahce.unlp.edu.ar/trab_eventos/ev.8571/ev.8571.pdf (accessed January 2023).
Sklodovska, E. (1996) Spanish American testimonial novel: Some afterthoughts. In G.M. Gugelberger (ed.) *The Real Thing: Testimonial Discourse and Latin American*. Duke University Press.
Sommer, D. (1991) Rigoberta's secrets. *Latin American Perspectives* 18 (3), 32–50.

Stetsenko, A. (2023) Knowledge production as a process of making mis/takes, at the edge of uncertainty: Research as an activist, risky, and personal quest. In P. Dionne and A. Jornat (eds) *Doing CHAT in the Wild* (pp.15–45). Brill. See https://doi.org/10.1163/9789004548664_002 (accessed October 2023)

Stover, E. (2005) *The Witnesses: War Crimes and the Promise of Justice in The Hague.* University of Pennsylvania Press.

Strejilevich, N. (2006) El testimonio: Más allá del lenguaje de la verdad. *Human Rights Quarterly* 28 (3) 701–713.

Suárez, J. (2011) La literatura testimonial de las guerras en Colombia: Entre la memoria, la cultura, las violencias y la literatura. *Universitas Humanística* 72, 275–296.

Vélez-Rendón, J.C. (2003) Violencia, memoria y literatura testimonial en Colombia. Entre las memorias literales y las memorias ejemplares. *Estudios políticos* 22, 31–57.

Villa-Gómez, J.D. (2016) Recordar para reconstruir: El papel de la memoria en la reconstrucción del tejido social. Una perspectiva psicosocial para la construcción de memorias transformadoras. In E. Arrieta (ed.) *Grupo de Investigación sobre Estudios Críticos; Conflicto, justicia y memoria: 1. Teoría crítica de la violencia y prácticas de memoria y resistencia* (pp. 183–214). Universidad Pontificia Bolivariana.

Vinyes, R. (2009) La memoria como política pública. In J. Guixé and M. Iniesta (eds) *Políticas públicas de la memoria.* I Coloquio Internacional Memorial Democrático. Editorial Milenio.

Violi, M.P. (2014) *Paesaggi della memoria, il trauma, lo spazio, la storia.* Bompiani.

Vivas, S. (2007) La experiencia de la violencia en Colombia. *Universitas Humanística* 63 (1), 269–286.

Vives-Riera, A. (2011) Conflicto cultural y construcción del conocimiento: Del choque de civilizaciones a la hibridación creativa. En VVAA. *Formas-Otra: Saber, nombrar, narrar, hacer. IV Training Seminar de jóvenes investigadores en Dinámicas Interculturales* (pp. 65–78). CIDOB.

Yúdice, G. (1996) Testimonio and postmodernism. In G.M. Gugelberger (ed.) *The Real Thing: Testimonial Discourse and Latin America* (pp. 42–57). Duke University Press.

Yúdice, G. (2002) Testimonio y concientización. In J. Beverley and H. Achugar (eds) *La voz del otro: Testimonio, subalternidad y verdad narrativa* (pp. 221–242). Papiro.

Zerillo, A. (2006) *Prácticas de escritura en el campo de la salud mental. La escritura en el Taller de Letras del Frente de Artistas del Borda.* Universidad de Buenos Aires.

Zerillo, A. (2008) *La escritura terapéutica.* XI Congreso de la Sociedad Argentina de Lingüística. Facultad de Humanidades y Ciencias, Santa Fe.

Zerillo, A. (2014) Escritura reparadora: El caso de las Madres de Plaza de Mayo. Traslaciones. *Revista latinoamericana de lectura y escritura* 1 (2), 82–103.

Part 2

Narratives of the Colombian Armed Conflict

3 Narrative as an Emotional Resource for the Empowerment of the Survivors of the Colombian Armed Conflict

Blanca Yaneth González Pinzón

> ¿Para qué escribe uno si no
> es para juntar sus pedazos?
> Eduardo Galeano, 1989

> Why does one write if not to
> gather our scattered pieces?
> Eduardo Galeano, 1989

Introduction

In this chapter, I examine collective and community actions rooted in using narrative as a resource for 'Symbolic Reparation'. These actions were promoted by various public and private entities and involved survivors of the different actors implicated in the Colombian armed conflict (military, guerrilla, paramilitary) and, of course, civilian society.

It is crucial to understand the concept of 'Symbolic Reparation' within a legal framework to comprehend the importance and aims of these actions and the interest they arouse in the current post-agreement context. To provide this understanding, I first clarify the concept from the perspective of Law 1448 and Law 975. Then, I outline the reasons for conducting exploratory research, describe the main methodology used and present the results in three sections. The comments and reflections are based on *testimonios* extracted from the documents produced by each of the selected community actions.

Like other chapters in the book, this chapter reveals the multiple forms of producing *testimonios* in Colombia, the reasons that motivate their production and sharing, their contributions to the recovery of Memory and the growing interest in giving a place of consideration and respect to those who have suffered.

The Concept of 'Symbolic Reparation'

The symbolic dimension of reparation has been mentioned in various works on Memory since the 1990s (Barreto-Moreno, 2004; Bustamante-Danilo & Carreño-Calderón, 2020; Wills, 2007). Moral reparation, collective reparation or integral reparation are the terms used to describe the obligations of States towards victims in transitional justice processes. In Colombia, the concept of 'Symbolic Reparation', which has been used for different forms of redress, came to the fore before the peace dialogues (2012–2016) when the Congress of the Republic enacted Law 1448 of 2011, known as the *Ley de víctimas y restitución de tierras* [*Law of victims and land restitution*]. The law sets out ways to provide support, assistance and comprehensive reparations to victims of the internal armed conflict. This legal provision resulted from a lengthy discussion and eventual consensus between the national government, various political sectors and civil society. The content of the Law is unequivocal: most of its articles reiterate its aim of providing 'integral reparation' to victims and guaranteeing 'non-repetition'. 'Symbolic Reparation' was included in this holistic approach; it went almost unnoticed at the time but gained momentum five years after the Law's promulgation. This Law was preceded by Law 975 of 2005, *Ley de justicia y paz* [*Law of Justice and Peace*], which also dealt with the issue.

Article 8 of Law 975 and Article 141 of Law 1448 define the concept of 'Symbolic Reparation' as:

> Any provision made in favour of victims or the community in general **that tends to ensure the preservation of historical memory**, the non-repetition of the victimising events, the public acceptance of the facts, the request for public forgiveness and the **restoration of the dignity of the victims**. (Emphasis added)

In turn, Article 3 of Law 1448 states:

> For the purposes of this Law, victims are considered to be those who, individually or collectively, have suffered harm as a result of events occurring on or after 1 January 1985, as a consequence of breaches of International Humanitarian Law or severe and gross violations of International Human Rights Law, which occurred as a result of the internal armed conflict (10).

Paragraph 4 of the same article clarifies:

> People who have been victims of events that occurred before 1 January 1985 have the right to the truth, **measures of symbolic reparation** and the guarantees of non-repetition provided for in this Law as part of the social conglomerate and without the need to be individualised. (Emphasis added)

Among the forms of reparation mentioned in the laws are '**actions** that promote restitution, compensation, rehabilitation, satisfaction; and guarantees of non-repetition of the conduct'. Specifically concerning rehabilitation, it is proposed to 'take **actions** aimed at the recovery of victims who suffer physical and **psychological** trauma as a consequence of the crime' (Article 8, Law 975, 2005) (Emphasis added).

Research on workshops and collective 'actions' dealing with reparation and mediated by written, oral and pictorial narratives are scarce in Colombia precisely because 'Symbolic Reparation' has only been recognised for the past two decades. Nevertheless, the country has a 40-year history of research on Testimony in literature, as seen in Chapter 2. Exploring narrative from the point of view of 'Symbolic Reparation' sheds light on narrative as a means of reconstructing Memory and as a reparative action in post-conflict environments.

Exploratory Research

This chapter analyses the effect that narrative has on three key dimensions: reparation and healing in relation to the individual and collective; the country's generation of Memory; and the transformative effect of the conflict. Exploring these three essential dimensions provides guidance for future reparations, emotional empowerment and dignification of survivors.

I conducted exploratory research (Adelman *et al.*, 1980; Cohen *at al.*, 2000; Hernández *et al.*, 2010; Yin, 1984) on the nature and impact of community-based actions centring on reparation because of the limited available knowledge about such actions. The research was guided by questions about the actions carried out, the objectives pursued, the organisations developing them, the people involved, the products created, the regions and locations and the methods used.

I took the period from 2011 (the year the Victims and Land Restitution Law was enacted) to 2019 (when the research began) as a chronological frame of reference. It includes the period of peace dialogues between the FARC guerrillas and the government between 2012 and 2016.

I began by searching the pages of the Centro de Memoria, Paz y Reconciliación [Centre of Memory, Peace and Reconciliation](CMPR),[1] created in 2008. This entity mapped publications and experiences of diverse actions favouring such reparation. The compilation revealed that 435 workshops, meetings, community actions and other activities had been organised by the State and various governmental and non-governmental organisations (NGO) nationwide. These actions were concentrated in regions where the conflict had had the most impact.[2]

Furthermore, I examined the documents produced by the CNMH,[3] which was established following the enactment of Law 1448. Almost two hundred of these compiled actions used narrative (oral, audiovisual, pictorial) as the driving force behind the work with the communities.

In total 10 actions were selected for analysis in this chapter, all of which met the following conditions: they took place in the chosen period (before, during and after the Peace Agreement); they were published to facilitate the reading of the *testimonios* and other descriptions of actions; they had 'Symbolic Reparation' as a goal; they involved survivors who had experienced the conflict from different positions of representation (ex-guerrillas, ex-paramilitaries, exiles, hired assassins, soldiers, civilian population), and they were located in different regions of Colombia.

Data Analysis and Organisation

To begin the analysis, I created an organising matrix with various data (Tables 3.1 and 3.2). In addition to the data organised in the tables, the complete reading of the published and publicly accessible *testimonios* – selected during the exploration phase – revealed a number of key aspects: the types of effects, the subjects' perceptions of the conflict, the most frequently used words, the memories, the changes in their lives, the impact of the war on their existence and their territories.

Tables 3.1 and 3.2 provide contextual data that help to give insight into the selected actions.

While narratives of 'Symbolic Reparation', such as those mentioned in this chapter, constitute the essential material of these *testimonios*, they are only one aspect of the process and product. Prior to their production, several resources and activities were used to prepare the ground for the elicitation of these emotionally charged narratives (see Table 3.2):

- orality, dialogue, the use of metaphors, reading other *testimonios* and chronicles to identify and activate the narrative rhythm itself;
- the use of objects of memory (letters, toys, recipes, photographs, etc.);
- techniques such as interviews, workshops, documentation of stories, roundtables;
- the activation of the senses, emotions and feelings through artistic expressions such as theatre, cinema, photography, murals and songs.

The use of these resources and activities is not trivial, as working with lacerating pain and disruptive trauma requires care, preparation, repetition and time. It is also important to avoid an abrupt arrival at the *testimonio*, as this can re-victimise. Re-victimisation prolongs suffering and hinders recovery because people experience new suffering as a consequence of the response from institutions, society, or people close to them. Most of what I refer to as core 'mobilising concepts' driving the actions (see Table 3.2) have been taken from the objectives defined in the projects or the documents produced by each action, and show the intention of reparation.

The analysis and discussion I present below emerged from my analysis of the mobilising concepts present in the stated objectives of the actions and a detailed reading and analysis of the published *testimonios*. The selected fragments come from oral or written *testimonios*, with the title

Table 3.1 Contextual data of the actions selected for exploration

Name of the action and year of publication	Year(s) of development/ context	Geographical location	Participants	Managing organisation(s)
1. *De su puño y letra: Polifonía para la memoria. Las voces de las víctimas del conflicto armado en Medellín* [In Their Own Words: Polyphony for Memory. The Voices of the Victims of the Armed Conflict in Medellín]	2006–2009 Urban	Medellín[4]	Approximately 100 people, with different trades and professions, organised in three groups.	Programa de Atención a Víctimas de la Secretaría de Gobierno de la Alcaldía de Medellín [Victim Attention Programme of the Government Secretariat of the Medellín Mayor's Office]
Three e-books				Vice-rectory of Outreach, University of Antioquia
a. *Jamás olvidaré tu nombre* [I will never forget your name] (2006) https://issuu.com/museocasadelamemoria/docs/jamasolvidare				Faculty of Communications, University of Antioquia
b. *El cielo no me abandona* (2007) [Heaven does not Abandon Me] https://issuu.com/museocasadelamemoria/docs/elcielo				
c. *Donde pisé aún crece la hierba* [Where I stepped, the grass still grows] (2009)[5] https://issuu.com/pr ograma-atenciona victimas/docs/dondepisecrecelah ierba/138				
2. *Retomo la Palabra, relatos de violencia y reconciliación* [Taking back the Word, Stories of Violence and Reconciliation] (2009) https://issuu.com/mariasanchezisaza/docs/retomo_la_palabra	2008 Rural and urban	Urabá Sucre Cordoba Cesar Bajo Cauca Antioqueño	Around 140 ex-paramilitaries took part in a reintegration programme.	Alta Consejería para la Reintegración Social y Económica de Personas y Grupos Alzados en Armas (ACR) [High Council for Social and Economic Reintegration of Armed Groups and Individuals] Centro Regional para el Fomento del Libro en América Latina y el Caribe [Regional Center for the Promotion of Books in Latin America and Caribbean]

(*Continued*)

Table 3.1 (Continued)

Name of the action and year of publication	Year(s) of development/context	Geographical location	Participants	Managing organisation(s)
3. *Memorias, la voz de los sobrevivientes* Capítulo V del informe ¡Basta ya! [*Memories, the Voice of Survivors Chapter V of the Enough Already! Report*] http://centrodememoriahistorica.gov.co/descargas/informes201/bastaYa/capitulos/basta-ya-cap5_328-395.pdf	2009–2011 Rural and urban	Several regions of the country	More than 1000 people	Grupo de Memoria Histórica del CNMH [CNMH Historical Memory Group]
4. *La verdad de las mujeres: Víctimas del conflicto armado de Colombia* [*The Truth of Women: Victims of Colombia's Armed Conflict*] Two volumes https://www.rutapacifica.org.co/publicaciones/198-la-verdad-de-las-mujeres-victimas-del-conflicto-armado-en-colombia-informe-de-comision-de-verdad-y-memoria	2013 Rural and urban	Different regions	More than 1000 women of different ethnicities (mestizo, Afro-descendant and indigenous).	CEV project Feminist movement Red de organizaciones *La Ruta Pacífica de la mujeres* [*The Pacific Route of Women* network of organisations]
5. *Narrativas del desplazamiento para la construcción de identidad* [*Narratives of Displacement for the Construction of Identity*] https://www.museocasadelamemoria.gov.co/wp-content/uploads/2019/04/Narrativas-1.pdf	2014 Urban and marginal urban	Medellín	Four population groups: El Cañón and San Gabriel communities, San Cristóbal municipality Ave Fenix and Mandala women organisations	Governmental institutions Medellín's Casa de la Memoria Museum Caro y Cuervo Institute Medellín Municipal Unit for Victims' Services

(Continued)

Table 3.1 (Continued)

Name of the action and year of publication	Year(s) of development/ context	Geographical location	Participants	Managing organisation(s)
6. *Exilio colombiano: Huellas del conflicto armado más allá de las fronteras* [Colombian Exile: Traces of the Armed Conflict Beyond Borders] https://centrodememoriahistorica.gov.co/e xilio-colombiano- huellas-del-conflicto-armado-mas-alla-de- las-fronteras/	2014 to 2017 Urban	Cúcuta Medellín Pasto Pereira Bogotá	Colombians in exile abroad	Government and CNMH Victims' organisations abroad International Victims Forum (FIV) Oficina del Alto Comisionado de Naciones Unidas para los Refugiados (ACNUR) [Office of the United Nations High Commissioner for Refugees] Organización Internacional para las Migraciones (OIM) [International Organisation for Migration]
7. *Recetas para olvidar la guerra* [Recipes to Forget the War] Printed booklet	2016 Rural	Chaparral, Tolima	Victims of the conflict that occupied an entire neighbourhood in Chaparral, Tolima Elders, youth and children from Tolima, Caquetá, Putumayo and Huila	Ministry of Culture
8. *Narrativas de paz al final de la guerra: Experiencia de reconciliación y diálogo en la I.E. San Vicente de Paúl (S.V. dP.)* [Narratives of Peace at the End of the War: Experience of Reconciliation and Dialogue in the Education Institution San Vicente de Paúl (S.V. dP.)] Printed book *Abrazar en vez de castigar* [Hugs, not punishment] (Ruiz-Lozano et al, 2016).	2017 Urban	Medellín	School students	José Manuel Segura Institutional Library (I.E. S. V.dP) Humanities Area I.E. S. V.dP.

(Continued)

Table 3.1 (Continued)

Name of the action and year of publication	Year(s) of development/ context	Geographical location	Participants	Managing organisation(s)
9. *Almas que escriben memorias y esperanzas* [Souls writing memories and hope] http://www.victimasbogota.gov.co/sites/default/files/documentos/LIBRO%20ALMAS%20QUE%20ESCRIBEN.pdf	2018 Urban	Different cities in the country	11 people Survivors People in the process of reintegration Retired soldiers Relatives of people who disappeared at different times	Alta Consejería para los Derechos de las Víctimas, la Paz y la Reconciliación [High Counsellor's Office for Victims' Rights, Peace and Reconciliation] Mayor of Bogotá Centro Nacional de Memoria Histórica [National Centre of Historical Memory]
10. *Escritura viva para la paz* [Live writing for peace] http://colecciones.museocasadelamemoria.gov.co/repositorio/handle/mcm/625	2018 Urban	Medellín	Victims Victims of the armed conflict in Colombia who belong to Medellín's 8th Commune	Call for Art and Culture Stimuli 2018. Medellín's Casa de la Memoria Museum

Source: Compiled by the author based on the analysis of the actions selected for exploration.

Table 3.2 Mobilising concepts in each action

Title of the action	Activities/resources	Mobilising concepts
1. *In Their Own Words: Polyphony for Memory. The Voices of the Victims of the Armed Conflict in Medellín*	Joint construction workshops, led by journalists, based on oral narratives (written in the memory), which were later written down Active 'one to one' searches over several months Neighbourhood workshops Support through gestures, drawings, words, toys, colours, pictures, papers and songs *Testimonios* written at different times, mostly on paper, later transcribed for publication	Recovery Memory Testimony
2. *Taking back the Word, Stories of Violence and Reconciliation* (2009)	Continuous reading in the meetings, then moving on to writing The themes of the chapters respond to the recurrences in them	Reintegration Memory construction Symbolic reconciliation Forgiveness
3. *Memories, the Voice of Survivors* Chapter V of the Enough Already! Report	Consultation of primary and secondary sources (24 previous research, local and national archives, court records and media archives) Participation of survivors as witnesses and researchers Selection of emblematic cases Hundreds of *testimonios* (through interviews and Memory recovery workshops)	Historical Memory Non-repetition Oral testimony
4. *The Truth of Women: Victims of Colombia's Armed Conflict* (I and II)	Documenting stories Oral testimony Interviews between women	Women's narrative Silenced women's *testimonio* Factual truth vs narrative truth Memory
5. *Narratives of Displacement for the Construction of Identity*	Narrative exchange Building word maps Letters Use of metaphors to re-signify words (peace, forgiveness, powerlessness, violence, resistance, hope, fear, oblivion, displacement, security, victims, heroes)	Rebuilding the community's social fabric Identity theft Catharsis Reconciliation Memory Writing for healing

(*Continued*)

Table 3.2 (Continued)

Title of the action	Activities/resources	Mobilising concepts
6. *Colombian Exile: Traces of the Armed Conflict Beyond Borders*	Working tables in stages Interviews Dialogues Narrative exchange Exercises to reconstruct the Historical Memory of the Colombian exile Workshops for the reconstruction of Memory, reparation and dignity	Collective Memory Memory reconstruction
7. *Recipes to Forget the War*	The creation of menus and recipes based on emotions Murals Dialogues between neighbours	Emotion Memory recovery Ancestral knowledge Collective construction Reconciliation Remedy
8. *Narratives of Peace at the End of the War: Experience of Reconciliation and Dialogue in the Education Institution San Vicente de Paúl (S.V. dP.)*	Workshops with students Systematising narrative experiences Audio stories Letters (to a child returning from war) Praxeological technique focusing on remembering Hugs as a symbolic materialisation of affection	Return Memory Affection Crisis Protection Writing Narrative experiences
9. *Souls writing memories and hope*	Ten workshops Regular exchange of views on each other's activities	Forgiveness Solidarity reconciliation Writing as a process dialogue Writing as restorative action
10. *Live writing for peace*	Photography Binding Writing Negotiation dialogue Public deliberation	Historical Memory Reconciliation Transitional justice Catharsis Social transformation Silenced tragedy

Source: Compiled by the author based on documentary analysis.

of the action from which they were produced indicated in each case. I have organised the presentation of the analysis under three key headings: *Narrative as a Liberating and Healing Action*; *'I' and 'We' in Narratives as a Contribution to Memory and the Search for Truth and Justice*; and *The Consequences of War as an Engine of Transformation and the Elaboration of Imaginaries of the Future*.

Narrative as a Liberating and Healing Action

<blockquote>
Si hubiéramos estado en otro lugar, nuestras palabras habrían sido diferentes.

Mujeres Ave Fénix, 2014

If we had been somewhere else, our words would have been different.

Phoenix Women, 2014
</blockquote>

The selected narratives, whether written by the survivors in the specific actions or as a result of subsequent interviews, show a diversity of forms, places of development, agents, actors, moments and strategies. Nevertheless, they all share a healing and pacifying intention in the context of assisted solitude, when pains and sorrows are shared and listened to (CNMH, 2019: 8). All of the narratives emphasise the liberating power of *testimonios*, the possibility of becoming protagonists of future stories, and the role of *testimonios* in giving a voice to survivors to those who have none without (Beverley, 2005; Dupláa, 1996; Housková, 1989; Narváez, 1986; Strejilevich, 2006). Many of their authors have testified as survivors in court proceedings and Memory recovery and reparations workshops, as exemplified in the experiences recounted by one woman:

<blockquote>
Me siento liviana porque acabo de hablar, de contar esas cosas que me han pasado, me siento realizada y siento como que descansé de poder sacar todo ese dolor que sentía adentro. Saber que alguien lo escucha, sin juzgarlo, porque lo que ha pasado no es solamente la violencia con todos estos grupos, mire que ha habido violencia familiar y todo. Asumir todo eso y aguantar y tenerlo aquí dentro oprimido. No todos los días de la vida uno habla de lo que hablamos hoy. Yo desde que declaré allá, solamente declaré lo que fueron las muertes y todo eso, pero mi vida nunca, a mí nunca me preguntaron por mi vida. (Acción 4: 27. Tomo I. Entrevista a mujer de Primavera, Arauca [número 3 en el mapa], 2013)

I feel a sense of lightness after sharing my story. I feel fulfilled and like I've taken a load off and found a bit of rest from the pain I've been carrying around inside. It's been a relief to have someone listen to me without judgement. I've been through a lot, including violence from various groups and family violence. It's been challenging to cope with all that and to keep it bottled up inside. It's not every day in life that you talk about what we're talking about today. Since I testified, I only talked about the deaths and all that, but they never asked me about my life. (Action 4: 27. Volume I. Interview with a woman from Primavera, Arauca [number 3 on the map], 2013)
</blockquote>

Genuine listening allows for the creation of a space of intentional communion, which is of great importance for Symbolic Reparation (Chapter 2 in this book). This process enables survivors to occupy different statuses of social representation. As illustrated in Tables 3.1 and 3.2, various resources and activities were used in each action to facilitate writing, graphic and oral narration; however, using these resources was only encouraged when people felt ready (Chapter 10 in this book). Patricia Nieto (2007) discusses the role of writing workshops in Action 1. According to Nieto, 'writing is a mirror, and therefore it caresses, hurts, sacrifices, searches and also heals, soothes, liberates and comforts'.

Similarly, Hernández (2011: 21) posits the emotive role of narratives:

> Narrative is close to the emotional and intricate dimensions of experience. As Bolívar (1998) asserts, narrative enables the capture of the multifaceted meanings of human experience, encompassing the desires, feelings, beliefs, and values that individuals share and negotiate within the context of their learning communities, where they develop as subjects.

Many scholars (Adorna, 2013; Caruth, 1996; De Salvo, 1999; Di Meglio, 2022; Henke, 1998; Orfaley *et al.*, 2019; Pennebaker, 1990; Vélez-Rendón, 2003; Zerillo, 2006, 2008, 2014) have acknowledged the therapeutic value of *testimonios*. They argue that this approach allows subjects, often marginalised and isolated, to overcome the condition of being only part of statistics and to emerge from the humiliating condition of invisibility to which the passage of time and the transformation of societies would condemn them. It enables them to express the feeling that they are not isolated in this experience. As Pablo Montoya (2022) posits, there is a collective liberation with each individual's emancipation.

Connerton (1989) emphasises the power of any activity with a ceremonial and commemorative character to bring back the past, covering it with a representational mask that captures it anew. This transfiguration has undergone an internal mutation, which, when made public seeks forms of expression other than horror to achieve solidarity and attention. Thus, the subject can let go of what they consider insurmountable and turn it into a call to the present and the future.

El Yanama ha sido romper y volver a llegar, tratar de curar no solamente la parte ritual asociada con el llanto a los muertos, sino la determinación de no dejarse despedazar culturalmente. (Acción 3: 394. Testimonio escrito por una mujer para el GMH. Taller Memorias en tiempo de guerra. Depto. de la Guajira, Bahía Portete [Número 18 en el mapa], 2011)	The Yanama[6] has been about breaking and returning, trying to heal, not only with the ritual part associated with weeping for the dead, but also the determination not to be torn apart culturally. (Action 3: 394. *Testimonio* by a woman for the GMH. Workshop Memories in Wartime. Department of Guajira, Bahía Portete [Number 18 on the map], 2011)

Carrying out spaces of communion to share with others who have suffered the same or worse highlights the representational power of the encounter. The following emotional *receta*, recipe, written by an elder woman, rather than describing a step-by-step guide to prepare food, expresses the value of neighbourliness and conversation with others in the community. In Colombia, the tradition of talking with a neighbour over coffee (*tinto*) makes much sense. In each meeting of this Action (7), the attendees worked from 12 noon until 6pm, with the help of officials from the Ministry of Culture, as many attendees were illiterate or had only primary school education. Each short written text was entitled according to the emotion people wanted to express.

Receta para estar de buen genio | Recipe for a good mood

- Me pone contento que halla [sic] que comer
- Tomarse un tinto
- Que halla [sic] leche para echarle al tinto
- Que cuando venga un vecino poder brindarle un tinto para conversar.

(Acción 7: 14. Mujer adulta mayor, que escribe una receta en un taller comunitario en el barrio Santa Helena. Dpto. del Tolima, Chaparral [Número 29 en el mapa], 2016)

- It makes me happy that there is something to eat.
- Drinking a cup of coffee.
- Let there be milk to put in the cup of coffee.
- When a neighbour comes over, we can give them a cup of coffee to talk.

(Action 7: 14. Elder woman writing a recipe in a community workshop in the Santa Helena neighbourhood. Department of Tolima, Chaparral [Number 29 on the map], 2016)

The organisers of actions for Symbolic Reparation (actions 1, 2, 5, 7, 8, 9, 10) try to ensure that freedom of expression prevails, which is why the narratives act as an emotional means of liberation (Feliu, 2007; Garzón, 2014; Muñoz-González, 2012). This liberation is produced differently depending on the role from which the conflict was experienced (victim, survivor or victimiser) – the place the subject occupied in the conflict. However, forgiveness, the discharge of hatred and the separation of the need for revenge are constant themes in these actions. In the following two fragments, religious beliefs support a transitional experience.

Quiero decirles que a pesar de las adversidades y contratiempos que la vida nos brinda, tenemos que sanar y continuar adelante... la cicatriz queda pero que ella sea solo un recuerdo, duro y amargo, pero que con ayuda de Dios y la Santísima Virgen debemos continuar adelante y darles a entender [a] los malvados que los buenos y los que deseamos la paz

I want to tell you that despite the adversities and setbacks that life brings us, we have to heal and move forward... the scar remains, but it should only be a hard and bitter memory. However, with the help of God and the Blessed Virgin, we must move forward and make the wicked understand that there are more of us who are good and

para nuestro barrio y nuestra Colombia somos más. (Acción 5: 8. Testimonio escrito por una mujer en Taller con Mujeres de El Cañón para resignificar la Esperanza. Depto. de Antioquia [Número 2 en el mapa], 2014)

who want peace for our neighbourhood and our Colombia. (Action 5: 8. *Testimonio* by a woman in a workshop with women from El Cañón to re-signify Hope. Department of Antioquia [Number 2 on the map], 2014)

El destino del ser humano solamente lo conoce Dios, y de pronto a los enclenques se les desea suerte, a los buenos se les desea éxito. Porque toda suerte es inestable. De pronto esto que me sucedió fue para hacer un pare en el camino, para reparar cosas, y con esto no quiero decir que fue Dios quien lo causó. De pronto, fueron los afanes de la vida. Es una oportunidad de volver a vivir, de compartir lo que me pasó con otras personas, sin odio, sin rencor. Mi alma está sana. (Acción 1c: 181. Testimonio escrito por hombre víctima de una mina antipersona, Medellín (Antioquia) [número 2 en el mapa], 2009)

The destiny of human beings is known only to God, and maybe the weak are wished luck, and the good are wished success. Because all luck is unstable. Maybe what happened to me was a call to make a stop along the way, to repair things, and by this, I don't mean that it was God who caused it. Suddenly, it was the hustle and bustle of life. It is an opportunity to live again and share what happened to me with other people without hatred or resentment. My soul is healthy. (Action 1c: 181. *Testimonio* by a male landmine victim, Medellín (Antioquia) [number 2 on map], 2009)

The narrative elaboration process encompasses both the interaction with the other (society, mediator, organisation) – which allows the construction of a social narrative – and a permanent relationship with the past – sometimes close up, and sometimes with distance. Returning to an extreme situation, and coming back from it, play an essential role in the production of *testimonios* (Bello-Tocancipá & Aranguren-Romero, 2020; Carmona, 2023; Cervantes, 2020; Garzón, 2014; Jelin, 2001; Ramírez, 2021).

In Colombia, the overwhelming majority of survivors experienced internal displacement, which affected an estimated 7 million individuals (CNMH, 2019; Lara, 2022). Consequently, abandoning territory was a pervasive theme in accounts. The concepts of family, customs, the house, home and relatives are repeatedly evoked. The house is where familial love, roots and belonging converge; it is the space to safeguard what is physically or emotionally acquired. Consequently, house and home are places which figure strongly in acts of remembrance:

La hija de ella se fue hace poquito, el sobrino de ella se fue hace poquito, igual mucha gente por miedo se va para otros barrios… al igual, como uno siempre tiene su casa por acá o

Her daughter left a little while ago, her nephew left a little while ago, and many people leave for other neighbourhoods out of fear… at the same time, since you always

> al menos su familia, si uno tiene una necesidad, una aguapanela me la da cualquier persona por acá. Eso para mí es desplazamiento, tener que huir, no porque alguien lo amenazó, sino porque los muchachos de diez años en adelante están corriendo peligro... (Acción 5: 13. Testimonio escrito por mujer de El Cañón, que acude a taller de resignificación del desplazamiento. Depto. de Antioquia [número 2 en el mapa], 214)
>
> have your house around here or at least your family, if you are in need, anyone around here will give you *aguapanela* [sugar cane beverage]. That, for me, is displacement, having to flee, not because someone threatened you, but because from age ten onwards, the boys are in danger... (Action 5: 13. *Testimonio* by a woman from El Cañón in a workshop on the resignification of displacement. Department of Antioquia [number 2 on the map], 214)

The conflict has also shifted how we define and use words to describe an unnamed and unspeakable loss. As the ¡*Basta Ya!* [*Enough already!*] report indicates: 'Home' is no longer a simple signifier for those who have lost theirs, and 'path' no longer means the same for those who have had to flee for good, leaving behind their territory, their family and their roots (Action 3: 1). And what does 'family' mean when a man dies of anguish in a small town park, after spending days in the cold, waiting for the return of his three tortured and massacred sons?

From Action 3, collected by the GMH, this narrative, about life before the 2000 Bojayá massacre and the relocation of the village, demonstrates how losses go beyond material possessions:

> Estas son las ruinas [las de Bellavista viejo]... La verdad es que yo después de lo que pasó no me gusta venir acá, es muy duro, es muy triste... hay muchas cosas que uno no las entiende, y como no las entiende pues eso le pega muy duro. Yo en especial siempre me pregunto: ¿por qué a nosotros?, ¿por qué tuvo que pasar lo que pasó? Y todo se va acabando... se han ido perdiendo muchas cosas en nuestra comunidad, las costumbres... como dice uno, su ideología, ya no la hay... Acá éramos de pronto más pobres porque vivíamos en unas casitas de madera, pero teníamos todo lo que queríamos... El río, que es la vida de uno acá, el río para nosotros ahora está muerto... solo lo utilizamos para transportarnos y no para saciar los deseos, como
>
> These are the ruins [those of old Bellavista]... The truth is that after what happened I don't like to come here, it's very hard, it's very sad... there are many things that one doesn't understand, and since one doesn't understand them, well, it is very hard. And I especially ask myself: why us? Why did this have to happen? And it all falls apart... many things in our community are being lost, the customs... what you would call its ideology, now there isn't any... Here we were poor perhaps because we lived in little wooden houses, but we had everything we wanted... The river, that is our life here, the river that is now dead for use... we only use it for transportation and not to satisfy our wishes, like bathing, fishing,

bañarse, pescar, lavar los platos, cepillar la ropa, que uno bajaba y lavaba su ropa y se sentía bien encontrarse con las otras mujeres... [...] No tenemos nada. (Acción 3: 337. Entrevista a mujer adulta, habitante de Bellavista, 2009)

washing dishes, doing the laundry. You'd go and wash your clothes and it felt good to be with the other women... [...] We have nothing. (Action 3: 337. Interview with an adult woman, an inhabitant of Bellavista, 2009)

Garzón (2014: 75) states that narratives of return are an appropriate framework for 'reconstructing the experience of violence, taking distance, revisiting, transforming and turning it into a political platform on which it is possible to reclaim lives of dignity and peace'.

En medio del dolor, también hay alegría, porque estamos nuevamente en nuestro territorio comiendo, durmiendo con nuestros muertos, estamos caminando, no tenemos ese miedo que teníamos tres años atrás, ahora nos sentimos como si nos quisiéramos quedar para siempre acá [...]. (Acción 3: 394. Testimonio de hombre o mujer para el GMH. Taller Memorias en tiempo de guerra. Depto. de la Guajira [Número 18 en el mapa], 2011)

In the midst of sorrow, there is also joy, because we are in our territory once again eating, sleeping with our dead, we are walking. We don't have that fear we had three years ago, now we feel as if we could stay here forever [...]. (Action 3: 394. *Testimonio* by a person for the GMH. Workshop Memories in Wartime. Department of Guajira [Number 18 on the map], 2011)

Returning allows for a more immediate possibility of recovery and the elimination of fear, arguably the most significant obstacle to overcoming the conflict. However, not all survivors could return to their original territories, as evidenced by the community in Action 7, which was forced to relocate because it was so utterly displaced. In this case, it could be said that emotional liberation depends on adapting to a new life and abandoning the old one, with the remembrance undergoing numerous stages until it allows for healing. In terms of adaptation, this survivor offers these insights from exile:

Hay otro tema especial que es el de la adaptación. Lo definimos así porque son personas que salen de un contexto georreferencialmente muy diferente al del territorio donde los recepcionaron. Cambia la gastronomía, cambia la cultura, cambian las costumbres, cambia absolutamente todo. Y es esa capacidad de adaptación que tienen estos connacionales lo que hace que, de alguna manera, hayan tenido lo que hoy se conoce, desde el punto de vista psicológico, como resiliencia,

There is another special issue, which is that of adaptation. We define it this way because they are people who left a very different georeferential context from that of the territory where they were received. Gastronomy, culture, customs, and everything else change. And it is this capacity for adaptation that these compatriots have that has given them what is known today, from a psychological point of view, as resilience; they are very resilient, have

ellos son muy resilientes, tienen una coraza muy grande y están afrontando todo lo que pueda venir a futuro. (Acción 6: 226. Testimonio escrito por hombre adulto, exiliado, retornado del Ecuador, taller de Memoria. Nariño, Pasto [Número 21 en el mapa], 2016)

very strong armour and face everything that may come in the future. (Action 6: 226. *Testimonio* by an adult man, exiled, returnee from Ecuador, in a Memory workshop. Nariño, Pasto [Number 21 on the map], 2016)

Forgetting can also be considered a constituent part of memory, as it is a process of subtracting elements of what is evoked. Reyes-Aparicio (2013: 253) states that 'Forgetting could appear as a way out, as a possibility of erasing events you do not want to remember'. Whether as a process of subtraction from memory or as a form of forgiveness, it facilitates the healing process in both instances. In the following fragments, one of the women makes an unsettling statement regarding the concept of healing. She asserts that while the heart can heal, memory cannot:

[El olvido]Es algo que añoramos pero está muy lejos de algunos... muchos creen que no existe pero si ponemos de nuestra parte lo podemos lograr. (Acción 5: 4. Testimonio escrito por mujer del colectivo Mujeres de El Cañón, participante en taller para resignificar el olvido. Depto. de Antioquia [número 2 en el mapa], 2014)

[Forgetting] is something we long for, but it is very far for some... many believe that it doesn't exist, but if we do our part, we can achieve it. (Action 5: 4. *Testimonio* by a woman from the Mujeres de El Cañón collective, participant in a workshop to re-signify forgetting. Department of Antioquia [number 2 on the map], 2014)

And the same woman comments:

[El olvido]Nos permite sanar, reflexionar, sanar el alma. Nos permite sobrevivir y fortalecernos como personas... el corazón sana pero la memoria no... porque es la lucha como sobrevivientes del conflicto armado. (Acción 5: 4. Testimonio de mujer del colectivo Mujeres de El Cañón, participante en taller para resignificar el olvido. Depto. de Antioquia [número 2 en el mapa], 2014)

[Forgetting] allows us to heal, reflect, and heal the soul. It allows us to survive and become stronger... the heart heals, but memory does not... because it is the struggle of survivors of the armed conflict. (Action 5: 4. *Testimonio* by a woman from the Mujeres de El Cañón collective, participant in a workshop to re-signify forgetting. Department of Antioquia [number 2 on the map], 2014)

In the above fragments, the concept of forgetting is presented as synonymous with both forgiveness and healing. Notably, this process can be initiated in the short, medium or long term. Vélez-Rendón (2003: 22) states that 'there are cases in which the faults are too serious, or too recent, and do not allow for an easy way out, sometimes not even a a temporary sticking plaster (...). These are countries where history repeats itself because the lessons of the past do not derive from the maxim "never again!"[7]

The past can be brought back to the present through imagination, experience, emotion, spirituality and rationality (Arroyave, 2013). Memory can thus be considered a moveable reservoir of resignification it reinvents itself over time. As Garzón (2014) asserts, one must be ready to narrate, and the narrative must be controlled, which can only be achieved by returning to the topic as often as necessary. Some *testimonios* must be distanced from, remembered and returned to when the passage of time has played a filtering role. The following fragment of *testimonio* from an exile who left the country as a child is so macabre that it must have been revisited several times for the words to appear so precisely. Indeed, there were moments closer to the event when words were not easily said. But in her adulthood, the evocation can now be made:

> En Acandí [Depto. del Chocó, número 12 en el mapa] eso fue horrible, a las personas las mataban, les cortaban las piernas y las dejaban allí. A uno le tocaba ver a esas personas. Eso fue algo impresionante, yo temblaba, vomitaba, me acuerdo, yo vomitaba del miedo, de los nervios. Todos los días a las seis de la tarde, las balas se veían rojitas que llegaban a la pared, al techo y al otro día uno se asomaba y veía los huecos. (Acción 6: 163. Testimonio de mujer adulta, exiliada en Panamá, entrevistada en 2017)

> It was horrible in Acandí [Chocó, number 12 on the map]; they killed people, cut their legs off and left them there. You had to see those people. That was shocking; I was shaking, I was vomiting, I remember, I was vomiting from fear, from nerves. Every day at six o'clock in the evening, you could see the reddish bullets reaching the wall and the ceiling; the next day, you looked out and saw the holes. (Action 6: 163. *Testimonio* by an adult woman, exiled in Panama, interviewed in 2017)

For many of these individuals, particularly combatants of one of the warring parties (guerrillas, military and paramilitaries), the process of healing and reconciliation is inextricably linked. It is not only the narrative and the community and collective work that contribute to this process but also the willingness of a country to offer second chances:

> Ya han pasado cinco años de la muerte de M. Gracias a Dios he organizado nuevamente mi vida con Orlando, que respeta a mi hija y a mi sobrino y tengo con quien contar en estos momentos. Doy gracias por haber salido con vida a reintegrarme. Hoy en día conforme un nuevo hogar, somos una familia feliz; cuando hay confianza y respeto, hay felicidad. Esto fue todo lo que ha sido y lo que fue. No es más. (Acción 2: 134. Testimonio escrito por mujer exparamilitar. Depto. de Córdoba [número 13 en el mapa], 2010)

> It has been five years since M.'s death. Thank God I have organised my life again with Orlando, who respects my daughter and nephew, and I have someone to count on now. I am thankful that I got out alive and reintegrated. Today, we have a new home; we are a happy family. When there is trust and respect, there is happiness. This is all it has been and all it was. There is nothing else. (Action 2: 134. *Testimonio* by ex-paramilitary woman. Department of Córdoba [number 13 on map], 2010)

Returning to a specific remembrance, understanding it and expressing it is a process of elaboration that requires multiple conscious activations before it can be externalised or narrated. When left alone, a person's sense of frustration, defeat and pain is unlikely to be transformed, but in a consciously planned space, it is highly likely to become transformed towards processing pain.

'I' and 'We' in Narratives as a Contribution to Memory and the Search for Truth and Justice

> Each individual *testimonio* evokes an absent polyphony of other voices, other possible lives and experiences
> John Beverley, 2005

In addition to disclosing the most intricate details of the Colombian tragedy, the narratives created by survivors offer a multifaceted account of the country's history (Piña, 1986). Facilitating the articulation of narratives allows for the rescuing of significant truths and the pursuit of justice for future generations, despite amnesia or denial on the part of dominant historical narratives (Chase, 2005; Muñoz-González, 2012; Nance, 2006) or other citizens who did not directly experience the conflict.

Despite the efforts of the multiple perpetrators to suppress these narratives – facilitated by the acquiescence of the military, judges and rulers – the production of these accounts reveals the nature of the perpetrators' domination, the cruelty, the intentions, the forms of torture, the populations affected and the excesses. The asymmetry of war is made manifest in the faces and names of the perpetrators, as is the acknowledgement of the defencelessness of victims and survivors. In individual *testimonios*, there is often a demand for justice and for the restoring of the dignity of those affected:

> Yo espero que se haga justicia en este sentido de que nosotros quedemos reivindicados porque la excusa que ellos [paramilitares] sacaron para matarnos a nosotros era que nosotros éramos dizque los jefes de la guerrilla del pueblo cuando en ese entonces nosotros no conocíamos un pueblo, ni siquiera había bajado guerrilla al pueblo ni nada y ellos entraron acusándonos de guerrilleros para podernos matar porque cuando eso estaban pagando por cada guerrillero que mataban. Les pareció muy fácil acusarnos de guerrilleros para matarnos [...]. (Acción 3: 356. Testimonio de mujer adulta. Depto. del Magdalena [Número 19 en el mapa], 2010)
>
> I hope that justice is done in this sense, that we would be vindicated because the excuse that they [paramilitaries] used to kill us was that we were supposedly leaders of the guerrilla in the town, when at that time we didn't know any town [like that]. The guerrilla hadn't even come to the town or anything and they came in accusing us of being *guerrilleros* so they could kill us, because at that time they were paying for every guerrilla soldier they killed. [When they wanted] to kill us, they found it very easy to accuse us of being *guerrilleros* [...]. (Action 3: 356. *Testimonio* of an adult woman. Department of Magdalena [Number 19 on map], 2010)

> [...] yo quisiera que en algún lugarcito de ese libro que ustedes van a escribir [el del GMH], se dijera que mi esposo era un hombre trabajador, buen padre y buen marido, que no era un guerrillero ni un malhechor... eso es lo que yo más quiero y que ojalá mis hijos lo pudieran leer y mostrárselo a todos los demás. Sí, eso es muy bueno [la recuperación de la memoria de las víctimas] porque [...] hay millones de personas que no los conocieron y no saben a qué se dedicaban realmente, y con eso van a saber qué clase de gente eran. La mayor parte se imagina que eran guerrilleros, que eso no es así, que eran personas de bien, trabajadoras. (Acción 3: 356. Testimonio de Mujer para el Grupo de Memoria Histórica. Valle del Cauca, Trujillo [Número 30 en el mapa], 2011)
>
> [...] I would like it if, in a little place in that book that you're going to write [GMH book], you would say that my husband was a hardworking man, a good father and a good husband, he was not a *guerrillero* or a wrongdoer... that's what I most want and hopefully my children could read it and show it to everyone else. Yes, that's very good [the recovery of the victims' memory] because [...] there are millions of people who did not know them and don't know what their work actually was, and this way they will know what kind of people they were. The majority imagine that they were *guerrilleros*, that's not so, they were good people, hard-working. (Action 3: 356. *Testimonio* by a woman for the GMH. Valle del Cauca, Trujillo [Number 30 on map], 2011)

It is essential to disseminate the overall narrative to the general public. Regardless of whether any individuals are apprehended or prosecuted for their involvement in the events, the revelation of the truth represents a form of justice for the citizen survivors. The collective account of survivors contributes to the Collective Memory that must be gathered by the people who have been at war (Acedo, 2017) as indicated by many survivors:

> Que se conozca lo que pasó con el desplazamiento y los efectos que generó. Que el gobierno sepa que el Baudó existe. Que se reconozca que hubo desaparecidos, asesinatos y muchas violencias. Se conozcan todos los hechos de violencia que ocurrieron en el Baudó. Se conozcan los hechos. Que el gobierno aplique la justicia. Que los victimarios digan dónde enterraron a los desaparecidos. Que el gobierno investigue sobre la violación de los derechos humanos. (Acción 4: 291. Tomo II. Entrevista a mujer afrodescendiente por el proyecto Ruta Pacífica de las Mujeres. Depto. del Chocó [número 12 del mapa], 2013)
>
> What happened with the displacement and the effects it generated needs to be known. The government has to recognise that Baudó exists. There needs to be recognition that there have been disappearances, assassinations and a lot of violence. All the acts of violence that occurred in Baudó have to be known. The facts have to be known. The government has to apply justice. The perpetrators have to say where they buried the disappeared. The government has to investigate the violation of human rights. (Action 4: 291. Volume II. Interview with an Afro-descendant woman done by the *Ruta Pacífica de las Mujeres* project. Department of Chocó [number 12 on map], 2013)

The use of the plural in the *testimonios* indicates the subjects' awareness that they were not alone in their experiences (they also involved families, neighbours and friends). The singular is almost impossible. This necessitates a societal examination of the gravity and dimensions of the events. It is a call to be aware that all of us could have been part of this 'we' (Rivara-Kamaji, 2007):

[…] construimos una comunidad de memoria viniendo de diferentes lugares del país… […] Cuando mataron a nuestros esposos, nuestros hijos estaban muy pequeños, no conocieron a sus papás, todas las familias estaban en proceso de construcción, estábamos casi todos recién casados. Esto fue lo que nos llevó a trabajar por la justicia; para que nuestros hijos sepan que no les pueden matar a sus seres queridos y nosotros quedarnos indiferentes. Nosotros estamos luchando por nuestros seres queridos. También estamos luchando para que nuestros hijos sepan, y la sociedad en general, que se debe hacer justicia. Nosotros nos hemos convertido como en una familia. (Acción 3: 335. Testimonio de mujer que participa en el taller *Memorias en diálogo y construcción*. Depto. de Santander, Cúcuta [Número 27 en el mapa], 2011) […]

we built a community of memory with people who came from different places in the country… […] When they killed our husbands, our children were very small, they didn't get to know their fathers, all our families were just starting to grow, we were almost all recently married. That is what got us to work for justice; so that our children would know that they can't kill our loved ones and we would just stand by, indifferent. We are fighting for our loved ones. We are also fighting so that our children, and society in general, would know that justice should be done. We have become like one family. (Action 3: 335. *Testimonio* by a woman participating in the workshop *Memories in dialogue and construction*. Department of Santander, Cúcuta [Number 27 on the map], 2011)

Beverley (2005: 548–549) states that 'a common form of variation of *testimonio* in the first-person singular is a polyphonic *testimonio* composed of accounts from different participants in the same event'. Consequently, the collective experiences of survivors become a public heritage whose imprint on Colombian society contributes to the consolidation of a commitment to 'non-repetition' (CNMH, 2019).

Deseo difundir entre las personas que conozco estos hechos, para que no se vuelvan a repetir 'el pueblo que no conoce su historia, está condenado a repetirla' para que nuestro país tenga un mejor futuro, en el cual podamos encontrar la paz, seguridad y confianza para que juntos logremos construir una

I want to share these events among the people I know to make sure they don't happen again because 'a people who doesn't know its history are condemned to repeat it.' We can create a better future for our country, where we can all find peace, security, and trust. We can build a Colombia where everyone has opportunities, where we are aware that duties and rights belong to everyone and not only to a few, and where men and women can work together to create change. (Action 10: 36. *Testimonio* by a woman participant in a workshop to construct narratives of memories. Department of Antioquia, Medellín [Number 2 on map], 2019)

Forgetting as a result of doing nothing? Is there an obligation to repeat the history we don't want to remember? Absolutely not. We want to reconstruct this history and turn it into memory, not oblivion... What happens when someone kills? What happens when someone is murdered for their ideas, for what they thought? What was it, who were they and who had that sole reason, knowingly murdering an everyday man, Hernando, even in the way he dressed? (Action 1b: 279. *Testimonio* by a woman participant in a workshop on narratives of memories of loved ones. Department of Antioquia, Medellín [Number 2 on map], 2007)

I think that history has to be known so that it does not repeat itself. Hopefully, my contribution will help future generations to approach things differently, so that they don't have to go through what we did. (Action 4: 69. Volume I. *Testimonio* by a woman about human rights violations. Popayán, Department of Cauca [Number 10 on the map], 2013

The call for 'non-repetition', strongly proclaimed by the survivors, is also expressed in Law 1448 and reiterated in the CEV reports. Those who participate in actions towards recovering Memory are empowered to demand their rights and in the process acquire a voice, which was silenced while they were suffering the abuse.

> La importancia de recordar o hacer memoria es para no olvidar y que no nos olviden, para seguir siendo colombianos, personas con derechos, con necesidades, con identidad cultural, moral, religiosa, para seguir siendo contados y valorados, porque pertenecemos a una familia, a un lugar y a un Estado. Porque nos vimos inmersos en una condición que no escogimos, pero que hace parte de nosotros, de nuestra vida. Somos refugiados para superarnos cada día, para no olvidar nuestro punto de partida ni nuestro punto de llegada. Para estar siempre presentes en cada uno de los nuestros, familiares y amigos, para vivir los buenos momentos, para sustentarse, para liberarnos, para seguir viviendo. (Acción 6: 147. Testimonio escrito por mujer exiliada en Panamá, taller de Memoria, Ciudad de Panamá, 2017)

> Remembering is important to not forget and not to be forgotten, to continue being Colombians, people with rights, with needs, with cultural, moral and religious identity, to continue being counted and valued, because we belong to a family, to a place and to a State. We were immersed in a situation we didn't choose, but it's part of us and part of our lives. We are refugees in order to improve ourselves every day, in order not to forget our point of departure and our point of arrival. We want to be present in our family and friends' life, to enjoy the good times, to look after ourselves, to free ourselves, to keep living. (Action 6: 147. *Testimonio* by exiled woman in Panama in a Memory workshop, Panama City, 2017)

The appeal to others to be part of a collective history has great value in amnesic societies such as ours, which, through the horror, seems to have lost an interest in knowing. Social amnesia serves as a shield against misfortune, preventing individuals from being touched by it, and is a deformation caused by external attempts to hide the truth (Nora, 2008; Vélez-Rendón, 2003). The construction of testimonial material reflects the confrontation of one person (the reader and/or immediate interlocutor) with another (the direct narrator(s)) on the plane of possible solidarity (Chase, 2005). The humble and those abandoned by the State who have lived through the war do not have that shield; however, they are endowed with forgiveness, and for this reason, they call for understanding from the perpetrators to stop the horror.

> El día del accidente, el muchacho, después de recoger la yuca, salió tres metros del yucal para armar una trampa que detuviera a una guagua que le estaba arrancando las yucas. En ese momento, se paró sobre la mina que lo partió por la cintura. Luego de

> On the day of the accident, the boy was harvesting cassava[8] and went three metres from the plant to set up a trap to stop a *guagua*[1,2] from eating the cassava. He stepped on a landmine and broke his waist in two. After arriving at the hospital

llegar al hospital de Caucasia, murió. Por eso yo les digo a las personas del conflicto armado que nosotros los civiles no sabemos el porqué de la guerra, entonces les pido de corazón que no siembren más minas antipersonales, pues somos los civiles los que sufrimos. (Acción 1c: 62. Testimonio escrito por hombre sobreviviente de mina antipersona, que refiere la historia de otro hombre joven víctima. Depto. de Antioquia, Caucasia [Número 2 en el mapa], 2009)

in Caucasia, he died. That's why I tell people involved in the armed conflict that we, civilians, don't know the reasons for the war, so I ask them to please stop planting landmines. It's us, the civilians, who suffer. (Action 1c: 62. *Testimonio* by a male landmine survivor, who tells the story of another young male victim. Department of Antioquia, Caucasia [Number 2 on map], 2009)

The Ave Fénix collective, established in 2015, predominantly comprises women and LGBTIQ+ individuals who have been victims of conflict and sexual violence in the Antioquia Department (number 2 on the map). They have conducted several workshops utilising literary writing as a therapeutic tool. The collective considers writing a 'powerful mechanism for the emotional recovery of victims, a means to remember and to contribute to their Symbolic Reparation' (CNMH, n.d.: paragraph. 1).

Hay dos tipos de olvidos…está el que viene mi amiga y me hace una ofensa… esa es una cosa muy distinta frente a lo que hemos vivido… es que ESO no se olvida, y nos corresponde a nosotras que las generaciones futuras conozcan lo que pasó para que no se vuelva a repetir… eso es diferente. (Acción 5: 10. Testimonio escrito por mujer en taller con Mujeres Ave Fénix para resignificar el olvido. Depto. de Antioquia [Número 2 en el mapa], 2014)

There are two types of forgetting… One is when my friend comes and offends me… that's something very different from what we've lived through. THAT can't be forgotten, and it's up to us to make sure future generations know what happened so that it doesn't happen again… that's different. (Action 5: 10. *Testimonio* by woman in workshop with Ave Fénix Women to re-signify forgetting. Department of Antioquia [Number 2 on the map], 2014)

Collectively, these *testimonios* constitute a call to pierce oblivion and to dignify the human person who has endured pain, torture, trauma and physical and moral suffering. The demand to all of us is simple: to demonstrate empathy at this time of transition in the country and to signal that we are willing to keep these memories as part of the Collective Memory. The *testimonios* can thus be read as a call for solidarity and empathy.

The Consequences of War as an Engine of Transformation and the Elaboration of Imaginaries of the Future

> Stories have been used to dispossess and to malign,
> but stories can also be used to empower and to humanize.
> Stories can break the dignity of a people,
> but stories can also repair that broken dignity.
> Chimamanda Ngozi Adichie, 2018

All forms of reconstruction are achieved through an interpretation of the past, where abandonments, displacements, ruptures, silences and losses serve as a motive for reflection and, discursively, allow for the reuniting, relating and even reconciling of all that was previously separated (Ferry, 2001; Muñoz-González, 2012; Piña, 1986). In summary, this intellectual interpretative operation in the survivors constitutes a way of assuming new roles and a possibility of transformation. In most cases, their *testimonios* position them as citizens aware of the causality of destiny and, consequently, as agents in constructing a better life.

One of the mediators' decisions evident in the documentation of each action is to organise the workshops and the *testimonios* in a temporal sequence (Table 3.3). This sequence may be understood as a transition from the past to the future, or from before to after, from darkness to light, from horror to hope. In some of the documents, this structure is expressed in their table of contents. In others, it is inferred from their structures.

In numerous accounts from Action 2, *Retomo la palabra, historias de violencia y reconciliación* [*Taking back the word, stories of violence and reconciliation*], the survivors reflect on their past experiences and the challenges they faced before joining a paramilitary group, from the perspective of those who recognise the opportunity for another chance on earth (Chapter 7 in this book). Furthermore, they discuss their lives in the context of the ongoing conflict and their current circumstances. From the most immoral (looting, murder, kidnapping, rape, extortion) actions to a life in peace filled with gratitude, reflection and a desire for well-being, which occurs not only on a personal level but also at the level of family and collective, the following accounts show that despite the scars, especially of shame, there are glimpses of salvation.

Entonces comencé a darme cuenta de que esa vida no era la que me merecía. Cuando nos mandaron a bajar y nos dieron la buena noticia de la desmovilización, no lo dudé. Fui uno de los primeros que aceptó la propuesta para cambiar de vida. Luego de la entrega me fui a tomar	Then I began to realise that this was not the life I deserved. When they sent us down and told us the good news of demobilisation, I didn't hesitate. I was one of the first to accept the proposal to change my life. After the handover, I went out for a drink and had an

Table 3.3 Structure and progression of narratives during the workshops

Action	Structure
1. *Where I stepped, the grass still grows*	The narratives encompass a spectrum of emotions, ranging from confessions and lamentations to self-recognition and the potential for viewing the traumatic and humiliating event as a possibility for the future. After being victims of landmines, they hope that 'grass will grow' where a device of destruction was sown.
2. *Taking back the Word, Stories of Violence and Reconciliation (2009)*	The *testimonios* are organised in four steps: *Starting Point, On the Way to War, Amid the Storm, Back Home,* and *Footprints*.
3. *Memories, the voice of survivors Chapter V of the Stop it now! Report*	The narratives are organised into three categories: *Memories of suffering, Claims and interpretations derived from memories,* and *Labours of dignity and resistance*.
4. *The Truth of Women: Victims of Colombia's Armed Conflict*	The *testimonios* range from the impact on women's bodies, minds, and emotions to strategies for protection to rebuild their lives and transform their roles.
5. *Narratives of displacement for the construction of identity*	The words not only define the tragedy (powerlessness, violence, fear, oblivion, displacement) but also transcend the recognition of the actors (victims, heroes) and the life that is being claimed (security, resistance, hope, forgiveness, peace).
6. *Colombian Exile: Traces of the Armed Conflict Beyond Borders*	Part 1 organises *testimonios* that locate Colombian exile(s) and their place in the world. Part 2 locates exiles between borders. Part 3 examines the resistance and resilience of exiles, exploring their struggles to construct peace and Memory.
7. *Recipes to Forget the War*	The recipes recall ancestral traditions and knowledge and narrate events that involve different emotions. There is an exciting closure: the traditional recovery of the use of medicinal plants as part of the 'Remedy'.
8. *Narratives of Peace at the End of the War: Experience of Reconciliation and Dialogue in the Education Institution San Vicente de Paúl (S.V. dP.)*	As this is an institutional experience with students, the vast majority of whom are minors, it follows a step-by-step approach, commencing with symbolic moments, progressing to letter writing, and concluding with the embrace of hope, calm and reconciliation.
9. *Souls writing memories and hope*	The letters written by the attendees are organised to move from remembrance of people who are no longer with us, to portraits of them, to accounts of violence and hope, to letters of gratitude.
10. *Live writing for peace*	The workshops and *testimonies* are organised into three sections: before the war, during the war and after the war.

Source: Compiled by the author based on analysis of the documents produced during the actions.

trago y tuve un accidente. Estaba en la casa de descanso cuando llegó una amiga de mi hermana a hacer unos pasteles y nos conocimos, nos gustamos y comenzamos un romance, muy diferente al anterior. Ella ha sido lo más lindo que me ha pasado, me dio dos hijos. Todo lo que he hecho es por ellos y mi cambio ha sido por mi familia para no caer en el error de nuevo. (Acción 2: 125. Testimonio escrito por hombre desmovilizado de las AUC. [Ubicación no especificada], 2010)

accident. I was staying at a rest house when a friend of my sister's arrived to bake some cakes. We met, liked each other and started a romance. It was a very different experience from before. She's been the nicest thing that's happened to me. She gave me two children. Everything I've done since has been for them, and my change has been for my family, so I don't repeat the same mistake. (Action 2: 125. *Testimonio* by a demobilised AUC man. [Location not specified], 2010)

Un día muy triste me fui para la bahía y me puse a tomar porque ya no quería seguir viviendo, pero ese mismo día llegaron unos muchachos y me ofrecieron trabajo en una finca. Les dije que me iba con ellos y enseguida me llevaron, a las dos horas me encontraba en la Sierra Nevada. Cuando llegué a la finca había pura gente armada y me asusté mucho, le pregunté a los muchachos que dónde era la finca y ellos me respondieron: 'Nosotros somos paramilitares y desde hoy perteneces a nuestro grupo'. Un año después nos desmovilizamos. Hoy día me estoy capacitando y me encuentro estudiando, gracias a esto me estoy recuperando y con la ayuda de Dios seré alguien en la vida. (Acción 2: 148. Testimonio escrito por hombre joven desmovilizado. Depto. del Magdalena [número 19 en el mapa], 2010)

One very sad day, I went to the bay and started drinking because I didn't want to go on living. But that same day, some boys arrived and offered me a job on a farm. I told them I'd go with them, and they immediately took me; two hours later, I was in the Sierra Nevada. When I arrived at the farm, there were only armed people, so I got very scared. I asked the boys where the farm was, and they said, 'We're paramilitaries, and from today, you're part of our group.' A year later, we demobilised. Today, I'm training and studying, and I'm getting better thanks to this. With God's help, I'll be someone in life. (Action 2: 148. *Testimonio* by a young demobilised man. Department of Magdalena [number 19 on map], 2010)

These narratives reveal that alongside the more sinister elements, there also exists a sense of humility, lack of knowledge, a yearning for escape from the quagmire, and an inexhaustible reservoir of forgiveness and reconciliation.

En fin, a mí esta dura y dolorosa experiencia me ha traído una enseñanza importante para la vida. Comprendí que existir es maravilloso, que hay que tener siempre el

In short, this hard and painful experience has taught me a valuable lesson for life. I realised that life is marvellous, and that you have to be brave to keep moving

> coraje para querer salir adelante, para sobreponerse de las adversidades y continuar con optimismo, con empuje como decimos los paisas, porque la vida es una sola y hay que vivirla con alegría. Dios me ha dado otra oportunidad y pienso aprovecharla, seguir caminando siempre hacía adelante aunque sea con un solo pie. (Acción 1c: 205. Testimonio escrito por hombre joven, víctima de mina antipersona. Depto. de Antioquia, Ituango [Número 2 en el mapa], 2009)

> forward, to overcome challenges and stay positive, with drive – as we 'paisas' say –, because life is only one and you have to live it with joy. God has given me another chance, and I intend to take advantage of it, to keep walking forward, even with only one foot. (Action 1c: 205. *Testimonio* by a young man, landmine victim. Department of Antioquia, Ituango [Number 2 on map], 2009)

The actions develop in a sequence, which is why they can be narrated. They also involve people in a fundamentally life-affirming way: like narratives, human beings are born, grow, develop and die. In all of them, one goes to the past, understands the present and hopes for the future, almost always as the ideal of closure and the possibility of a better life. Those who promote these actions intentionally or unintentionally, take the experiences through the core structures of narrative: temporal organisation, orientation and coda or closure (Labov, 2010).

These narratives empower the subjects by making them participants in the reconstruction of a history for all. One of the analyses made by the researchers in *La verdad de las mujeres* [*The truth of women*] puts it this way:

> For many of them, the Collective Memory of their experiences becomes the possibility of transforming suffering, abandonment and neglect into hope for dignity. They're seeking redress for their violated rights from a society that for many years turned a blind eye to the atrocities they suffered. (Action 4, 2013: 179)

In this fragment from *Almas que escriben memorias y esperanzas* [*Souls writing memories and hope*], a son writes a letter to his father, who was a victim of the attack on the El Nogal club. In the letter, the son describes his current position as a contributor to the memory process.

> Tic, tac, tic, tac, tic, tac, tic. No sé cuántas veces el planeta le ha dado la vuelta al Sol. Tic. No sé cuántas veces la Tierra ha girado sobre su eje. Tac... Dicen que el tiempo todo lo cura, solo que no nos dijeron que la cura era el olvido. Tac. Tic, tac, tic, tac. El tiempo se detiene y se transforma. Pero llegará la hora en la que todo el dolor se volverá un

> Tick, tock, tick, tock, tick, tock, tick, tock. I'm not sure how many times the planet has gone around the sun. Tick, tock, tock, tock, tock, tock. I'm not sure how many times the Earth has spun on its axis. Tick... They say that time heals everything, but they didn't tell us that the cure was oblivion. Tick, tick, tick, tick. Tick, tick, tick,

caluroso y fortísimo abrazo de reencuentro...Cuando las manecillas de mi reloj hayan dado todas sus vueltas y mi alma pase al lugar donde estás, cuando el tic tac solo sea recuerdo de esas veces en que lloraba recordándote, podré despertar de este sueño en el que no estás... Mientras tanto seguiré aquí, dando lo mejor de mí, persiguiendo mis sueños, apoyando a mi familia y aportando mi grano de arena para la construcción de un mejor país. (Acción 9: 33–36. Testimonio escrito por Joven que le escribe a su padre muerto. Bogotá [número 14 en el mapa], 2018)

tick, tick. Time stands still and changes. But one day, all the pain will turn into a warm and strong embrace of reunion. When my watch hands have turned over and my soul passes to the place where you are, when the ticking is only a memory of those times when I cried remembering you, I'll be able to wake up from this dream where you are not here... In the meantime, I'll still be here, giving it my all, chasing my dreams, supporting my family and doing my bit to help build a better country. (Action 9: 33–36. *Testimonio* by a young man, a letter to his dead father. Bogotá [number 14 on map], 2018)

The attack on the El Nogal Club in an urban area was one of the actions of the now-defunct FARC guerrillas. A car bomb had been placed in the car park of one of the most prominent clubs for wealthy people in Bogotá. Its target was political and military: 36 people tragically died, and 198 were injured, including members, guests and workers.

The *testimonio* is a loving one, indeed. Rather than expressing rage, impotence and injustice (the father worked as a security guard), the son wishes for the well-being for an entire country. There is a constant thread in many of the narratives, to move from defeat, frustration, pain and humiliation to the creation of imaginary futures, always calm, always peaceful.

Tuve miedo y lo enfrenté, tuve tristeza y la vencí, intenté levantarme y caí mil veces, me decepcioné y me di cuenta que perdiendo también se gana. (Acción 5: 10. Testimonio escrito por mujer en Taller con Mujeres de San Gabriel para resignificar el Miedo. Depto. de Antioquia [Número 2 en el mapa], 2014)

I was scared and I dealt with it; I was upset and I got through it; I tried to get up and I fell a thousand times; I was disappointed but I realised that losing also means winning. (Action 5: 10. *Testimonio* by a woman in a workshop with women from San Gabriel to re-signify fear. Department of Antioquia [Number 2 on the map], 2014)

To not falter, to resist, to persist, to fight, to advance: these words apply both within the theatre of war and outside of it, and are highly potent. Both sides (survivors from civil society and those who come from the armed struggle) employ these terms with equal force. War can be an engine for transformation and the elaboration of imaginaries of the future (Chapter 7 in this book).

> Esta historia termina quince años después. Episodios como éste han servido para desarrollar propuestas de intervención que disminuyan la vulnerabilidad personal ante el conflicto que vive nuestro país. Actualmente, historias como las que vivimos en El Dos sirven de orientación a socorristas y médicos, quienes vivimos el conflicto, a veces como espectadores, y otras, como víctimas directas. El fin, como dice Eduardo Galeano, es 'recuperar el pasado para que sirva para la transformación del presente'. (Acción 1b: 177. Testimonio escrito por hombre y mujer, voluntarios de la Cruz Roja que cuentan a dos voces, la retención por parte de la guerrilla. Depto. de Antioquia, Turbo [Número 2 en el mapa], 2007)

> This story ends fifteen years later. These kinds of incidents have helped to develop proposals for interventions to reduce personal vulnerability in the face of the conflict in our country. These days, stories like the ones we lived through in El Dos are a guide for aid workers and doctors, as we also lived through the conflict, sometimes as spectators and sometimes as direct victims. As Eduardo Galeano says, the goal is to 'recover the past so that it can be used to transform the present'. (Action 1b: 177. *Testimonio* written by a man and a woman, Red Cross volunteers, who tell their experience being retained by the guerrillas. Department of Antioquia, Turbo [Number 2 on map], 2007)

This survivor from Putumayo, one of the areas most severely affected by the conflict, exemplifies the strength required to acknowledge the challenges faced and invites others to recognise it as well:

> Es importante recordar, para que nuestros hijos, nuestros vecinos y todos los que nos rodean algún día puedan decir que lo que se vivió aquí no fue algo tan fácil, fue algo muy difícil. Que [en algunos] días nos tocaba salir de nuestras casas, que teniendo propiedad teníamos que abandonar nuestras casas. Pero aquí estamos, fuimos valientes y resistimos a esos altibajos que hubo. (Acción 3: 359. Testimonio de un hombre adulto recogido en el Tigre. Depto. de Putumayo [número 23 en el mapa], 2010)

> It is important to remember, so that our children, our neighbours and all those around us will someday be able to say that what we experienced here was not so easy, it was very difficult. That there were days when we had to leave our houses, that owning the property, we had to leave our homes. But here we are, we were brave and we resisted those ups and downs. (Action 3: 359. *Testimonio* by an adult man collected in El Tigre. Department of Putumayo [number 23 on map], 2010)

The following fragment of a *testimonio* is moving in portraying the subject's recognition of his disadvantaged and ignorant position. It also demonstrates the value placed on the solidarity of others in similar vulnerable circumstances, including women who offered him support and welcomed him. He humbly shows his willingness to learn and his comforting sensation of feeling helpful to his family, even with the constraints of his situation:

> Entonces el mayordomo me dijo 'el único que trabajo que hay es para recoger café, voy a dejarlo para que ensaye'. Esa misma tarde me entregó las herramientas de trabajo y al día siguiente, a las 4:00 de la mañana, todos los trabajadores estaban en pie organizando sus instrumentos. A las 5 de la mañana salimos para el cafetal. En ese primer día de trabajo me fue muy mal; como no estaba acostumbrado, mis manos me quedaron hinchadas y peladas. Ese día cogí dos cuartillados de café y las muchachas recogieron de veinticinco a treinta. Al día siguiente, madrugamos otra vez y cuando llegamos al corte yo me hice en medio de las jóvenes, miraba para todos lados y no podía hacer nada porque mis manos no me acompañaban, pues las tenía hinchadas. En la hora del almuerzo se reunieron las mujeres y me dijeron: 'niño, venga', yo fui y cuando vieron mis manos hinchadas se sorprendieron y me dijeron: 'Eugenio a usted lo vamos a poner de garitero para que nos traiga agua y almuerzo todos los días hasta que termine la cosecha'. Empecé a trabajar con las muchachas. Esa tarde me sentí muy feliz, contento, porque entre ellas me reunieron el jornal, que equivalía a lo que una de ellas ganaba en un día de trabajo. Continué trabajando hasta que se terminó la cosecha y después me fui con ellas a trabajar a otra finca. Estuve con las muchachas 6 meses, en ese poca empecé a coger plata y cada 15 días mandaba para mi casa. (Acción 1c: 47–48. Testimonio escrito por hombre víctima de mina antipersona. Depto. de Antioquia [número 2 en el mapa], 2009)
>
> The estate steward said: 'The only work there is to pick coffee; I'm going to leave you to practise'. That afternoon, he gave me the tools I needed to do the job. The next day, at 4 in the morning, all the workers were up, organising their tools. At 5am, we left for the coffee plantation. On my first day, I didn't do well. I was new to it, so my hands were swollen and skinned. I picked two *cuartillados* of coffee, while the young women picked twenty-five to thirty. The next day, we got up early again, and when we arrived at the plantation, I chose to work with the young women. I was looking everywhere, but couldn't do anything because my hands didn't feel right, as they were swollen. At lunchtime, the young women got together and said to me, 'Come here, kid.' When they saw my swollen hands, they were surprised and said: 'Eugenio, we're going to put you as a *garitero* so that you can bring us water and lunch every day until the harvest is over.' I started working with the young women. That afternoon, I was really happy because they paid me what I would have earned in a day's work. I kept working until the harvest was over, and then I went with them to work on another farm. I stayed with them for six months, during which I started earning money, and every 15 days I sent money home.(Action 1c: 47–48. *Testimonio* by a male landmine victim. Department of Antioquia [number 2 on map], 2009)

To contribute to the rebuilding of what has been destroyed and the construction of new foundations on the ruins, the coordinators and facilitators of the actions worked both symbolically and materially. Symbolically they proposed several keywords as part of their objectives, including 'rebirth', 'regeneration', 'reintegration', 'reconstruction', 'reconstitution', 'recomposition', 'restoration', 'recovery', 'reconciliation', 'reparation' and 'non-repetition'. Materially they worked collaboratively with participants to organise the spaces for the actions. Collective practice underscores the value of pluralism, which entails the possibility of empowerment and learning with others.

[...] Hablamos con el coordinador del programa y le dijimos que había un grupo de más o menos ochenta personas que no sabían leer ni escribir, que eran un grupo de reinsertados que se habían desmovilizado en el año 2006. Bueno, ahí fue lo duro, porque en esa época, recién desmovilizados, nadie nos quería ayudar [...] Con las motos cerramos la calle, para que no molestaran ni interrumpieran nuestra labor. Prestamos sillas a los vecinos e iniciamos las clases para enseñarles a leer y escribir. Les dije: 'Compañeros, vamos a tener un cambio, no tengan miedo que les va a ir bien'. Y no me equivoqué, se me han graduado varios y algunos ya van para la universidad. (Acción 2; 146. Testimonio escrito por hombre desmovilizado de un grupo paramilitar. Sin referencia del lugar, 2008)

[...] We spoke to the programme coordinator and told him that a group of about eighty people couldn't read or write. They were a group of people who had been demobilised in 2006. That was the tricky bit. At the time, we were getting back on our feet after demobilisation, and nobody was willing to help us. [...] We closed the street with our motorbikes to keep the neighbours out and to make sure we could get on with our work. We lent our neighbours some chairs and started teaching them to read and write. I told them: 'Compañeros, we're going to make a change. Don't be afraid; you're going to do well.' And I was right. A few of them have graduated, and some are already attending university. (Action 2: 146. *Testimonio* written by a man demobilised from a paramilitary group. No location reference, 2008)

Another example is the Ave Fénix collective, which published the book *El refugio del Fénix: El final de una noche de agonía* [*The Phoenix Refuge: The End of a Night of Agony*] and, subsequently, they have continued to strengthen their interest in writing to keep showcasing their talent and their realities in multiple communities.

Numerous examples exist of how the survivors have attempted to come to terms with their experiences to take other paths, perhaps less distressing, after unloading such unbearable burdens through narrating their experiences.

Las cosas suceden porque tienen que suceder y no porque uno quiera. Ahora estoy feliz porque estoy rehaciendo mi vida y tratando de olvidar todo el dolor y el sufrimiento del pasado, ese que no quiero volver a recordar, o tal vez sí, para no cometer los mismos errores del pasado. (Acción 1a: 186. Testimonio escrito por mujer joven, cuya familia fue víctima de la violencia urbana de sicarios de Medellín. Depto. de Antioquia, Medellín [Número 2 en el mapa], 2006)	Things happen because they have to happen, not because you want them to. Now, I am happy because I am rebuilding my life and trying to forget all the pain and suffering of the past, which I don't want to remember again, or maybe I do, so as not to make the same mistakes. (Action 1a: 186. *Testimonio* by a young woman whose family was victim of urban violence by hired assassins in Medellín. Department of Antioquia [Number 2 on map], 2006)
Después de un mes de terapias en casa me trasladaba al consultorio al lado de la estación Shaio de Transmilenio. Allí las rutinas de ejercicios eran más exigentes, pero al mismo tiempo eran muy agradables. Lo tomé como ir al gimnasio, cosa que no podía hacer antes por falta de tiempo. Me veía y me sentía diferente cada día. Me exigía más porque había podido superar algunos de mis miedos. Me tocó aprender a caminar de nuevo. A los seis meses aprendí a manejar las muletas y ser independiente. También me motivó ver a otros compañeros y socios que estaban en peores condiciones que yo. Vi su recuperación, que para mí fue un ejemplo de vida. Me dije: si ellos pueden, yo también puedo. (Acción 9: 86–87. Testimonio escritor por mujer que participó en Talleres con sobrevivientes del Club el Nogal. Bogotá, 2018)	After a month of therapy at home, I started going to the clinic next to the Shaio station of Transmilenio [public transportation system in Bogotá]. The exercise routines were more challenging, but also really enjoyable. I treated it like going to the gym, which I couldn't do before due to lack of time. I felt and looked different every day. I pushed myself harder because I had been able to overcome some of my fears. I had to learn to walk again. After six months, I learned to use the crutches and to be independent. I was also inspired by seeing other compañeros and partners who were in worse shape than me. I saw their recovery, which for me was a great example of what's possible. I told myself: if they can do it, so can I. (Action 9: 86–87. *Testimonio* by a woman who participated in workshops with survivors of Club el Nogal. Bogotá, 2018)

Just as places and events continue, people see themselves as active participants in the world that also continues. Their rootedness in hope represents the conviction that, to continue, life must be better. Hopeful and optimistic *testimonios* are far from being a naive illusion that it will be so; rather, they signal the daily struggle for life.

Notes

(1) See http://centromemoria.gov.co/
(2) According to the UN, there are 125 municipalities (out of 1102 in Colombia) where the conflict is concentrated. Cauca, number 10 on the map (20 municipalities); Antioquia, number 2 on the map (15 municipalities); Caquetá, number 8 on the map (14 municipalities); Chocó, number 12 on the map, and Nariño, number 21 on the map (12 municipalities each); Norte de Santander, number 22, Putumayo, number 23 and Meta, number 20 (8 municipalities each); Valle, number 30 (6 municipalities); Tolima, number 29 (5 municipalities); Arauca, number 3, and Huila, number 17 (4 municipalities each); Bolívar, number 5, Casanare, number 9, Córdoba, number 13, and Guaviare, number 16 (2 municipalities each), and La Guajira, number 18 (one municipality) (Corporación Nuevo Arco Iris, 2015). See https://www.arcoiris.com.co/2015/01/estos-son-los-125-municipios-del-posconflicto-segun-la- onu/
(3) See https://centrodememoriahistorica.gov.co/
(4) One of the most affected regions (the second with the second largest number of municipalities affected) is Antioquia (number 2 on the map), whose capital is Medellín. This city has been characterised by its Symbolic Reparations activity. It has a museum of memory that predates the CNMH, which has developed numerous narrative workshops for survivors of the conflict and has disseminated them through books, websites, brochures, etc. Hence, in eight of the ten experiences, the city or the department is named.
(5) This action is the subject of Chapter 6, by Claudia Bungard.
(6) The annual commemoration of the Yanama (collective work) undertaken by the Wayuu women of the Bahía Portete community and by relatives of the victims of the 2004 massacre. For the commemoration, members of the displaced community return to the territory in the company of other indigenous people and companions. The meaning of the Yanama can be condensed in the idea of re-inhabiting, which means recovering and restoring the link with the territory to recover life (CNMH, 2013a: 394).
(7) The author employs the phrase 'Nunca más' [Never again], utilised by the prosecutor Julio César Strassera, in their closing argument against the military councils of Argentina's military dictatorship. The report of the National Commission on the Disappearance of Persons (Conadep) (1984) bore the same name. Much of the information presented in the report was utilised as evidence to convict the accused. In Colombia, one of the CNMH reports, presented in Experience 3 of this chapter, was similarly entitled ¡Basta ya! [Enough Already!].
(8) A tuber that is white on the inside, rich in starch, and an essential part of rural and urban diet, from America and is consumed from Mexico to the north of South America.
(9) This rodent is about 60 to 79 cm long, 35 cm tall, and has a 2 to 3 cm tail. It weighs between 7 and 10 kg. It has different names in Central and South America.

References

Acedo, N. (2017) El género testimonio en Latinoamérica. Aproximaciones críticas en busca de su definición, genealogías, y taxonomía. Mirador Latinoamericano. *Latinoamérica* (64), 39–69.

Adelman, C., Kemmis, S. and Jenkins, D. (1980) Rethinking case study: Notes from the Second Cambridge Conference. In H. Simons (ed.) *Towards a Science of the Singular. Centre for Applied Research in Education* (pp. 45–61). University of East Anglia.

Adorna, R. (2013) *Practicando la escritura terapéutica*. Editorial Desclée de Brouwer.

Alcaldía Mayor de Bogotá (2018) *Almas que escriben memorias y esperanzas*. Secretaría General – Imprenta Distrital.

Arroyave, M. (2013) Objetos de la memoria en el destierro: El presente del pasado. Tesis de maestría inédita, Universidad Nacional de Colombia, Sede Medellín.

Barreto-Moreno, A. (2004) Función de la responsabilidad civil en Colombia en el marco de las acciones populares y de las acciones de grupo. Tesis de maestría inédita, Universidad de los Andes.

Bello-Tocancipá, A.C. and Aranguren-Romero, J. (2020) Voces de hilo y aguja: Construcciones de sentido y gestión emocional por medio de prácticas textiles en el conflicto armado colombiano. *H-ART* 6, 181–204.

Beverley, J. (2005) Testimonio, subalternity, and narrative authority. In N.K. Denzin and Y.S. Lincoln (eds) *The Sage Handbook of Qualitative Research* (3rd edn, pp. 547–558). Sage Publications.

Bustamante-Danilo, J. and Carreño-Calderón, A. (2020) Reparación simbólica, trauma y victimización: La respuesta del Estado chileno a las violaciones de derechos humanos (1973–1990) *Íconos. Revista de Ciencias Sociales* 67 (24), 39–59. See https://doi.org/10.17141/iconos.67.2020.4231 (accessed September 2022).

Carmona, O. (2023) Narrativas y testimonios de la verdad en Colombia El testimonio y su emergencia en tiempos difíciles. In AA.VV *Perspectivas y retos en la construcción de verdad: Miradas desde lo narrativo, educativo y metodológico* (pp. 109–133). Universidad Tecnológica de Pereira.

Caruth, C. (1996) *Unclaimed Experience: Trauma, Narrative, and History*. Johns Hopkins University Press.

Cervantes, A. (2020) Testimonios. In L. Comas-Díaz and E. Torres Rivera (eds) *Liberation Psychology: Theory, Method, Practice, and Social Justice* (pp. 133–147). American Psychological Association.

Chase, S. (2005) Narrative inquiry: Multiple lenses, approaches, voices. In N.K. Denzin and Y.S. Lincoln (eds) *The Sage Handbook of Qualitative Research* (3rd edn, pp. 651–679). Sage Publications.

CNMH (n.d) Organización de víctimas Ave Fénix. See https://accioneseiniciativas.centrodememoriahistorica.gov.co/s/inicio/item/222 (accessed November 2024).

CNMH (2013a) *Informe ¡Basta ya! Colombia. Memorias de guerra y dignidad.* CNMH.

CNMH (2013b) *La verdad de las mujeres. Víctimas del conflicto armado en Colombia.* CNMH.

CNMH (2019) El conflicto armando en cifras. See http://micrositios.centrodememoriahistorica.gov.co/observatorio/portal-de-datos/el-conflicto-en-cifras/ (accessed August 2022).

Cohen, L., Manion, L. and Morrison, K. (2000) *Research Methods in Education*. Routledge.

Conadep (1984) *Informe Nunca Más*, Capítulo II, Título Primero: Víctimas. See http://www.desaparecidos.org/nuncamas/web/investig/articulo/nuncamas/nmas2_01.htm (accessed September 2023).

Connerton, P. (1989) *How Societies Remember.* Cambridge University Press.

Corporación Nuevo Arco Iris (2015) Estos son los 125 municipios del posconflicto, según la ONU. See https://www.arcoiris.com.co/2015/01/estos-son-los-125-municipios-del-posconflicto-segun-la-onu/ (accessed September 2023).

De Salvo, L. (1999) *Writing as a Way of Healing. How Telling Our Stories Transform Our Lives.* HarperCollins

Di Meglio, E. (2022) Hablar desde el silencio: la escritura autoficcional como elaboración discursiva de lo traumático. *Revista del Centro de Letras Hispanoamericanas* 44, 118–133.

Dupláa, C. (1996) *La voz testimonial en Montserrat Roig: Estudio cultural de los textos.* Icaria.

Feliu, J. (2007) Nuevas formas literarias para las ciencias sociales: El caso de la autoetnografía. *Athenea Digital* 12, 262–271. See http://psicologiasocial.uab.es/athenea/index.php/atheneaDigital/article/view/447 (accessed October 2020).

Ferry, J.M. (2001) *La ética reconstructiva*. Biblioteca Francesa de Filosofía. Universidad Nacional de Colombia y Siglo del Hombre.
Galeano, E. (1989) *El libro de los abrazos*. Siglo XXI Editores.
Garzón, M.A. (2014) Las narrativas del retorno. *Revista Encuentros* 12 (2), 67–77. Universidad Autónoma del Caribe.
Henke, S. (1998) *Shattered Subjects: Trauma and Testimony in Women's Life-Writing*. St. Martin's Press.
Hernández, F. (2011) Las historias de vida en el marco del giro narrativo en la investigación en Ciencias Sociales: Los desafíos de poner biografías en contexto. In F. Hernández, J.M. Sancho and J.I. Rivas (Coord.) *Historias de vida en educación: Biografías en contexto* (4 edn, pp. 13–22). Esbrina.
Hernández, R., Fernández, C. and Baptista, L. (2010) *Metodología de la investigación*. MacGraw Hill.
Housková, A. (1989) El testimonio como género literario. *Iberoamericana Pragensia* 22, 11–20.
Jelin, E. (2001) *Los trabajos de la memoria*. Serie Memorias de la represión. Siglo XXI Editores.
Labov, W. (2010) Oral narratives of personal experience. *Cambridge Encyclopedia of the Language Sciences*, 546–548.
Lara, P. (2022) *Un informe final para leer muchas veces*. El Espectador. See https://www.elespectador.com/opinion/columnistas/patricia-lara-salive/un-informe-final-para-leer-muchas-veces/ (accessed January 2024).
Montoya, P. (2022) *Una patria universal*. Editorial Universidad de Antioquia.
Muñoz-González, G. (2012) El alcance metodológico de las narrativas. In S. Soler Castillo (Comp.) *Lenguaje y Educación: Perspectivas metodológicas y teóricas para su estudio* (pp. 161–182). Universidad Distrital Francisco José de Caldas.
Nance, K.A. (2006) *Can Literature Promote Justice? Trauma Narrative and Social Action in Latin American Testimonio*. Vanderbilt University Press.
Narváez, J. (1986) El testimonio. Transformaciones en el sistema literario. In R. Jara and H. Vidal (eds) *Testimonio y literatura* (pp. 235–279). Institute for the Study of Ideologies and Literature.
Nieto, P. (Comp.) (2007) *El cielo no me abandona*. Alcaldía de Medellín.
Nora, P. (2008) Entre memoria e historia. La problemática de los lugares. In *Los lugares de la memoria*. Trilce.
Orfaley, M., Bedoya, M. and Díaz, V. (2019) *Escribir para reinventarse*. Universidad de Antioquia.
Pennebaker, J. (1990) *Opening Up: The Healing Power of Expressing Emotions*. University of Texas.
Piña, C. (1986) Sobre las historias de vida y su campo de validez en las ciencias sociales. *Revista Paraguaya de Sociología* 23 (67), 143–162.
Ramírez, Y. (2021) George Lavarca, hilar el alma. *The Wynwoodtimes*. See https://www.thewynwoodtimes.com/george-lavarca-artista-entrevista/ (accessed February 2021).
Reyes-Aparicio, P. (2013) Narrativa, violencia y memoria: Rupturas y secuencias. In A. Castillejo and F. Reyes (eds) *Violencia, memoria y sociedad: Debates y agendas en la Colombia actual* (pp. 237–256). Ediciones USTA.
Rivara-Kamaji, G. (2007) El testimonio: Una forma de relato. *Revista Bajo Palabra* 2, 111–118.
Strejilevich, N. (2006) El testimonio: Más allá del lenguaje de la verdad. *Human Rights Quarterly* 28 (3), 701–713.
Vélez-Rendón, J.C. (2003) Violencia, memoria y literatura testimonial en Colombia. Entre las memorias literales y las memorias ejemplares. *Estudios políticos* 22, 31–57.
Wills, M.E. (2007) *Inclusión sin representación: La irrupción política de las mujeres en Colombia (1970–2000)*. Editorial Norma.

Yin, R.K. (1984) *Case Study Research: Design and Methods*. Sage Publications.
Zerillo, A. (2006) *Prácticas de escritura en el campo de la salud mental. La escritura en el Taller de Letras del Frente de Artistas del Borda*. Universidad de Buenos Aires.
Zerillo, A. (2008) *La escritura terapéutica*. XI Congreso de la Sociedad Argentina de Lingüística. Facultad de Humanidades y Ciencias, Santa Fe.
Zerillo, A. (2014) Escritura reparadora: El caso de las Madres de Plaza de Mayo. Traslaciones. *Revista latinoamericana de lectura y escritura* 1 (2), 82–103.

4 'Walking the Word' with the Nasa People: A Perspective from the Narrative of *The Strength of the Umbilical Cord* (*La Fuerza del Ombligo*)[1]

José Navia Lame

Caminando la palabra los hermanos andan, llevando la semilla de la Vida custodiada por la Guardia, y con sus bastones de arco iris se enfrentan a las armas sin más armas que la sabiduría de la palabra. Margarita González, 2008	Walking the word the brothers [brothers and sisters] walk, carrying the seed of Life protected by the Guard, and with their rainbow sticks they face the guns without further weapons than the wisdom of the word. Margarita González, 2008.[2]

Where it all Happens

At an unpaved crossroad in the mountains of southwestern Colombia, a yellow sign proclaims the importance of this place for the indigenous movement: '*Weçx Yuwe'kwe* – V. La Susana – Cuna del CRIC'.[3] [Welcome to La Susana village, in Nasa Yuwe language – cradle of the CRIC-in Spanish] (see Figure 4.1).

The sign, written on three rustic boards near the village of Tacueyó, in the municipality of Toribío, fulfils two objectives: to keep the places and other symbols of the Nasa or Paez people[4] in the memory of the *comuneros* (inhabitants of the *resguardo*[5]), and to mark the territory with their narratives. This sign stands in sharp contrast to the posters with violent and proselytising narratives that the guerrilla groups have placed in villages and rural roads in the Department of Cauca (number 10 on the

Figure 4.1 Photograph of welcome to La Susana Village
Source: Author's personal collection.

map), where they have been active for more than 50 years. Three indigenous *resguardos* are located in this municipality: Toribío, Tacueyó and San Francisco, with more than 95% inhabited by Nasa indigenous people (numbering around 40,000). The rest are *mestizos* (mixed ancestry between indigenous and settler) who live in small urban areas and work mainly in commerce. The total population of the Nasa People of Cauca is around 130,000 indigenous people.

Most of the stories I reflect on in this chapter took place in the three *resguardos* of Toribío. I published them between 1985 and 2015 in various news outlets and institutions related to the subject (*Casa Editorial El Tiempo, Publicaciones Semana, Revista Soho, Revista El Malpensante, Fescol, Colprensa, Revista Magazín al Día* and *Centro Nacional de Memoria Histórica*). They are a collection of chronicles and journalistic reports[6] on current events and fragments from the unfinished social processes related to the armed conflict that this area of the Cauca Department has historically experienced; above all, they are related to the resistance of the Nasa People trying to defend their territory. I included the 23 chronicles compiled by the University of Cauca under the title *La fuerza del ombligo, crónicas del conflicto en territorio nasa* [*The strength of the umbilical cord, chronicles of the conflict in the Nasa Territory*] and *Los nuevos enemigos de los Nasa* [*The new enemies of the Nasa People*], a report published in 2019 in *Semana* magazine. These publications aimed to show the evolution of the conflict in this region after the signing of the Peace Agreement between the government and the FARC in 2016. In this chapter, I include fragments from the interviews conducted as ethnographic work prior to writing the chronicles.

Walking the Word

I have visited the three *resguardos* of Toribío about 40 times to research journalistic stories, but also to do what the indigenous people call *caminar la palabra* or 'walking the word', seeking answers to questions such as What happened to...? What is happening now? What are the new dynamics of the conflict? Or to talk informally with some acquaintances and take part in their daily lives (Hoyos, 2003). 'Walking the word' is a daily practice that the Nasa People begin to develop as children during family conversations around the wood stove and the cooking pot, especially at night, when they talk about what happened during the day and plan the next day's activities. This practice is transferred to the organisational scenarios where, if necessary, the problems of the community are discussed for many hours or days, or to special sessions such as walks to discuss the boundaries of their territory, their history or the leaders who have been assassinated.

Sometimes the Nasa carry out protests or hold meetings with other social groups, with the government or with the armed groups operating in their *resguardos* to seek solutions through the word. This practice involves a process of permanent reflection and analysis of their territory as a physical and cosmogonic space, their history, thought and emblematic leaders, with the participation of schools and universities, and countless organisations – environmental, economic and corporate, artistic, women's, youth, elderly and human rights. I have participated in some of these collective exercises, almost always as a witness, after explaining to the people, even with a microphone in my hand, who I am, why I am in their territory, what my intentions are, how long I am going to be with them and, on some occasions, I have explained that not all journalists go in search of scandalous, distorted or superficial news. The Nasa then take the floor to explain why they accept or reject the journalist's presence in the room. These verbal exchanges are conducted in Spanish, a second language they all master.

The objective of my trips has been to stay up to date with the changes occurring in the territory, gain a deeper understanding and enhance future reportage with more effective participatory tools. This objective is also one of the reasons for including reflection in this chapter, written from my perspective as the journalist/chronist, in a book such as this, which is mainly testimonial. A second reason is that the Nasa People, to which I have dedicated my narrative efforts, and of whom I am a descendant, are historically the people most affected by the armed conflict in Colombia.

The Journalist: Returning to my Roots

In the first quarter of 1985, I had my first contact with the Nasa indigenous territory when, after four or five visits to the municipalities of Toribío and Jambaló, I managed to interview combatants of the Movimiento Armado Quintín Lame (MAQL), a guerrilla group made up almost entirely of Nasa indigenous people. This group was named after Colombia's prominent indigenous leader in the 20th century, Manuel Quintín Lame (1883–1967), who fought for indigenous rights through legal and *de facto* means at the beginning of the century. This organisation proclaimed its indigenist character in defence of their territories and their leaders, who had been assassinated mainly for promoting the 'recovery' of ancestral lands that had passed into the hands of landowners.

Romir, a medium-sized, straight-haired man and Quintin Lame movement leader, recalls that the group came into being

como forma de autodefensa ante los atropellos de terratenientes y bandas de 'pájaros'..., debido a la impunidad en que ha quedado la muerte de más de un centenar de dirigentes indígenas del Cauca. (Entrevista de la crónica *En el campamento del Quintín Lame*: 26)	as a form of self-defence against the outrages of landowners and gangs of 'birds' [pajaros- hired killers]..., due to the impunity in which the death of more than a hundred indigenous leaders in Cauca had gone unpunished. (Interview from the chronicle *In the Quintin Lame Camp*: 26)

My initial attempt to chronicle people's lived experience was guided primarily by traditional journalistic criteria, that is, by the variables that determine whether an event is newsworthy in the mass media (Martini, 2000); in this case, the beginning of the first known indigenous guerrilla movement in Colombia. The only journalistic precedent was a report, *La Quintinada*, the name given to the followers of Manuel Quintín Lame, who, armed mainly with machetes, occupied some towns in Cauca in rebellion against the *terraje* (days of work that indigenous people had to pay landowners for allowing them to live on smallholdings on land taken from their ancestors). However, during my interaction with the Nasa and in the years that followed, several things changed my perspective, both as a journalist and as a person: their history, their cosmogony, their heroism in defending the land, the majesty of their mountains, their level of organisation and their festive and arduous daily life. In addition, I discovered that the village where I was born (in 1959) had been an indigenous *resguardo* until 1926 and that my maternal grandfather had been one of the last governors, the highest-ranking position in these places.

After six years working in different news outlets in Bogotá, I returned to the mountains of north-eastern Cauca. By then (1991), the conflict landscape in the region had changed (see Chapter 1). The Ricardo Franco group, Quintín Lame's partner in some of the attacks, had disappeared as a result of an internal purge that left more than 150 dead. Quintín Lame and the *Movimiento 19 de abril* (M-19), another guerrilla group with a strong presence in the indigenous territories of Cauca, had laid down their arms thanks to the peace agreement with the government (Celis, Chapter 1 in this book). While ex-combatants struggled to reintegrate into civilian life and consolidate a political space, the FARC gained strength in the areas abandoned by the other groups, swelling its ranks by recruiting indigenous youth.

Several of the interviews I did for the chronicles I wrote bear evidence of what was experienced at the time:

Cuando vinieron los del Cabildo les tocó sacarlo [mi hijo] por allá abajo, por esa hondonada, no ve que ya la guerrilla andaba por la parte de arriba buscándolo porque decían que había desertado. (Entrevista a madre de joven indígena, de la crónica *Regreso a casa*: 104)	When the people from the *Cabildo* came, they had to take him [my son] out down there through that gully, the guerrillas were already looking for him higher up because they said he had deserted. (Interview with the mother of a young indigenous man, from the chronicle *Return Home*: 104)
Ellos [los guerrilleros] podrían pensar que se trata de un proyecto contrainsurgente [Proyecto propio Regreso a casa] y lo único que queremos es que nuestros niños y jóvenes que se han ido a empuñar las armas, así sea en el Ejército o la guerrilla, regresen a la comunidad. (Entrevista a líder nasa de la *Cxab Wala Kiwe*, Asociación de Cabildos Indígenas del Norte del Cauca (ACIN), en idioma nasa yuwe, de la crónica *Regreso a casa*: 104)	They [the guerrillas] may think that this is a counter-insurgency project [Own project *Regreso a casa*], and the only thing we want is for our children and young people who have taken up arms, whether in the army or the guerrillas, to return to the community. (Interview with Nasa leader of the *Cxab Wala Kiwe*, Association of Indigenous Cabildos of Northern Cauca (ACIN), in Nasa Yuwe language, from the chronicle *Return Home*: 104)

Since the 1990s, the dynamics of the conflict and also the daily life of the indigenous *resguardos* have undergone both minor and major changes, some of them almost imperceptible and silent, such as the appearance in Toribío of restaurants offering meals, cocktails and other drinks for urban consumption. Their customers are primarily young. They wear sneakers and fashionable clothes, have mobile phones and haircuts in the style of European football players. Also ubiquitous are the dozens of small family and community businesses producing everything from handicrafts to vacuum-packed trout, homemade salves, wine and *aguardiente*. The war has also been transformed and recycled: Dagoberto Ramos and Carlos Patiño, guerrilla commanders killed in battles with the army, now lend their names to two of the FARC's most bloodthirsty dissident columns, accused of fostering 'creepy' marijuana crops,[7] recruiting children and young people, and over the past six years murdering dozens of people, most of them indigenous. The cultural practices of 'incorporation' – that is, the way people retain culturally learned ways of acting – have been significantly affected by the conflict and the cultivation of illicit crops. Practices which would naturally guarantee the recreation of the past and the safeguarding of Memory are being replaced by new practices (Connerton, 1995).

The Nasa People, Survivors of the Conflict

The CEV Final Report (2022: 235), chapter *Violencias y daños contra los pueblos étnicos de Colombia* [*Violence and harm against the ethnic peoples of Colombia*], notes that:

> In accordance with the indigenous peoples' own cosmovision and their sacred conception of Mother Earth, and by virtue of the special and collective bond they hold with the territory as living integrity and sustenance of identity and harmony, the Commission determined that it had suffered multiple (damages) and was desecrated by the armed groups.

In the report *Pueblos indígenas, víctimas de violencias de larga duración* [*Indigenous peoples, victims of long-term violence*], published on the anniversary of the International Day of Indigenous Peoples, the Observatory of Memory and Conflict (OMC) states that 'among the victims, there are 736 indigenous leaders and authorities' (2020: para. 1). According to this report, up to 20 June 2020, 1008 murders of indigenous people had been committed in the department of Cauca. In addition:

> Between 1958 and 2019 indigenous peoples have been attacked. There have been 5.011 victims during the conflict. Selective assassination is the main victimising event, with 2,300 victims during the recorded period. (CNMH, 2020, para. 4)

Likewise, '431 homicides of indigenous people from 25 August 2016 to 31 December 2021, with a growth rate of 200%; in Colombia, an indigenous person is murdered every four days' (CNTI, 2022: 13). Furthermore, 'during the year 2021, homicides against indigenous people at the departmental level were again concentrated in the Cauca Department with 42.9% (49 cases)'. Figure 4.2 shows the number of homicides of indigenous people in different departments, with the Cauca region suffering most of all.

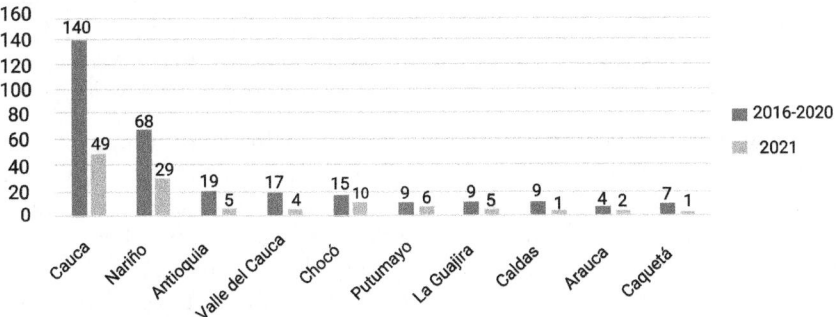

Figure 4.2 Comparison of homicides at the regional context, cumulative period 2016–2020 and 2021

Source: SIVOSPI of the Observatory of Territorial Rights of Indigenous Peoples (ODTPI) of the CNTI (5 August 2022).

This violence has continued, particularly against the Nasa People, to the point that on 24 March 2022, the United Nations publicly called on the Colombian government to investigate the killings and threats, and to eliminate

> the groups generating violence that seek to control the territory of the Nasa People. The Government must also adopt actions for the prevention and protection of the communities, as well as strengthen the Nasa People's own self-protection strategies and organisational forms. (ONU, 2022, paragraph 6)

The Magical-Political

In the territories of the Nasa People, spiritual leaders called the *Thê Walas* have issued warnings that few have heeded. They are concerned about the loss of certain traditions owing to customs adopted from social media and television and by the influence of nearby urban centres, with which the indigenous people of Toribío have consistently interacted. This interaction is a result of the Colombian government paving the road leading to the plains of northern Cauca in the early 2000s. The improvement of the road has led to the growth of three municipalities with a combined population of several thousand, fostering a rich exchange between indigenous, Afro-Colombian and mestizo communities and facilitating interaction with Cali (capital of Valle del Cauca Department, number 30 on the map), the third largest city in the country.

Despite the advance of modernity, the word of the *Thê Walas* still holds great value within the community, especially among the elders, who consider these spiritual guides to be

> Intermediarios ante los espíritus del trueno, del viento y del arco iris y protectores del pensamiento del mítico cacique Juan Tama. (Entrevista a Bernardo UI, de la crónica *Kiwe Thegnas: guardianes de la tierra*: 64)

> Intermediaries with the spirits of thunder, wind and rainbows and protectors of the thoughts of the mythical chief Juan Tama. (Interview with Bernardo UI, from the chronicle *Kiwe Thegnas: the guardians of the land*: 64)

However, the cosmogonic world is also being undermined by the emergence of new powers based on the extravagance that money from illicit crops (marijuana and coca) enables, as opposed to the traditional way of life of the *Thê Walas* and other elders, who are attached to their relationship with the land and all the beings that inhabit it.

In the face of these circumstances, the *Thê Walas* strive to maintain the ancient secret rituals which, according to them, help to counteract the disharmony in the territory through the use of plants whose characteristics are only known to them and which have been inherited from their ancestors. These rituals include the harmonisation of the spaces where the community will carry out any activity; the cleansing of the sticks or 'the refreshing of the sticks', symbols of those who hold a position within the government; and the *pulseo*, a test that those who aspire to occupy essential positions must pass to guarantee that the candidates seek the good of the community and not their personal interests.

> El 'pulseo' 'consiste en tantear los impulsos de la sangre en algunas arterias a medida que van haciendo preguntas al examinado. De esa forma, los *thê walas* determinan si la persona dice la verdad. Algunos chamanes nasa se entrenan durante muchos años en esta técnica' y, a juzgar por lo que dicen los indígenas, es tan efectiva como una prueba de polígrafo. (Navia Lame, 2015: 65, de la crónica *Regreso a casa*)
>
> The 'pulseo' 'consists of testing the blood pulses in certain arteries as they ask the examinee questions. In this way, the *Thê Walas* determine whether the person is telling the truth. Some Nasa shamans train for many years in this technique' and, judging by what the indigenous people say, it is as effective as a polygraph test. (Navia Lame, 2015: 65, from the chronicle *Return Home*)

The harmonisation of the space, which typically lasts several days, is conducted exclusively at night. They use handmade drinks, coca leaves and other plants grown in both cold and warm temperatures. The objective of this practice is to harmonise the energies of the location, ensuring that the activities are beneficial to the community and that there are no significant disagreements. For example, when a young man returns from guerrilla activities, he is cleansed with a 'remedy,' because the Nasa believe that if a person violates the community's rules, this is attributed to 'mala energía':

> Se le aposentó una mala energía que lo hace actuar de manera incoherente con el resto del pueblo nasa. (Entrevista a dirigente de la ACIN, de la crónica *Regreso a casa*: 105)
>
> A bad energy has settled in him that makes him act incoherently with the rest of the Nasa People. (Interview with ACIN leader, from the chronicle *Return Home*: 105)

> Hay que hacer dos tipos de remedios con los muchachos que vienen de la guerra…Hay que proteger el cuerpo y la mente. El cuerpo se protege dándole seguridad para que no le pase nada y con el remedio que les hace el *thê wala*. Pero la parte más difícil es el trabajo en la mente del muchacho. (Entrevista a dirigente de la ACIN, de la crónica *Regreso a casa*: 104)
>
> There are two types of remedies for the boys who come from the war. You have to protect the body and the mind. The body is protected by giving it security so that nothing happens to it, and with the remedy that the *thê wala* gives them. But the most difficult part is working on the boy's mind. (Interview with ACIN leader, from the chronicle *Return Home*: 104)

The cleansing of the sticks takes place on the banks of a river or a pond, to wash these symbols of the impurities that, according to the *Thê Walas*, are collected during the activities of those who carry them and which often have to do with the resolution of internal conflicts or with armed groups.

Among the Nasa, cosmogony is the basis of their customary law. It is an inexhaustible universe connected to the uses and customs that govern the daily lives of the indigenous people of the *resguardo*. These practices are transmitted orally, mainly through the elders.

The *testimonio* of Eibar Fernández Chocué embodies the enduring hold of the Nasa on their territory. Despite being threatened by illegal armed groups, he says he would prefer to die in his village rather than live in exile. Like the rest of the Paeces, he has a profound connection to the mountains, a connection to which he is bound physically as well as spiritually, so deep that his umbilical cord is buried in them.

> Yo tengo enterrado el mío [el ombligo] en la vereda Loma Gruesa. Comenta que su madre se lo contó a los 17 años, cuando quiso irse a coger café al Valle del Cauca con unos amigos 'Mamá... ¿por qué será que yo alisto la maleta pa' irme y al otro día ya se me quitan las ganas?', 'Usted no se puede ir, mijo, porque yo le enterré el ombligo para que no se mueva de aquí'. (Entrevista de la crónica *La fuerza del ombligo*: 86–87)

> Mine [umbilical cord] is buried in the village of Loma Gruesa. He says his mother told him this when he was 17 years, when he wanted to go and get coffee in Valle del Cauca with some friends. 'Mum... why is it that I pack my suitcase to leave and the next day, I do not feel like going', 'You cannot leave, *mijo* [my son], because I buried your umbilical cord so that you will not move from here'. (Interview from the chronicle *The strength of the umbilical cord*: 86–87)

The dynamics of resistance and the strengthening of the Nasa's political organization have enabled the magical stance of their cosmovision to extend and accompany these processes. For example, a general assembly (the highest decision-making body of a *resguardo*) decided that the *Thê Walas* (Shamanes) should examine candidates for *Kiwe Thegna*s or Guardians of the land. Previously, this was only an administrative procedure. The *Thê Walas* were also tasked with deciding on the reintegration into the *cabildo's* jurisdiction of an indigenous person who had previously deserted the guerrillas:

> Cuando un muchacho se vuela de uno de esos grupos y nos dice que quiere volver a ser parte de su resguardo, primero hay que llevarlo al *thê wala*. Y él nos dice si el muchacho en realidad tiene voluntad para cumplir con el Cabildo o se va a devolver pa'l monte o les va a llevar información. (Entrevista a líder nasa de la ACIN del Norte del Cauca, de la crónica *Regreso a casa*: 142)

> When a boy leaves one of these groups and tells us that he wants to return to his *resguardo*, we first have to take him to the *thê wala*. He tells us if the boy is really willing to comply with the *cabildo*, if he is going to go back to the forest or if he is going to bring them information. (Interview with a Nasa leader from the ACIN of Northern Cauca, from the chronicle *Return Home*: 142)

Ellos tienen que volver a entender que la propiedad del territorio es colectiva y que aquí hay una identidad cultural basada en un gobierno y en una justicia propias y que las cosas funcionan mediante acuerdos y bajo la orientación de la asamblea general. (Entrevista a líder indígena, de la crónica *Regreso a casa*: 106)	They have to understand over and again that the ownership of the territory is collective and that here, there is a cultural identity based on their government and justice and that things work through agreements and under the guidance of the general assembly. (Interview with indigenous leader, from the chronicle *Return home*: 106)

The *Thê Walas* also leave their mountains to accompany, even if for only several days, the hundreds or thousands of villagers who travel to the cities to participate in assemblies or protest days. They are responsible for harmonising the energies of the lodgings, meeting places, and even the *chivas* (handcrafted adapted vehicles) in which the protestors travel (Figure 4.3).

The *Thê Walas* are also involved in political decisions. For instance, a candidate for governor cannot be appointed if he or she performs poorly in their rituals. The *Thê Walas* also determine the time or manner in which certain actions should be carried out. In general, they function as a permanent consultative body.

Fueron los *thê walas* del resguardo de San Francisco, quienes aconsejaron, en diciembre pasado, el nombramiento de Luz Dary Pazú como gobernadora de ese territorio donde habitan seis mil paeces y hay presencia de grupos armados ilegales. Después de varias noches de consultas a los espíritus, determinaron	In December of last year, the *Thê Walas* of the San Francisco *resguardo* recommended the designation of Luz Dary Pazú as governor of this territory where six thousand Paeces live and where illegal armed groups are present. After several nights of consultations with the spirits, they decided that a

Figure 4.3 Photograph of a *Chiva*, handcrafted adapted vehicles
Source: Author's personal collection

| que una mujer podía traer algo de armonía ante los tiempos difíciles que estaban por venir. (Navia, 2015: 68, de la crónica *El blindaje de los hijos del trueno*) | woman [Luz Dary Pazú] could bring some harmony to the difficult times that were to come. (Navia, 2015: 68, from the chronicle *The shielding of the sons of thunder*) |

Coexisting with War

The 24 chronicles and reports that I generated enabled me to trace some of the insurgent groups within the indigenous territory of the northern Department of Cauca. They show how the Nasa became involved in the armed conflict, almost always as civilian victims, but in some cases as combatants and even as victimisers of their own people.

A significant number of leaders have been threatened and killed by illegal groups for opposing the occupation of territory by armed organisations. This situation is discussed in the chapter *Resistir no es aguantar* [*Resisting is not enduring*], dedicated to the ethnic peoples of Colombia by the CEV (2022: 224):

> Indigenous leadership and authorities were seriously affected during the military occupations and armed confrontations between the FARC-EP and ELN guerrillas, paramilitary groups and the security forces, as it was these people who had to take the political positions of their communities and express their disagreement with the presence of armed groups in their territories.

In the chronicle *Los eternos conflictos en el territorio nasa* [*The eternal conflicts in the Nasa territory*] (Navia-Lame, 2015: 23–34), I recount the circumstances of the first guerrilla action in the indigenous territories of Cauca, which took place in March 1965 on the outskirts of Inzá. A recently formed rebel column in Riochiquito, Cauca, called Bloque Sur (South Bloc, an embryo of the FARC), which intended to take over the town, responded in the darkness of the early morning to shots fired at them by a policeman from a public service vehicle full of passengers. Sixteen people, including two nuns, were killed by the insurgents that day.

The area of Cauca gradually became attractive to other guerrilla groups because of its inaccessible mountains, strategic location, the ease of supply and the desirability of recruiting indigenous people because of their recognised warrior tradition. In the 1970s and 1980s, in particular, their weaponry evolved from using old shotguns to high explosives, automatic rifles and even rustic artillery capable of firing handmade grenades that were as destructive as they were inaccurate. These grenades sometimes landed in civilian homes.

| Desde que llegó la guerrilla a esta zona, hace unos 30 años, llevamos más de 600 hostigamientos y 14 han acabado cuatro veces con el | Since the guerrilla war arrived in this area approximately 30 years ago, we have been harassed more than 600 times and attacked 14 |

cuartel de la policía y en unas cuatro tomas el pueblo ha quedado destruido en parte. (Entrevista a Ezequiel Vitonás, de la crónica *El pueblo más atacado por la guerrilla*: 125)	times, the police headquarters has been destroyed four times, and the village has been partially destroyed in four takeovers. (Interview with Ezequiel Vitonás, from the chronicle *The village most attacked by guerrillas*: 125)

The people of Toribío have particular memories of the *'chiva bomba'*, a bus-sized vehicle loaded with explosives that the FARC used to blow up the police headquarters on 9 July 2011.

Cuando se disipó la humareda, había más de cien personas heridas. El cerrajero, el carnicero y un gallero estaban muertos. Un sargento de la policía quedó destrozado. Solo hallaron una pierna. (Navia, 2015: 127 de la crónica. *El pueblo más atacado por la guerrilla*)	When the smoke cleared, more than a hundred people were injured. The locksmith, the butcher and a man engaged in cockfights were dead. A police sergeant was mangled. Only one leg was found. (Navia, 2015: 127 from the chronicle *The village most attacked by guerrillas*)

In Colombia, an image of Toribío, Tacueyó and hundreds of other villages in conflict zones has been constructed by the media, who only visit these places when there are massacres or natural tragedies. 'The Colombian population is more familiar with the violent aspects of the country than with its positive aspects, such as its people, landscapes and natural resources' (Salazar, 2001: 142).

In this sense, the value of the interviews and *testimonios* that I reflect on in this chapter, in terms of reconstructing the Memory or History of those years, can be located in the descriptions and narratives (2015) of what can be called the everyday life of the war (Bergalli & Rivera, 2010; Chase, 2005) in places like Jambaló:

La primera sensación que se tiene al llegar a este poblado, perdido entre desfiladeros y montañas, a unos cien kilómetros de Popayán, es la de estar entrando en una zona de guerra. Al doblar la primera calle aparecen las trincheras y zanjas de arrastre que rodean el cuartel de policía. Algunos uniformados caminan por la calle armados de fusiles Galil. Por lo general, el pueblo permanece en silencio, solo y con las puertas cerradas. La mayor parte de sus habitantes se van a trabajar de madrugada a los minifundios que rodean el caserío.	The first impression upon arrival at this village, situated between gorges and mountains, approximately 100 kilometres from Popayán, is that of entering a war zone. As you turn into the first street, you observe the trenches and dragging ditches surrounding the police headquarters. Uniformed personnel walk down the street armed with Galil rifles. For the most part, the village remains silent, isolated and with its gates closed. The majority of the population commutes to work in the early hours of the morning on

> Un viento frío que baja por la garganta de la cordillera barre la única calle pavimentada que atraviesa el pueblo. Unos metros más allá de donde termina el pavimento aparecen más trincheras y zanjas de arrastre. Por esa carretera se sigue hacia Toribío, otro municipio donde los policías viven al acecho de los francotiradores que las FARC apostan en los montes vecinos. (Navia, 2015: 83, de la crónica *La fuerza del ombligo*)
>
> the small farms that surround the hamlet. A cold wind blowing down the gorge of the mountain range sweeps the only paved road through the village. A few metres beyond where the pavement ends, more trenches and dragging ditches appear. This road leads to Toribío, another municipality where the police live on the lookout for snipers posted by the FARC in the neighbouring mountains. (Navia, 2015: 83, from the chronicle *The strength of the umbilical cord*)

This daily life is marked by the inhabitants' behaviour, which results from living with the war on a daily basis and on which they may depend to survive:

> Los 3,500 habitantes del área urbana se han acostumbrado a la fuerza al tastaseo nocturno de los fusiles y a los rafagazos. Los que viven cerca del cuartel se acuestan con ropa cómoda o en sudadera y dejan los zapatos listos al pie de la cama. (Navia, 2015: 126, de la crónica *El pueblo más atacado por la guerrilla*)
>
> The 3,500 inhabitants of the urban area have become forcibly accustomed to the strength of the nocturnal *tastaseo*[8] of the rifles and the bursts. Those who live near the barracks go to bed in comfortable clothes or sweatshirts and leave their shoes ready at the foot of the bed. (Navia, 2015: 126, from the chronicle *The village most attacked by guerrillas*)

In the midst of the daily life marked by the conflict, a relationship between death and fiesta dominates the lives of the inhabitants of Toribío, a behaviour that may provide a psychological barrier against the horrors of war in these remote mountains (Chronicle *Aquí se llora, pero también se baila* [Here we cry, but we also dance]). There is no corner of this municipality where dance music is not heard at some time of the day. In fact, the town's traditional dance hall, the Discotk Manolo, was one of the first businesses to reopen its doors after the most powerful explosive attack by the FARC, the *chiva bomba*, which killed four people and destroyed or rendered useless hundreds of homes and businesses.

> [El bailadero] lo reconstruyeron y al mes ya estaba funcionando. (Entrevista a Mary Martínez, de la crónica *El pueblo más atacado por la guerrilla*: 131)
>
> [El *bailadero* (The dance hall)] was rebuilt and was ready for use within a month. (Interview with Mary Martínez, from the chronicle *The village most attacked by guerrillas*: 131)

Amid this panorama, different and renewed forms of resistance of the Nasa People emerge to safeguard their territory in three dimensions: as a physical space, as an integral part of the being that inhabits it and as a place of ancestral practices (Garzón, 2014; Muñoz-González, 2012; Orozco *et al.*, 2013; Vives-Riera, 2011).

Multiple Forms of Resistance

El pasado es raíces, conciencia y vivencias. Por eso hacemos tanto honor a la gente que se va a otro espacio. Le hacemos mucho homenaje a la memoria porque nos permite existencia y resistencia, y, sobre todo, mantenernos como pueblos en diferentes lugares	The past is roots, awareness, and experiences. That's why we honor so much the people who move on to another place. We pay great tribute to memory because it allows us to exist and resist, and, above all, to maintain ourselves as communities in different places..
(Feliciano Valencia, líder nasa, entrevista en Verdad Abierta.com)	(Feliciano Valencia, Nasa leader, interview on Verdad Abierta.com)

The current process of indigenous resistance in Cauca became official with the birth of the CRIC on 24 February 1971 in the village of La Susana. As mentioned, this process had other manifestations in the early and mid-20th century, with an organised movement against paying taxes to landowners and later against land dispossession. Indeed, almost all of the Nasa's public actions are linked to resistance, not only to defend the life and autonomy of their judicial and governmental organs, but also to preserve or recover their cultural forms that survived the imposition of the new order brought by the Spanish conquerors since the 15th century (Almendra, 2017). Thus, they promote schools of *Nasa Yuwe* (the ancestral language), workshops for weaving backpacks and other clothing accessories, rituals such as those of the seeds[9] and the Day of the Dead, the construction of ceremonial houses, the creation of artistic collectives and audiovisual and written communication, activities of control and authority within the *resguardo*, the exchange of agricultural products and the production of medicines, as well as dance, music and the production of alcoholic beverages. With the expansion of these lines of resistance, the female figure in particular has gained strength.

Although the role of women has been significant in the historical resistance of the Nasa People, especially in terms of culture, they have tended to remain excluded from leadership positions. In addition to transmitting ancestral practices such as the *Nasa Yuwe* language, weaving and their relationship with cosmogony to other generations, Nasa women have participated in all the activities of their community, including difficult ones such as serving in the Indigenous Guard, sowing and harvesting, or participating in the massive occupation of land.

The education of Sofía Valencia, a farmer from the Tacueyó *resguardo* and mother of five, may partly explain why Nasa women have been marginalised. Sofía can neither read nor write:

Como a los dos días de haber entrado a la escuela mi papá cogió un libro y me dijo: 'Lea aquí, a ver qué fue lo que aprendió', y como no podía me daba rejo (fuete). Yo mejor me retiré y me puse a trabajar. Ahora, mirando los libros de los muchachos, es que aprendí a firmar, pero no más. (Entrevista de la crónica *Los hijos de la Gaitana siguen creciendo*: 110)	About two days after I started school, my father picked up a book and said: 'Read here, show what you've learnt', and when I couldn't, he hit me with a belt (*fuete*). So I withdrew and went to work. Now, looking at the boys' books, I learned how to write my signature, but nothing more. (Interview from the chronicle *The children of La Gaitana continue to grow*: 110)

In recent years, Nasa women with experience in political spaces and with university degrees and postgraduate studies have begun to occupy important positions including governor or *Nejwes'x* in the new governing councils known as *Kueque Nejwes'x* and in other spaces of political representation at the national level.

However, this higher-level participation in public positions has also increased their risk in terms of armed opponents. Almost all of the indigenous people murdered during the period in which the chronicles referred to in this chapter were written were men. The same is true of their historical martyrs: Benjamín Dindicué, José María Ulcué, Álvaro Ulcué, Cristóbal Secue and Marden Betancur. However, the situation has changed as women have moved into positions of greater responsibility. As I write, Yermi Chocué, treasurer of an indigenous *resguardo* in the municipality of Morales, Cauca, has been assassinated, and Aída Quilcué, the most recognised leader of the Nasa People, who sits in the Colombian parliament, escaped an attack unharmed. In 2021, Sandra Peña, the governor of the Nasa reservation of La Laguna Siberia, was killed; in 2019, the governor or *Nejwes'x* of the Tacueyó *resguardo*, Cristina Bautista, was killed along with five indigenous guards; and in 2017, indigenous journalist María Efigenia Vásquez Astudillo was shot dead during a confrontation between indigenous people and a police riot squad.

This mother's defiant attitude in the face of the guerrillas is a testament to the Nasa women's self-defence and the defence of their territory.

Un domingo me cogieron en el camino unos milicianos. Yo los conocía porque eran de aquí de la vereda. Me dijeron que era mejor que les entregara por las buenas al muchacho [mi hijo]... '¿Y yo por qué se los voy a entregar?', les dije. 'Si	One Sunday, some militiamen picked me up on the street. I knew them because they were from this village. They told me it would be better if I handed the boy [my son] over to them... 'And why should I hand him over to them?' I told them:

cuando yo estaba en dieta ustedes no me tiraron ni una libra de sal… si quieren, mátenme que si me tengo que morir por un hijo…pues me muero'. (Entrevista a madre de un joven que desertó de la guerrilla, de la crónica *Regreso a casa*: 107)	'When I was in childbirth, you did not even throw a pound of salt at me [metaphor about providing food in solidarity]… if you want to kill me, if I have to die for my son… then I will die'. (Interview with the mother of a young man who deserted from the guerrilla, from the chronicle *Return Home*: 107)

The victimisers of the indigenous people include guerrilla groups, paramilitaries, '*pájaros*' (birds-hired killers) in the service of landowners, and even the army and police. 'If we keep quiet, they kill us, and if we speak out, they kill us too. Then we speak', said the *Nejwes'x* Cristina Bautista months before she was murdered.

The history of the Nasa People explains, in part, the Nasa's present-day commitment to defending their territory and autonomy. Records exist from the 16th century of battles with the Spanish troops that entered the Nasa territories during the so-called Conquest of America. The first reference to this resistance in these south-western mountain ranges emphasises the role of a woman: La Gaitana, a *cacica* whom the Nasa claim as their heroine. La Gaitana led an army of around 8000 indigenous people from different tribes. The indigenous people inflicted several defeats on the Spaniards, but were eventually routed. Faced with a new reality, the Nasa continued their struggle by political means, negotiating with the authorities of the viceroyalty. Their main objective was to maintain a degree of autonomy and control over the lands granted by the King through public deeds.[10]

Although at the beginning of the 20th century, as mentioned, Quintín Lame combined the legal struggle in favour of the Nasa with a short-lived uprising of indigenous people, the most organised acts of resistance since the founding of the CRIC have taken place in four key ways:

(1) recovering the lands of their *resguardos* from the hands of the landowners;
(2) rejecting the assassination of their leaders by 'pájaros', public forces and guerrillas;
(3) rescuing and sustaining the ancestral culture;
(4) opposing the presence and interference of insurgent groups in the daily life of the *resguardos*.

The most elaborate mechanism of resistance of the Nasa People to peacefully confront the armed conflict took shape at the beginning of the millennium with the emergence of the Civic Guard, later called the Indigenous Guard (National Peace Prize, 2004). It later shared its name in the Nasa *Yuwe* language: *Kiwe Thegnas* (Figures 4.4 and 4.5).

Kiwe Thegnas: The guardians of the land, explains where and how this name was defined. It was one of the points of debate at a meeting of

Figure 4.4 Photograph of a boy who wears a vest of the Indigenous Guard
Source: Author's personal collection

elders who were discussing the future of their indigenous guardians. One of the elders suggested:

Debería llamarse *Kiwe Thegnas*, que quiere decir cuidanderos de la tierra. Otro de los presentes complementó: Estaba pensando que sería mejor *Kiwe Thegnas Wala* porque wala es grande y esta tierra es grande porque	It should be called *Kiwe Thegnas*, which means guardians of the land. Another of those present added: I thought that *Kiwe Thegnas Wala* would be better because 'Wala' is big and this land

Figure 4.5 Photograph of a detail of the vest with the name of the Indigenous Guard woven in yarn
Source: Author's personal collection

tiene historia y aquí está el pensamiento y el espíritu del pueblo nasa. (Entrevista de la crónica *Kiwe Thegnas; guardianes de la tierra*: 48)	is big because it has history and here is the thought and spirit of the Nasa People. (Interview from the chronicle *Kiwe Thegnas: The guardians of the land*: 48)

The *testimonio* of the leader, Arquímedes Vitonás, gives an account of the first actions of the indigenous guard to exercise control over the territory:

Taponamos las carreteras que venían de El Palo y de Corinto y nos turnábamos para controlar la entrada de extraños... allí comenzamos a tener roces. Primero con la misma comunidad porque los requisábamos y les pedíamos papeles [solicitar los documentos de identidad] para entrar y salir del resguardo; y después con los milicianos y con la guerrilla, porque querían andar pa' rriba y pa' bajo como si esto fuera de ellos. (Entrevista de la crónica *Los hijos de la Gaitana siguen creciendo*: 111)	We blocked the roads coming from El Palo and Corinto and took turns controlling the entry of outsiders. That's when we started to have friction. First, with the community itself, because we searched them and asked for their identity cards to enter and leave the *resguardo;* and then with the militia and the guerrillas, because they wanted to go up and down as if it were theirs. (Interview from the chronicle *The children of La Gaitana continue to grow*: 111)

The Nasa claim that the Guard has always existed in various forms, which is what their leaders teach in political training workshops:

El primer antecedente de la Guardia fueron las huestes paeces que organizó la cacica La Gaitana, en 1535, para resistir al ejército invasor del	The first forerunners of the Guard were the Paeces forces organised by the *cacica* La Gaitana, in 1535, to resist the invading army of the

conquistador español Sebastián de Belalcázar. (Entrevista a Ezequiel Vitonás, de la crónica *Los hijos de las Gaitana siguen creciendo*: 79)

Spanish conqueror Sebastián de Belalcázar. (Interview with Ezequiel Vitonás, from the chronicle *The children of La Gaitana continue to grow*: 79)

The contemporary Indigenous Guard is a powerful and peaceful autonomous defence system against the actions of various forces in the *resguardos*, governed by the elders' mandate and whose members are subjected to ongoing rituals to avoid 'disharmony'.

La fuerza de la guardia radica en la unidad de la comunidad. Es un instrumento de vida que en ningún momento se va a armar. La guardia está para cuidar a la comunidad y los bienes públicos. (Entrevista a Arquímedes Vitonás, de la crónica *Guardianes de sus montañas*: 51)

The strength of the guard lies in the unity of the community. It is an instrument of life that at no time is going to be armed. The guard is there to look after the community and public goods. (Interview with Arquímedes Vitonás, from the chronicle *Guardians of their mountains*: 51)

Rechazamos con vehemencia a todos los actores armados de la guerra que se libra en nuestro territorio. (Entrevista a Luis Acosta, de la crónica *El coronel no asistió al juicio indígena*: 56)

We vehemently reject all armed actors in the war being waged in our territory. (Interview with Luis Acosta, from the chronicle *The colonel did not attend the indigenous trial*: 56)

Sofía Valencia, who had been a guard for eight years when I wrote the chronicle, remembers how she experienced the birth of the organisation:

En esa época no sabíamos bien qué era la guardia. Nos metimos no más para cuidar el territorio, porque decíamos que los grupos armados se iban a meter para llevarse a los hombres para matarlos. Ya habían desaparecido a gente del pueblo. (Entrevista de la crónica *Los hijos de la Gaitana siguen creciendo*: 110)

At that time we didn't really know what the guard was. We got involved just to look after the territory, because we said that the armed groups were going to come in and take the men away to kill them. They had already made people from the village disappear. (Interview from the chronicle *The children of La Gaitana continue to grow*: 110)

Sofía was one of the 2000 people from the *resguardos* of Tacueyó, Toribío and San Francisco who attended the official inauguration of the Indigenous Guard, where they were sworn in:

De La Playa bajamos como ochenta personas hasta El Tierrero. Era como un día de fiesta. Todos los guardias llevábamos los bastones; el mío yo misma lo había hecho con un

From La Playa, we went down to El Tierrero with about eighty people. It was like a holiday. All of us guards carried our walking sticks; I had made mine out of a 'yellowflower'

palo de floramarillo. Lo corté, le quité la cáscara, lo puse a secar como quince días y, con ayuda de mis hijos, le abrí dos huecos con una broca y le puse dos cordones para cargarlo sin que me estorbe. (Entrevista de la crónica *Los hijos de la Gaitana siguen creciendo*: 113)

stick. I cut it, removed the skin, left it to dry for about fifteen days, and then, with the help of my children, drilled two holes in it and put two cords in it so that I could carry it without it getting in the way. (Interview from the chronicle *The children of La Gaitana continue to grow*: 113)

Although in these mass assemblies and small meetings, the Nasa listen to various musical compositions alluding to the resistance, two of them have become specific symbols of this process. They are played at every activity the Nasa carry out. One is the anthem of the Paez (Nasa) people, composed by Rosa Elena Toconás, a school teacher with another guerrilla group, who was murdered by the FARC in 1985, along with six others accused of collaborating with another organisation. The anthem of the Paez people, also known as *Hijos del Cauca* [*Sons of Cauca*], reaffirms the warrior spirit:

Vivimos porque peleamos,
contra el poder invasor,
y seguiremos peleando,
mientras no se apague el sol.

We live because we fight,
against the invading power,
and we will continue to fight,
as long as the sun does not go out.

However, the anthem that the Nasa chant with fervour and raised sticks is that of the Indigenous Guard, a more recent composition influenced by *rayni* (Ecuadorian ritual music) and the festive rhythms of Cauca. Its lyrics are close to heroic poems and make the hair on the back of your neck stand up, because of the effect of the content and the sound: all the words end with the letter 'a' in Spanish, which gives the declaration its power.

¡Guardia! ¡Guardia!
¡Fuerrrza! ¡Fuerrrza!
¡Por mi raza!
¡Por mi tierra!

Guard! Guard!
Force! Force!
For my race!
For my land!

Some lines of the anthem (*Compañeros han caído, pero no nos vencerán. Porque por cada indio muerto, otros miles nacerán* [*Comrades have died, but we will not be defeated. Because for every Indian killed, thousands more are born*]) remind me of my conversation with Luis Alberto Menza, one of Toribío's most hardened and menacing guards, who has no hope of dying of old age. Nor do some of the *Kiwe Thegnas* hope to die in their beds, often singing the words of their anthem.

Pa' delante compañeros,
dispuestos a resistir.
Defender nuestros derechos,
así nos toque morir...

Forward, comrades,
willing to resist.
Defend our rights,
even if we have to die...

In addition to the Indigenous Guard, the Nasa have created other forms of resistance, perhaps accounting for why there are no 'ghost villages' in their territory, as there are in other parts of Colombia where massacres and assassinations have forced their inhabitants to flee (as described in the following chapter). The Nasa have learned to 'live with the conflict, they integrate it into their daily lives, they also consider it part of their lives and look for mechanisms to resist it, and in this way they manage to survive it without abandoning their territory' (Navia-Lame, 2015: 23). Acting together as a community is the essence of their strength.

> Cada vez que desaparecían a alguno salíamos a la loca, a buscar pa' arriba y pa' abajo. Buscábamos todo el día y dormíamos en chozas, en medio de los cañaduzales o donde nos agarrara la noche. La gente por donde pasábamos nos regalaba comida, yuca, plátanos... Como no teníamos plata para comprar radios, usamos postas, unos indígenas jóvenes que corrían a avisar a la vereda más cercana y ahí arrancaba a correr otro muchacho con la noticia de lo que hubiera pasado. (Entrevista Arquímedes Vitonás, de la crónica *Los hijos de la Gaitana siguen creciendo*: 75)
>
> Whenever someone was disappeared, the rest of us would go out aimlessly, searching up and down. We searched all day and slept in huts, in the middle of the sugar cane plantations or wherever the night took us. The people we passed gave us food, cassava, bananas... As we had no money to buy radios, we used *postas*, some young indigenous people ran to the nearest village, and another boy ran with the news of what had happened. (Interview Arquímedes Vitonás, from the chronicle *The children of La Gaitana continue to grow*: 75)

One of these mechanisms is the temporary shelters known as Sitios de Asamblea Permanente (Permanent Assembly Sites), which were set up around 1998 as hostilities intensified in the north of the region. I have been to two of these places where it is astonishing to see the meticulous internal planning of each activity and the logistical groups that keep the people sheltered and supplied with water and food.

> La selección del lugar de asamblea permanente se ajusta a la lógica de la guerra: que se pueda abastecer de agua, leña y comida; que sea visible y que tenga trochas y caminos por los cuales huir. El sitio, además, debe tener buenas energías para evitar enfermedades o peleas entre los miembros de la comunidad. La energía del lugar la miden los *thêe walas* o chamanes. También les dicen los 'mayores'. Son ellos quienes determinan si el punto que eligieron las autoridades del resguardo es
>
> The selection of the permanent assembly site follows the logic of war: that it can be supplied with water, firewood and food; that it is visible; and that it has paths and roads to flee along. The site must also have good energy to avoid illnesses or fights between community members. *Thê Walas* or Shamans measure the energy of the site. They are also called the 'elders'. They are the ones who determine whether the spot chosen by the authorities of the *resguardo* is appropriate. They do

apropiado. Lo hacen mediante un ritual que llaman de armonización e incluye el uso de la coca. (Entrevista a Oswaldo Imbachí, de la crónica *El arte de la resistencia*: 137–138)	this through a ritual they call harmonisation, which includes the use of coca. (Interview with Oswaldo Imbachí, from the chronicle *The art of resistance*: 137–138)

Some of these strategies fell into disuse with the demobilisation of the FARC and the departure of combatants from indigenous territories. However, the post-conflict period (since 2016) has brought other forms of violence, and indigenous peoples have resorted to new mechanisms. The reappearance of dissident groups dedicated to the cultivation of illicit crops (marijuana and coca) has led to an increase in resistance. These groups recruit young people, threaten and kill their opponents, and fight among themselves for control of routes and cultivation areas, as explained by one of the leaders of the *Guardia de Toribío*, who has been threatened:

Quieren el dominio completo del territorio para poder manejar el comercio de la marihuana. (Entrevista de la crónica *Los nuevos enemigos de los nasas*. Revista Semana, 2019)	They want complete control of the territory in order to manage the marijuana trade. (Interview from the chronicle *The new enemies of the Nasa People*. Semana Magazine, 2019)

At the current time, however, the situation for the Nasa resistance appears to be more complex. In addition to the increase in killings, the boom in illicit crops has also led to an increase in the circulation of cash. In Toribío, shops selling high-end mobile phones, music consoles, electronic equipment and clothes, sneakers and fashion accessories have become ubiquitous. The places where indigenous people used to tie up their mules and horses are now filled with Enduro-type motorbikes, and the dusty roads are lined with 4 × 4 pick-up trucks.

This onslaught of external threats, combined with increased alcohol consumption, will demand new and creative forms of resistance, ones that the leaders, accustomed to facing guns all their lives, have not found so far. The new licit and illicit dynamics seem indecipherable to them, even though they have spent nights discussing the issue around the fire in ceremonial huts.

The Italian priest Antonio Bonanomi, who lived with the Nasa for almost 20 years, warned of one of these phenomena:

Para sobrevivir como etnia, los Nasa deben superar un inmenso desafío que se llama 'el indio moderno'. Existe un choque con la modernidad. El gran reto es cómo conjugar la modernidad sin traicionar la tradición, los rituales. (Entrevista de la crónica *El padre Antonio se cansó de enterrar muertos*: 73)	In order to survive as an ethnic group, the Nasa have to overcome an immense challenge called 'the modern Indian'. There is a clash with modernity. The great challenge is how to combine modernity without betraying tradition and rituals. (Interview from the chronicle *Father Antonio got tired of burying the dead*: 73)

Cauca, A Social Laboratory for Other Struggles in the Country

The complex organisational structure and mobilisation capacity of the indigenous peoples of Cauca and, in the case I have analysed here, the Nasa, have positioned this group as a national reference point. The Nasa have created, strengthened and transferred mechanisms and symbolic elements of resistance to other social movements in the country. Since its creation in 1971, the CRIC has had a significant impact on the Colombian indigenous movement, thanks to the political training its leaders received during the agrarian struggles of the 1960s in the south-west of the country. For about nine years, the CRIC facilitated meetings with indigenous peoples from other regions until 1980, when it led to the creation of the National Indigenous Organisation of Colombia (ONIC). Its first president was an indigenous Cauca of the Guambiano or Misak people. Sixty years earlier, Quintín Lame and José Gonzalo Sánchez, another indigenous man from Cauca, travelled to Tolima (number 29 on the map), where he led the local indigenous people in their struggle against the landowners who had taken over the lands of the great *resguardo* of Ortega and Chaparral.

These transfers of the Cauca indigenous movement's rebelliousness and forms of organisation to other indigenous peoples have been the most significant in the 20th century. In this millennium, the main export has been the Indigenous Guard, its methods and the symbols with which this body is identified: the anthem, the wooden sticks, a vest with the name of the community woven in thread and, of course, its battle-hardened stance:

> Matarán uno; matarán dos… matarán cien, pero a todos no nos matan…Ellos quieren mandar en nuestros territorios y nosotros no nos dejamos. (Entrevista a Albeiro Quiguanás, gobernador del Cabildo Jambaló, de la crónica *La fuerza del ombligo*: 57)

> They will kill one; they will kill two… they will kill a hundred, but they won't kill us all… They want to rule in our territories and we won't let them. (Interview with Albeiro Quiguananás, governor of the *Cabildo* Jambaló, from the chronicle *The Strength of the Umbilical Cord*: 57)

One woman explains the meaning of the red and green colours, symbols of the CRIC, used on the ribbons of their walking sticks and on some of their hats (Figure 4.6):

> El verde representa a las montañas y el rojo, la sangre derramada por nuestros líderes asesinados por defender los derechos de los indígenas. (Entrevista a Sofía Valencia, de la crónica *Los hijos de la Gaitana siguen creciendo*: 73)

> The green represents the mountains and the red the blood shed by our leaders assassinated for defending indigenous rights. (Interview with Sofía Valencia, from the chronicle *The children of La Gaitana continue to grow*: 73)

Figure 4.6 Photograph of a **headscarf** on which is written the word 'Fuerza, Fuerza' which is part of the chorus of one of the anthems
Source: Author's personal collection.

The forms of organisation developed by the Indigenous Guard and passed on to other social movements in Colombia result from the evolution of a centuries-old process developed by the Indigenous Guard, reinforced by the need to protect themselves against the increasing aggressions of illegal armed groups; hence it is vital for them to provide ongoing training for the *Guardia* on issues essential to their preservation. This *testimonio* by Luis Acosta, whom I interviewed when he was the general coordinator of the Indigenous Guard of Cauca, describes part of the training that the traditional authorities provide to these defenders of their territory. Acosta has been attending community meetings for as long as he can remember:

> La capacitación comenzará por profundizar, entre otras cosas, en el origen de los nasa, su territorio, la legislación indígena, su cosmogonía y las formas de resistencia ante la evangelización, la cultura de los no indígenas y la presión de los grupos armados. (Entrevista a Luis Acosta, coordinador general de la Guardia, de la crónica *Kiwe Thegnas: guardianes de la tierra*: 64)

> The training will begin by delving into, among other things, the origin of the Nasa, their territory, indigenous legislation, their cosmogony and forms of resistance to evangelisation, the culture of non-indigenous people and pressure from armed groups. (Interview with Luis Acosta, general coordinator of the Guard, from the chronicle *Kiwe Thegnas: The guardians of the land*: 64)

The transfer of resistance methods developed in northern Cauca began with the creation of peaceful bodies of guards in a large part of Colombia's 115 indigenous peoples. This task was facilitated by ONIC, which brought in Luis Acosta, former coordinator of the *Kiwe Thegnas* from the ACIN, and leader of the Nasa, with experience of dozens of activities carried out by the indigenous guards of the Cauca. The expansion of the *Kiwe Thegnas* model has been facilitated by media coverage that has reproduced images of long human chains of guards holding their sticks, keeping thousands of indigenous protesters in perfect order in the streets of Cali, Bogotá and other cities.

Symbolically, the anthem of the Indigenous Guard has also left the sphere of Cauca to become the hymn of all Indigenous Guards in the country. It is even played on other stages, after the iconic rock group Aterciopelados, winners of three Latin Grammy Awards, recorded a version to accompany the group that first played it, the Parranderos del Cauca 4+3.[11] In 2020, it was performed by the Bogotá Philharmonic Orchestra[12] as a tribute to the defence of life made by the Indigenous Guard.

The indigenous peoples of Cauca might be the most politically educated in Colombia and have demonstrated the greatest capacity for mobilisation. The conflict and resistance in the region have produced numerous leaders, many of whom are university graduates. These leaders advise other indigenous movements throughout Colombia or even in consultative bodies of the national government. A significant part of the CRIC's efforts is directed towards education. As a result, Cauca serves as the headquarters of the Intercultural Autonomous Indigenous University (UAIIN), with 10 programmes, including administration and management, intercultural law, pedagogy for the revival of native languages and good community life. Students from different regions and other Latin American countries attend the university.

The Nasa People are in permanent construction or reconstruction, constantly adapting to new circumstances within the *resguardo* and to external conditions, 'endogenous and exogenous', as some leaders call it, having adopted these terms from one of the NGOs visiting their territories. These processes are nourished by the ancestral knowledge of their *Thê Walas* or spiritual guides and by the experiences of other peoples in resistance, which they adapt to their cosmogonies and export to other indigenous peoples.

Despite the well-known organisational strengthening of the CRIC and other regional organisations (ACIN (*Cxhab Wala Kiwe*) or *Nasa Cxhacxha*, from Tierradentro), the emergence of new armed groups in Nasa territory, which are less political and more violent, and changes in their customs and consumption habits, heavily linked to illicit crops, seem to be creating cracks in some sectors of the Nasa People and in the role of the traditional authority.

'Walking the Word' to Keep on Living

The fragments that formed part of the chronicles on which this chapter is based enable us to see some of the transformations of the Nasa People. Key aspects include: the change of name from Paez People to Nasa People and from the *cabildo* to *Kueque Nejwes'x;* the birth and strengthening of resistance mechanisms; the rise of women to leadership positions and the subsequent violence against these leaders; the metamorphosis of the conflict; the shift from subsistence agriculture to the creation of community enterprises, but also the emergence of illicit economies and even the rapprochement and interaction with urban centres; the rise of motorised transport to the detriment of the horse (which has practically disappeared in Toribío) and the replacement of traditional construction materials by industrially produced ones, which sometimes threaten the environment.

The armed conflict and indigenous organisation and resistance have developed in parallel, although in recent years the warlords have imposed conditions through threats and assassinations. The Nasa, who have baptised themselves 'guerreros milenarios' ['ancient warriors'], are constantly innovating their resistance and organisational mechanisms, protecting themselves differently in each situation. As a result, they have become a national reference point, even for urban social sectors involved in street protests against the government (Figure 4.7). This recognition is

Figure 4.7 March of indigenous people
Source: Author's personal collection [translation of banner: Indigenous Guard forever in the millenary resistance]

attributable to their continuous practice of 'walking the word', which, as described above involves constant reflective conversation and questioning. The cultural and natural environment of the Nasa thus functions as a vast laboratory in which they analyse and learn, refreshing their thinking in the context of the present, which allows them to survive, to endure or to continue living despite time, problems or difficulties. This is the approach described in the anthem of the *Kiwe Thegnas*:

Indios que con val**entía**	Indians who with bravery
y fuerza en sus coraz**ones**	and strength in their hearts
Por justicia y perviv**encia,**	For justice and survival,
hoy empuñan los bast**ones**.	today they wield the sticks.

Notes

(1) *La fuerza del ombligo: cróncas del conficlto en teriotiro Nasa* [*The strength of the umbilical cord, chronicles of the conflict in the Nasa Territory*] is the title of a compilation of 23 chronicles authored by me and published by the University of Cauca. This title is based on one of the chronicles called *La fuerza del ombligo* [*The strength of the umbilical cord*] which in turn is based on the belief that attachment to the land is linked to the tradition of burying the umbilical cord of newborns somewhere in or near the mother's home. It is important to clarify that for the Nasa People, the navel refers both to the scar left on the abdomen and the piece of umbilical cord that remains once it is cut.
(2) Poem published in *Enlace indignea [Indigenous connection]* magazine. See https://movimientos.org/pt-br/node/13458 -Translation by the author.
(3) The Regional Indigenous Council of Cauca (CRIC) was created on 24 February 1971.
(4) Until the mid-2000s, the Nasa were known, even among themselves, as the Paeces. Nasa is part of the evolution of the resistance process, in which they have saved part of their cosmogony, language, traditional medicine, and forms of justice and government.
(5) *Resguardo* are collectively owned territories, recognised and protected by law, designed to protect and guarantee the rights of indigenous peoples over their ancestral territories. Their administration is usually carried out by an indigenous *cabildo* or council, which is the traditional and administrative authority of the community. *Resguardos* cannot be sold or divided and often have a role in environmental protection. Within them, indigenous communities have a significant degree of autonomy to govern themselves according to their own rules and customs.
(6) The chronicle and the report are part of what is known as narrative journalism to distinguish it from journalism devoted to the simple and brief reporting of daily news, from which it also differs in that it incorporates elements such as greater depth of reportage (investigation), the use of multiple and diverse sources, the voice of the narrator and the appropriation of literary tools such as free structures and the construction of scenes and dialogues while maintaining total adherence to truthful and verifiable data.
(7) According to the Colectivo de Estudio Drogas y Derecho (CEDD) (2019), this type of marijuana has genetic modifications to increase the level of Tetrahydrocannabinol (THC). While traditional marijuana has an octane rating of between 2% and 7%, 'creepy' marijuana has an octane rating of between 12% and 22%. See https://www.dejusticia.org/wp-content/uploads/2020/01/Cartilla_CEED_Cannabis.pdf
(8) Verb derived from an onomatopoeia *Tas, Tas*! which imitates the sound of bullets.

(9) The seed ritual is a spiritual and cultural practice that integrates the connection with the earth, nature and the cycles of life. Key elements of this ritual are: connection with Mother Earth (Pachamama), purification and preparation, choice of place and time, planting ritual, thanksgiving and offerings, care of the harvest and celebration.
(10) A summary of La Gaitana can be read at https://dbe.rah.es/biografias/10029/la-gaitana.
(11) See https://www.youtube.com/watch?v=uwR6VgQ1mOE.
(12) See https://www.youtube.com/watch?v=wsIrR4wZy00.

References

Almendra, V. (2017) *Entre la emancipación y la captura. Memorias y caminos desde la lucha Nasa en Colombia*. Grietas Editores.
Bergalli, R. and Rivera, I. (coords.) (2010) *Memoria colectiva como deber social*. Anthropos.
Chase, S. (2005) Narrative inquiry: Multiple lenses, approaches, voices. In N.K. Denzin and Y.S. Lincoln (eds) *The Sage Handbook of Qualitative Research* (3rd edn, pp. 651–679). Sage Publications.
CNMH (2020) *Pueblos indígenas, víctimas de violencias de larga duración*. See https://centrodememoriahistorica.gov.co/pueblos-indigenas-victimas-de-violencias-de-larga-duracion/ (accessed August 2023).
Comisión para el Esclarecimiento de la Verdad, la Convivencia y la No Repetición (2022) *Hay futuro si hay verdad: Informe Final de la Comisión para el Esclarecimiento de la Verdad, la Convivencia y la No Repetición*. See https://www.comisiondelaverdad.co/hay-futuro-si-hay-verdad (accessed February 2023).
Connerton, P. (1995) *How Societies Remember*. Cambridge University Press.
Garzón, M.A. (2014) Las narrativas del retorno. *Revista Encuentros* 12 (2), 67–77. Universidad Autónoma del Caribe.
González. M. (2008) Poema Caminando la palabra. *Revista Enlace indígena*. See https://movimientos.org/pt-br/node/13458 (accessed August 2024).
Hoyos, J.J. (2003) *Escribiendo historias – El arte y el oficio de narrar en el periodismo*. Universidad de Antioquia.
Martini, S. (2000) *Periodismo, noticia y noticiabilidad*. Grupo Editorial Norma.
Muñoz-González, G. (2012) El alcance metodológico de las narrativas. In S. Soler Castillo (Comp.) *Lenguaje y Educación: Perspectivas metodológicas y teóricas para su estudio* (pp. 161–182). Universidad Distrital Francisco José de Caldas.
Navia-Lame, J. (2015) *La fuerza del ombligo, crónicas del conflicto en territorio Nasa*. Universidad del Cauca.
Observatorio de Derechos Territoriales de la Comisión Nacional de Territorios Indígenas (CNTI) (2022) *El eterno retorno de la violencia política contra los pueblos indígenas*. Secretaría Técnica Indígena.
Organización de la Naciones Unidas (2022) Colombia: Asesinatos de defensores indígenas Nasa, incluidos los niños, son muy preocupantes y deben cesar inmediatamente – Experta de la ONU. Comunicado de prensa. See https://www.ohchr.org/es/press-releases/2022/03/colombia-un-expert-says-killings-nasa-indigenous-human-rights-defenders (accessed November 2023).
Orozco, M., Paredes, M. and Tocancipá, J. (2013) Territorio y cosmovisión. Una aproximación interdisciplinaria al problema del cambio y la adaptación en los nasa. *Boletín de Antropología* 28 (46), 244–271. Universidad de Antioquia.
Salazar, A. (2001) Arboleda, pueblito de mis cuitas. En VVAA (2021) *Años de fuego, grandes reportajes de la última década* (pp. 141–145). Planeta.
Vives-Riera, A. (2011) Conflicto cultural y construcción del conocimiento: Del choque de civilizaciones a la hibridación creativa. En VVAA. *Formas-Otras: Saber, nombrar, narrar, hacer. IV Training Seminar de jóvenes investigadores en Dinámicas Interculturales* (pp. 65–78). CIDOB.

5 Narratives to Transform War Imaginaries in Colombia: An Animation Workshop with Ex-Guerrilla Children

Cecilia Traslaviña González

Introduction

In 2019, Mathew Charles,[1] professor and researcher at the Faculty of International, Political and Urban Studies at the Universidad del Rosario in Bogotá, invited me to participate in the project, *Mi historia: la niñez que peleó la guerra en Colombia* [*My Story: the children who fought war in Colombia*]. Mathew Charles has been engaged in two main initiatives in Colombia for several years. The first is creating and running workshops in collaboration with various civil organisations to prevent vulnerable children and young people from being recruited by armed groups and gangs. The second is journalism and audiovisual production training for young people between 14 and 18 who come from violent contexts.

The Global Challenges Research Fund, awarded by the UK Arts and Humanities Research Council, funded the initiative in partnership with the University of Leeds, Rosario University, CEV [the Commission for the clarification of the Truth] and Benposta, a foundation which offers support to children and young people at risk or in danger of being at risk. The latter is a community-based charity known as 'La *Ciudad de los Muchachos*' [*The City of the Youth*]. In Colombia, this initiative welcomes young people from different regions who are at risk of participating in the armed conflict.

Mi historia: la niñez que peleó la guerra en Colombia [*My Story: the children who fought war in Colombia*] is an animated series in Spanish and English that resulted from visual storytelling workshops with former child combatants.² It comprises short films recounting instances of forced recruitment during the Colombian armed conflict. The project was launched at the beginning of 2021 as part of the CEV's *testimonio* documents and as tools to promote reconciliation and to contribute to peace-building.

The production process for the short films was developed in three stages. The first explored the lives of former child soldiers from different regions of Colombia. The second stage concentrated on the indigenous communities of the Department of Vaupés (number 31 on the map) which is part of the Amazon region (numbers 1, 8, 16, 23, 23, 31 on the map), whose war experiences have often been overlooked, along with the impact on indigenous youth. The third stage, centred on the experiences of young people from Benposta (Table 5.1). The focus of this chapter is this latter experience and is part of the *Changing the Story*³ programme, a project based at the University of Leeds, UK, that uses arts to facilitate participatory practices that benefit young people in 12 post-conflict countries.

The key focus in this chapter is on the potential of animation to reveal the effects of traumatic events and its capacity to transform perceptions of violence. While describing the procedural aspects of the workshops, this chapter also presents our reflections that emerged from them. The various layers of violence and their convergences are revealed in the animation creation process.

The animations were made in collaboration with two students and two recent graduates from Pontificia Universidad Javeriana's Arts Degree programme who had significant experience in their artistic practice. With this group of students, a short film was made for the project *Cartas de la selva* [*Letters from the jungle*], based on texts by former FARC combatants in a writing workshop. Different universities worldwide – such as KHM, Germany; NID, India; CAFA, China; UNAM, Mexico; and PUJ, Bogotá – also participated in creating animations from those texts. The students and graduates acted with Mathew and I as workshop leaders, taught the boys and girls of Benposta various animation techniques and narrative strategies, and guided them through the whole process, including editing. A sound engineer was also involved, coordinating sessions to guide the sound production and recording of the oral narratives that complemented the animations.

This project was an important opportunity, both for the Javeriana students and workshop participants, to approach Colombia's social and historical reality. It involved enabling the girls and boys of Benposta learning about animation as a medium rich in techniques to tell their *testimonios*. At the same time, it involved the students weaving a respectful relationship with the girls and boys, one mediated by the responsibility of

Table 5.1 *Testimonios* themes developed for the animations

Title of the animation / year of joining Benposta	Geographical origin of the participant	Gender, age and first name initial (preservation of anonymity)	Summary of the support *testimonio* for the voice-over
Uno se acostumbra a la violencia, 2016 [One gets used to violence] https://www.youtube.com/watch?v=CQcBsGz8FoU	Norte de Santander (number 22 on the map)	Male, 16 years old. P.	The boy evokes his place of origin, family life, the territory, the coca cultivation and the drug trafficking business to which most inhabitants are dedicated. He also evokes the moment when friends who lived with many luxuries and comforts induced him to join the Popular Liberation Army (EPL); he remembers his arrival to the group and his camouflage clothing; he describes his disappointment because after belonging to the group, he never received money. He also remembers the confrontations, the camp, the murder of one of his companions and his change of perspective to leave the camp and give himself up to the police. Finally, he tells how his mother helped him, for security reasons, to move to another city to join the Benposta programme. He longs to return to the land but knows it is dangerous.
El día que vi la luz, 2018 [The day I saw the light] https://www.youtube.com/watch?v=oUhSZD4aUWE	Meta (number 20 on the map)	Female, 15 years old. M.	The girl recalls her life at school and her love of football, and the warnings their teachers gave them at school about the dangers of being recruited. She also evokes how a young man from the community, who became her boyfriend, tried to recruit her into the FARC; then, this organisation threatened to kill her if she did not recruit someone else. She remembers how all of this disappointed her, how fortunate she was not to have been deceived by her boyfriend's manipulation, and how her brother prevented her from being recruited into the group. She ends her *testimonio* by regretting losing her interest and ability in football.

(Continued)

Narratives to Transform War Imaginaries in Colombia 111

Table 5.1 (Continued)

Title of the animation / year of joining Benposta	Geographical origin of the participant	Gender, age and first name initial (preservation of anonymity)	Summary of the support *testimonio* for the voice-over
Rojo y negro, 2017 [Red and Black] https://www.youtube.com/watch?v=sws7LgEbHX0	Chocó (number 12 on the map)	Female, 15 years old. L.	The girl recalls her life with her grandmother in a very humble wooden house and the moment when men from ELN arrived in her region, offering money to children to join this armed group. She describes the exact moment they found her alone washing clothes in the ravine, and they offered her money, which she accepted. She describes her disappointment as she was deceived, for they never gave her any money, only clothes and a weapon; on the contrary, she had to endure forced labour. She also describes moving around at night for long hours to change camps, along with other children who were also recruited. She recalls how she escaped, taking advantage of an opportunity to hide when they passed through one of the communities where they helped her and moved her to Bogotá to avoid being found.
Estaba dejando atrás mi vida como la conocía, 2017 [I was leaving behind my life as I knew it] https://www.youtube.com/watch?v=vSNZ-ZJbg_k	Norte de Santander (number 22 on the map)	Female, 14 years old. G.	The girl recalls pleasant memories of where she spent her childhood and the difficult situations they had to go through, such as clashes between different armed groups. Specifically, she recalls the time a bomb exploded very close to where she was with her brother, the death of neighbours, and the arrival of armed men at her school to recruit children by offering them money. She remembers that when she told her mother, who asked the parish priest for help, the priest told them where to place her in Bogotá; she remembers her sadness at having to leave her friends, family and town.
The Saviours, 2017 https://www.youtube.com/watch?v=kgLyWGBKYq0	Meta (number 20 on the map)	Male, n.d. C.	The boy tells his *testimonio* through the adventures of superheroes (*Right Man* and *The Saviours*) who were well trained as human rights defenders and headquartered in Bogotá. In parallel, it narrates a confrontation between the army and the FARC just as the children are leaving school to take their break. With sadness, he also talks about why the military barracks did not know what had happened and why painful things continue to happen. He tells how, after the death of Juan's brother, Lucas, and with the help of technology, Juan was able to warn the superheroes. The superheroes then go to the region to try to resolve many situations of injustice but lose their powers when the young people do not want to save themselves and decide to join the illegal groups. *The Saviours* thus recruit Juan to help the other kids in the future.

(Continued)

112 Part 2: Narratives of the Colombian Armed Conflict

Table 5.1 (Continued)

Title of the animation / year of joining Benposta	Geographical origin of the participant	Gender, age and first name initial (preservation of anonymity)	Summary of the support testimonio for the voice-over
Todos sabíamos que volverían por mí, 2015 [We all knew they would come back for me] https://www.youtube.com/watch?v=ogx0tt93E68	Valle del Cauca (number 30 on the map)	Female, 14 years old. N.	The girl evokes the beauty of her region. She contrasts it with the situations of violence caused by armed groups, the recruitment of children and the creation of invisible borders, which are places that cannot be crossed due to the absence of the police and the State in general. She recalls how she refused to join these groups on several occasions, but also how one day she was drugged at a party, and they tried to recruit her to become a prostitute forcibly. She tells how she was saved because some neighbours noticed, and they all joined to prevent them from taking her away. The next day, she was uprooted from the region because it was known that they would come back for her.
El negocio de la coca, 2018 [The coca business] https://n9.cl/sj03k	Norte de Santander (number 22 on the map)	Female, 14 years old. S.	The girl evokes situations that led her family and all the men in the region to become involved in the cultivation of coca and the subsequent manufacture and negotiation of cocaine. She recounts how it all began with her grandfather and the workers he hired for these trades, including her father, who, in turn, bought a huge farm to expand the business. She mentions this was very peaceful at first, but then her grandfather was persecuted. She recalls that in order to 'solve' these problems, her grandfather had to meet with the ELN commander, who demanded he not take coca out of the territory and told him that if he wanted to stay alive, he had to sell it to the armed group. She recalls the images of dead and tortured people and the disappearance of women working in bars. Finally, she recounts how she had to leave the region because of the death of her father and the threats against her life.

Source: Compiled by the author based on the data accompanying the short films in the mihistoria.co repository.

listening and exploring the best ways to bear witness to their harsh experiences.

Our goal was to encourage the boys and girls to delve deeper into their *testimonios* and use images and writing (*voice-over* in the animation) to contribute sensitive information that would help us as citizens understand their *testimonios*, and to feel and experience them. Most of the members of the mediating team were also young people, which fostered a more equal relationship with the boys and girls participating. The open atmosphere created in most sessions allowed the boys and girls to act freely; they could listen to music, talk, move around to work, take breaks and be spontaneous, in contrast to the usual norms of discipline and rigor in more formal educational settings.

As several of the voice-over fragments show, the narratives are difficult; sometimes, when the team of mediators felt that situations were tense or challenging to narrate, we had to stop, change the activity and continue later. Thanks to the fact that the girls and boys in Benposta have permanent psychological support, this support could be called on at moments of extreme stress. Despite the caution and shyness, the atmosphere of closeness and trust that developed allowed the boys and girls to ask the university students questions: about their artistic work and whether it was possible to make a living from art and more generally about films and music. This way, the atmosphere that developed was pleasant and relaxed; the exercises were fun, and young people talked while learning the creative techniques.

In order to participate in the workshops, girls and boys had to have their parents' permission. In this case the Benposta Foundation was authorised to represent them. At Benposta's request, the identity of participants who are referred to in this chapter are anonymised. Fragments of *testimonios* included in this chapter use pseudonymous initials.

One exciting aspect of the process was the way in which it became an exercise in ownership and co-creation. One of the participants put it this way:

> Nosotras no nos conocemos desde hace mucho tiempo y, aunque venimos de lados opuestos de Colombia, compartimos una pesadilla que nos ha hecho cercanas. (Testimonio de M., creadora de *El día que vi la luz*)
>
> We have not known each other for a long time, and although we come from opposite sides of Colombia, we share a nightmare that has made us close. (*Testimonio* by M., creator of *The day I saw the light*)

The titles of the seven animations[4] outline the themes they discussed in the short texts they wrote and then narrated using *voice-overs* (Table 5.1). In this chapter, fragments from the voice-overs written by the young creators during the workshops to weave the *testimonios* together are included.

Expressive and Technical Possibilities of Animation to Depict Traumatic Events

> But what does memory 'look like,' and
> how does it get from mind to linguistic articulation to screen?
> Suzanne Buchan, 2019

Animation has expressive potential even for people who have never practised it; relatively recently, its contributions in the field of reality have begun to be studied. One might think that it is impossible for such a 'fictional' medium, in which everything has to be created to tell something, to account for reality. Patrick (2008: 36) puts it this way: 'For years, animation was incorrectly considered too artificial a technique to present non-fiction content with sufficient authority'. Ward (2008: 14) argues that animation openly allows for reconstructing aspects of reality beyond mere illustration:

> The underlying dialectical relationship between 'appearances' and 'reality' is therefore of the utmost importance to human understanding of the real world and our place within it. And, arguably, a form such as animation can give us access to exactly those 'hidden' or obscured 'real relations', precisely because its constructedness is foregrounded. Even at its relatively mimetic moments (e.g. the rotoscoping in *Old Glory*), we are not watching something that is simply trying to mimic the world.

Since the beginning of the 20th century, animation has been used as a vehicle for representing reality; Winsor McCay's *Sinking on the Lusitania* (1918) is considered the first animated documentary. Its animated illustrations visually recreate the tragic sinking of an ocean liner during the First World War. The film presents powerful and detailed images of the disaster, capturing the tragedy and loss of lives. In *Animated Documentary* (2013), Anabelle Roe provides a comprehensive overview of research on documentary animation. She proposes three functions that contribute to the understanding of how animation works with image: by mimetic substitution, by non-mimetic substitution and through evocation. In the first case (by mimetic substitution), the animation tries to follow the *testimonio* or events as faithfully as possible; in the second (by non-mimetic substitution), it moves away from the fidelity of the story and interprets the events by highlighting other aspects of reality that are not so obvious; finally, in the case of evocation, it brings images of the events from poetic, metaphorical suggestions that respond to the different types of limitation for representation. The seven animations made by the girls and boys in this workshop have elements of all three functions but particularly the third, the evocative poetic. Working with this dimension was crucial given that the girls and boys arrived in Bogotá with only fragments of their stories in their minds and hearts.

Animation can create relationships or reconstruct places and situations, as in the case of the renowned films *Vals con Bashir* [*Waltz with Bashir*] (2008) by the Israeli director Ari Folman or *Persepolis* (2007) by the French-Iranian graphic artist and animator Marjane Satrapi, both of which have given documentary animation a prominent place. As with other forms for narrating violence, a key value of animation lies in its evocative representation of how the survivor is conceived and recognised, and in providing a mechanism for achieving social justice (Bergalli & Rivera, 2010; Bungard, 2019; González, in this book; Maldonado, 2008; Nance, 2006).

The functions proposed by Roe help understand the animations created by the girls and boys in this project as a dynamic process. In all cases, there was no archival material, no trace from which to start. Therefore, drawings, particular objects, dolls and toys became the tools that allowed us to see and understand what happened: they became the objects of memory, necessary when narrating painful events (Arroyave, 2013; Bahntje *et al.*, 2007; Garzón, 2014; Virno & Sadier, 2003).

In addition to representation, the materiality of the techniques we used also offered information, as is evident in *Rojo y negro [Red and Black]* and *The Saviours*. Using charcoal (Figure 5.1) to draw the story provided insights into how memory works. By sketching directly on paper, erasing the previous drawing and associating the trace that persists, the old image remains blurred, with the imprecision of remembrances, the drawing replaced the image of the facts. Remembering, however it manifests itself, coexists with a fact. By evoking it later, the animation returns by translating whatever the perception has elaborated at the time (Virno & Sadier, 2003). In these cases, we can go back to Halbwachs's (2004b: 35) comment:

> It is not only because the passage of time increases the distance between a period of our lives and the present moment that many remembrances become inaccessible, but we no longer interact with the same people: many of the individuals who could have provided us with information about past events have disappeared.

The workshop to create animations had two parts. The first part of preproduction, which lasted two months, consisted of teaching techniques

Figure 5.1 Frame from *The Saviours*
Source: Mihistoria repository. See https://mihistoria.co/testimonios/

such as cut-out, paint- and sand-on-glass animation, charcoal-on-paper drawing, rotoscoping, stop-motion and pixelation. These techniques were practiced twice a week in two-hour sessions. All these techniques have an artisanal character and are an encounter between the qualities of the materials and the animator's intentions.

In the second part of the workshop, the entire team of mediators guided the girls and boys in creating animations based on their personal experiences of recruitment or violence by armed groups in their places of origin. This process was guided by viewing reference animations that directly addressed the issues at hand and included: the Colombian animations *Migrópolis* by Karolina Villarreaga, *Cuentos de viejos* [*The elders' stories*] by Carlos Smith, and the short film *Todos somos inmigrantes* [*We are all immigrants*] by Catalina Matamoros. These animations served as powerful examples of how animation can effectively represent and address real-world problems.

In the next two sections, I delve deeper into each part of the workshop which led to the creation of the seven animations.

The Workshop. A Meeting to Create Collectively

Practical exercises helped girls and boys familiarise themselves with the characteristics of the different materials and to become familiar with the technical requirements of animation (planning the duration of each action, calculating how many movements each shot requires, how many frames per second to work with, etc.).

Cut-out animation is a form of stop-motion animation in which flat characters, props and backgrounds are cut out of materials such as paper, cardboard, stiff fabric or photographs. Paint-on-glass, sand-on-glass, pastel or charcoal drawing and other direct under-camera techniques can be described as 'experimental' or 'alternative' animation. The medium is placed directly under the camera and recorded frame by frame. Each frame appears to merge with the previous one, creating a seamless transition into the next. The result is a fluid and organic movement akin to a continuous process of metamorphosis. Rotoscoping is the frame-by-frame tracing of live-action images. In rotoscoping, actors and live objects are filmed frame by frame to simulate movement. The result is a film with an animated look, in which people and objects around them move without being touched. In stop-motion, puppets and objects are physically manipulated in small increments between individually photographed frames. This manipulation allows them to appear to move independently or to change as the series of frames is played back.

Classical animation works at 24 frames per second, which means that 24 drawings or positions were needed to complete one second; in our case, we asked participants to work at 12 frames per second, which means two shots per drawing or movement, although their animations show that this guideline was not fully met. Similarly, we introduced them to the universe of sound, teaching them about different types of microphones, how sounds (Foley – the name given to the reproduction of everyday sound effects that are added to films) and characters (character animation) are created, and to software for capturing and editing drawings or figures. This process helped participants to understand the different stages involved in animation production.

In the narrative workshops, the use of referents has a healing power in two ways: on the one hand, it allows people to acknowledge that telling a *testimonio* is worthwhile, as the status of the marginalised and isolated subject is set aside to give way to visibility and dignity, and on the other hand, it allows them to see in the *testimonios* of others, that they are not alone and can have a glimmer of hope to change their lives (Acedo, 2017; Caruth, 1996; Castillejo, 2010, 2013; Jensen, 2005; Muñoz-González, 2012; Pennebaker, 1990; Semprun, 1995). In this context, animation became a bridge between what the young people felt, what they remembered and what they found difficult to articulate. The environment allowed them to get closer to deep places of personal and Collective Memory, both because of the versatility of the techniques and the narrative strategies they offered. Animation techniques, which are diverse, served as mediators of traumatic experiences because they are so efficient in visually articulating the mental forms of memory and complex processes such as remembering painful situations. In fact, according to Halbwachs (2004b: 39), 'all that is found is that the mind in memory is oriented towards an interval of the past with which it never comes into contact'.

The exercise of remembering the events experienced through writing and images revealed that the evocations came in a fragmented form. It was sometimes difficult to express what happened before or after the event the young people were narrating since what was recovered were mainly fragments that were then transformed into images and sounds. Without exception, the narratives in which the voice-over was recorded, have jumps owing to the attempt to narrate several situations in a few words or to narrate them as the mind brought them, without a defined sequence; in several of the animations, there are points of departure and return that seem to break the narrative sequence.

In *Uno se acostumbra a la violencia [One gets used to violence]* (Table 5.1), in less than 100 words, the boy talks about himself, the place where he lives, the danger of the region, the businesses that operate, abandonment by the state, the peace process that has not touched them, the lack of fear in people, the easy money and how violence becomes embedded until it becomes a habit.

Yo tengo 18 años y soy de Norte de Santander donde vivía junto con mi familia hasta 2018. Tenemos una	I am 18 years old and come from Norte de Santander, where I lived with my family until 2018. We have

casa en Catatumbo. Es un lugar peligroso, es un espacio de guerra donde se puede ver el movimiento de narcotráfico. Allá no hay apoyo del Estado. Allá la paz no ha llegado. Los grupos armados son los que controlan la zona, pero no creo que la gente tenga miedo. La mayoría trabaja con coca. Es la mejor manera para hacer dinero y seguir adelante. Uno se acostumbra a la violencia. (P. *Uno se acostumbra a la violencia*)

a house in Catatumbo. It is a dangerous place; it is a war zone where you can see the drug trafficking movement. There is no government support there. Peace has not arrived there. The armed groups control the area, but I do not think the people are afraid. Most of them work with coca. It is the best way to make money and keep going. You get used to violence. (P. *One gets used to violence*)

We knew that this was not the first time that the girls and boys had participated in a memory exercise, and for this reason, it was difficult for images to emerge in a non-rationalised way; it was difficult for their unconscious to free itself because it was not easy for them to differentiate the discourse they had learned from their own and many other's experiences. The fact that these remembrances were to form the basis of an animation, a medium in which they had not worked before, helped them approach the fragments of their experiences differently. Feindt *et al.* (2014: 24, cited by Buchan, 2019), in this sense, state:

> In a synchronic perspective, memory's entangledness is presented as twofold. Every act of remembering inscribes an individual in multiple social frames. This polyphony entails the simultaneous existence of concurrent interpretations of the past. In a diachronic perspective, memory is entangled in the dynamic relation between single acts of remembering and changing mnemonic patterns.

The girls' and boys' remembrances had many overlapping layers, which made it difficult to uncover them quickly. The process required us to ask them for more precise descriptions, as any detail could open up a way to refine the understanding of what happened, as well as the personal and collective dimensions, both for them and for us. We also understood their fears, insecurities and dreads because memory is changeable; it adapts to what we are living, it even hides, it sets traps so that we can survive (Jensen, 2005), especially when we start a new life, which is what Benposta offered them.

Some participants struggled to socialise with the other workshop members. Although they knew each other, many of them did not want to read out loud or show their first drawings but sharing was considered important in the workshop so was gradually encouraged and, as discussed below, central to the practical activities. Benposta insisted that the regular teacher leading the group should be present in the sessions; this was fortunate in many instances, but in others, it was an interference as she tried to make chronological sense of what was coming up in the recall exercise, which was very different from what we had hoped to explore with the technique. Undoubtedly, the events were similar; recruitment and violence have clear ways of operating, but the way the wounds remain are very different in each individual, and it was this individual experience that we wanted girls and boys to express in the animation. We asked participants to keep in their minds the images that came to them of how the recruitment and other violence they had suffered happened, the impact of these events on their lives and family relationships, whether they were aware of what was happening to them at the time or whether it was revealed to them at a later stage. For example, the offer of money and better opportunities is repeated in several of the narratives as the background to recruitment, but each person recalls and expresses this in different ways:

La mayoría trabaja con coca. Es la mejor manera para hacer dinero y seguir adelante. Uno se acostumbra a la violencia. Hace dos años, cuando tenía 16 años, todo cambió. Me gustaba estudiar y me encantaba jugar fútbol, hasta el día que empecé a tomar actitudes diferentes con mi familia. Me aburrí. Estaba discutiendo mucho con mi mamá. No me gustaban las normas que había en mi casa. Creí que ya estaba lo suficientemente grande como para defenderme a mí mismo, y es cuando empecé a salir a trabajar solo. Dejé el estudio y las cosas que me gustaban a un lado. Quería mi propia plata para comprar mis cosas. (P. *Uno se acostumbra a la violencia*).

Most work with coca. It is the best way to make money and move on. You get used to violence. Two years ago, when I was 16, everything changed. I liked studying and playing football until the day I started to take a different attitude towards my family. I got bored. I argued with my mum a lot. I did not like the rules at home. I thought I was old enough to stand up for myself, and that's when I started going out to work on my own. I left my studies and the things I liked aside. I wanted my own money to buy my own things. (P. *One gets used to violence*)

Empezó en el 2016, cuando el ELN – el Ejército de Liberación Nacional – llegó al Litoral de San Juan en el Chocó. Yo tenía 13 años. Iniciaron ofreciendo dinero a los niños y las niñas para irnos con ellos al grupo armado, pero cuando algunos no querían, los obligaban. Mi comunidad es Chagpien Tordo. Yo vivía con mi abuela y mi casa era de madera, teníamos unas cinco ollas de acero. Había cucharas, platos, vasos. Al final de todos los días poníamos una cobija en el piso y así pasábamos las noches. (L. *Rojo y Negro*).

It started in 2016 when the ELN – the National Liberation Army – arrived in the Litoral de San Juan in Chocó. I was 13 years old. At first, they offered the boys and girls money to go with them to the armed group, but when some of them didn't want to, they forced them. My community is Chagpien Tordo. I lived with my grandmother, and my house was made of wood; we had about five steel pots. We had spoons, plates, and glasses. At the end of the day, we would put a blanket on the floor, and that's how we spent the nights. (L. *Red and Black*)

Un día llegaron unos hombres uniformados a interrumpir la paz de nuestro colegio, iban armados, ellos no tenían buenas intenciones. Escuché que le estaban diciendo a mis compañeros que les darían dinero si se iban con ellos, la primera vez fue demasiado extraño, pero esa situación empezó a repetirse todos los meses. (G. *Estaba dejando atrás mi vida como la conocía*)	One day, some men in uniform came to disrupt the peace of our school. They were armed, and they did not have good intentions. I heard that they told my classmates that they would give them money if they left with them. The first time, it was too strange, but this situation began to repeat itself every month. (G. *I was leaving behind my life as I knew it*)
De regreso a su casa, Juan se encontró con un retén de guerrilleros. Le ofrecieron un buen pago a cambio de sus servicios, pero este no aceptó [...] Otro niño, al día siguiente, pisó una mina y perdió la pierna, fue trasladado al hospital. (C. *The Saviours*)	On his way home, Juan came across a guerrilla roadblock. They offered him good money for his services, but he refused [...] The next day, another boy stepped on a mine and lost his leg; he was taken to hospital. (C. *The Saviours*)

Encouraging the writing that later became part of the voice-over in the animations was a task that Mathew Charles undertook based on his experience as a journalist and his work with at-risk young people in various countries worldwide. This was based on conversations he had with each of them, after which he invited them to write about their experiences. This process of writing and remembering helped them understand a little more about what had happened to them. In the act of writing, they found a way to make sense of their experiences (Muñoz-González, 2012). Writing became a mechanism for decanting what had happened, confronting memories and looking for ways to approach them so that another person could understand them as well as possible. This involved expressing the complexity of the experiences in a metaphorical, symbolic or direct way. For M., for example, it meant understanding the events that had taken place in a romantic relationship with a male partner (Figure 5.2):

Nosotros estuvimos juntos durante seis meses hasta que un día después del entrenamiento, cuando estábamos solos, me agarró y me dijo que tenía que ir con él. Estaba sorprendida y triste. Tenía mucho miedo y le dije que no. Me dijo que, si no lo acompañaba a la guerrilla, lo matarían. Me di cuenta que el chico que pensé que era mi novio había estado tratando de reclutarme todo el tiempo. Quería ganarse mi confianza y luego entregarme al grupo armado. (M. *El día que vi la luz*) (Figura 5.2)	We were together for six months, until one day after training, while we were alone, he grabbed me and told me I had to go with him. I was shocked and sad. I was terrified, and I said no. He told me that if I didn't go with him to the guerrillas, they would kill him. I realised that the boy I thought was my boyfriend had been trying to recruit me all along. He wanted to gain my trust and then hand me over to the armed group. (M. *The day I saw the light*) (Figure 5.2)

Figure 5.2 Frame of *El día que vi la luz [The day I saw the light]*
Source: Mihistoria repository. See https://mihistoria.co/testimonios/. The short films are translated into English, so the screenshot shows English-medium subtitles.

In all these instances (remembering, writing, drawing, recording the *testimonio*), several events are intertwined simultaneously and intermittently, with many blurred or hidden in the memory, refusing to emerge; the reconstruction of a traumatic event can be liberating but also confrontational; it means touching issues in the unconscious that can constitute a powerful shock.

> For Agamben (2000), *testimonio* carries within itself the signs of its own limitation, its own lacuna, since those who could offer the most accurate account of how the acts of violence took place are precisely those who cannot testify, that is, the murdered, the disappeared. In this way, *testimonio* attempts to make intelligible something that by nature cannot be intelligible, and from this point of view, its place is configured between the said and the unsaid; therefore, the truth about the past can only be configured, to echo Castillejo (2008), as a spectral manifestation. (Martínez, 2013: 49)

Agamben's approach makes one wonder how much of what the boys and girls had heard from their relatives and people close to them, who had died or were disappeared, filtered into what they recounted. The young people had in common that they were survivors of violent experiences; they carried their ghosts on their backs and were at Benposta because their lives were in danger. They had been torn away from their family nucleus, another episode of violence that added to a life about which they were trying to join fragments together:

> Era 24 de octubre del 2016. Mataron a mi papá. Inmediatamente mi mamá y yo nos pusimos muy mal, empezamos a llorar mucho. Después empe

> It was 24 October 2016. They killed my dad. Immediately, my mum and I were in a very bad state; we started crying a lot. Then the

zaron las amenazas contra nosotras y a mí me tocó salir del pueblo porque un grupo armado me iba a matar también. (S. *El negocio de la coca*)

threats against us started, and I had to leave the village because an armed group was going to kill me too. (S. *The coca business*)

El gobierno de mi comunidad me ayudó a salir del grupo pero no fue fácil porque del grupo no nos dejaban salir, pero cuando vi la oportunidad, me escondí en una de las comunidades por las que pasamos, pero nos enteramos que el grupo me estaba buscando. Entonces me sacaron para Bogotá. (L. *Rojo y negro*)

The government of my community helped me to leave the group, but it wasn't easy because they wouldn't let us leave the group, but when I saw the opportunity, I hid in one of the communities we passed through, but we found out that the group was looking for me. So they took me out to Bogotá. (L. *Red and Black*)

Cuando pasaba esto corría asustada a mi casa a contarle todo a mi mamá, porque me daba miedo que estos hombres se acercaran a mí, ella bastante preocupada por todo lo que venía pasando en las Mercedes decidió pedirle ayuda al padre del pueblo, él escuchó a mi mamá y de inmediato le habló de un lugar donde yo podía estar segura, pero eso significaba que tenía que dejar mi pueblo, mis amigos y mi familia porque este lugar se encontraba en Bogotá. (G. *Estaba dejando atrás mi vida como la conocía*)

When this happened I ran scared to my house to tell my mother everything because I was afraid that these men would come near me, she was quite worried about everything that was happening in Las Mercedes and decided to ask the priest of the village for help, he listened to my mother and immediately told her about a place where I could be safe, but that meant that I had to leave my village, my friends and my family because this place was in Bogotá. (G. *I was leaving behind my life as I knew it*)

Me salvé sólo porque algunos vecinos se dieron cuenta y todos se unieron para evitar que me llevaran. Al siguiente día, me tuve que ir. (N. *Todos sabíamos que volverían por mí*)

I was only saved because some neighbours noticed, and they all joined together to stop them from taking me away. The next day, I had to leave. (N. *We all knew they would come back for me*)

As part of the process of creating the animations, the team of mediators faced questions such as: how effective is it to write to remember and try to make sense of a violent experience? Who are/should they be addressing in their writing -themselves, us? How can we gain their trust to have the necessary closeness and thus achieve a sincere *testimonio* far from the commonplaces they have often had to rely on to feel that they are being heard?

Owing to the discourse learned by the citizens in general – from what is reported in the news, radio or print media – often essential issues of life stories are obscured. The media encourage people to tell their stories to benefit a political sector and thus continue to justify the war. Those involved often learn particular codes of verbal and body language, and, in this way, the media achieve what they want (Restrepo, 2019). The whole country has heard such stories for several generations, creating an emotional shield that prevents people from sensitively approaching people's actual lived pain, perhaps for fear of having to deal with the events that have happened. For this reason, also, as mediators, we asked ourselves: What tools should we use to bring out other kinds of images and discourses? How to confront the unknown? How to make the unmentionable appear, explain, or name it? How to create animations that attract the attention of those who are often indifferent?

Because of the type of relationships that this technique promotes for group work, we chose to use analogue animation because we could engage directly with the materials: touching them, feeling them, 'listening' to them, cutting them out, kneading them, drawing, erasing, painting, etc. This approach not only helped us to get to know each other's skills but also made the relationships more horizontal, as the collective exercises allowed the *testimonios* not only to be personal but to be embraced by everyone.

To do the work of animation, the body needs to contort into unusual postures: bending down for a long time to move a character or a stage; stretching to hold something while taking a shot; taking a few steps repeatedly to shut off the camera; changing one role in the team for another; organising the work environment; staying in front of a screen for many hours, when the eyes and hands are very busy, and the body itself sometimes provides the support on which the animation is done. In addition, some techniques require the use of the body to relate to others, to see and recognise oneself in the other body with which one interacts, to stand close to each other and make repetitive movements, to stay in one position for a few seconds and then change it very slightly while the partner takes the pictures.[5] In the process, the girls and boys formed a kind of overarching body, as a result of the wounds of war, where they recognised each other's experiences.

Just as the writing helped girls and boys to understand what had happened, creating the images gave them a way to forge an account of these experiences from another place, giving them another layer of meaning to their experiences (Muñoz-González, 2012; Salazar-Henao & López-Moreno, 2016). They had to go back to the first sessions in which they remembered and look again at the drawings that emerged from those sessions, then to carefully choose the initial images without concern to match them with the accounts. The image could be a simple '*matacho*' [poorly drawn picture] or something more elaborate; the idea was to take these images from the unconscious and then question them: What was behind what was put on paper?

The trusting relationship established between the young mediators and the young participants proved invaluable in creating a storyboard of their *testimonios* for the animations. Storyboarding enabled them to understand and organise the key moments in the images, which in turn allowed them to give nuance to the narrative and aesthetic form to the story, as well as to determine the time that each action would take, the role of sound, and the intentions, effects, ambient sound, voice. This work was accompanied by instances of silence, in which the young mediators and the girls and boys needed to work together. Instances of silence and evasion, typical of the recollection of traumatic events, were present. Figure 5.3 illustrates a fragment of P.'s storyboard.

Figure 5.3 Excerpt of storyboard from *Uno se acostumbra a la violencia* [*One gets used to violence*]
Source: Mihistoria repository. See https://mihistoria.co/testimonios/

As animation is a medium of expression that was unfamiliar to the girls and boys and, to a large extent, to the mass media, it is able to destabilise the act of storytelling and become a kind of counterpoint offering the possibility of narrating from a different place than traditional textual accounts. Though the films we showed them as references were unfamiliar and the images difficult to codify, the participants enjoyed them despite their strangeness. In these experimental films, the narrative and technique have an expressive sense that enriches the audiovisual experience and thus engages the viewers actively. Some were animated documentaries, such as *Anzoátegui* by Bibiana Rojas. By showing others, we wanted to illustrate the relationship between technique and experimental narratives, as in the pieces by Gianluigi Tocafondo and William Kentridge.

Some of the reference film examples may have seeped into young people's imagination, either owing to the strength of the stories or the diversified and dynamic use of techniques. For example, in *Estaba dejando atrás mi vida como la conocía* [*I was leaving behind my life as I knew it*], techniques such as cut-outs are used to show the quiet life of the village. Then, to portray the violent actions of the different armed groups that attacked the village, charcoal is used to draw saturated layers on which bullets are drawn, creating a strong effect on the viewer. Figures 5.4 and 5.5 show these techniques.

Narratives to Transform War Imaginaries in Colombia 125

Figure 5.4 Frame expressing the quiet life in *Estaba dejando atrás mi vida como la conocía* [*I was leaving behind my life as I knew it*]
Source: Mihistoria repository. See https://mihistoria.co/testimonios/. The short films are subtitled in English.

Figure 5.5 Frame showing the use of black charcoal to express violent events in *Estaba dejando atrás mi vida como la conocía* [*I was leaving behind my life as I knew it*]
Source: Mihistoria repository. See https://mihistoria.co/testimonios/. The short films are subtitled in English.

The Possibilities of Animation to Expand Imaginaries Around Violence

After the initial experimental phase, in which participants prepared the storyboard for pre-production, the second stage of the workshop involved the creation of the animation. It was an intense moment. The joyful atmosphere of the workshops did not last into the stage of creating the animated *testimonios*. Sometimes participants seemed no longer sure that they wanted to tell their stories, or at least not in the way they had previously planned; sometimes, partly because they were tired of returning to these complex and painful fragments of their lives, we felt they wanted to avoid them by talking about their present life in Benposta, the new friends and relationships they were creating.

Animation involves a long and sustained process. Given that the personal story and games, which constituted the experimental part, had taken up a large part of the planned time and had to be put aside in the interest of producing the animated testimony, we needed the girls' and boys' full attention and investment. Some girls and boys felt ambivalent in having to be faithful to the *testimonio* they had recorded and visually structured about their lives amid the armed conflict, and also discovered that with animation they could weave that same *testimonio* in different ways. When they returned to what they had written, some felt some distance from it; perhaps at that point they felt that what they had said did not tell the precise *testimonio* of what they had experienced, so they wanted to do something else. Memory changes over time (Halbwachs, 2004a) and perhaps they felt they were not the same people who recounted those episodes.

The girls' and boys' imagination regarding how to tell their own *testimonio* was expanded thanks to the range of possibilities that the processes of animation offer. As facilitators, we brought a lot of randomly chosen materials, objects and puppets to stimulate their curiosity about making the short films. We used objects that we had kept throughout our professional lives or that other people had given us: broken superheroes, dwarfs, plastic animals of different sizes, cardboard houses and figures. These objects aroused the participants' interest when they saw them, they related to these objects with considerable familiarity and immediately incorporated them into their *testimonios* as characters. They also made their own characters, such as the spaceship in *The Saviours*. These 'characters' and artefacts allowed participants to depict the events they experienced in a fictionalised way, with their own 'Hollywood'-style commercial audiovisual influences mixed in with their experiences. Far from detracting from the seriousness of their *testimonio*, being able to choose the objects freely allowed participants to distance themselves from their story and tell it playfully, which may have helped them manage their pain.

The animations created by the girls and boys offer an eclectic, unconventional universe. The expressive configurations of their experiences in the animations showed how young people themselves had to adapt to difficult and unusual situations. As an example, in *Uno se acostumbra a la violencia* [*One gets used to violence*], the creators use figures as characters that do not correspond to the universe being narrated (among the characters were some dwarves, a camel, a broken superhero), showing their own sense of dislocation from the world. Figures 5.6 and 5.7 show the varied resources used: cardboard, string and tape to make a spaceship, and different toys to represent a camp fight.

In these created narratives, instead of being portrayed as victims, people are shown as survivors, strong people who have rebuilt their lives by finding a place where they have agency in their history memories, and lives. The protagonists and the voices that narrate the animations are survivors, hopefully trying to change the course of events that were painful

Figure 5.6 Frame from *The Saviours*
Source: Mihistoria repository. See https://mihistoria.co/testimonios/

Figure 5.7 Frame from *Uno se acostumbra a la violencia* [*One gets used to violence*]
Source: Mihistoria repository. See https://mihistoria.co/testimonios/

and incomprehensible to them (Yúdice, 2002). In this way, the animations of the young people of Benposta show how their manipulation of a previously unfamiliar technique could free them from the 'official' narrative and provide tools for the telling of a different story.

> Me di cuenta que esa no era la vida que quería. Entonces decidí dejar todo lo que me habían dado y marcharme para hacer una nueva vida sin ellos. Dejé el campamento y corrí hasta el pueblo. (P. *Uno se acostumbra a la violencia*)
>
> I realised that this was not the life I wanted. So I decided to leave everything they had given me and leave to make a new life without them. I left the camp and ran to the village. (P. *One gets used to violence*)

Al ingresar me di cuenta que todo lo que me decían no era verdad, me tocó trabajar de manera forzada, cargaba tanques de gas de una loma a otra y eran muy pesados. También cortaba la leña que se usaba para cocinar pero nunca me pagaron. La ropa, sí me la dieron, y toda era negra. También me dieron un arma. Era como una pistola, yo no me acuerdo cómo se llama. Nunca disparé ese arma. (L. *Rojo y negro*)

When I joined, I realised that everything they told me was not true; I had to work in a forced way, carrying gas tanks from one hill to another, and they were very heavy. I also cut the firewood used for cooking, but they never paid me. They did give me clothes, and they were all black. They also gave me a weapon. It was like a gun; I don't remember what it was called. I never fired that gun. (L. *Red and Black*)

Juan es el primero que decide salir de su vereda, así que convence a un grupo de jóvenes a unírsele y huir. Algunos entran a estudiar en colegios buenos, de calidad. Pero Juan es el único que es capturado por *The Saviours*, por su gran fuerza de voluntad, valentía, honestidad, ganas de hacer el bien y demás valores buenos que puede tener un ser humano. Incluso algunos lo veían raro por lo que hacía. Fue llevado al cuartel de *The Saviours* para entrenarse al lado de los mejores y así inició su duro entrenamiento para luego ayudar a los necesitados. (C. *The Saviours*)

Juan is the first to decide to leave his village, so he convinces a group of young people to join him and run away. Some of them go on to study in good, quality schools. But Juan is the only one whom *The Saviours* capture because of his great willpower, bravery, honesty, desire to do good and other good values that a human being can have. Some people even looked at him funny for what he did. He was taken to the *Saviours*' base to train alongside the best and thus began his hard training to help those in need. (C. *The Saviours*)

While it is unclear how conscious the participants were of the impact of their narrated animations on their *testimonios*, they clearly discovered ways of narrating themselves that differed from the hegemonic forms configured in our nation's imagination (CNMH, 2019; Chase, 2005; Rueda, 2022). These girls and boys are part of the creation of our nation's imagination; they created small *testimonios* that, when considered together, create a tapestry, a network that differs from Memory as institutional narrative, as the historian Paolo Vignolo (2019: 11) discusses:

> Memory as a connection mocks the solemnity of History with a capital H, revealing a plethora of other stories with small hs. And it necessarily refers us back to its counterpart: 'Is there a place for a memory of dissidence'. Rufer asks. Disrupting the shelves of museographic taxonomies, unbinding history manuals, removing statues from their pedestals: it is through the continuous assembly and disassembly of the logics with which the politics of cultural heritage and historical memory operate in the public sphere that other cycles and other landscapes can emerge.

This 'continuous assembly and disassembly' requires society, including all of us, to sharpen its/our capacity for analysis, help broaden its/our vision of the country, and take a step forward by delving deeper into what these *testimonios* offer. If the people who tell their *testimonios* expose themselves by opening up their personal histories to create new imaginaries about their experiences, we all have to do our work too. We have to find ways to create and disseminate these experiences. Rivara-Kamaji (2007: 113) argues that narratives have a surprising historical consciousness by challenging the reader; there is an implicit 'we' in the self, for a historical event cannot be understood 'only from the perspective of the individuals who endured it'.

Facilitating young people's *testimonios* through animation enabled some participants to make public horrific practices, as in N.'s animation, in which the voice-over tells of a specific event:

Un día me invitaron algunos amigos a una fiesta. En esta época tenía 14 años. Ahí fue cuando me drogaron. Pusieron algo en mi bebida y trataron de llevarme. Creo que querían hacerme trabajar como prostituta. (N. *Todos sabíamos que volverían por mí*)	One day some friends invited me to a party. I was 14 years old at the time. That's when they drugged me. They put something in my drink and tried to take me away. I think they wanted to make me work as a prostitute. (N. *We all knew they would come back for me*)

The horrific practice of forcing young women to work as prostitutes is widespread in Colombia and the gangs that kidnap the women profit from the use of their bodies (Ruta pacífica de las mujeres, 2013a). Although this story is repeated in different corners of the country, hearing it in N's voice and seeing how she resolves it makes us face what she has experienced in a unique way. Knowing that she was being persecuted, she had to flee her beloved territory in the Colombian Pacific and save her life by living in a place very different from her home. The emotional consequences of this event and having to leave her family and social group on this young woman left deep wounds.

It is important to look at these animations from within the context in which they were made, that is with their technical 'flaws' alongside their expressive power: their authors are not animators and this is the first time they have tried this form of expression. The participants did not choose to tell their *testimonios* through this medium; rather, our experience in film led us to believe that animation could be an effective means of communicating experiences which were not easy to express. Although the girls and boys wanted to tell their *testimonios*, at the same time there was a certain resistance. In addition, animation requires dedication, and when the results were not achieved quickly, some participants got upset. Yet the young people also showed a great capacity for concentration when animating and for working alongside others: they came to understand their *testimonios* as also coming from other places, it was no longer just their personal story but that of the group being woven together while they were animating.

Participants' nervousness and impatience in the workshop also reflects of course the pain and tension of constantly having to relive the past. Though we do not know what was going on inside their minds and emotions, for some it seems that the process was cathartic (Jensen, 2005). A case in point is that of S., the author of *El negocio de la coca* [*The coca business*] (see Figure 5.8), who wanted to avoid finishing her *testimonio*. The other members of the group supported her, but unquestionably, she was suffering. We had to help her so that she felt supported to finish the *testimonio*; we came to understand that the sequence she was avoiding was the one that referred to the violent death of her father and her subsequent escape with her mother to avoid being murdered.

Lo que jamás imaginamos es que la muerte iba a tocar a nuestra puerta. Era 24 de octubre del 2016. Mataron a mi papá. Inmediatamente mi mamá y yo nos pusimos muy mal, empezamos a llorar mucho. Después empezaron las amenazas contra nosotras y a mí me tocó salir del pueblo porque un grupo armado me iba a matar también. (S. *El negocio de la coca*)	What we never imagined was that death would come knocking on our door. It was October 24 2016. They killed my dad. Immediately my mum and I got very upset, we started to cry a lot. Then the threats against us started and I had to leave the village because an armed group was going to kill me too. (S. *The coca business*)

In these animations and *testimonios* we can find relationships between historical, collective and personal remembrances. If we look closely, the animations give an account of a personal experience inscribed in the historical context of our violence and, at the same time, they tell us about

Figure 5.8 Frame of *The coca business*
Source: Mihistoria repository. See https://mihistoria.co/testimonios/

what happened to communities that were marginalised, forgotten by the State and remained faceless in the official narrative. When the narrator of *Todos sabíamos que volverían por mí* [*We all knew they would come back for me*] ends her *testimonio*, she says: 'The next day, I had to leave. We all knew they would come back for me'. She is describing the situation in a specific region, Buenaventura, where there is still a high level of violence caused by different groups of drug traffickers, paramilitaries and guerrillas, among other gangs responsible for daily violence.[6]

To understand what happens in this process of making memory, writing, drawing, and animating, it is important to follow Suzanne Buchan's (2019: 28) question: How does memory work?

> As neurological and cognitive processes, memory and its recall, and its companion, forgetting, are at work constantly in our waking and unconscious lives. These are experiences that remain invisible, subjective, and personal until their interpretation and expression through some form of communication. In her writings on the mental, social, and material features of memory culture, Astrid Erll (2011: 104) notes that 'media not only connect [these] three dimensions of memory culture; they are also the interface between the collected and collective, the cognitive and the social/media level of memory,' and she observes that there are 'different modes of remembering identical past events' as individuals, society, political, or family history.

The animations made by the girls and boys must become an essential part of the big picture of our recent history of Colombia. We, those who have not experienced the wounds of war first-hand, are the ones called upon to complete the collective history by listening to those who have.

It is difficult to know how the young people's participation in the creation of animation might shape any future experience. However, as Benposta's Facebook page shows, the workshop had a significant impact on some participants: G., who was an active and curious member of the group later took up journalism:

> [G] is a Benposteño who has stood out for his talent in the handling of photographic equipment, earning the position of Chief Correspondent of *Mi Historia: periodismo por y para jóvenes* [*My Story: journalism by and for young people*] in Tierralta, Córdoba (number 13 on the map), where he trains future young journalists of this territory. We are very proud of his achievements.[7]

Can these young people's accounts of Colombia's armed conflict gain the attention of people unaware of what has happened and what is happening in many places? For their *testimonios* to reach different sectors of the population, they must be disseminated. Alongside the efforts of the CEV, the CNMH, a publication such as this book may help promote conscious remembrance (Muñoz-González, 2012) and may help to re-shape the nation's Memory.

Notes

(1) Mathew Charles is also a journalist who has worked for the BBC in London and currently writes a column for *The Telegraph* on social and political issues. See https://www.telegraph.co.uk/authors/m/ma-me/mathew-charles/
(2) See https://mihistoria.co/testimonios/.
(3) To learn more about the macro project, which is being implemented in 20 countries, see https://changingthestory.leeds.ac.uk/.
(4) Access to the seven animations of the third project entitled *Mi historia Benposta*, see https://mihistoria.co/testimonios/.
(5) This is especially true in the case of Pixilation, where people and objects are worked with as if they were 'enchanted'.
(6) Buenaventura has become a laboratory for reconciliation. This is part of the current government's policy of 'Total Peace'.
(7) See https://www.facebook.com/benpostacolombia/. Last visited on 22/06/24.

References

Acedo, N. (2017) El género testimonio en Latinoamérica. Aproximaciones críticas en busca de su definición, genealogías, y taxonomía. Mirador Latinoamericano. *Latinoamérica* (64), 39–69.
Arroyave, M. (2013) Objetos de la memoria en el destierro: El presente del pasado. Tesis de maestría inédita, Universidad Nacional de Colombia, Sede Medellín.
Bahntje, M., Biadiu, L. and Lischinsky, S. (2007) Despertadores de la memoria. Los objetos como soportes de la memoria. En II Jornadas de Humanidades. Historia del Arte. 'Representación y Soporte'. Octubre, 2007. Bahía Blanca, Argentina. Recuperado de CD-ROM.
Bergalli, R. and Rivera, I. (coords.) (2010) *Memoria colectiva como deber social*. Anthropos.
Buchan, S. (2019) Memoria rerum: Animated materiality, memory, and amnesia. In M. Van Gageldonk, L. Munteán and A. Shobeiri (eds) *Animation and Memory*. Palgrave Macmillan.
Bungard, C. (2019) Writing by heart. Victims of the Colombian armed conflict write their testimonies. Electronic thesis, University of Arizona.
Caruth, C. (1996) *Unclaimed Experience: Trauma, Narrative, and History*. Johns Hopkins University Press.
Castillejo, A. (2010) Iluminan tanto como oscurecen: De las violencias y las memorias en la Colombia actual. In E. Barrero and J. Salas (eds) *Memoria, silencio y acción psicosocial. Reflexiones sobre por qué recordar en Colombia* (pp. 21–60). Ediciones Cátedra Libre.
Castillejo, A. (2013) La ilusión de la palabra que libera: Hacia una política del testimonio en Colombia. In A. Castillejo and F. Reyes (eds) *Violencia, memoria y sociedad: Debates y agendas en la Colombia actual* (pp. 21–40). Universidad Santo Tomás.
Chase, S. (2005) Narrative inquiry: Multiple lenses, approaches, voices. In N.K. Denzin and Y.S. Lincoln (eds) *The Sage Handbook of Qualitative Research* (3rd edn, pp. 651–679). Sage Publications.
CNMH (2019) El conflicto armando en cifras. See http://micrositios.centrodememoriahistorica.gov.co/observatorio/portal-de-datos/el-conflicto-en-cifras/ (accessed August 2022).
Errl, A. (2012) *Memoria colectiva y culturas del recuerdo*. Estudio introductorio. Universidad de los Andes.
Folman, A. (Director) (2008) *Waltz with Bashir* [Film]. Sony Pictures Classics.
Garzón, M.A. (2014) Las narrativas del retorno. *Revista Encuentros* 12 (2), 67–77. Universidad Autónoma del Caribe.

Halbwachs, M. (2004a) *La memoria colectiva*. Prensas Universitarias de Zaragoza.
Halbwachs, M. (2004b) El sueño y las imágenes-recuerdos. *Los marcos sociales de la memoria* 39, 13–56.
Jensen, S. (2005) Del viaje no deseado al viaje de retorno. Representaciones del exilio en Libro de Navíos y Borrascas y Tangos. El exilio de Gardel. In E. Jelin and A. Longoni (comps.) *Escrituras, imágenes y escenarios ante la represión* (pp. 167–202). Siglo XXI Editores.
Maldonado, J. (2008) *El intelectual y el sujeto testimonial en la literatura latinoamericana*. Editorial Pliegos.
Martínez, F. (2013) El arte como archivo, lo otro como testimonio, el artista como testigo. In A. Castillejo and F. Reyes (eds) *Violencia, memoria y sociedad: Debates y agendas en la Colombia actual*. Universidad Santo Tomás.
Matamoros, C. (Directora) (2021) *Todos somos inmigrantes* [Animación]. Artefecto producciones.
McCay, W. (Director) (1918) *Sinking of the Lusitania* [Film]. Winsor McCay. See https://youtu.be/wq7hMuiz1mI (accessed January 2023).
Muñoz-González, G. (2012) El alcance metodológico de las narrativas. In S. Soler Castillo (Comp.) *Lenguaje y Educación: Perspectivas metodológicas y teóricas para su estudio* (pp. 161–182). Universidad Distrital Francisco José de Caldas.
Patrick, E. (2008) La representación de la realidad. *Magazine Animac* 3. Editorial Milenio.
Pennebaker, J. (1990) *Opening Up: The Healing Power of Expressing Emotions*. University of Texas.
Restrepo, O. (2019) Los medios en el conflicto, un papel en discusión. See https://hacemosmemoria.org/2019/05/02/medios-en-el-conflicto/ (accessed November 2023).
Rivara-Kamaji, G. (2007) El testimonio: Una forma de relato. *Revista Bajo Palabra* 2, 111–118.
Roe, A.H. (2013) *Animated Documentary*. Palgrave Macmillan.
Rueda, E. (2022) Orígenes y trayectorias de la humanidad: Narraciones originarias y emancipación. In E. Rueda, A. Larrea, A. Castro, O. Bonilla, N. Rueda and C. Guzmán (eds) *Retornar al origen. Narrativas ancestrales sobre humanidad, tiempo y mundo*. CLACSO-UNESCO.
Ruta pacífica de las mujeres (2013a) *La verdad de las mujeres. Víctimas del conflicto armado colombiano*. Tomo I. Comisión de Verdad y Memoria de Mujeres Colombianas.
Ruta pacífica de las mujeres (2013b) *La verdad de las mujeres. Víctimas del conflicto armado colombiano*. Tomo II. Comisión de Verdad y Memoria de Mujeres Colombianas.
Salazar-Henao, M. and López-Moreno, L. (2016) Las narrativas como método de investigación en las ciencias sociales: Una mirada a la investigación transformadora. *V Encuentro Latinoamericano de Metodología de las Ciencias Sociales. Memoria Académica*. See http://www.memoria.fahce.unlp.edu.ar/trab_eventos/ev.8571/ev.8571.pdf (accessed January 2023).
Semprún, J. (1995) *La escritura o la vida*. TusQuest Editores.
Vignolo, P. (2019) Prólogo. En C.J. Salamanca and J. Jaramillo (eds) *Políticas, espacios y prácticas de memoria. Disputas y tránsitos actuales en Colombia y América Latina* (pp. 8–17). Editorial Pontificia Universidad Javeriana.
Virno, P. and Sadier, E. (2003) *El recuerdo del presente: Ensayo sobre el tiempo histórico*. Paidós.
Ward, P. (2008) Animated realities: The animated film, documentary, realism. *Reconstruction: Studies in contemporary culture* 8 (2), 1–27. See http://reconstruction.digitalodu.com/Issues/082/ward.shtml (accessed November 2022).
Yúdice, G. (2002) Testimonio y concientización. In J. Beverley and H. Achugar (eds) *La voz del otro: Testimonio, subalternidad y verdad narrativa* (pp. 221–242). Papiro.

6 *Testimonios* of Armed Conflict Survivors: Participants in Narrative Workshops in Medellín

Claudia Bungard

Introduction

After more than 60 years of armed conflict, Colombia is currently undergoing a period of transition. As described by Celis in Chapter 1 and expressed by the CEV (2022), this transition involves the building of a more nuanced picture of the conflict than the hegemonic one typically presented by the mass media. This has led to the emergence of several versions that, in addition to revealing social and political truths, also depict a fragmented country (López, 2012; Ortiz, 1994; Palacios & Safford, 2002). The collection of people's *testimonios* through different media across the country has been a crucial part of this process.

In the last two decades, thousands of survivors have begun to participate in Memory projects that challenge the 'subaltern *testimonio*' practices discussed in Chapter 2. Whereas subaltern *testimonios* are heavily mediated by others, e.g. journalists, and tend to homogenise subjects and experiences, the more recent shift towards collecting 'direct *testimonios*' emphasises the importance of recording survivors' experiences in their own words. As López (2013: 33) states:

> It is crucial to rethink the theories that are currently taken for granted about *testimonios*. This will allow us to rescue them from the framework that has been imposed on them and to expand it to make room for other historical realities and other subjects of expression that do not fit within the narrow parameters of the subaltern.

This chapter works with the idea of 'direct *testimonio*' and is based on a study I carried out exploring the perceptions of people who had taken part in testimonial Memory workshops some seven years previously (Bungard, 2019). The workshop was one of the first in Colombia, *De su puño y letra. Polifonía para la memoria. Las voces de las víctimas del conflicto armado en Medellín* [*In their own handwriting: Polyphony for memory. The voices of the victims of the armed conflict in Medellín*] (2006–2010), organised by academics and journalists and funded by the Colombian State.

I begin by outlining how the workshops in Medellín were organised, my interview-based study, my role as an external researcher who did not participate in the original workshops, and the approaches that led to the findings and reflections I share in this chapter.

Although my study did not involve a detailed analysis of the stories originally written by the workshop participants, I include some fragments of their written *testimonios* to provide a contrast between what participants felt and wrote at the time of the workshops (2006–2010) as compared with what they had distilled seven years later (2017). In this chapter I use verbatim the translations I made at the time, from the interviews, for my research work.

The Organisation of the Original Workshops (2006–2010)

This initiative to recover Memory and writing was instigated by the first director of the Programme of Attention to the Victims of the Armed Conflict in Medellín, Gabriel Bustamante, who asked, 'What about the victims?' This complex and multifaceted question motivated a group of Colombian academics, human rights activists and humanists to come together and seek answers.[1] By 2010, the programme became an official office with legal, psychotherapeutic and Memory-building approaches, as a result of joint discussions and analyses.

From this centre, Patricia Nieto designed a Memory project with the aim of collecting written *testimonios* from 'victims'. Questions that guided this project included: How to conceive of narratives from the 'inside' of the war that will privilege the subjects who have suffered through the war? What is the spatial and temporal territory for the development of these narratives? Who could narrate this hidden face of the Colombian conflict? What is the social and political relevance of a proposal of this nature? What are the most appropriate methods to enable narrators to put anecdotes about their suffering into writing?

The goal of the workshops was to cross-reference different kinds of experiences and to thus to enable each person to recognise their *testimonio* in the stories of others. As one of the organisers put it in her interview:

Las señoras que siempre estaban juntas supieran que los niños también tenían historias para contar, o que la gente del barrio Villa Lillyam pudiera conocer a la gente del barrio La Sierra. Hubo un poco de	The ladies who were always together knew that the children also had stories to tell, or that the people of the Villa Lillyam neighborhood could meet the people of La Sierra neighborhood. There was kind of tension

| tensión por eso, pero, al final pudieron construir estas historias juntos. (**Entrevista** # 9 a Lina María Martínez, parte del equipo de organizadores desde el primer taller, 2017) | because of that, but in the end they were able to build these stories together. (**Interview** with Lina María Martínez, part of the organising team since the first workshop, 2017) |

Table 6.1 summarises the criteria used to organise the three workshops. Initially, the workshops had no names; the names given in the table are the titles of the books in which the written products of each workshop were compiled.

Table 6.1 Organisational criteria for each workshop

Writing experience/ publication	Places where participants were recruited	Recruitment managers	Criteria for participation	Meeting time	Number of participants
Jamás olvidaré tu nombre [*I will never forget your name*]	Marginalised and impoverished neighbourhoods of the city	Journalism student group	People who have been displaced or who have experienced various forms of harassment (looting and loss of land, murder and disappearance of Family members, loss of work or productive activity, etc.).	4 months	4 men 17 women
El cielo no me abandona [*Heaven does not abandon me*]	Through the office of the Victims' Programme or by the Prosecutor's Office, several young people found out about the project at school, and others were part of organised groups.	Journalism student group	Mainly professionals from the middle and upper classes of the city who have been affected by the armed conflict	Approximately 4 months	11 men 17 women
Donde pisé aún crece la hierba [*Where I stepped, the grass still grows*]	National Network of Landmine Victims and women's associations	Journalism student group	People affected by anti-personnel mines	Approximately 1 month	15 men 4 women

Source: Compiled by the author based on workshop data.

Methodology of the Research

In 2010 workshops were carried out with 55 people in Medellin. Some seven years later, in the summer of 2017 (thanks to a grant from the Tinker Foundation) I went to Medellín to contact people who had participated at the time as facilitators and authors of the *testimonios* in the workshops. The first contact was with the journalist Patricia Nieto, an organiser and facilitator of the workshops, who gave me access to the database of attendees and to various documents from the workshops (from the first drafts to the final versions of the *testimonios*). After several attempts to contact workshop attendees, 17 agreed to take part in interviews: 10 survivors/writers (whose occupations were farmers, teachers, artists, accountants, journalists, social workers, and whose ages were between 25 and 60) and seven facilitators (see Table 6.1). I met with them in their homes or public places in their neighbourhoods.

Each interview lasted between 60 and 90 minutes. The questions focused on three main themes:

- the experience of being a 'victim';
- the impact of writing *testimonios*;
- the contribution of *testimonios* to the country's social and political transformation (Table 6.2).

Table 6.2 Respondents and questions

Interview questions	Interviewee's name
What is your perception of being considered a 'victim'?	Patricia Nieto/Facilitator
	Jorge Mario Betancur/Facilitator
	Victor Casas/Facilitator
What impact (positive, negative, neutral) has participating in a *testimonio* writing workshop had on you as a person who directly experienced the conflict?	Helly Johana Blandón/Participant
	Jorge Iván López/Participant
	Iván Darío Arroyave/Participant
	María Theresa Giraldo/Participant
	Luz Adriana Ruiz/Facilitator
	Lina Maria Martinez/Facilitator
What is the contribution of the production and collection of *testimonios* from 'victims' of the conflict to political and social transformation in Colombia?	Laura Guzman/Participant
	Octavio Úsuga/Participant
	Gabriel Bustamante/Facilitator
	Orlando de Jesús Guarín M./Participant
	Fabiola Lalinde/Participant
	Cristian Camilo Úsuga/Participant
	Jhon Elkin Úsuga/Participant

Source: Compiled by the author based on interview questions and interviewees.

Thus, concepts such as victimhood, family, community, trauma and justice emerged from the written *testimonios* and recurred in different interviews, reflecting survivors' and facilitators' perceptions of the complex meaning of 'victimhood', the healing effects of producing a *testimonio*, and the ways their narratives could contribute to Colombian sociopolitical transformation, which I develop later in this chapter.

Since attendees' names have been made public and they agreed to the use of their names without pseudonyms in the original publications, I use them in this chapter. Only one requested not to make their name public for the interview (he is not included in Table 6.2).

In addition to carrying out and analysing interviews, I also re-read the contents of the three books published as a result of the initial workshops: *Jamás olvidaré tu nombre* [*I will never forget your name*] (2006); *El cielo no me abandona* [*Heaven does not abandon me*] (2007), and *Donde pisé aún crece la hierba* [*Where I stepped, the grass still grows*] (2010). These 55 narratives were written by residents of Medellín, in the Department of Antioquia (number 2 on the map). I also read Patricia Nieto's doctoral thesis and Colombia's Victims and Land Restitution Law (Law 1448 of 2011), among other documents, all of which helped me contextualise the original workshops and my subsequent interviews.

The value of the interviews that I discuss in this chapter lies in the survivors' distillation of the meaning of the *testimonios* they had produced as participants in the Memory Workshops, seven years earlier.

In this chapter I include extracts from interviews and of what survivors wrote in the original workshops. At the end of each fragment, I bold '***Testimonio***' (2006–2010) or '**Interview**' (2017) to differentiate them.

Reflections on Being a 'Victim'/'Victimisation'

It is important to note that the workshops took place before the enactment of Law 1448 of 2011, or *Ley de víctimas y restitución de tierras* [*Law on Victims and Land Restitution*], and that the concept of 'victim', as explained in the introduction to this book, was only redefined years later on the basis of academic discussions on the subject. For those who promoted the concept in 2007, the distinction between who could be considered a 'victim' and who could not was a major conceptual challenge. Even for the people who were directly implicated, it was difficult to identify whether they considered themselves to be 'victims'. In an interview, Patricia Nieto, who facilitated a writing workshop, put it this way:

Poco a poco los participantes empezaron a reconocer que habían sido maltratados; que perder su casa, un hijo, su tierra no era normal y no debía aceptarse. Entonces, al saber	Little by little the participants began to recognise that they had been abused; that losing their home, a son, their land was not normal and should not be accepted.

que el victimismo era una condición, empezaron a mirarse de otra manera. (**Entrevista** a Patricia Nieto, directora del piloto, 2017)	Then, by knowing that victimhood was a condition, they began to look at themselves in a different way. (**Interview** with Patricia Nieto, director of the pilot, 2017)

At the time of the workshops, the law had not been enacted and participants were not recognised as 'victims'. Therefore, it made a lot of sense to ask them, seven years later and based on the law, what it now meant for them to be considered as 'victims'. For this reason, one of the questions that guided the interviews in 2017 had to do with their perception of being called 'victims' under the law. Their answers varied. Some of the participants used the word in general terms and according to what was discussed in the workshops; others referred specifically to the events that led to their particular experience of 'victimisation'.

One woman who had lost her husband after he was kidnapped by paramilitaries, said:

Antes se pensaba: secuestraron a fulano, ¿qué haría? Se pensaba que el culpable era uno. Nunca se hablaba de víctimas. (**Entrevista** a María Theresa Giraldo, 2017)	In the past, people used to think: so-and-so has been kidnapped, what should I do? It was thought that the culprit was the one who was guilty. They never talked about the victims. (**Interview** with María Theresa Giraldo, 2017)

This fragment indicates a change in her perspective about the concept of 'victim' in particular a need to make 'victims' and their experiences visible. This recognition of the need to make 'victims' visible contrasts with what María Theresa wrote 10 years previously in *El cielo no me abandona* (2007) [*Heaven does not abandon me*] where what is articulated is a sense of resignation and defeat in the face of hopelessness:

A veces pienso: ¿Para qué investigué tanto si al final no obtuve nada? En fin. No siento odio ni rencor por nadie. Dios los juzgará, y en cuanto a mi hijo seguiré viviendo con él el día a día con sus crisis frecuentes y con mucha fe en Dios, a quien también pido mucha fortaleza, pues no es fácil convivir con una persona enferma sin esperanzas de recuperación. (**Testimonio** escrito por María Theresa Giraldo '*Sin respuestas*' para *El cielo no me abandona.*, 2007: 194)	Sometimes I think: Why did I do so much research if I didn't get anything in the end? Anyway, I don't feel hatred or resentment towards anyone. God will judge them, and as for my son, I will continue to live with him day by day, with his frequent crises, and with a lot of faith in God, to whom I also ask for a lot of strength, because it is not easy to live with a sick person who has no hope of recovery. (***Testimonio*** by María Theresa Giraldo '*No answers*' in *Heaven does not abandon me*, 2007: 194)

However, the notion of 'victim' is contested. In another case, a man who was besieged and threatened by paramilitaries, and who remained anonymous for the interview, had to leave his job and home to save his life, said: 'I am not a victim. I have only been affected by the conflict'. His comment highlights a resistance to being labelled a 'victim', where 'victim' seems to negate a strong sense of agency and control: here, 'victim' is only meaningful if it signals someone who survives and consciously works on their situation to reconfigure it (Feliu, 2007; Muñoz-González, 2012; Vélez-Rendón, 2003). This chapter works with this latter notion of 'victim' and 'victimisation', one which recognises the importance of using the term 'victim' to acknowledge people's lived experiences of violence, while at the same time attributing strength, power and agency to the people implicated. The workshops were conducted between 2006 and 2010. The law was enacted in 2011, and as we saw in Chapter 3, Law 1448, Article 3, defined a victim as those individuals or groups who have suffered harm as a result of breaches of International Humanitarian Law or violations of international Human Rights standards that occurred owing to the internal armed conflict. Additionally, for legal reasons, it sets 1 January 1985, as the starting point for this consideration.

The lived experience of being a 'victim' or 'victimisation' is not limited to the personal and individual, but is also a collective phenomenon. Behind a *testimonio* can be the history of an entire family, a whole village, a city or a region. This is how Memory of 'victimisation' emerges, because it comes from a group that it unites. There are as many distinct 'victim' memories as there are individuals and groups, which is why they can be multiple or standardised, collective, plural or individualised (Bergalli *et al.*, 2010; Errl, 2012; Halbwachs, 2004; Herrera, 2008; Nora, 2008; Rueda, 2013; Vélez-Rendón, 2003; Villa-Gómez, 2016; Vinyes, 2009).

Several workshop participants wrote their *testimonio* with two or three other members of their family. Cristina and Yury Guzmán Pérez wrote a *testimonio* recounting the mistreatment of the women in their family, including themselves.

Mama ha sido víctima de la violencia varias veces y ha quedado viuda tres. La primera vez que fue víctima y quedó viuda fue cuando asesinaron a mi papá en Villa Hermosa por líos amorosos. La segunda, cuando mataron un hermano de ella, mi tío Jaime, unos hombres encapuchados. La tercera, cuando se ahogó un esposo de ella en el río Cauca. La cuarta, cuando mataron a Wilson, un hijastro de ella, en Tarso. Y la quinta, cuando desapareció su	Mum has been a victim of violence on several occasions and has been widowed three times. The first time she was a victim and was widowed was when my father was murdered in Villa Hermosa because of love affairs. The second was when a brother of hers, my uncle Jaime, was killed by hooded men. The third, when her husband drowned in the Cauca River. The fourth, when Wilson, her stepson, was killed in Tarso. And the fifth, when

último esposo, en Bolombolo. En estos cinco casos mi madre ha sido víctima y la han marcado tanto a ella como a sus hijos. (**Testimonio** escrito por Cristina y Yury Guzmán, 'Historia del conflicto' para *Jamás olvidaré tu nombre*, 2006: 167)	her last husband disappeared in Bolombolo. In these five cases my mother has been a victim and they have marked her and her children. (***Testimonio*** by Cristina and Yury Guzmán 'Conflict history' in *I will never forget your name*, 2006: 167)

In *Donde pisé aún crece la hierba* [*Where I stepped, the grass still grows*] (2010: 73), Cristian Camilo, Jhon Elkin and Octavio Úsuga wrote the *testimonio La esperanza de los hermanitos Úsuga* [*The hope of the Úsuga brothers*], in which they recount how they fell 'victim' to landmines one day while undertaking a routine activity, looking for scattered cattle.

A los quince minutos volví donde mis tres hermanos. Ya estábamos los cuatro juntos y nos íbamos a ir para la casa, pero un hermano dijo que siguiéramos buscando el ganado del otro señor; le hicimos caso y nos fuimos a buscarlo de la casa para arriba, y llegamos a un morro desde donde se veían unas pineras y unos montes muy bonitos; ahí fue cuando uno de mis hermanos se subió a un palo para poder divisar mejor las montañas que se veían, el palo se quebró y explotó la mina. No sabemos si nos paramos del suelo ahí mismo o al rato; el caso fue que cuando nos paramos nos preguntamos si estábamos bien y todos pensábamos que sí. Yo les dije a mis hermanos que nos fuéramos ligero para la casa. Nos demorábamos cuarenta minutos para bajar a la casa, y ese día en quince minutos llegamos. En el camino, mi hermano Octavio dijo que le estaba doliendo una mano, se alzó la manga de la camisa y estaba herido. Entonces Jhon Elkin dijo que le estaba doliendo mucho una pierna, pero nosotros no le hacíamos caso porque la sudadera no estaba rota. Pero cuando íbamos llegando a la casa se levantó la bota de la sudadera y estaba muy herido, entonces fuimos a	Fifteen minutes later I returned to my three brothers. The four of us were already together and we wanted to go home, but one brother told us to go and look for the other man's cattle; we listened to him and went to look for them from the top of the house, and we came to a hill from where we could see some pine trees and some very beautiful mountains; that's when one of my brothers climbed up a pole to get a better view of the mountains that could be seen, the pole broke and the mine exploded. We don't know if we got up from the ground immediately or later; the fact is that when we got up we asked ourselves if we were all right and we all thought we were. I told my brothers and sisters to hurry home. It took us forty minutes to get down to the house, and that day we got there in fifteen minutes. On the way my brother Octavio said his hand hurt, he lifted the sleeve of his shirt and he was wounded. Then Jhon Elkin said his leg was really hurting, but we didn't listen to him because his trousers weren't torn. But when we got to the house he lifted up the boot of his trousers and he was really injured, so we went inside and told my mum what had hap-

la casa y le dijimos a mi mamá lo que había pasado. (**Testimonio** escrito por Cristian Camilo, Jhon Elkin y Octavio Úsuga, '*La esperanza de los hermanitos Úsuga*' para *Donde pisé aun crece la hierba*, 2010: 73)

pened. (***Testimonio*** by Cristian Camilo, Jhon Elkin y Octavio Úsuga, '*The hope of the Úsuga brothers*' in *Where I stepped, the grass still grows*, 2010: 73)

Rosmira, Luis Enrique and Salomón Chavarría Mesa wrote the *testimonio Éramos los niños del Jordán* [*We were the children of El Jordán*], in *Donde pisé aún crece la hierba* [*Where I stepped, the grass still grows*] (2010: 198), where they narrate how their lives changed when two members of the same family were affected by landmines in events that happened about a year apart.

Pues bien, hablando de minas les cuento que aquella tarde del día 27 de febrero del año 2008, por ser fin de mes y como de costumbre, emprendí el camino que conduce al corregimiento de La Granja, con el propósito de hacer el mercado. Había recorrido un trayecto extenso y aproximadamente a las dos de la tarde di un paso y no supe qué pasó. Desperté un largo rato después y aún no sabía qué pasaba. Me encontraba en un gran hueco y a mi alrededor había ramas despedazadas, sangre y tierra removida... Como esta violencia parece no terminar, el 7 de enero del año 2009 a las ocho de la mañana, mi hermano Salomón se encontraba desmalezando cuando cayó en una mina que igual que a mí le destrozó la pierna izquierda. A él los compañeros de trabajo y su hijo lo llevaron al centro de salud de La Granja. Desde allí un helicóptero de la Cruz Roja Internacional los trasladó a Medellín. En estos momentos está en rehabilitación. Los dos vivimos en la casa de Rosmira. Ella lo cuida como lo hizo conmigo y lo lleva a todas las citas y terapias. (**Testimonio** escrito por Rosmira, Luis Enrique y Salomón Chavarría Mesa '*Éramos los niños del Jordán*' para *Donde pisé aún crece la hierba*, 2010: 198)

On the afternoon of the 27 February 2008, as it was the end of the month I set off, as usual, on the road that leads to the village of La Granja to go to the market. I had walked a long way and at about two o'clock in the afternoon I took a step and didn't know what had happened. I woke up a long time later and still didn't know what had happened. I was in a big hole and all around me there were broken branches, blood and disturbed earth... Because this violence never seems to end, on 7 January 2009, at eight o'clock in the morning, my brother Salomón was weeding when he fell on a mine that destroyed his left leg, just like mine. His work mates and one of their sons took him to the health centre in La Granja. From there, an International Red Cross helicopter took him to Medellín. He is now undergoing rehabilitation. We both live in Rosmira's house. She looks after him like I do and takes him to all his medical appointments and therapies. (***Testimonio*** by Rosmira, Luis Enrique and Salomón Chavarría Mesa '*We were the children of El Jordán*', in *Where I stepped, the grass still grows*, 2010: 198)

The interviews gave some insight into how the *testimonios* in the original workshops were produced. In this interview, the participant recounts how he turned to relatives to reconstruct his story:

> Para escribir sobre la situación de desplazamiento, tuve que decir que mi padre había sido cocalero (cultivaba hojas de coca) y que mi madre era distribuidora [de cocaína]. Cuando escribía, le preguntaba cosas a mi abuela, que es muy buena narradora. Había muchas cosas que no sabía de mi madre y me dolía saberlo. (**Entrevista** a participante anónimo, 2017)
>
> To write about the displacement situation, I had to say that my father had been a cocalero (grew coca leaves) and my mom was a distributor [of cocaine]. When I wrote, I asked things to my grandmother, who is a very good storyteller. There was a lot that I did not know about my mom and it was painful to know. (**Interview** with anonymous participant, 2017)

In another case, Iván Darío Arroyave, 47 years old, an accountant and one of the eight brothers of a priest (José Luis Arroyave) killed by paramilitaries, mentioned in an interview how his family helped him to write a more complete *testimonio*, sharing memories of the tragic moment and parts of his brother's life:

> Los contables no somos buenos escritores. Pero tuve una ayuda muy grande: mi hermano, que es médico y ha publicado varios libros. Él me ayudó a escribir. También visité a mi hermana para preguntarle cosas y poder mejorar la historia. Ella me dio información y comentarios. (**Entrevista** a Iván Darío Arroyave, 2017)
>
> We accountants are not good writers. But I had a very big help: my brother who is a doctor and has published several books. He helped me write. I also visited my sister to ask things so I could improve the story. She gave me information and feedback. (**Interview** with Iván Darío Arroyave, 2017)

In the *testimonio* written at the workshop (2007), Iván recounts as follows:

> A las diez llamó a mi hermana para decirle que ya subía para la comuna 13. Se comunicaba constantemente con ella, parecían esposos. Cuando subían, vieron que una vía estaba cerrada. Los recibieron dos encapuchados y los hicieron bajar del carro. Al conductor lo separaron a un lado y a José Luis se lo llevaron para hablar con el jefe de los guerrilleros. Después de un rato los dejaron continuar para repartir las donaciones
>
> At ten o'clock he called my sister to tell her that he was on his way to the Commune 13. He communicated constantly with her, they were like husband and wife. On the way up, they saw that a road was blocked. They were met by two hooded men who forced them to get out of the car. The driver was pushed to one side and José Luis was taken away to talk to the guerrilla leader. After a while they were

que llevaban a las escuelas y a las parroquias de Juan XXIII y La Quiebra. Llevaban cuadernos, lápices, colores, tizas y volantes para las misas. Cuando llegaron a la parroquia de La Quiebra le entregaron los volantes al padre Juan Manuel. Se despidieron y salieron para el parqueadero. Al subirse al carro llegaron dos encapuchados y le pidieron a José Luis que se identificara. Mi hermano se rio. El conductor les dijo: '¡Es el padre José Luis!' Le dispararon con un fusil en la cabeza. Yo quedé mudo al conocer la noticia. (**Testimonio** escrito por Iván Darío Arroyave para *'Septiembre Negro'* para *El cielo no me abandona*, 2007: 146)

allowed to continue distributing the donations they had taken to the schools and parishes of Juan XXIII and La Quiebra. They carried notebooks, pencils, crayons, chalk and leaflets for the masses. When they arrived at the La Quiebra parish, they gave the flyers to Father Juan Manuel. They said goodbye and went to the car park. As they were getting into the car, two hooded men arrived and asked José Luis to identify himself. My brother laughed. The driver told them, 'This is Father José Luis!' They shot him in the head with a rifle. I was speechless when I heard this. (**Testimonio** by Iván Darío Arroyave *'Black September'* in *Heaven does not abandon me*, 2007: 146)

Each of the *testimonios* written in the workshops shows a particular vision of the complex concept of 'victim' that, in some cases, challenges and exceeds the meaning imposed by national law. Subsequent interviews with survivors allowed them to add further complexity to their accounts and their impact, and therefore to nuance the concept of 'victim' itself. In Colombia, the layers of violence have overlapped to obscure the past, such that the possibility of clarifying the truth and the faces of the perpetrators was hindered until the peace dialogues began (2012–2016) (CEV, 2022). As Iván expresses, in the workshop he attended, there were victims of both the guerrilla and the army, which could have led to divisions in perceptions about who is more of a victim than another or which perpetrators deserve punishment. However, the understanding was that, in the end, everyone was equally affected:

Me enfrenté a un gran conflicto: a mi hermano lo mató la guerrilla, y luego habla una madre y dice: 'a mi hijo lo mató el ejército'. Lo primero que pensé fue: ¡Bien! Tenemos que matar a los guerrilleros. Pero más tarde comprendí que no podía culpar a la madre por eso, y, al final, todos en el grupo se hicieron amigos y se querían y se entendían. (**Entrevista** a Iván Darío Arroyave, 2017)

I faced a big conflict: my brother was killed by the guerrillas, and then a mother speaks and says: 'my son was killed by the army.' So the first thing I thought was: Good! We have to kill the guerrillas. But later on I understood that I could not blame the mother for that, and in the end everyone in the group became friends and liked and understood each other. (**Interview** with Iván Darío Arroyave, 2017)

When survivors met with others in the workshops, some mentioned those who had caused the events they were referring to. The concept of 'victimhood' becomes more visible when it is talked about and made official in the law; that is, when the government enacts a law to recognise it, it helps citizens emerge from the darkness of their tragedy and begin to feel they are not alone. However, through shared discussion, the concept simultaneously transforms and starts to carry a more complex and profound meaning.

The Diverse Effects of Writing *Testimonios*

The healing potential of writing, underlined in Chapter 3, is evident in people's accounts of the Memory workshop.

Ahí es donde uno ve que [este espacio] ayuda a sanar. Porque uno cree que el problema es sólo mío, pero ahí ves que hay gente con problemas mucho mayores (…) Después, cuando salió el libro, vimos que las historias de todos eran muy diferentes y muy duras. (**Entrevista** a Iván Darío Arroyave, 2017)

That is where you see that [this space] helps you heal. Because one believes that the problem is only mine, but there you see that there are people with much greater problems. (…) Later when the book came out, we saw that everyone's stories were very different and very hard. (**Interview** with Iván Darío Arroyave, 2017)

Después de oír estas historias, uno piensa: 'Vaya, esta gente ha pasado por situaciones muy malas. A mí no me ha pasado nada'. (**Entrevista** a Octavio Úsuga, 2017)

After listening to these stories, you think, 'My goodness, these people have been through really bad situaions. Nothing has happened to me'. (**Interview** with Octavio Úsuga, 2017)

Mientras escribía, sentía tristeza y luego alivio. Escribir quita el dolor del alma. Si tuviéramos más oportunidades de escribir, el mundo no sería así. (**Entrevista** a Laura Guzmán, 2017)

While writing, I felt sadness, then relief. Writing takes away the pain of the soul. If we had more opportunity to write, the world would not be like this. (**Interview** with Laura Guzmán, 2017)

Escuchar esas historias de vida me parecía increíble porque sabía que eran situaciones que habían vivido. Deja mucha huella relacionarse con personas tan diferentes y saber que sufrieron, pero que salieron adelante. (**Entrevista** a Helly Johana Blandón Uribe, 2017)

Listening to those life stories seemed incredible to me because I knew they were situations that they lived. It has a huge impact to relate with such different people and know that they suffered, but that they went ahead. (**Interview** with Helly Johana Blandón Uribe, 2017)

These fragments, which signal the trauma experienced by the survivors and carried in their bodies, remarkably illustrate how one's own suffering is often minimised when one recognises that one is not alone in misfortune; how solidarity and empathy are born when one puts oneself in the souls and bodies of others, above one's own, even when fragile and wounded.

The facilitators witnessed this healing process, referring to the fact that by the end of the workshops, writers described a kind of 'transformation' that occurred during and after the writing process. From the facilitators' perspectives, some survivors clearly experienced writing as a way of coping with trauma and as a way of initiating forgiveness and reconciliation:

> Ves cómo la víctima afronta su historia -dijo un editor- pero también cómo la familia le ha ayudado o no a sobrellevar su dolor. Hay muchos sentimientos de culpa, rabia o resentimiento, y también un momento en el que el autor encuentra una especie de luz en su interior. (**Entrevista** a Luz Adriana Ruiz, comunicadora social, mediadora y editora, 2017)

> You see how the victim deals with their story —said one editor— but also how the family has helped them or not to cope with his pain. There are many feelings of guilt, anger or resentment, and there also a moment when the author finds sort of a light within. (**Interview** with Luz Adriana Ruiz, journalist, mediator and editor, 2017)

In this interview Orlando explicitly mentions the pain caused by the land mine and how his writing helped to minimise the pain but he also questions the value of such writing to his life:

> Qué va a importar escribir si uno tiene que levantarse todos los días, con este dolor en la pierna, y coger el carro para salir a la calle [a vender refrescos] en busca de dinero. Esta pierna me duele todos los días de mi vida, y de todos modos tengo que salir de casa porque si no, no como. ¿Y quién me ayuda? (**Entrevista** a Orlando de Jesús Guarín Morales, 2017)

> What will it matter to write if one has to get up every day, with this pain in my leg, and take the cart to go on the street [to sell sodas] looking for money. This leg hurts me every day of my life, and anyway I have to leave the house because if not, I won't eat. And who helps? (**Interview** with Orlando de Jesús Guarín Morales, 2017)

Writing about trauma does not work in the same way for everyone. In the workshops, Orlando had recounted in his written text an unfortunate family tragedy, as a 'victim' of an anti-personnel mine, whose accident occurred on the very day that he had to look for his son in another village where a massacre had taken place. As well as hearing the news of his son's disappearance, he fell on a landmine in the same place, completely destroying his left leg:

> Para mí es algo muy duro haber sido víctima de una mina antipersona, puesto que mi vida dio un giro de 180 grados. En una palabra me siento solo. Antes tenía un trabajo

> It is very hard for me to be a landmine victim because my life has been turned upside down. In a word, I feel alone. I used to have a stable job, but after this I lost it.

estable, y después de esto lo perdí. A veces siento que cada día se me cierran más las puertas, **pero sé que con la ayuda del Señor y la Virgen podré salir adelante.** (**Testimonio** escrito por Orlando de Jesús Guarín '*En busca de mi hijo*' para *Donde pise aún crece la hierba*, 2010: 117)

Sometimes I feel that the doors are closing more and more every day, **but I know that with the help of God and the Virgin I will be able to go on.** (***Testimonio*** by Orlando de Jesús Guarín '*In search of my son*' in *Where I stepped, the grass still grows*, 2010: 117)

Despite the optimistic conclusion of Orlando's written *testimonio* – highlighted in boldface above – seven years later, the circumstances that gave rise to this narrative have not been significantly transformed and Orlando does not share the same hope.

In an interview, Iván expresses in the present tense what he felt when he had to face writing in the workshop:

Respiro profundamente. Sé que ha llegado el momento de escribir esta historia, aunque en el fondo, quiero esconder mis miedos para no enfrentarme a esta mezcla de sentimientos: tristeza, esperanza, dolor. A veces intento evadirme en una u otra actividad. Pero esta vez no será fácil. Tendré que parar, secarme las lágrimas y ser fuerte. (**Entrevista** a Iván Darío Arroyave, 2017)

I breathe deeply. I know that the time has come to write this story, although depth inside, I want to hide my fears to not facing this mixture of feelings: sadness, hope, pain. Sometimes I try to escape in one or another activity. But this time it will not be easy. I will have to stop, dry my tears, and be strong. (**Interview** with Iván Darío Arroyave, 2017)

The reticence of another participant is reflected in the length of his text, the shortest in the three collections.

Preferiría no escribir lo que sentí o lo que siento. Por cierto, no hay palabras que digan lo que sentí. No me interesa participar en una catarsis pública. (**Testimonio** escrito por Felipe Hernando Restrepo Giraldo '*Cuando era niño*' para *El cielo no me abandona*, 2007: 292)

I would rather not write what I felt or what I feel. Certainly, there are no words to express what I felt. I am not interested in participating in a public catharsis. (***Testimonio*** by Felipe Hernando Restrepo Giraldo '*When I was a child*' in *Heaven does not abandon me*, 2007: 292)

While there is ambivalence towards the value of writing for some, for others writing provides a way of documenting and sharing about specific experiences. Laura, like thousands of other Colombians, had lost her property and land to extortion, to which she and several of her neighbours had been 'victims'.

Bajé bruscamente su mano y les aseguré con firmeza: 'Ay, señor, vea: Con mis hijos...' Me reboté, pero muy brava. 'A mis hijos que los crie

I abruptly lowered his hand and assured them firmly, 'Oh, sir, you see: With my children...' I was angry, but very brave. 'My chil

haciendo empanadas, no voy a tirárselos a ustedes para que los maten por allá. A mis hijos, no. Me matan, pero no se llevan a mis hijos ni a mí'. Nunca entregaría a ninguno de los dos. Los había criado con mucho sacrificio e innumerables esfuerzos económicos, que implicaron largas jornadas de trasnocho para entregar, al amanecer, pequeños y grandes pedidos de empanadas y pandequesos, todo esto durante los años de su infancia, para ahora venir y entregárselos a un grupo de hombres armados. Ante todo era una madre y me haría matar antes de que eso sucediera. (**Testimonio** escrito por Laura Guzmán para *El Cielo no me abandona. Ni mis hijos ni yo,* 2007: 266)

dren, who I've brought up to make empanadas, I'm not going to throw them to you so you can kill them over there. Not my children. You can kill me, but you can't take me or my children'. I would never give them up. I had raised them with much sacrifice and countless economic efforts, long days of late nights to deliver at dawn small and large orders of empanadas and *pan de quesos*, all this during their childhood years, to now come and hand them over to a group of armed men. I was first and foremost a mother, and I would have let myself be killed before that happened. (***Testimonio*** by Laura Guzmán *Ni mis hijos ni yo* [*Neither my children nor I*] in *Heaven does not abandon me,* 2007: 266)

Quedé muy marcada después de todo esto. Me cambió la vida porque antes mi felicidad era irme para una finca; ahora es leer y ver televisión. En los libros encuentro mucha compañía. Esa tarde me despedí de la tierra, de la que iba a cultivar, de mis frutas, de mis hortalizas, de mis matas. Era yo quien las sembraba. Lo hacía por amor. Trabajaba allá, porque era algo muy lindo de la naturaleza. Lo aprendí desde muy pequeña estando con mi papá cuando sembraba las paperitas y los fríjoles. (2007: 274–275)

I was very affected by all this. It's changed my life, because before, my happiness was going to a farm; now it's reading and watching television. I find a lot of companionship in books. That afternoon I said goodbye to the land, to the land I was going to cultivate, to my fruit, my vegetables, my bushes. I was the one who planted them. I did it for love. I worked there because it was something very beautiful in nature. I learnt it from a very young age, when I was with my father when he sowed *paperitas* [sic – little potatoes] and beans (2007: 274–275).

One experience illustrates the value of writing despite the difficulties, and the need for support and mediation. This is the experience of Mrs María Teresa Giraldo and her son Alejandro, who produced their *testimonios* in the second writing workshop. When Alejandro was 13 years old, he and his father were kidnapped by a paramilitary group. They were kept in a dark place, in a small room, for 20 days. In the end, the paramilitaries decided to release the son, but not the father, whom they killed a few days later. As a result of his ordeal, Alejandro has never spoken since, suffers from post-traumatic stress disorder and takes daily medication to control his schizophrenia. When Mrs Giraldo heard about the writing workshops, she wanted to take her son. Although it was not easy to convince him, she was so persistent that he finally started writing. As she wrote her own version of the *testimonio*, she developed an editorial capacity to support her son.

> Le dije: Alejandro, cuéntame lo que pasó el primer día [del secuestro]. Él tiene ese recuerdo muy vívido, así que empezó a hablar. Luego le pedí que lo escribiera y día a día le hice escribir. Yo no conocía muchos detalles del caso y aprendí leyendo sus palabras. ¿Cómo fue? me preguntó. 'Esa es tu versión', le dije. [Después de escribir], mi hijo me dijo que se sentía más ligero. Llevaba un gran peso sobre los hombros. Aunque escribir no le curó del todo (él es extremadamente reticente y asocial). (**Entrevista** a María Theresa Giraldo, 2017)
>
> I told him: Alejandro, tell me what happened on the first day [of kidnapping]. He has that memory too vividly so he started to talk. Then I asked him to write that and day by day I made him write. I did not know many details of the case, and I learned by reading his words. 'How was it?' He asked me. 'That's your version,' I told him. [After writing] my son told me that he felt lighter. He was carrying such a weight on his shoulders. Although writing did not totally cure him (he is extremely reticent and asocial). (**Interview** with Maria Theresa Giraldo, 2017)

Mrs Giraldo also says that writing helped her son to heal:

> Estaba muy agresivo y desplazado con todo el mundo; a partir de ahí empezó a calmarse. (**Entrevista** a María Theresa Giraldo, 2017)
>
> He was very aggressive and displaced [sic] with everyone; from there he began to calm down. (**Interview** with Maria Theresa Giraldo, 2017)

The last paragraph of Alejandro's *testimonio* illustrates the power of the workshops to enable some survivors to write and articulate what they would like to happen (in boldface):

> Del secuestro me quedaron recuerdos tristes y dolorosos. El hecho de dejar un padre que suplicaba que le dejaran a su hijo, y ver a unos muchachos que gritaban para que no los golpearan, me causó nerviosismo e inquietud. **Lo que más deseo** es que se sepa qué pasó con mi padre, que se haga justicia y que yo pueda ser una persona normal algún día. (**Testimonio** escrito por Alejandro 'Mi secuestro' para *El cielo no me abandona*, 2007: 199)
>
> I had sad and painful memories of the kidnapping. Seeing a father begging for his son to be left with him and seeing some boys screaming for them not to be beaten made me nervous and uncomfortable. **What I want most** is for what happened to my father to be known, for justice to be done and for me to be able to be a normal person one day. (**Testimonio** by Alejandro 'My kidnapping' in *Heaven does not abandon me*, 2007: 199)

Of course we cannot take for granted that writing does or does not help healing, because all utterances are produced on a human, individual scale and are affected by each person's subjectivity (Arias, 2018,) and the timing of the writing within their own trajectory. Thus while one person experienced writing in the workshop as cathartic:

> La catarsis [que se consigue escribiendo] forma parte de la elaboración del dualismo, para decir: esto es parte del pasado. (**Entrevista** a Laura Guzmán (facilitadora), 2017)

> The catharsis [achieved by writing] is part of elaborating the dualism, to say: this is part of the past. (**Interview** with Laura Guzmán (facilitator), 2017)

For another person it was neither the right action nor the right timing:

> El taller fue demasiado. No estaba preparada para ello en aquel momento. En lugar de escribir, necesitaba apoyo psicológico. (**Entrevista** a Helly Johana Blandón, 2017)

> The workshop was way too much. I was not prepared for that at that time. Instead of writing, I needed psychological support. (**Interview** with Helly Johana Blandón, 2017)

For some, a range of complex feelings surface in the midst of writing as illustrated by Maria Teresa's comments on forgiveness and rage:

> Sentí el perdón mientras escribía, no antes. Antes me moría de rabia. Si veía a Ramón Isaza [un paramilitar] en las noticias, quería que se muriera porque era el único miembro vivo del grupo que secuestró a mi hijo. Pero luego pensaba: este hombre también tiene familia, también va a envejecer, no sabemos la razón por la que lo hizo… es imposible meterse en el corazón de la gente. Así que me di cuenta de que lo mejor para mí es perdonar. Para sanar mi corazón, tengo que encontrar el perdón. (**Entrevista** con María Theresa Giraldo, 2017)

> I felt forgiveness while I was writing, not before. Before I was dying of anger. If I saw Ramón Isaza (a paramilitary) in the news, I wanted him to die because he was the only living member of the group that kidnapped my son. But then I thought: this man also has a family, he is also going to get old, we do not know the reason why he did it … it is impossible to get into people's hearts. So I realised, the best thing for me is to forgive. To heal my heart, I have to find forgiveness. (**Interview** with María Theresa Giraldo, 2017)

The paradox of feeling both relief and pain was common among survivors. One interviewee, Iván, at one point in the interview reported feeling relief when he wrote his *testimonio*, yet seven years later his feeling is of anger:

> Este enero [2017] fui a la audiencia de apelación del tipo que mató a mi hermano. Mató a 24 personas; 24 que por lo menos saben que mató. Han pasado más de quince años. Seguí adelante y escribí sobre lo que pasó, pero lo sigo odiando. No le he perdonado ni le voy a perdonar. Moriré así. (**Entrevista** a Iván Darío Arroyave, 2017)

> This January (2017) I went to the appeal hearing for the guy who killed my brother. He killed 24 people, 24 who at least they know he killed. It has been more than fifteen years. I went ahead and wrote about what happened, but I still hate him. I have not forgiven him nor am I going to forgive him. I will die like this. (**Interview** with Iván Darío Arroyave, 2017)

For some participants, being with other survivors in the workshops helped them to heal, forgive or reconcile, but in the interviews they agreed that in the end everyone has to go their own way and find healing within themselves.

The organisation of the workshops was premised on the idea that writing *testimonios* would involve a complex set of emotions and responses. The way the workshops were conducted also influenced the survivors' perceptions. The methodology of testimony production in the Medellín workshops, therefore, included attention to the importance of the 'how' in dealing with trauma. Nieto (2007: 10), one of the organisers says:

> The writers came together to read their stories, to question them, to add to them [...] There were cries, tears, hugs. Then the *tertulia* (the group conversation) led to the examination of other corners of intimacy that the readers had not yet read.

The organisers designed pedagogical and support strategies to help the writers engage with their *testimonios* and those of the other survivors.

The Inscription of *Testimonio*, its Importance for the Recovery of Memory and its Contributions to Sociopolitical Transformation

In Colombia, Vélez-Rendón (2003: 11) posits, a 'plurality of autobiographical memories' exist that, although they do not represent a model Collective Memory, allow for a 'partial recovery of the past and the construction of a social Memory'. These memories, although they may not be dominant or representative, persist in society despite lacking broad dissemination mechanisms. The objective of Testimony is to serve as a means of preserving an essential aspect of history, without which the narrative of the Colombian conflict would be distorted and biased (Nora, 2008). John Beverley (2010, as cited in Acedo, 2017) posits that *testimonio* is 'an art of memory'. However, this is not to suggest that it is centred on the action of evoking or memorialising a past. Its value is amplified when it contributes to the constitution of more egalitarian, democratic and diverse nation states.

Approximately 5000 copies of each publication derived from the workshops were printed. Some were donated to public libraries in Medellín, while others were distributed at the launch of the books. A significant number were also given to the authors and their families. Electronic versions can be accessed via the Colombian Virtual Archive of Human Rights.[2] Additionally, the website of Diario de Paz,[3] a news programme I established in 2017, is available for consultation. Its objective is to disseminate information and narratives that facilitate the identification of alternative sources of information to those typically provided by the mainstream media, and to encourage reflection on the country's transition towards peace and diversity.

The impact of the publication and dissemination of people's *testimonios* must be evaluated at individual, family, local and national levels. Perhaps the most conspicuous impact of such dissemination is the restoration of dignity. At the individual, local and family levels, these survivors express their experiences in the following ways:

Todavía tengo mi libro en casa. A veces leo las historias de los demás. Me ayuda a no sentirme solo en mi dolor. (**Entrevista** a Iván Darío Arroyave, 2017)	I still have my book at home. Sometimes I read other people's stories. It helps me feel not alone in my pain. (**Interview** with Iván Darío Arroyave, 2017)
No puedo creer que mi nombre esté en un libro. Es increíble que pudiera escribir la historia de mi familia y que aún esté ahí para que otros lectores la conozcan. (**Entrevista** a Octavio Úsuga, 2017)	I cannot believe my name is in a book. It is incredible that I could write my family story and that it is still there for other readers to know. (**Interview** with Octavio Úsuga, 2017)
Cuando salió el libro, mi familia se sintió bien al saber que otras personas conocerían nuestra historia. Incluso para nosotros, volver a contar la historia en voz alta nos sirvió para conocernos más. (**Entrevista** a Helly Johana Blandón, 2017)	When the book came out, my family felt good to know that other people will know our story. Even for us, re-counting the story out loud served to get to know us more each other. (**Interview** with Helly Johana Blandón, 2017)

According to Connerton (1989), inscribing these stories reaffirms the importance and impact of writing on Social Memory and offers the possibility of returning to and working on understanding as often as necessary. Oral *testimonio* can be significant, as it has been in many court cases, but if the events become less widespread and seem less immediately relevant, it can also fade over time. For this reason, it is important to repeat the question: 'What is the purpose of remembering?'. Todorov (2008) speaking of the subsequent use of what is remembered, warns that the evocation of the past in itself has no function, and thus distinguishes between 'exemplary memory' and 'literal memory', to differentiate between those who use memory to promote social justice and the involvement of others, and those that fixate on that past without processing and managing it.

Jelin (2002) also distinguishes, in terms of narrative itself, between ordinary memories, which do not contribute to the social, and narratives that drive a reconfiguration of events and of the subjects themselves. Hence, from the collectivity that was formed in the workshops, and from the products created, it is possible to speak of Social Memory. The existence of the published works facilitates a dialogue between those who have suffered and the rest of society, as happened with *Memoria del silencio* [*Memory of silence*] (the report by the Commission for Historical Clarification of Guatemala in 1999). In this way, survivors' productions (whether written, or film as in Chapter 5, or weaving as in Chapter 8) contribute to a more public discussion of the war, which is fundamentally important as Colombian society has not yet fully assimilated the conflict.

Prior to law 1448 (*Ley de víctimas y restitución de tierras* [*Law of victims and land restitution*]) the congress had issued law 975 (Law of justice and peace). Law 975 established the State's guidelines on the concepts of truth, justice, reparation and victims, and contributed to Memory beginning to have value. As a guideline for transitional justice, it facilitated the adoption of a 'certain type of language', which Castillejo (2010, cited in Muñoz, 2013: 338) identifies as 'the conceptual and universal logic of the idea of transitional justice' or 'the gospel of reconciliation, truth and forgiveness'. Whatever the case, it is good to use a language to interpret what has happened to a society that facilitates understanding and a shared consciousness, without which it would be much more difficult to move forward and overcome tragedies.

The following comments make clear what workshop participants see as the value to truth and memory of what is produced as written testimony:

> En estos tiempos de posconflicto, si el país realmente va a hacer un recuento histórico y una construcción de la verdad histórica, deberíamos escribir más. Y los testimonios deben ser escritos por cada uno de los que han sido afectados. (**Entrevista** a Jorge Iván López, 2017)

> In these post-conflict times, if the country it really going to build a historical recount and a construction of historical truth, we should write more. And the *testimonios* should be written by each one of those that have been affected. (**Interview** with Jorge Iván López, 2017)

> Para mí es bueno ver que este libro está escrito sólo por personas que tuvieron un accidente con minas antipersonales porque refleja lo malo que ha pasado y toda la violencia que hay en el país. Esto hace que la gente tome conciencia y vea que puede haber otras formas de vivir. (**Entrevista** a Octavio Úsuga, 2017)

> For me, it is good to see that this book is written only by people that had an accident with landmines because it reflects the bad that has happened and all the violence in the country. This makes people become aware and see that there that there can be other ways to live. (**Interview** with Octavio Úsuga, 2017)

In terms of justice, for many survivors, writing about their loved ones was their own form of justice (Nance, 2006; Rivara-Kamji, 2007). As one facilitator put it:

> A medida que los autores avanzaban en el proceso de escritura, descubrían la necesidad de escribir bien, les preocupaban las palabras que

> As the authors progressed in the writing process, they discovered a need to write well, they were worried about the words they were

> utilizaban o el estilo del relato. Creo que algunos se dieron cuenta de que escribir no sólo les ayudaba a lidiar con todas esas cargas y pesos que tienen en la cabeza, sino que era la oportunidad de honrar la memoria de sus hijos o familiares fallecidos. Su pregunta era: ¿cómo contar la vida de mi ser querido? (**Entrevista** a Lina María Martínez, asistente de edición en las tres obras, 2017)
>
> using or the story style. I believe some realised that writing not only helped them to deal with all those burdens and weights they have in their heads, but it was the opportunity to honor [sic] the memory of their children or relatives who have died. Their question was: how to tell the life of my loved one? (**Interview** with Lina María Martínez, assistant editor of the three works, 2017)

For some survivors, however, reparations for 'victims' seemed to be a condition of justice.

> No habrá paz en Colombia mientras las víctimas no reciban una reparación justa: una casa donde vivir, un trabajo, beneficios reales para salir adelante.'(**Entrevista** a Laura Guzmán, 2017)
>
> There won't be peace in Colombia as long as victims do not receive a just reparation: a house to live in, a job, real benefits to move forward. (**Interview** with Laura Guzmán, 2017)

Today, the *Ley de víctimas y restitución de tierras* [*Law of victims and land restitution*], these experiences recounted in *testimonios*, the CNMH documentation and the CEV reports have turned the country's hegemonic history on its head by providing a record for posterity. The attempt by one of the country's former presidents to convince society that there had never been a conflict in Colombia is fading away, giving way to a clearer awareness that there was not just one conflict, but many, overlapping and buried by the simultaneous action of forces of different orders.

Conclusion: The Value of *De su puño y Letra* [*In their own handwriting*] and its Contributions to other Experiences

De su puño y letra [*In their own handwriting*] was a project of great significance to the region, attracting international attention. Fragments of the books were exhibited at the Museo Casa de la Memoria in Medellín in 2015. In 2012, six Colombian artists adapted some of the *testimonios* into art that was exhibited in a New York gallery.

The phrase 'De su puño y letra' contains a metaphor: this expression is used generically to refer to the act of hand writing, but at the same time it has two suggestive images: 'puño' the fist, represents the force imposed on the closed hand to strike a blow; 'letra' letters or words, signals that words emerge with force in order to make themselves heard.

The Colombian context presents an opportune moment to encourage the practice of testimonial writing among 'victims'. In contrast to the assumption that some people lack the necessary tools to write, the public

Figure 6.1 Book covers that are part of *De su puño y letra* [*In their own handwriting*]
Source: Diario de Paz. See https://diariodepaz.com/2019/06/13/de-su-puno-y-letra/

writing workshops demonstrated that it is possible to explore methodologies to turn a perceived barrier into an opportunity. Following the organisation of numerous workshops in which dozens of 'victims' were assisted in the production of their narratives, the organisers concluded that individuals who have suffered as a result of war are indeed capable of writing their *testimonios*. The collection of first-hand accounts of the war, written without the intervention and interpretation of a mediator, is of profound significance. (One exception was made in this workshop for reasons of sensitivity.)

It is pertinent to cite Rueda (2013: 20) on the theoretical-methodological proposal of 'Reasoned Historical Memory,' which encourages the active participation of 'victims' in the construction of Colombian history.

> The conceptual proposal is relevant not only for the dissemination of the stories of victims of the internal armed conflict, but also for the promotion of their active participation. The concept is that victims and reasearchers will collaborate to analyse the narratives and construct collective memory to resist marginalisation, denial, silence and forgetting imposed by centres of power and contemporary society.

One of the facilitators believes that these workshops should be continued because:

> Cuando te sientas a hablar de lo que pasó, te das cuenta, primero, de que hay gente que está lidiando con historias o enemigos más duros que los tuyos y que, después de una experiencia transformadora, son capaces de perdonar o, al menos, de hablarlo de una manera más tranquila. (**Entrevista** a Luz Adriana Ruiz, 2017)

> When you sit down and talk about what happened, you realise, first, that there are people who are dealing with harder stories or enemies than yours and that, after a transformative experience, are able to forgive or, at least, to talk about it in a calmer way. (**Interview** with Luz Adriana Ruiz, 2017)

This experience of writing collective *testimonios* ended in 2010 with the publication of the last book. But 'when should a writing workshop end?' asked Gabriel Bustamante, former director of the Victim Assistance Programme (2005–2010). For him, there has been a general lack of follow-up to such initiatives, which means that after months of hard work, building trust, getting to know each other and sharing intimate stories, there is an abrupt end. This closing inevitably has an impact on attendees and organisers. In addition to the administrative logistics of such projects, he mentions external conditions such as timing and bureaucratic decisions:

> Los tiempos políticos del gobierno [2017] son muy diferentes de los de la academia. Creo que vale la pena tener más tiempo para hacer el seguimiento, pensando en una estrategia de acompañamiento. (**Entrevista** a Gabriel Bustamante, 2017)
>
> The political times, of the government [2017], are very different from those of the academy. I think it's worth having more time to follow up, thinking of an accompanying strategy. (**Interview** with Gabriel Bustamante, 2017)

There is also a pressing need not only to disseminate these stories, but also to include 'victims' perspectives on Memory, justice and peacebuilding. *Testimonios* serve to pluralise narratives of war and facilitate the voices of individuals who have suffered the effects of violence to be heard. However, it is crucial to be mindful of the numerous expectations surrounding their production.

Finally, and in line with what Testimony studies suggest, this Collective Memory project questions the traditional way of conceiving literature as the work of art of a professional writer, who offers us their 'particular' way of interpreting the world and a private and unique experience within it (Sotelo, 1995). The *testimonios* of survivors, protagonists in the conflict, as has been said elsewhere in the book, help weave, whatever the different beginnings and endings, the great story to be known, about Colombia, with and through the people who have lived that story.

Notes

(1) Some of them were: María Teresa Uribe (political scientist and historian at the University of Antioquia); Horacio Arango (from the Programa por la Paz), and Juan Luis Mejía (rector of the Eafit University in Medellín).
(2) See https://www.archivodelosddhh.gov.co/saia_release1/ws_client_oim/menu_usuario.php.
(3) See https://diariodepaz.com/2019/06/13/de-su-puno-y-letra/.

References

Acedo, N. (2017) El género testimonio en Latinoamérica. Aproximaciones críticas en busca de su definición, genealogías, y taxonomía. Mirador Latinoamericano. *Latinoamérica* (64), 39–69.

Arias, B. (2018) Subjects suffering in resistance: An approach to the subjectivities of the Colombian armed conflict. *Social Medicine* 12 (12), 1–7.

Bergalli, R. and Rivera, I. (coords.) (2010) *Memoria colectiva como deber social*. Anthropos.
Betancur, J. and Nieto, P. (comps.) (2006) *Jamás olvidaré tu nombre*. Alcaldía de Medellín.
Comisión Nacional de Territorios Indígenas (2022) *El eterno retorno de la violencia contra los pueblos indígenas en Colombia*. Informe del Observatorio de Derechos Territoriales de los Pueblos Indígenas. CNTI.
Connerton, P. (1989) *How Societies Remember*. Cambridge University Press.
Feliu, J. (2007) Nuevas formas literarias para las ciencias sociales: El caso de la autoetnografía. *Athenea Digital* 12, 262–271. See http://psicologiasocial.uab.es/athenea/index.php/atheneaDigital/article/view/447 (accessed October 2020).
Halbwachs, M. (2004) *La memoria colectiva*. Prensas Universitarias de Zaragoza.
Herrera, A. (2008) Memoria colectiva y procesos de identidad en el Movimiento Nacional de Víctimas de Crímenes de Estado. Tesis de maestría inédita, Universidad Nacional de Colombia.
Jelin, E. (2002) *Los trabajos de la memoria*. Fondo de Cultura Económica.
López, C. (2012) *Trauma, memoria y cuerpo: El testimonio femenino en Colombia (1985–2000)*. Asociación Internacional de Literatura y Cultura Femenina Hispánica.
Muñoz, C.A. (2013) Acercamiento al concepto de memoria desde la visión crítica de la democracia. In A. Castillejo and F. Reyes (eds) *Violencia, memoria y sociedad: Debates y agendas en la Colombia actual* (pp. 375–387). Universidad Santo Tomás.
Muñoz-González, G. (2012) El alcance metodológico de las narrativas. In S. Soler Castillo (Comp.) (2012) *Lenguaje y Educación: Perspectivas metodológicas y teóricas para su estudio* (pp. 161–182). Universidad Distrital Francisco José de Caldas.
Nance, K.A. (2006) *Can Literature Promote Justice? Trauma Narrative and Social Action in Latin American Testimonio*. Vanderbilt University Press.
Nieto, P. (Comp.) (2007) *El cielo no me abandona*. Alcaldía de Medellín.
Nieto, P. (Comp.) (2010) *Donde pisé aún crece la hierba*. Alcaldía de Medellín.
Nora, P. (2008) Entre memoria e historia. La problemática de los lugares. In *Los lugares de la memoria*. Trilce.
Ortiz, C. (1994) Historiografía de la violencia. *La historia al final del milenio: Ensayos de historiografía colombiana y latinoamericana* 1, 390–92.
Palacios, M. and Safford, F. (2002) *Colombia: País fragmentado, sociedad dividida*. Norma.
Rivara-Kamaji, G. (2007) El testimonio: Una forma de relato. *Revista Bajo Palabra* 2, 111–118.
Rueda, A.J. (2013) Reasoned historical memory. A proposal to include victims of Colombian internal armed conflict. *Revista de Historia Regional y Local* 5 (10), 17–51.
Sotelo, C. (1995) El testimonio: Una manera alternativa de narrar y de hacer historia. *Texto y Contexto* 28, 67–97. Universidad de los Andes.
Todorov, T. (2008) *Los abusos de la memoria*. Paidós.
Vélez-Rendón, J.C. (2003) Violencia, memoria y literatura testimonial en Colombia. Entre las memorias literales y las memorias ejemplares. *Estudios políticos* 22, 31–57.
Villa-Gómez, J.D. (2016) Recordar para reconstruir: El papel de la memoria en la reconstrucción del tejido social. Una perspectiva psicosocial para la construcción de memorias transformadoras. In E. Arrieta (ed.) *Grupo de Investigación sobre Estudios Críticos; Conflicto, justicia y memoria: 1. Teoría crítica de la violencia y prácticas de memoria y resistencia* (pp. 183–214). Universidad Pontificia Bolivariana.
Vinyes, R. (2009) *El Estado y la memoria. Gobiernos y ciudadanos frente a los traumas de la historia*. RBA libros.

7 The Memory of the Future: Voices of FARC-EP Reincorporated Combatants in the Construction of Peace Imaginaries

Mario Ramírez-Orozco

Introduction

As part of the Agreement signed between the Colombian State and the FARC-EP guerrillas in 2016, the then-government allocated 24 temporary Espacios Territoriales de Capacitación y Reincorporación (ETCR) [*Territorial Spaces for Training and Reincorporation*] to establish the process of reintegrating former combatants into society (Agencia Gubernamental para la Reincorporación y la Normalización – ARN [Governmental Agency for Reincorporation and Normalisation], 2022). These spaces are located in different regions of the country and represent a significant effort towards the consolidation of peace and reconciliation in Colombia. The purpose of the ETCR is to provide ex-combatants with training and education, psychosocial support, economic assistance and security. The official number of people participating in the reincorporation process (accredited by the Office of the High Commissioner for Peace) is 12,729; another 9770 live outside the territories, while 774 live inside them and are waiting to be relocated. The territorial space where the study reported in this chapter took place was in San José de Oriente, in Tierra Grata, Cesar Department (number 11 on the map).

The interviews referred to in this chapter were part of the corpus of the research project, *Transiciones sociales y políticas de las FARC. Una mirada en perspectiva de construcción de paz y educación para la paz* [*Social and Political Transitions of the FARC: A Perspective on Peacebuilding and Peace Education*], carried out by La Salle University between 2018–2020 with Dr Esperanza Hernández, Mg. Angélica Rocha (research assistant) and I as researchers.

This chapter centres on the *testimonios* of the nine reincorporated combatants currently or formerly living in the area, and is part of the research I carried out to explore the significance of changes in the reincorporated combatants' daily routines. I collected information through observation, formal interviews and informal conversations that took place with the reintegrated individuals, over a period of two weeks, to explore the ways in which they were conceptualising peace, that is, their peace-related imaginaries. Speaking with them during this period in the territorial space as part of their daily routines, allowed me to get to know their plural truths, much if not all of which were previously unheard in mainstream Colombian society.

Their *testimonios* indicate that for them, the transition to civilian life has been and continues to be challenging and complex, with doubts and questions arising from issues such as gender, age, change of identity and the political situations related to the fulfilment or non-fulfilment of what was negotiated in the Agreement that brought the combatants back into civilian life. As Beverley (2005, as cited in Acedo, 2017) puts it, within the construction of a new idea of life, in addition to the acceptance of non-violent action, combatant-survivors need to create a narrative of a 'meaningful life experience'. Or, as Narváez (1986: 64, as cited in Acedo, 2017) says, in the collective expression of *testimonios*, 'the true history of groups without an official historical voice' is revealed: the *testimonios* contain ideas that strongly contest those of the traditional elites, as we see in the fragments of their narratives.

The reality expressed by combatant-survivors involves imaginaries that are different from those of people who do not understand the ways 'the others' think (Hobsbawm, 1996: 89) and who refuse to recognise the spaces of opportunity offered to reincorporated people within a genuine democracy. To understand the new social reality with which combatants are struggling, it is important to recognise their fundamental and existential link with territory, given that their main claim has been the struggle for land, particularly rural land ownership. Consequently, the establishment of the temporary zones by the government (ETCR) created a state of uncertainty because the agreed-upon commitments in 2016 were not immediately fulfilled, as is discussed in this the chapter.

To guarantee the confidentiality and security of ex-combatants, the interview extracts used throughout the chapter are anonymised, with numbers used to refer to each participant.

The Context of the Agreement Signed Between the Colombian State and the FARC-EP Guerrillas in 2016

It is important to note that before the signing of the 2016 Agreement that aimed to bring reincorporated people into the transition zones, many

Colombians opposed the peace dialogues. The peace plebiscite promoted by the government (of 2 October 2016), whereby Colombians were asked to vote on whether or not to sign the Agreement, produced a surprising result, especially for the international community. The 'no' vote received 50.21%, while the 'yes' vote received 49.78% (RNEC, 2016). Many voters in the plebiscite expressed scepticism about the potential of reintegrated combatants to transform their lives. This scepticism stems from experiences with past peace processes, which led to concerns that the process might facilitate new forms of aggression and violence (see Celis, Chapter 1).

The disquiet and debate around the reincorporation of combatants into civil society echoed public discourse around previous peace processes in Colombia (Ortiz-Sánchez, 2020). In particular, right-wing and ultra-right-wing political leaders, with the collaboration of the mass media, promoted the fallacy that the guerrillas had been defeated on the battlefield and, above all, in the negotiations. The stigma attached to the reincorporated combatants created the perception that their signing of the accords was an act of surrender, and that they should therefore renounce their political ideals and receive lengthy prison sentences (García-Gómez, 2022).

However, even today, it is essential to remember that the FARC-EP was the 'other party' at the negotiation table, on an equal footing with the government and with full negotiating rights. Because the FARC-EP were never militarily defeated, they maintained the right to exercise an ideology and disseminate their political objectives through a new party: the Revolutionary Alternative Force of the Common FARC, later called the Party of the Common 2022. Thus with the signing of the Agreement, the FARC-EP undertook an immediate transition from armed combatants to electoral combatants without weapons. In the words of one reincorporated combatant:

Para el gobierno era imposible acabarnos, pero también era imposible para nosotros tomarnos el poder por la vía armada. Porque esa era la lógica, esa era la parte objetiva. (Entrevista # 2, 2019)	It was impossible for the government to finish us off, but it was also impossible for us to take power by armed means. Because that was the logic, that was the objective part. (Interview #2, 2019)

By signing the Agreement, the FARC-EP accepted the rules of the civilian political game, with all its virtues and difficulties. Moreover, they tacitly accepted that their struggle was no longer against 'the system' but that they would become an integral part of the formal democratic system they had been violently fighting for more than five decades.

In the face of ongoing challenges and stigmatisation, and with the authority of being signatories to an agreement, one of the fundamental FARC-EP demands was to change the discourse with regard to their identity. They sought to be acknowledged publicly as 'reincorporated' individuals instead of as 'ex-combatants', a term that carries significant weight within the legal framework of 'civilian life'. This term 'reincorporated' signifies their arrival on the legal political stage under equal conditions, a stark contrast to their past of political, economic and social exclusion. Since the signing of the 2016 Agreement, they have declared themselves combatants in political discourse, with the aim of defending social rights in the electoral arena (Ortega, 2013). They firmly believe that they continue to be combatants, but in a different sense: instead of being armed combatants, they see themselves as combatants for the rights of all, from a civilian position.

The three axes I develop in this chapter emerge from the most recurrent themes evident in the discourse of the reincorporated combatants, shaped by this new condition of transition: the difficulties of transition, obstacles to the construction of new imaginaries, and Memory as the future. Rather than experiencing certainties, the reincorporated combatants have constructed positive imaginaries of what their lives will be like in the near future. The use of the term 'imaginary' in this article is based on the perspective of Cornelius Castoriadis (2007: 4), who states that:

> The imaginary of which I speak is not an image of. It is an incessant and essentially indeterminate (socio-historical and psychic) creation of figures/forms/images, of which it can only be 'something'. What we call 'reality' and 'rationality' are its products.

This is precisely why I agree with Castoriadis (2007: 131) in that there is a deep and real basis in imaginaries:

> It is useless to stress that the social imaginary, as we understand it, is more real than what is 'real'. From a strictly symbolic or 'linguistic' point of view, it appears as a displacement of meaning, a combination of metaphor and metonymy.

It is with this notion of social imaginary that I explore the perspectives of reincorporated combatants in this chapter.

The Difficulties of Transition from Combatants Armed with Rifles to Combatants Armed with Discourse

One of the most complex aspects of the reincorporation process has been managing the aid for acquiring or adjudicating land and subsistence allowances for ex-guerrilla members and their families, as outlined in the 2016 Agreement. The deadline for these adjudications was 1 August 2019, also the date of the legal handover of land. However, as Chapter 1 in this book shows (see *The Second Decade of the 21st Century: Illusions of Peace and A New Cycle of Violence*, p. 11), the government of President Iván Duque has not fully complied, leaving the reincorporated in a legal limbo that has been difficult to resolve because of a lack of alternative places to live, as one reincorporated combatant explains:

> Ahorita, el 15 de agosto se elimina la figura de ETCR. Se termina la indemnización, la renta básica de comida, y quedamos con lo que tenemos puesto y nos convertiríamos en nómadas. Toca empacar el morral y buscar el horizonte, o debajo de un puente, o alguien que nos pueda acoger para trabajar, porque no tenemos ni siquiera un gramo de arena que diga esta tierra es mía. No tenemos nada absolutamente y nosotros llegamos a este espacio territorial porque creemos en este proceso. (Entrevista # 2, 2019)
>
> Now, on 15 August, the legal structure of the ETCR will be abolished. Compensation, the basic food income, will end and we will be left with what we have, and we will become nomads. We'll have to pack our rucksacks and look for the horizon, or under a bridge, or for someone to take give us work, because we don't even have an ounce of sand to say that this land is mine. We have absolutely nothing and we came to this territorial space because we believe in this process. (Interview #2, 2019)

The attitude of most reincorporated individuals was to look for practical solutions, so some moved to other ETCR territories where land and aid had been allocated to other reincorporated people. To keep up their spirits and avoid losing motivation, they built community kitchens and collectively set up protection for their children while receiving funds that were almost always delayed (Interview #4, 2019).

The ARN, which is responsible for providing contributions to reincorporated persons, indicated that from 2016 to 30 September 2022, more than 94,646,000,000 Colombian pesos (approximately USD $24.5 million) had been allocated to more than 9887 reincorporated persons on a one-time basis for such projects (ARN, 2022). At the same time, it had enrolled 13,886 people in the national health system and 12,175 in pension accounts, per the Agreement. ARN also highlighted that, as of August 2022, the ARN had assisted several reincorporated individuals through the *Arando la Educación* [*Ploughing Education*] model, the *UNAD Maestro Itinerante* [*UNAD Itinerant Teacher*] model, the Adult Education model; the Public Offer model; and the Universidad Élite and OEI scholarship programme. Also 13,312 reincorporated individuals received a basic income, 13,272 received a one-off payment, 12,369 received a monthly allowance and it was reported that 13,312 had opened a bank account. In August and September 2022, with the new government of President Gustavo Petro, the ARN accelerated distribution of funds and paid out 20,294 million pesos [approximately USD $5 million] in just one month (ARN, 2022).

The ARN points out that the Tierra Grata ETCR was established in a rented six-hectare area devoid of basic amenities such as an aqueduct, internet connections, or electrical connections. In accordance with the

Agreement, reincorporation actions are meant to be a product of joint decision-making and planning between the authorities and the reincorporated individuals (ARN, 2022). However, as men and women transition to a life in peacetime, their *testimonios* showed that they do not have total control over their immediate futures, which concerns them, especially given the history of non-compliance in several of the ETCR. Hence, they constantly demand the economic resources to which they are entitled, the provision of work materials and the facilitation of many bureaucratic procedures.

The first reincorporated people decided to improve essential services by signing contracts for providing drinking water by a water tank truck, purchasing an electric generator and a sewage treatment plant, supplying gas and organising the ecological collection of solid waste. Furthermore, they built a health centre, a library and recreational areas, with priority given to children's areas. They also built a communal kitchen, urinals, showers, a fenced-in area, concrete steps, large work tables, children's games, a covered chicken coop and recreational areas such as a pool table, a shuffleboard court and a small football pitch (ARN, 2022). With the help of several organisations, they bought land to build a town which would have all public utilities in the future:

> Aquí vamos a construir 150 casas y estamos aprendiendo, capacitándonos con el SENA porque este proyecto es de autoconstrucción autoasistida. Nosotros vamos a poner la fuerza de trabajo y la fuerza calificada. La parte técnica la van a colocar universidades como la Andina, el mismo SENA y la Universidad del Norte. La sociedad de arquitectos también se ha ofrecido para ayudarnos aquí a hacernos, no solamente el estudio de suelos, sino el diseño de lo que vamos a llamar Ciudadela de Paz. (Entrevista # 1, 2019)
>
> We will build 150 houses here and are learning; we are training with SENA [National Apprenticeship Service][1] because this is a self-assisted self-building project. We will provide the manual labour and the skilled labour. Universities like the Andina [University], SENA and the Universidad del Norte will provide the technical component. The Association of Architects has also offered to help us here with the soil study and the design of what we will call the Ciudadela de Paz [Citadel of Peace]. (Interview #1, 2019)

Under point 1 of the Agreement (2016: 10), the reincorporated combatants are invited to engage in collective and rural development under the guidelines of '*Hacia un Nuevo Campo Colombiano: Reforma Rural Integral*' [*Towards a New Colombian Countryside: Integral Rural Reform*]. The recent acquisition of 53 hectares allows them to expand their arable land. With the construction of an aqueduct, these lands can be transformed into productive land with irrigation.

Another objective of the reincorporated combatants is to be valued as human beings, after having been dehumanised by State agents during the war. The mainstream media mainly reported on combat operations, using a discourse which positioned combatants as bandits, drug traffickers and terrorists all of which are latent in the public imagination. Although the guerrillas' actions caused casualties, international standards require media coverage to distinguish between the actions of criminal gangs without political objectives and groups that have taken up arms for political reasons (see DIH Glossary for Media Professionals, International Committee of the Red Cross, May 2016: 2).

Reincorporated combatants face difficulties in this transitional period, given the ambiguity of their identity as unarmed combatants. Before, they were 'owners' of a theatre of operations for their struggle that the media appropriated. Now, they are owners of a situation of peace but without legal ownership of the territory they inhabit (Cairo & Ríos, 2019); this circumstance has created a problematic situation that leads them, in some cases, to constantly ask themselves whether their Peace Agreement 'was worth it' (Interview #1, 2019).

As they are aware of the imaginaries constructed around them, reincorporated combatants see the need for society at large to transform its perception of them:

> La gente creía que nosotros éramos narcotraficantes, que éramos terroristas, bueno todo lo que se escuchaba por los medios de desinformación. (Entrevista # 3, 2019)

> People believed that we were drug traffickers, that we were terrorists, well, everything they heard in the disinformation media. (Interview #3, 2019)

They see the need for society in general, and the urban population in particular, to know their true characteristics. In this context, their *testimonios* reveal the construction of new identities and new imaginaries, as the reasons for their democratic struggle – which include a multiplicity of factors (socioeconomic, ethnic, political, illegal, religious, etc.) are being defined.

An existential problematic was the transition from a guerrilla life of constant displacement, constant anxiety and uncertainty resulting from the fighting, towards tranquillity and daily routines. This was the first challenge for many: accepting that their goals went beyond immediate military success. This led them to accept that they would also have to focus on other tasks, such as legalising their identity documents or filing petitions, matters in which they faced new challenges, such as being stalled by impassive bureaucrats who, on many occasions, denied them their rights to these procedures, despite the fact that these rights had been negotiated. The need for all civil society to engage with specific details of the Peace Agreement is underlined by one of the reincorporated women:

> Es bueno leer el Acuerdo de paz, conocerlo y mirarlo bien porque mucha gente en la actualidad piensa que es solo para los exguerrilleros; pero no, él es el resultado de la participación de muchas personas y de muchos sectores; ese acuerdo de paz es para todo el pueblo, no solo para las FARC. (Entrevista # 5, 2019)
>
> It is good to read the Peace Agreement, to know it and to look at it carefully because, at the moment, many people think that it is only for ex-guerrilla members, but no, it is the result of the participation of many people and many sectors; this peace agreement is for all people, not only for the FARC. (Interview #5, 2019)

Transition and identity are closely related, as the reincorporated combatants become subjects in reconstruction constantly moving 'through action and thinking' (Sandoval-Álvarez, 2000: 72). At the same time, they seek recognition for other subjectivities in the transition phase (Garzón, 2014). This highlights the importance of assuming the quality of 'social subjects with a discourse under construction' (Salazar-Henao & López-Maren, 2016: 71), which empowers them as citizens incorporated into a relationship charged with intersubjectivity, transforming them from guerrillas to reincorporated combatants. Thus, they are involved in an identity in transit with the help of social practices manifested in their projects, opening up physical and political spaces for them, until they become a new identity with a novel discourse (Chase, 2005; Muñoz-González, 2012; Rivara-Kamaji, 2007).

The vitality that the reincorporated combatants bring to developing projects, practices and new subjectivities transforms their discourses, which are no longer confrontational but inclusive. Despite this transformation, one thing remains an essential part of their past existence: the doctrinal consciousness that justified their political struggle for so long. For some reincorporated individuals, understanding their new situation involves explaining that they are 'still doing the same thing' but with other means, now non-violent, which gives validity to their past actions toward creating greater political awareness:

> El mecanismo es que lo mismo que nosotros hacíamos cuando estábamos en armas – de hacer que el pueblo entrara en conciencia, de que peliara, que luchara por sus derechos, de que exigiera sus derechos – lo mismo lo vamos a hacer ahora, lo estamos haciendo ahora, pero ya en las plazas públicas [...] Hoy en día [...] no tenemos ninguna limitante
>
> The mechanism is the same that we used when we were armed – to make the people aware, to make them fight, to fight for their rights, to demand their rights – we are going to do the same thing now. We are doing it now, but now in the public squares [...] Today [...] we have no limits to go into the public squares to make known the

> para ingresar en la plaza pública dando a conocer la metodología y el cambio que todavía se está buscando y que se seguirá buscando y que hemos querido tener. Que haya igualdad social, beneficio para el pueblo, estudio, salud, vivienda de una manera gratuita, porque el Estado colombiano si tiene como solventar esas necesidades ante la población. (Entrevista # 9, 2019)
>
> methodology and the change that we are still seeking and that we will continue to seek and that we have wanted: that there be social equality, benefits for the people, education, healthcare, free housing, because the Colombian State has the means to meet these needs for the population. (Interview #9, 2019)

In the case of women, there is also a multifaceted struggle against a society that tries to integrate them into a machista environment, which for them is synonymous with backwardness and the past. Many women joined the guerrilla to confront the violent patriarchal domination of their family environment and dated rural traditions, based on the discourse of submission and total loss of autonomy (*Ruta pacífica de las mujeres* [*Women's peaceful path*], 2013). Therefore, they find it unacceptable to resume traditional roles, which deny their gains in independence and political decision-making, as part of their reincorporation. One woman stresses the need to recognise their significant achievements within the FARC movement:

> Las mujeres, acá dentro del movimiento, fuimos valoradas como personas y eso nos dio esa fortaleza de ser mujeres, de saber que estamos en este mundo y que como mujeres tenemos que ser fuertes, independientes, luchadoras. Y que, aparte de ser mujeres, somos madres, amigas, compañeras. Y que la mujer en todas estas luchas tiene un gran valor, un valor significativo. Y de eso me siento muy orgullosa, de haber llegado a las filas de las FARC, haber podido conocer y haber podido ser esa mujer que me siento hoy, una mujer libre… (Entrevista # 5, 2019)
>
> We women, here in the movement, were valued as people, and that gave us the strength to be women, to know that we are in this world and that, as women, we have to be strong, independent fighters. And that we are not only women but also mothers, friends, comrades. And that women have a great value, a significant value in all these struggles. And that is what I am very proud of, to have joined the ranks of the FARC, to have known and to have been able to be the woman that I feel I am today, a free woman… (Interview #5, 2019)

The general position of the reincorporated women is that they will continue to spread the political ideals that led them to take up arms; but now, from the platforms of the public square and without coercion, they seek to win followers for their newly created political party. More than anything, for them the exercise began with their own comrades, regardless of rank or hierarchy.

> Las mujeres no éramos menos, ni mucho menos ante los hombres. Los hombres eran conscientes de eso también y nos veían que éramos capaces cuando nos separaban de ellos pues entrábamos nosotras. Y el aprendizaje fue mutuo, era mutuo, de ellos como hombres y de nosotras como mujeres. Ellos aprendían de nosotras, y nosotras también aprendíamos de ellos. (Entrevista # 4, 2019)

> We women were no less in the eyes of the men. The men were aware of that, too, and they saw that we were capable, and when they separated us from them, later we joined in. And the learning was mutual, it was mutual, from them as men and from us as women. They learned from us, and we learned from them. (Interview #4, 2019)

Educational opportunities for women are emphasised as being crucial:

> Soy reincorporada, yo puedo salir, ya puedo, pero de ahí para adelante, para ser reincorporada totalmente a una vida civil, hace falta. No tengo tierra donde trabajar, no tengo casa donde vivir, la salud muy pésima, la educación es lo único bueno aquí, un proceso muy hermoso, un proyecto muy bonito el cual aquí ya van 15 graduados y el próximo ciclo vamos 19, entre esos yo. Supremamente importante para nosotros, cuándo pensé yo, después de haber perdido la esperanza siendo niña de poder al menos lograr bachillerato, después de 21 años, participar en una guerra y tener que pensar ahorita, verme graduada, eso es una experiencia muy hermosa, es muy importante, y continuar, claro. (Entrevista #4, 2019)

> I've reincorporated, I can leave, I can already leave, but to be fully reincorporated into civilian life, there is a way to go. I don't have land to work on, I don't have a house to live in and I have terrible health. Education is the only good thing here. It's a very beautiful process, a very nice project which already has 15 graduates and next year there will be 19, including me. It's really important for us. When I was a child, I thought I'd never make it to high school. After I was 21, I participated in a war and now I have to think about it. To see myself graduate is a beautiful experience. It's important to continue, of course. (Interview #4, 2019)

As the fragment shows, there is an ongoing comparison between the past and the present, including a consideration of how women's civil futures can encourage respect and equality.

Obstacles to the Construction of New Social Imaginaries

According to Jelin (2002: 2), an essential fact in creating a sense of the past is the need to understand the subjectivities of the reincorporated, given their state of permanent confrontation in a new type of conflict. Within the selection of memories, there are struggles between what they are transforming and the parallel realities and beliefs of other Colombians who remain indifferent to such political transformations. In this context, a crucial objective is to preserve a tangible legacy of political struggle among the reincorporated. This can be achieved by maintaining their status as combatants and defenders of their ideals, albeit employing different methods and within a framework of democratic participation. It is essential to acknowledge that their memory conflicts with the 'established memory' of those who fought against them. Jelin (2002: 6) emphasises that memories are used to counter forgetting or make visible what has been denied, and must be recognised as part of a struggle between different forms of Memory. From the perspective of the reincorporated combatants, they have a clear understanding of the imaginary that connects them to their past guerrilla work, as well as the potential for creating a different imaginary in the context of citizens who engage in political dialogue. Here, their lived experience as a period of transition from the past towards the future is just beginning.

> Hay que aclarar eso, que hayamos dejado las armas para emprender un nuevo camino que es otra cosa, pues vamos a iniciar un camino político. (Entrevista # 7, 2019)

> We have to clarify that we have laid down our arms to embark on a new path, which is something else because we are going to embark on a political path. (Interview #7, 2019)

> Ahora, el camino, el nuevo camino, lo que estamos empezando, porque es que esto apenas está empezando, hay que tener claro eso: qué son dos años (como reincorporados) frente a 53 de guerra. Eso no es nada. (Entrevista # 7, 2019)

> Now, the path, the new path, what we are starting, because this is just beginning, we have to be clear about that: what are two years (as reincorporated people) in the face of 53 years of war. That is nothing. (Interview #7, 2019)

Nevertheless, the strength of their stigmatisation by the dominant discourses is such that almost all are concerned about the negative perceptions of them held by the population of the big cities, far removed from areas of the armed conflict. The narrative created by the media is one which discredits them and which they feel it is difficult to counteract.

> Nos satanizaron como terroristas, violadores, narcotraficantes. Lo peor del mundo éramos nosotros... ahorita mismo, fíjate, una cosa con la otra, ahorita mismo ese mundo que nos vio como los malos de la película, ahora todo el mundo quiere venir a visitarnos [a los ETCR], tenemos esa ventaja ahora. (Entrevista # 7, 2019)

> They demonised us as terrorists, rapists, drug traffickers. We were the worst thing in the world... Right now, look, one thing with the other, right now that world that saw us as the bad guys in the movie, now everyone wants to come and visit us [in the ETCRs], we have that advantage now. (Interview #7, 2019)

As this interviewee says, the camps are visited by a few people, usually from the region where they are located, academics conducting research, non-governmental organisations (NGO), or government agencies responsible for carrying out population surveys.

There are still citizens who do not yet understand the perspectives and subjectivities of the reincorporated combatants because they have never really known what they were like before the 2016 Agreement, let alone what they are like now. For over half a century, the language used to refer to insurgent movements complied with the premise put forth by the Korean philosopher Byung-Chul Han (2016: 160), 'Language is not only relational but also diabolical, which generates enmity and offence'. In Colombia, this, as Estrada (2004: 123) notes, has resulted in a 'militarisation in the field of rhetoric', characterised by the uncritical reproduction of epithets and negative adjectives used to describe guerrilla members.

An account by a reincorporated combatant woman illustrates the extremes of dehumanisation perpetrated by officials and journalists who visited them when they first arrived at the Tierra Grata ETCR and the extent of the preconceived notions that were held about them:

> Para decirte que venía la gente desde allá, hasta aquí, nos hicieron dos líneas, pero no era porque ellos querían recibirnos, no mami, ellos querían saber si nosotros éramos peludos como un macaco, para ver si así bajábamos llenos de pelos, porque tantos años en el monte. Y yo les decía, 'por favor, si nosotros somos unos seres humanos como los son ustedes'. Sin embargo, mucha gente, pensaba que nosotros éramos así como los gorilas, en el monte, que en la montaña nos había crecido pelo. Era la inocentada del pueblo, de pronto ustedes como universitarios no pensaban eso, porque sea como sea ustedes tenían contacto con los jefes y miraban los guerrilleros. Pero los otros no tenían de nosotros ni videos, ni nada. No es como ahorita, tú te subes en YouTube y pides la página de las FARC y eso te mandan de todo, desde la historia de las FARC, todo, eso era distinto a antes. (Entrevista # 8, 2019)

> The people came from there to here, and they queued up to see us, not because they wanted to receive us, dear. They wanted to know if we were as hairy as monkeys. They wanted to see if we would come down covered in hair because we had been in the hills for so many years. I told them, 'Please, we are human beings like you are.' But a lot of people thought we were like gorillas in the hills, that we had grown hair in the mountains. It was a village joke, maybe you as university students didn't think that, because in any case you were in contact with the leaders and you watched the guerrilla members. But the others didn't have videos of us, or anything. It's not like it is now. You just go on YouTube and search for the FARC page and they send you everything, from the history of the FARC, everything. It was different back then. (Interview #8, 2019)

The reactions of people to the reincorporated combatants can be explained by the absence of a critical or pedagogical framework that would prepare society for the transitional process outlined in the Agreement (Oglesby, 2007). For the reincorporated combatants, it was necessary to adopt a humanising perspective and within an imaginary of a country at peace. Despite complying with the terms of the dialogues, they have endured constant attacks and the assassination of their leaders. According to the Institute of Development and Peace Studies (Indepaz), between 7 August 2018 and 1 August 2022, (during the government of President Iván Duque) 261 signatories of the Agreement were assassinated (Indepaz, 2022). The importance however of publicly evidencing their compliance was crucial:

> Nosotros como colombianos sabemos, desenmascaramos y sabemos cómo son las máscaras que tiene el gobierno colombiano. Para nosotros fue muy importante cumplir y que el mundo nos viera: los países garantes, los países aliados, los países que estaban interviniendo, los países testigos. Ellos sabían que si la queríamos [la paz] y sabíamos que ellos si saben que somos transparentes. (Entrevista # 6, 2019)
>
> As Colombians, we know, we unmask, and we know the masks of the Colombian government. It was very important for us to comply and for the world to see us: the guarantor countries, the allied countries, the intervening countries, the witness countries. They knew we wanted [peace], and we knew that they knew we were transparent. (Interview #6, 2019)

Even in Parliament, those who were supposed to be in favour of the 2016 Agreement have been discrediting and repeatedly attacking each other with metaphors and metonymies alluding to the war without understanding that they, as protagonists of national politics, should also reintegrate themselves into a new reality, like their counterparts who signed the Peace Agreement. Towards this aim, as Estrada (2004: 123) says, the media must change the 'rhetoric of war that has generated an unconscious inversion of the values that Colombians attribute to the reality that we share daily, and this inversion corresponds mainly to a modification of words and their meanings'. By leaving behind metaphors of combat, language can be brought to a level of sincerity until it reaches, as stated by Ramírez-Orozco and Roa-Mendoza (2017: 131), 'the open and critical recognition of the means and ends used, which, perversely, sustain the use of disqualifying discourses, riddled with dysphemisms and euphemisms'.

Therefore, it is necessary to underscore the power that discourses have in disseminating both false realities and objective realities, bearing in mind that in both cases, as Estrada (2004: 118) argues, 'words produce effective changes in the situations in which they are uttered'.

In this new situation of consciousness, the reincorporated combatants assume the importance and the necessity of changing their discourse to obtain a different vision of their new reality in the face of a past that means recognising that they are now different people. Moreover, it is from this new identity as unarmed citizens, as newly incorporated people, that they need to open up new imaginaries to facilitate their current exercise of citizenship with their full rights. Commenting on Homi Bhabha,

Byung-Chul Han (2018: 43) says that '[cultural] identity is always 'negotiated', 'agreed upon', again in an 'antagonistic' and contradictory intermediate space'. While reincorporated individuals have made a genuine and democratic exercise of openness to plurality, social acceptance by all Colombians has not yet been achieved.

Memory as the Future

All Memory searches in the shadows for a meaning to share with the society it addresses. Moreover, it resorts to *testimonio*, to those first-person words that transmit lived experiences to rescue them from the ephemeral (Beverley, 2005; Blanco, 2012; Muñoz-González, 2012; Rivara-Kamaji, 2007). Here, however, I am more concerned with Collective Memory, which seeks to find in its *testimonios* what Jelin (2002: 12) mentions: 'the meaning of the past in the present and in terms of a desired future'. That is, although *testimonios* record a remembrance that is always retrospective, they also aim to go forward until they come face to face with hope (Borja, 2015; Garzón, 2014; Jara & Vidal, 1986; Muñoz-González, 2012; Riaño, 2006).

The *testimonios* of the reincorporated combatants bring with their memories the justification of the aims of the political ideals that they still hold (Pardo-Abril, 2020: 485). Because of their past, and their situation at the time of the interviews, the *testimonios* add a significant weight to larger debates about social transformation. As indicated in other chapters in this book, reflecting on the war and making *testimonios* become a driving force for thinking differently about the future. The reincorporated combatants look towards the future at the same time that they recall painful events, such as the day of departure and the almost-permanent separation from their original families, the deaths of their comrades, battle wounds and the guilty realisation that those who died on the other side of the trench were peasants and poor people, just like them, siblings in the same social tragedy.

In their *testimonios*, the courage of past sacrifices and the imagined world of realisable peace are present simultaneously.

> Para mí no fueron perdidos los 40 años que estuve allá, porque estuve luchando por unos ideales que hoy siguen siendo todavía mi bandera de lucha. (Entrevista # 1, 2019)

> For me, the 40 years I spent there were not wasted because I was fighting for ideals that are still the aim of my struggle today. (Interview #1, 2019)

> Aquí dentro de los 30 años de mi carrera político militar, [esto] fue una universidad de conocimientos y aprendizajes. (Entrevista # 2, 2019)

> Here, in the 30 years of my political-military career, [this] was a university of knowledge and learning. (Interview #2, 2019)

Despite being anchored in the past, the reincorporated combatants have a *future memory* capable of building hope. Historicising memories of *what they were* from a critical perspective is instrumental in constructing an identity of *what they could become*. This dynamic generates in themselves and in their environment the possibility of being unarmed citizens, contributing from the spaces of inclusion that they conquer in their process of citizenship. Like other actors in the conflict, as Bustos (2010: 11) says they are 'bearers of Memory'; their *acts of memory* are necessary to resolve the vicissitudes of a difficult past and serve as the basis for reconstruction in the present. For this reason, being aware of past mistakes is a necessary act in this reconstruction, which is why asking for forgiveness becomes a genuine and necessary act to open up paths of hope. However, there is always a selective act of remembering, involving the capacity to construct a *memory of the future* (Halbwachs, 2004).

> Yo personalmente tuve la oportunidad [en una audiencia pública] de pedir perdón si a alguien que se encontraba ahí se encontraba víctima de nosotros. (Entrevista # 1, 2019)
>
> I personally had the opportunity [at a public hearing] to ask for forgiveness if someone who was there was a victim of our actions. (Interview #1, 2019)

In their speeches, the confrontation with the past is juxtaposed with the construction of new values necessary for fulfilling what was agreed upon in 2016. Therefore, what they were in the past becomes reconstructed with what they want for the future, with collective projects and a new political party:

> Nosotros luchamos por unos ideales, ideales que no hemos dejado a pesar de haber dejado las armas. Yo creo que dejamos una forma de luchar por esos ideales que nos llevaron a enfrentar al Estado y al establecimiento, pero que hoy siguen siendo vigentes. (Entrevista # 1, 2019)
>
> We fought for ideals, ideals that we have not given up despite having laid down our arms. I believe that we left behind a way of fighting for those ideals that led us to confront the State and the establishment, but that are still valid today. (Interview #1, 2019)

With reincorporation, they know that they are entering new territory, where a participatory democracy should prevail, where argument, not prejudice or discrimination, is the primary tool. However, they face obstacles from the parallel realities of other Colombians, who deny the existence of the conflict and therefore devalue peace.

> Aquí hay gente que únicamente vio la guerra por televisión, pero realmente no le tocó vivirla en el campo de batalla. Y me refiero a los dirigentes políticos de este país, que utilizan los micrófonos como una ametralladora, lanzando dardos contra el proceso de paz, lanzando ráfagas contra el proceso de paz, pero que realmente ellos no lo vivieron. (Entrevista # 3, 2019)
>
> There are people here who only saw the war on television but did not really experience it on the battlefield. And I am referring to the political leaders of this country, who use microphones like a machine gun, throwing darts against the peace process, shooting bursts of gunfire against the peace process, but they didn't really live it. (Interview #3, 2019)

There were constant allusions to their mission of what Acedo (2017: 46) calls 'reconstructing the different versions that exist about the historical course of a country'. It is important to stress that their memory fights against forgetting, to make visible what has been denied, where the confrontation between the Memory they possess and the Memory that is emerging. The reincorporated combatants try to rescue the positive aspects of their social demands from the established Memory, that of the system, which displays a negative state of submission and fear in its narrative. It is a distorted Memory (Nora, 2008) that needs to be overcome as one person underlines:

> La guerra de la desinformación, lo que ha impulsado es cambiar la mentalidad, la psique, el subconsciente, los patrones cerebrales, creando unos hábitos de ignorancia en el pueblo para que opine lo contrario: que nosotros éramos matones, sanguinarios, terroristas, violadores. Lo que quería el enemigo o el Estado, en ese entonces, en el conflicto era aislarnos del pueblo, aislarnos de la comunidad internacional y colocando calificativos negativos a la realidad por la cual luchaba yo. (Entrevista # 2, 2019)

> The war of disinformation has promoted a changed mentality, psyche, subconsciousness, and brain patterns, creating habits of ignorance among people so that they think the opposite: that we were thugs, bloodthirsty terrorists, and rapists. What the enemy or the State wanted, at that time in the conflict, was to isolate us from the people, to isolate us from the international community and to place negative labels on the reality for which I was fighting. (Interview #2, 2019)

The reincorporated people are also announcing their projects to create an imagined future in which the conformation of a place of situated reality will be central, with fixed coordinates, far from the movement of the *cambuches* of the past (*cambuches* were improvised shelters built with green tree branches and small dry trunks to protect from the weather and to hide for a night or more during military bombardments). They aim to realise projects such as neighbourhoods, parks, aqueducts, roads, highways and to participate in communal, cultural and educational activities and in the plans of the municipalities. Understandably, given their connection with land, they are keen to forge strong links with the new physical environment, thus laying the foundations for a non-traumatic coexistence. Their close proximity to other citizens allows them to become part of a social whole and be accepted as an integral part of the community (Muñoz-González, 2012).

> Lo positivo es porque uno vuelve a recuperar el seno de la familia, ya uno puede tener libertad de salir, de relacionarse, de hablar con la población civil ya abiertamente, explicarles como ha sido, como fue nuestra vida en el monte, como es ahora, esa es la parte positiva. (Entrevista # 9, 2019)

> The positive thing is that you can go back to the family, you can have the freedom to go out, to meet others, to talk openly with the civilian population, to explain to them what it has been like, what our life was like in the mountains, what it is like now, that is the positive part. (Interview #9, 2019)

The value of the new imaginaries lies in the capacity to create a present-future that includes reincorporated combatants as full citizens of society. Thus in their interviews, they frequently express great emotion when discussing their projects. Their eyes light up when they talk about what they want to do (Zapata *et al.*, 2021: 9). For instance, a former commander aims to complete his degree in public administration (Interview #1) at the Escuela Superior de Administración Pública (ESAP), the sole public institution training administrative cadres and State leaders. One of them, a former low-ranking guerrilla member, is also pursuing this course (Interview #7). Younger reincorporated combatants, both women and men, aim to complete their baccalaureate in Valledupar (Interviews #2, #4 and #5). Some individuals, such as a nurse, are interested in studying medicine in Cuba (Interview #5); a peasant farmer is hoping to cultivate his own land (Interview #3); a technician is aiming to provide water to the community and construct his neighbourhood (Interview #8); a woman is seeking to be reunited with her son, who is situated far from the war zone (Interview #4), and a long list of other aspirations exist that are now within reach. In some cases, the distance between their projects and their realisation is short, thanks to the reincorporated peoples' commitment and discipline.

> Estoy en el proyecto de la panadería, ahora yo soy panadera, hice una capacitación con Levapan, tengo mi cartón de Levapan y mi proyecto en Tierra Grata es tener mi panadería en un localcito. (Entrevista # 8)
>
> I am in the bakery project, now I am a baker, I did a training course with Levapan,[2] I have my Levapan diploma and my project in Tierra Grata is to have my bakery in a small shop. (Interview #8)

As noted, many reincorporated combatants' primary objective is to study to obtain an academic degree. This is a global, collective endeavour. They study in groups and help each other. While they spend time together, they discuss their future plans for their studies and new projects. One of the projects is already well underway: ecotourism,[3] which is expected to generate hard currency, allowing the expansion of services to a greater number of tourists.

> El proyecto de ecoturismo Tierra Grata Ecotur, en donde nosotros, a raíz de tanta visita, de tanta gente extranjera que vino a visitarnos cuando llegamos aquí, recién llegados del proceso, y fue a los mismos extranjeros a quienes les surgió la idea de un turismo sano. (Entrevista # 7, 2019)
>
> The ecotourism project Tierra Grata Ecotur, where we, as a result of so many visits, of so many foreign people who came to visit us when we arrived here, recently emerged from the process, and it was the foreigners themselves who came up with the idea of healthy tourism. (Interview #7, 2019)

This project has already resulted in constructing ecological trails in the jungle surrounding the ETCR. Notably, this project was initiated to integrate the community near the reincorporation camp. The objective is to foster closer ties with the community and to encourage a deeper understanding of the reincorporados/as' circumstances.

Acá en San José, arriba en Las Flores, estamos planteando nosotros o se está planteando [que esto se haga] con las comunidades, que sea un turismo en donde ellas también obtengan su beneficio. (Entrevista # 7, 2019)	Here in San José, up in Las Flores, we are proposing, or it's being proposed [that this be done] with the communities, that it be a form of tourism where they also benefit. (Interview #7, 2019)

The proposed collaboration with communities may go some way towards challenging the perception that they are outsiders or even land invaders with access to privileges their neighbours do not have, such as government aid and international cooperation. In the context of seeking harmony with the local community, reincorporated combatants have developed the 'One metre of water' campaign to build a 10-kilometre pipeline to bring drinking water to their future town. The remaining funds will be raised through raffles and bazaars until the contract with the water tankers can be terminated (Interview #7, 2019).

Almost all the projects they discuss with great enthusiasm and passion are in their initial stages. This allows them to consider future improvements, as one reincorporated woman explains:

Nosotros por iniciativa propia, con lo poquito que tenemos, hemos multiplicado 17 iniciativas de esperanza en marranerías, en pollos de engorde, en gallinas ponedoras, en una asociación de ganaderos. Pero también en cultivos de pan coger agrícolas cuando hay tiempo, como maíz, yuca, plátano, ají, tomate, que son iniciativas de cosechas a corto plazo. En 3, 4 meses ya hay un resultado, para tener un pequeño ingreso y saciar las necesidades de nuestra misma alimentación. No hay un proyecto que no abarque al colectivo, hay un pequeño proyecto sobre turismo, pero está por la primera fase, hacen falta más recursos, más logística, la preparación y la legalidad. (Entrevista # 2, 2019)	Through our own initiative, with what little we have, we have initiated 17 projects in the poultry farming sector, including broiler chickens, laying hens and an association of livestock farmers. Additionally, we have cultivated short-term harvest initiatives such as corn, cassava, bananas, peppers, and tomatoes. In three to four months, we have already achieved a positive result, generating a modest income and satisfying our own food needs. All our projects are collective in nature. While we have initiated a small tourism project, it is still in its early stages and requires additional resources, logistics, preparation, and legal support. (Interview #2, 2019)

This fragment demonstrates the power of words to prompt action and establishes a direct link with the concept of 'doing things differently' to gain new identities that reincorporate people into new imaginaries or identities as business administrators, doctors, nurses, bakers, farmers, pork producers, tourism promoters. Through their concrete inclusion within genuine democratic spaces, they hope to be recognised from the perspective of a new imaginary: of combatants of daily life, of everyday civilian work.

Final Considerations

Key points about the experience and imaginaries of reincorporated combatants can be summarised as follows:

- Reincorporated combatants are no longer what they were; reincorporation is a transitory identity, between a 'before' as an armed combatant and an 'after' as a civilian combatant.
- Their daily lives are changing from constant mobility in jungles and inhospitable areas to choosing a fixed territory, mostly rural or semi-urban.
- The participation in the struggle that led to the destruction of lives and infrastructure is being replaced by an imaginative present of producing vital and strategic projects for their individual and collective survival.
- The dignity of combatant-survivors is constantly being fought for, given the stigmatisation to which State agents and the media have contributed for decades. This positioning has led to their struggle for a place of respect in a society that knows little about the conflict, given the unidirectional perspective of the official discourse.
- The failure of the government to honour the terms of the agreement and the subsequent persecution and assassination of the now-unarmed leaders has not prevented the implementation of their projects. Instead, it has provided an opportunity to convince others of the value of peace for the progress of a country.

The peace dialogues that led to the 2016 Agreement lacked a strategy to prepare society to welcome the reincorporated combatants who, on equal terms at the negotiating table, signed an Agreement to lay down their weapons. Thanks to the transitional ETCR territories, reincorporated people have developed a vision of peace based on projects and hopes, in contrast to their lives during the war. Furthermore, Colombian society has the potential to imagine peace for the first time in half a century.

I want to conclude with a position repeated in informal conversations with reincorporated combatants. The process of reintegration is a two-way street. Many men and women have committed to achieving their political and social goals through the democratic electoral process. However, the old elites and the society that supports them have failed to enact commitments to changing structures of exclusion and unequal land ownership. Rather they continue to stigmatise and exclude. These old elites, who benefited from the war, must also embrace democratic principles, which include opening up opportunities for all members of society, rather than continuing to work within systems of nepotism and corruption that currently characterise them. If we, as a society, could begin to share these transformed imaginaries with less prejudice, we would see the value of having signed the 2016 Agreement and of unceasingly seeking total peace.

Notes

(1) The SENA is a national, public, multi-site training institution with its own assets and administrative autonomy attached to the Colombian Ministry of Labour. It is responsible for 'fulfilling the State's commitment to invest in the social and technical development of the Colombian workforce by offering and providing comprehensive vocational training for the integration and development of people in productive activities that contribute to the social, economic and technological development of the country' (Law 119/1994).
(2) Colombian multinational that specialises in producing and selling yeast, yeast extracts and flavour enhancers for the manufacture of bread and pastries.
(3) This project has a website: See https://www.facebook.com/TierraGrataET/.

References

Acedo, N. (2017) El género testimonio en Latinoamérica. Aproximaciones críticas en busca de su definición, genealogías, y taxonomía. Mirador Latinoamericano. *Latinoamérica* (64), 39–69.

Agencia para la Reincorporación y la Normalización (2022) *ARN en cifras*. See https://www.reincorporacion.gov.co/es/agencia/Paginas/ARN-en-cifras.aspx (accessed October 2022).

Beverley, J. (2005) Testimonio, subalternity, and narrative authority. In N.K. Denzin and Y.S. Lincoln (eds) *The Sage Handbook of Qualitative Research* (3rd edn, pp. 547–558). Sage Publications.

Blanco, M. (2012) Autoetnografía: Una forma narrativa de generación de conocimientos. *Andamios* 9 (19), 49–74.

Borja, M. (2015) Paz y estructura social. El nido de la paloma. *Análisis Político* 28 (85), 233–236.

Bustos, G. (2010) La irrupción del testimonio en América Latina: Intersecciones entre historia y memoria. *Historia Crítica* 40, 10–19.

Cairo, H. and Ríos, J. (2019) Las élites políticas y la paz territorial en Colombia: Un análisis de discurso en torno al Acuerdo de Paz. *Revista Española de Ciencia Política* 50, 91–113.

Castoriadis, C. (2007) *La institución imaginaria de la sociedad*. Tusquets.

Chase, S. (2005) Narrative inquiry: Multiple lenses, approaches, voices. In N.K. Denzin and Y.S. Lincoln (eds) *The Sage Handbook of Qualitative Research* (3rd edn, pp. 651–679). Sage Publications.

Estrada, F. (2004) *Las metáforas de una guerra perpetua: Estudios sobre pragmática del discurso en el conflicto armado colombiano*. Universidad Eafit.

García-Gómez, S. (2022) Memorias insurgentes: La parresía como saber disidente de las FARC–EP en tiempos de justicia transicional. *Trama, Revista de Ciencias Sociales y Humanidades* 11 (1), 72–110.

Garzón, M.A. (2014) Las narrativas del retorno. *Revista Encuentros* 12 (2), 67–77.

Halbwachs, M. (2004) El sueño y las imágenes-recuerdos. *Los marcos sociales de la memoria* 39, 13–56.

Han, B.C. (2016) *Topología de la violencia*. Herder Editorial.

Han, B.C. (2018) *Hiperculturalidad*. Herder Editorial.
Hobsbawm, E. (1996) La política de la identidad y la Izquierda. *Nexos* 24, 86–99.
INDEPAZ (2022) Cifras durante el gobierno de Ivan Duque - Balance de la violencia en cifras. See https://indepaz.org.co/cifras-durante-el-gobierno-de-ivan-duque-balance-de-la-violencia-en-cifras/ (accessed June 2022).
Jara, R. and Vidal, H. (1986) *Testimonio y literatura*. Sociedad para el Estudio de las Literaturas Revolucionarias Hispánicas y Lusófonas Contemporáneas.
Jelin, E. (2002) *Los trabajos de la memoria*. Fondo de Cultura Económica.
Muñoz-González, G. (2012) El alcance metodológico de las narrativas. In S. Soler Castillo (Comp.) *Lenguaje y Educación: Perspectivas metodológicas y teóricas para su estudio* (pp. 161–182). Universidad Distrital Francisco José de Caldas.
Narváez, J. (1986) El testimonio. Transformaciones en el sistema literario. In R. Jara and H. Vidal (eds) *Testimonio y literatura*. Institute for the Study of Ideologies and Literature.
Nora, P. (2008) Entre memoria e historia. La problemática de los lugares. In *Los lugares de la memoria*. Trilce.
Oglesby, E. (2007) Educating citizens in postwar Guatemala: Historical memory, genocide, and the culture of peace. *Radical History Review* 97, 77–98.
Ortega, P. (2013) Las FARC: De las armas a la política Conflicto, Drogas y Paz. *La Razón Pública*. See https://razonpublica.com/las-farc-de-las-armas-a-la-politica/ (accessed February 2023).
Ortiz-Sánchez, N.A. (2020) La palabra desarmada: Análisis de discurso de la UP (1986–1987) y la FARC (2018–2019) en el Congreso. Tesis de maestría inédita, Pontificia Universidad Javeriana.
Pardo-Abril, N.G. (2020) Memorialización y conflicto armado: La construcción de narrativas para la paz en Colombia. *Revista de Estudos da Linguagem* 28 (1), 479–506.
Ramírez-Orozco, M. and Roa-Mendoza, C.P. (2017) De los lenguajes del poder a los lenguajes de la no violencia. *Revista de la Universidad de La Salle* 72, 115–136.
Registraduría Nacional del Estado Civil (2016) Plebiscito 2 de octubre de 2016. See https://elecciones.registraduria.gov.co/pre_plebis_2016/99PL/DPLZZZZZZZZZZZZZZZZZZ_L1.htm (accessed September 2023).
Riaño, P. (2006) *Jóvenes, memoria y violencia en Medellín: Una antropología del recuerdo y el olvido*. Universidad de Antioquia. Icahn.
Rivara-Kamaji, G. (2007) El testimonio: Una forma de relato. *Revista Bajo Palabra* 2, 111–118.
Salazar-Henao, M. and López-Moreno, L. (2016) Las narrativas como método de investigación en las ciencias sociales: Una mirada a la investigación transformadora. *V Encuentro Latinoamericano de Metodología de las Ciencias Sociales. Memoria Académica*. See http://www.memoria.fahce.unlp.edu.ar/trab_eventos/ev.8571/ev.8571.pdf (accessed January 2023).
Sandoval-Álvarez, R. (2000) La dimensión política en la constitución de la identidad del sujeto. *Espiral* 6 (17), 71–83.
Zapata, E.A., Hernández, M.D. and Morales-Herrera, D. (2021) Discursos del trabajo en excombatientes de las FARC. Barreras sociolaborales en la reintegración. *América Latina Hoy* 88, 3–21.

8 Weaving Memory and Unweaving Trauma: Textile Narratives on the Conflict in Colombia

Emilia Perassi

The Blankets that do not let People Sleep

The blankets that do not let people sleep and are wrapped around Colombia have the quality of unforeseen, loving and dynamic objects/subjects. They emerge from imperceptible spaces inside homes, inspire the sharing of foundational and everyday writing such as textile writing – the focus of this chapter – occupy public spaces and provoke ever-larger networks: local, national and international. In this chapter, I explore a particular form of *testimonio*: that which is written with thread and needle on canvases and fabrics, with stitches that embroider the wounds and desires, the mourning and hopes of Colombian women who have survived the conflict.

The *text*imonial act combines a specific knowledge and a way of thinking that involves both an empirical practice and a highly symbolic projection: embroiderers, seamstresses and weavers come together to relate their experiences and those of their communities. They turn to share what we can think of as an *Esperanto*[1] of textile tasks that simultaneously unite, configure and reconfigure the pieces of the social fabric that have been broken by violence.

Embroidering, weaving and sewing are ways of giving form to thought through creative and reflexive physical action that brings order to the fractured and dispersed, recomposing it into a unity of meaning. Community scenes, traumatic memories, faces and names of the absent, dreams of the future and peace slogans populate this textile universe in which is written and inscribed a true visual history of wounded Colombia and, at the same time, a project of reparation. To provide an account of this endless and collective sense-making that aims to re-signify Colombian history, I draw on close reading and analysis of projects, films, accounts of weavers and seamstresses, and publications that have documented weaving practices and the profound healing value offered by 'textile narratives'. As his Wayúu grandmother told artist Jorge Lavarca: 'Weave when you are alone, and the ideas will flow, and the hands will do great things' (Ramírez, 2021: para. 7).

Violeta

In 2010, the Centre for Human Rights and International Litigation (CEDHUL), with the support of the Global Fund for Women, released an animated short film, *Violeta*.[2] The film tells the story of a mother and her daughters, 'las Amarillas' [The yellow girls], who were raped and disappeared by the 'Sin Sombras' [Men without shadows]. Inspired by her pain, Violeta begins to make a blanket with the memories of her daughters. The blanket has a peculiar quality, as those who are aware of it cannot sleep. The voice-over in the film states, 'Violeta's sadness, and the beauty of her daughters, lingered on in the minds of those who saw them, and soon the State became uneasy'. Despite threats, abandonment by the justice system and loneliness, Violeta persists in weaving her blanket. Even when she learns that the Amarillas – one of whom is 17 years old and loved the countryside, the other 19 and loved animals – will not return, she continues.

In the film, we observe the sisters walking, gently shedding colours that fill the earth, alluding to the angelic and innocent nature of those who become 'victims'. Of that beauty, only a shoe and a shirt remain, and the scraps or threads that we imagine will form part of the fabric of the blanket that Violeta will make, along with the remembrances of those young women, full of life and tenderness. The blanket displays suns, hearts, houses, mountains, trees, flowers and smiling faces. Two images, however, interrupt this succession of harmonious images, creating a sense of dissonance. One is a sad little face, and the other is a pair of handcuffs coming loose. At the bottom of the blanket, in one corner, a single word can be read: *libertad*/freedom (Figure 8.1).

Freedom can be defined as the absence of pain, allowing for its expression and manifestation. Alternatively, it can be the absence of evil, injustice and indifference, all three being hells lived by Violeta. Her story in the film is divided into two parts: the first, in which light reigns, triumphant in the time before, which is the time of a loving family, united by the affection between its members and with the earth; the second, where night reigns, is smudged by violence, which erases the colours along with the smooth sounds of life, to bring Violeta to the silence of absence, or the ferocious word of the wicked. When the Amarillas do not return to the house, night falls on Violeta: the end of the world comes, dragging her simple Eden with it. Moreover, night becomes the entrance to darkness: the awareness of pain, the flight from the known world, loneliness.

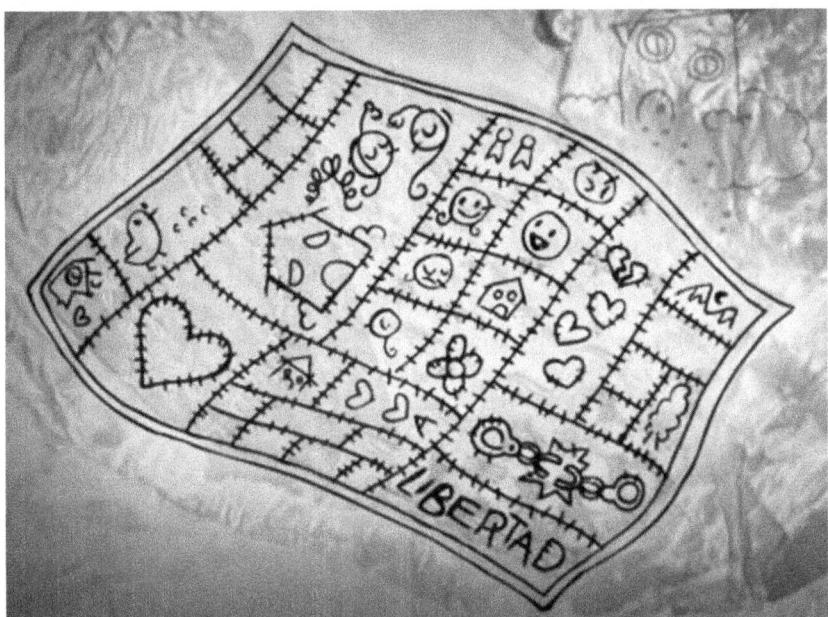

Figure 8.1 The blanket of the remembrances of Violeta, as shown in the animated film
Source: EnPánico! (2010) *Violet*. See https://www.youtube.com/watch?v=IL_7uUw7CFI&t=361s

We can interpret the figures of *Las Amarillas* as representing celestial symbolism. Violeta stands out as a 'suffering mother', sliced by the knives of anguish: 'A thorn has pierced her heart', we hear. The narrative thus has the tones of a parable in which violence sweeps over a small sacred family. However, in the third movement, the story – which at the beginning of the film claims to be 'a true story' – shows Violeta conquering a space of her own, inhabited by her inexhaustible search for justice and living Memory. A space is created from the affective map she designs in a blanket of remembrances. This blanket reunites what has been separated and broken, re-establishes the threads of the family story that were interrupted by the outbreak of violence and reminds the viewer of the beauty of what has been lost.

Violeta condenses a narrative practice that is emblematic of Colombian women's resistance to recover from the profound wounds caused in the subjectivities of individuals and communities by the armed conflict. The textile practice is employed as a possible form of writing to reveal the unspeakable damage. The blanket that the character weaves is not only a text that publishes an experience, it is also the performance of political action: by making Memory, it prohibits forgetting. The blanket is unsettling because it 'does not let you sleep', forcing 'those who see it' to become present in the scene of trauma, pain and Memory.

The subject's healing path begins when her wound is assigned social value; this wound can be inscribed in a common frame of reference and 'decibilidad/sayability', as Violi (2014) notes. Unravelling *Violeta's* symbolic core and weaving a blanket of memories involves a collective effort to construct Memory as a common frame of reference. For cooperative action to be effective, it must rely on the semiotisation of experience. This process transforms the experience into a 'sayable' story that articulates new coordinates of meaning. In the short film, the intention that significantly underscores the privileged use of textile practices in the context of post-conflict resonates profoundly. The words of Luz Dary Osorio, a woman weaver, effectively confirm the self-consciousness of the textile experience in terms of 'sayability' and the construction of shared Memory:

> Entonces eso fue un descanso, yo lloré mucho haciendo el bordado de cuando mataron a Mario y todo eso. Pero también siento que ahí dejé mucho en ese coso pues que ya no tengo que volver a contar, que la gente lo ve y dice 'ah ve', pues de pronto dirán que por qué esas matas de maíz, por qué eso, porque lo mataron en unas Fiestas del Maíz, pero también me hice unas parejas ahí bailando [...] ya no tengo que decir más. ¿Entonces eso fue una forma de uno contar lo que sentía sin tener que estar llorando cada que le preguntaran a uno ¿cierto? Entonces el contar nos iba liberando de todas esas cosas que teníamos que no nos atrevíamos a hablar con nadie. (Entrevista a Luz Dary Osorio. Rangel-Barragán, 2016: 39)

> So that was a rest; I cried a lot while embroidering when they killed Mario and all that. However, I also feel that I left a lot in that object that I do not have to tell anymore, that people see it and say, 'Ah see', well suddenly, they will say why those corn plants? Why that? Because they killed him at a corn festival, but I also made some couples dance there [...] I do not have to say anything else. So that was a way of telling what I felt without having to cry every time they asked me, right? So telling was freeing us from all those things we had that we did not dare to talk about with anyone. (Interview with Luz Dary Osorio. Rangel-Barragán, 2016: 39)

Materialising Absence

A multitude of documented accounts resonate with the fictionalized character of Violeta. However, one account in particular appears to embody the film's protagonist. The account of Blanca Nieves Meneses, as narrated by Manuela Ochoa (2017), is a case in point. Ochoa, along with Camilo Leiva, curated the Oropéndola project for the CNMH (2014–2017), a virtual platform that collected dozens of artistic exhibitions that tell the history of the armed conflict (Ramírez-Gómez, 2021). According to Manuela, from 2001 to 2011, Blanca Nieves and her only surviving daughter, Nancy, conducted a 10-year search for the bodies of her four daughters, who were kidnapped and disappeared by paramilitaries in 2000 in La Dorada (Putumayo, number 23 on the map). Their remains were found in 2011, bearing the marks of torture and rape.

After repeatedly experiencing dreams of her daughters with large bleeding wounds on their chests, the mother had the idea of sewing a quilt out of her daughters' clothes that she had kept. She cut the clothes into pieces, put them together and added fragments of photographs, as well as a poem written by Nancy, in which the memory of her sisters is metaphorized into seeds that turn into sunflowers (Figure 8.2). The blanket is not only a personal account of a traumatic experience but also a concise yet comprehensive encyclopaedia 'of the complex relationship,' says Manuela, 'between the peasants, their land and their territories amid the armed conflict. The work of cultivating the land has been disrupted and replaced

Figure 8.2 The Blanca Nieves Meneses quilt
Source: Courtesy of *Dissolve* magazine. See www.dissolvesf.org

by the search for their relatives under the earth' (Ramírez-Gómez, 2021: 7). The poem's words and images convey a tension between destruction and construction, despair, courage and love for the absent. This tension is recomposed in the blanket's iconic unity. Its weaving narrates the past and the present, bearing the imprint of the skins of those who wore the clothes. The blanket is full of time as it reassembles the multiple chronologies of the interrupted family narrative.

By composing in her quilt of memories, 'what remains' (Agamben, 1998) of her daughters, Blanca Nieves expresses her will and capacity to re-insert herself into history, to tell it, to visualise it for herself and others. Her narrative act, her 'narr'action', marks her as an active subject who reconstructs, sews and mends what is broken. She re-signifies and reconfigures it, thereby conferring upon it the agency of reparation, of Memory, of the right to truth and of the public demand for justice. The materiality of the fabric enables the mother to bring her daughters back into the world, reinstate their presence and biography and give shape to their absence. The quilt created by Blanca Nieves is structured as a narrative text that evokes a sense of mourning. At the same time, it functions as an act of tenderness, care and self-care, bearing witness on behalf of those who are absent, (re)presenting them to Memory and mourning.

In recounting her experience through sewing, adorning and piecing together scattered fragments, dismembered like the bodies of her daughters, Blanca Nieves reconstructs a space that is finally whole. This space is one in which what has been separated comes together again. In this context, it is helpful to consider the concept of an 'ontology of the textile' in the words of Rocha-Vivas (2018: 65) who developed the notion based on indigenous oral narrations. This mother, who sews and repairs her blanket that will not let her sleep, is engaged in the process of self-representational sovereignty; that is to say, she exercises her right to represent herself symbolically and politically. This process entails speaking for herself, making herself visible and engaging with others. It also involves breaking free from the silence and isolation that have previously characterised her life and using the blanket to narrate, denounce and remember. The blanket, and above all, the process of agency that led to its creation, will serve as a reference point for other family members in search of reparation, recognition and support. In her account, Nancy, the surviving daughter, recounts:

| Mucha gente del campo se me acercaba a pedirme ayuda, querían encontrar también a sus familiares desaparecidos, me escribían papelitos, me esperaban cuando volvía para preguntarme, todos desesperados igual que yo por encontrar a sus desaparecidos [...] eso era todos los | Many people from the countryside approached me to ask for help, they also wanted to find their disappeared relatives, they wrote me little notes, they waited for me when I came back to ask me, all desperate like me to find their disappeared [...] that was every day that |

días que se me acercaban, y yo me convertí como en la intermediaria, la vocera, y les trataba de ayudar y dar valor. Yo hablaba con ellos y les decía que si sabían dónde habían [sic] más fosas que hablaran, y si sentían miedo, yo iba hasta la casa de ellos para que me contaran con confianza. (Entrevista a Nancy, hija sobreviviente de Blanca Nieves Meneses para el CNMH, 2016: 358–359)

they approached me, and I became like the intermediary, the spokesperson, and I tried to help them and give them courage. I would talk to them and tell them that if they knew where there were more graves, they should talk, and if they were afraid, I would go to their house so that they could talk to me in confidence. (Interview with Nancy, surviving daughter of Blanca Nieves Meneses for CNMH, 2016: 358–359)

This paradigmatic account, which I selected as a representative example of the diverse array of narratives within the context of a simultaneously woven and unwoven mourning, aligns with the findings of Arias (2018: 1–5), who posits that studies of the relationship between political violence and mental health have not yet fully addressed the formation of subjectivities that emerge in the medium and long-term horizons of prolonged armed conflicts. Such subjectivities are instead medicalised, studied in the short term for 'post-traumatic stress disorder' and homogenised through 'the narrowness of labels such as the medical notion of <traumatised> or the legal notion of <victims>'. While acknowledging the significance of these labels, Arias (2018: 1–5) advocates for examining the multifaceted forms of resistance employed by individuals through survival strategies that require 'the constant rethinking and continuous reinvention of everyday knowledge'.

From the perspective of the field of testimonial studies, which is where I situate myself, in which the textile practices we are observing are inscribed, this approach is essential: in the deep layers of any testimonial, text is housed in the vertiginous displacements, dislocations, negotiations and changes to which the 'victims' are subjected. The 'victim'-survivors are not immobilised in their past; they are powerfully dynamic subjects who negotiate, readjust and modify the conditions of their survival, as we have seen throughout the chapters of this book. They articulate their conditions of survival from their 'intrapsychic tellurism' (psychic processes or phenomena that develop within the mind, often associated with internal experiences, emotional conflicts, or unconscious dynamics) and the intersubjective, the social and the relational. Their textual narratives rearticulate a grammar that has been taken away by the disappearance of names, bodies and narratives to stage the wound and seek ways of speaking it.

This quality of 'active life' (Arendt, 2015) of the witness as a survivor is determined by the huge work of individual and collective relocation/reparation. Witnessing moves ceaselessly between the sunken and the saved, what is missing and what is needed. It is a movement of reimagining and rewriting the world that is not only an immediate response to trauma but a permanent and tireless construction. Gloria Astrid Méndez of the collective *Madres de los Falsos Positivos de Soacha y Bogotá* (MAFAPO) [*Mothers of False Positives from Soacha and Bogotá*] (number 14 on the map), who are dedicated to seeking justice for their children, says:

> A veces guardamos muchas cosas pero haciendo un tejido usted saca todo eso y así permite que florezca la ternura y el amor que lleva dentro. (Entrevista a Gloria Méndez. Bello-Tocancipá, 2018: 195)
>
> Sometimes we keep a lot of things to ourselves, but by sewing, you bring it all out and allow the tenderness and love inside you to blossom (Interview with Gloria Méndez. Bello-Tocancipá, 2018: 195)

Lilia Yaya, a relative of one of the leaders of the Unión Patriótica [Patriotic Union] a political party which was systematically exterminated by paramilitary groups (see Chapter 1, this book) and a community leader states that:

> Tejer es elaborar y coser reconstruir, coser esos pedacitos y reconstruirlos. (Entrevista a Lilia Yaya. Bello-Tocancipá, 2018: 8)
>
> To weave is to elaborate and sew to reconstruct, to sew those little pieces together and rebuild them (Interview with Lilia Yaya. Bello-Tocancipá, 2018: 8)

Gledys López, a member of the collective *Mujeres tejiendo Sueños y Sabores de Paz* [*Women Weaving Dreams and Flavours of Peace*], resides in the village of Mampuján, a small Afro-Colombian community located within the municipality of María La Baja, in the Montes de María, in the north of the Bolívar Department (number 5 on the map), one of the areas most affected by forced displacement. In this region, on 10 March 2000, 245 families were forced to leave the region en masse as a result of paramilitary actions. The transformative power of the testimonial act as a reinstallation of subjectivities that have been displaced by violence is evident in her words:

> Cuando ya íbamos terminando el primer tapiz nos dimos cuenta de que logramos sacar todo lo que sentíamos y convivir con los recuerdos. Comenzamos a sacar risas del llanto y entendimos que lo que estábamos haciendo era una terapia. (Entrevista a Gledys López. Noguera-Montoya, 2018)
>
> When we finished the first tapestry, we realised that we had managed to express everything we felt and coexist with the remembrances. We started laughing about the tears and understood that what we were doing was therapy. (Interview with Gledys López. Noguera-Montoya, 2018)

Arias (2018: 2) provides us with the concept of 'suffering-resisting subjects' to argue 'that it is possible to suffer without disappearing as subjects'. The quilt of Blanca Nieves Meneses, the blankets, tapestries, scarves, sackcloths, burlaps, tissues and rag dolls that are being sewn, embroidered and woven throughout Latin America are powerful symbols of this suffering while resisting, being at the same time 'a modality of historical action in the face of violence' (Bello-Tocancipá, 2018: 36). Their testimonial – or rather **text**imonial – character is evident in their nature as unexpected objects. The textimonial subject is also an unexpected subject, that is, one who should not have been there, and who should have been either silenced or disappeared. The nuclear slopes of the act of Testimony (elaborating trauma, promoting justice, transmitting Memory) produce a discourse that should not have existed and is taking its place in that kind of 'distribution of the sensible' that programmed its absence.

Doris, another mother – whose son Óscar was arrested and disappeared in Cúcuta, Norte de Santander (number 22 on the map) in 2008 – has dedicated herself to denouncing and demanding justice for her son and all the young people extrajudicially executed in Bogotá and Soacha. Doris helps us understand how the affective relationship established with the material allows us to experience the return of those absent, especially when this process involves the resignification of the remains/clothes of the dead. Through this relationship, the material (threads, fabrics, colours, textures) enters into a relationship with a field of emotional forces that mould it (Ingold, 2010) to the rhythm of a body whose movements inhabit both the immaterial space of Memory and the material space of sewing, simultaneously walking through the spaces of life and death. Doris says:

> Yo a Óscar le había tejido un saquito amarillo y blanco, el saco era grande, de mangas grandes, porque él, desde pequeño fue fortachón ¡lo más de lindo! Tengo la idea de volverlo a hacer tal cual… es para tenerlo conmigo, para traer a mi hijo. Yo busqué y tengo cuatro pañales de tela de él, quiero bordarlos, son muy significativos […]. Yo todavía no me he desprendido de él, no lo he dejado ir, porque por medio de estas cosas yo puedo hablar con él cuando sea, puedo verlo, hablarle. Y hasta que su cuerpo no aparezca yo no lo voy a dejar ir. (Entrevista a Doris. Bello-Tocancipá & Aranguren-Romero, 2020: 191–192)
>
> I had knitted a yellow and white jumper for Óscar, the jumper was big, with big sleeves, because ever since he was a little boy, he was sturdy, the cutest thing! I have the idea of redoing it as it is… it's to have it with me, to bring my son. I looked for, and I found four of his cloth nappies, I want to embroider them, they are very significant […]. I still haven't let go of him, I haven't let him go, because through these things I can talk to him whenever I want, I can see him, talk to him. And until his body appears, I am not going to let him go. (Interview with Doris. Bello-Tocancipá & Aranguren-Romero, 2020: 191–192)

As Bello-Tocancipá and Aranguren-Romero (2020) observe, the narrative and the therapeutic potential of textile making allows both the enunciation of violence and the management of emotions, materialising the absence in the physical consistency of the fabric, witnessing it in its texture.

Blanca Nubia Díaz, a Wayúu woman, lost her husband and daughter in 2000 and 2001, respectively, at the hands of the Jorge 40's paramilitary group. For 17 years, Blanca has been demanding information about the disappearance, rape and murder of her daughter, Irina. Her words attest to the status of a 'magical object' that this affective investment and projection ascribes to the fabric. The act of weaving is thus imbued with the quality of a 'dwelling place where the spirit resides', as described by Marc Augé (1998: 22) in his analysis of the fetish object. This quality is generated by the reflective and meditative nature of the textile practice, as evidenced by the works of Raye-Garlock (2016) and Bello-Tocancipá and Aranguren-Romero (2020). This is how Blanca expressed her feelings during an interview:

> **Blanca:** Yo siento mucho alivio, siento que le estoy dando un acompañamiento a mi hija; al estar tejiendo estoy con ella. Como yo tengo sus cuadros, yo la miro y le digo 'Mija, te quiero, te amo, me haces falta'. ¡Eso es una cosa muy bonita para mí!
>
> **Entrevistadora:** ¿El tejido te permite sentirla a ella contigo?
>
> **Blanca:** ¡Sí! ¡Claro! Y como yo tengo tantas fotos y cosas de ella en la casa ¡Claro! Estoy tejiendo y me pongo a pensar en ella, en cómo era ella de chiquita, como era peleona con la otra hermana…Empiezo a recordar y es como si pudiera sentirla también. (Entrevista a Blanca Nubia Díaz. Bello-Tocancipá y Aranguren-Romero, 2020: 190–191)

> **Blanca:** I feel a lot of relief, I feel that I am accompanying my daughter; I am with her when I am weaving. As I have her paintings, I look at her and say, 'Mija [daughter of mine], I love you, I love you, I miss you'. That's a very nice thing for me!
>
> **Interviewer:** Does the fabric allow you to feel her with you?
>
> **Blanca:** Yes, of course! And as I have so many photos and things of her in the house, of course! I'm weaving and sewing, and I start thinking about her, about how she was when she was a little girl, how she quarrelled with her sister… I start to remember, and it's as if I can feel her too. (Interview with Blanca Nubia Díaz. Bello-Tocancipá & Aranguren-Romero, 2020: 190–191)

Community leader and human rights defender Virgelina Chará – a displaced woman from Suárez, Cauca (number 10 on the map) – assists displaced families and 'victims' of violence through the *Asociación para la Mujer y el Trabajo* [Association for Women and Work]. She arrived in Bogotá in 2003, having fled threats from paramilitaries. She is a member of the *Unión de Costureros de Bogotá* [Union of Bogotá Sewing Workshops] (Bello-Tocancipá, 2018: 46). In an interview, she reveals how the affective bond imbues the fabric with a life of its own, transforming it into an object-witness, a quasi-subject endowed with agency, a bio-object whose materiality is offered as a place for the incarnation of the mother's pain:

> Entrevistadora: Tú me decías que el tejido te permite sacar dolores. ¿Cómo? ¿Cómo saca esos dolores?
>
> Interviewer: You were telling me that weaving and sewing allows you to get rid of pain, how? How does it get rid of pain?
>
> Virgelina: Cuando yo empiezo a contarle a la tela y la tela empieza a hablar.
>
> Virgelina: When I start telling it to the fabric, and the fabric starts talking.
>
> Entrevistadora: ¿Cómo si la tela contara tu dolor?
>
> Interviewer: Is it as if the fabric is speaking your pain?
>
> Virgelina: Exactamente. Porque la tela empieza a hablar lo que yo estoy sintiendo, porque ella cuenta lo que yo estoy escribiendo en ella. Ahora, el dolor está en la tela y ella empieza a contar, empieza a viajar. (Bello-Tocancipá & Aranguren-Romero, 2020: 200)
>
> Virgelina: Exactly. Because the canvas begins to say what I am feeling, because it tells what I am writing on it. Now, the pain is in the cloth, and it starts to speak, it starts to travel. (Bello-Tocancipá & Aranguren-Romero, 2020: 200)

'To Embroider is to Unite'[3]

Let us consider the potential for generating links implicit in the textimonial task, as exemplified by Blanca Nieves' quilt of remembrances. Thanks to a meeting with her and other victims from the Putumayo Department (number 23 on the map), in 2013 Claudia Girón, then director of the Manuel Cepeda Vargas Foundation, Francisco Bustamante, from the Asociación Minga and Ana María Ramírez from the Federación Colombiana de Deporte Especial [Colombian Federation of Special Sports] (FEDES), initiated the *Costurero de la Memoria Kilómetros de Vida y Memoria* [*Sewing Workshop of Memory: Kilometres of Life and Memory*] project in Bogotá. The work's title alludes to the thousands of kilometres that victims of the armed conflict had to travel across the country. The project's primary objective was to produce kilometres of embroidered fabrics to wrap around the Palace of Justice.

This public action aimed to promote the right to truth, as Ochoa (2017) outlined. The extensive and intricate fabric of the Costurero initiatives is revealed in the digital 'skein book' *Textimoniando y haceres textiles* [*Textimoning and textile work*], 'a collective construction of all the people who have walked, inhabited and woven together in the Sewing Workshop of Memory: Kilometres of Life and Memory'. The prologue highlights the guiding principle that informs the Sewing Workshop's textilities production and processing activities and its associated networks:

> We must re-signify our memories so as not to forget what happened, we must weave other possible peace in order to confront all kinds of violence

and oppression, and we must come together to mend all the wounds of war. (*Costurero de la memoria*, 2022: 5)

These contents are again proposed in the declarations of the numerous Colombian and Latin American textile collectives, which reflect a shared approach to governing the universe of textimonial practices.

The importance of the work of the *Costurero de la Memoria Kilómetros de Vida y Memoria* [*Sewing Workshop: Kilometres of Life and Memory*] project was later emphasised during the exhibition of testimonial textiles *La vida que se teje* [The woven life], curated by Roberta Bacic, an eminent scholar of the heritage of precursor textiles such as those of the Chilean *arpilleras* [appliquéd burlap] created during the Pinochet dictatorship. The architect of the cataloguing, conservation and study of the immense narrative, political and poetic capital kept in the pieces made by the Colombian textile collectives was Beatriz Elena Arias López, a lecturer at the University of Antioquia. She is an outstanding scholar in mental health and the therapeutic value of textile work in conflict and post-conflict Colombia.

The exhibition, entitled *La vida que se teje* [*The woven life*] was held between 11 May and 10 July 2016. It brought together 85 pieces from Colombia, Chile, Mexico and Peru, demonstrating the diversity of the global textile community and the similarities between the various local experiences. In this context, the leaders of several regional sewing workshops in the country, convened by Isabel González Arango and Beatriz Arias López, came together to form the *Red de tejedoras por la Memoria y por la vida* [*Network of Weavers for Memory and Life*]:

To create collective and peaceful actions of political empowerment in order to promote reparative processes of civil resistance based on the narrative force and expressive richness of the fabric. (Arias, as cited in Ochoa, 2017: para. 14)

Other significant research processes and institutional alliances emerged from the flow and exchange of ideas from *La vida que se teje* [*The woven life*]. In the context of an academic degree project, Isabel Arango constructed a digital repository to document testimonial textiles of the armed conflict in Colombia (August 2017–November 2019). This project was developed with the support of the Museo Casa de la Memoria de Medellín and the Universidad de Antioquia to design a visual atlas of Memory: a digital repository of remembrances (July 2017–October 2019). The project *Remendar lo nuevo: Practicando reconciliaciones a través del quehacer textil y la memoria digital en la transición del posconflicto de la Colombia rural* [*Mending the new: Practising reconciliation through textile work and digital Memory in the transition of post-conflict of rural Colombia*] was conducted between September 2018 and September 2020. The Ministry of Science and Technology (Minciencias) and the UK Newton Fund funded the project.[4] This project facilitated networking among various social actors. Researchers from the National University, the University of Los Andes and the University of Antioquia participated, and the universities of Nottingham, Lancaster and Warwick supported the project. It involved these textile collectives:

- Artesanías Guayacán [Guayacan Handicrafts] (Bojayá, Chocó, number 12 on the map);
- Artesanías Choibá [Choiba Handicrafts] (Quibdó, Chocó, number 12 on the map);
- Costurero de Tejedoras por la Memoria [Sewing Workshop Weavers for Memory] from Sonsón (Antioquia, number 2 on the map);
- Mujeres tejiendo Sueños y Sabores de Paz [Women Weaving Dreams and Flavours of Peace] (María la Baja, Bolívar, number 5 on the map);
- Asociación de Mujeres Víctimas Artesanas e Innovadoras de Hoy para el Mañana [Association of Women Victims Craftswomen and Innovators of Today for Tomorrow](ASVIMARIN) (Valle de Guamuez, Putumayo, number 23 on the map);
- Asociación de Mujeres Defensoras del Agua y de la Vida [Association of Women Defenders of Water and Life](AMARÚ) (Ituango, Antioquia, number 5 on the map); and
- Muñecas Combatientes por la Paz y la Vida [Combatant Dolls Fighting for Peace and Life] (Miranda, Cauca, number 10 on the map).

In November 2019, the exhibition *Tiempos de la escucha* [*Times of listening*][5] was derived from *Mending the new*, in which each project is accompanied by audio and videos which, among other messages, reproduce messages of peace and reconciliation from their authors. The project was born out of an encounter between the transdisciplinary research team from Bogotá and Medellín and the women's collectives from Bojayá, Quibdó, Sonsón and Mampuján, who for years have been mending their wounds with thread and needle, fabrics and threads. It was organised by Artesanal Tecnológica, 'a feminist, intergenerational and interdisciplinary sewing/collective/laboratory that thinks from textile knowledge and digital technologies', active since 2014.[6]

The *Archivo Digital de Textiles Testimoniales* [*Digital Archive of Testimonial Textiles of the Armed Conflict in Colombia*][7] was created and coordinated by Isabel González Arango after the work carried out in *Remendar lo nuevo* [*Mending the new*]. It is a magnificent repertoire of textiles carefully and rigorously assembled and catalogued through images, information on the sociopolitical context and characterisation of the collectives, documents and related links, description and interpretation of the pieces. Isabel defines the theoretical framework from which to think about testimonial textiles, characterising them as 'non-textual documents', 'artefacts of Memory', 'repertoires of action' and 'multivocal documents' (González-Arango, 2019). Their narratives provide alternative forms of documentary information in which events, affections, gestures and emotions are stored. The Memory they preserve is particularly performative: the language of the textile implies the practice of the senses, as is well demonstrated by studies in the field of psychology and psychosocial accompaniment by Bello-Tocancipá (2018), Bello-Tocancipá and Aranguren-Romero (2020) and González-Arango et al. (2022). A clear definition can be found on the login page of the Digital Archive:

> Testimonial textiles are materialities and artefacts of memory that document or denounce events and experiences through embroidery, sewing and weaving as narrative supports and media in resignification and testimonial acts. This means they have a political and social dimension for the collectives that have made them and help configure shared meanings about the events they narrate in these formats.[8]

Textimonios serve as articulators and producers of meaning as they repair and unite. The journey that began with Blanca's story has proliferated into meetings and exchanges, the formation of networks and the realisation of ever more comprehensive projects, the production of knowledge and generative practices. All this taxonomic, investigative and participatory ferment has been produced from the textile narratives that women have been writing for a long time. Gargallo (2014: 54) notes that these narratives are 'humble and supportive' domestic and collective actions. They are generators of practical knowledge and symbolic action through which Colombian and Latin American women articulate their response to violence, their proposals for peace and their projects for the future.

Weaving a Common History

On 4 December 2016, approximately 30 weavers from all over Colombia gathered at Plaza Bolívar in Bogotá to unite all the weavings made so far and wrap them around the 420 metre perimeter of the Palace of Justice (Ochoa, 2017: para. 17). The blankets were interwoven with photographs of the disappeared in a powerful public act of denunciation and Memory.

Among the textiles that wrapped around the Palace of Justice was another emblematic and famous textile: the *Nuestras Víctimas [Our Victims]* tapestry, sewn and embroidered by the Guayacán Handicrafts Collective, made up of Afro and indigenous women from Bellavista, the principal town of Bojayá in the department of Chocó (Figure 8.3).

The group was established in the late 1980s as a Basic Ecclesial Community,[9] with the support of the Augustinian Missionary Sisters and Father Jorge Luis Mazo, who was assassinated in 1999. Crafts such as embroidery, weaving and baking enabled community members to resist the effects of the war in their territories. In 1997, coinciding with the entry of the paramilitaries into the territory of Medio Atrato (number 12 on the

Figure 8.3 *Nuestras Víctimas [Our Victims]* tapestry, 2 May 2002
Source: *Artesanías Guayacán* (Bojayá, Chocó) (2003). See http://www.textilestestimoniales.org/creadores/4. Courtesy of Isabel González Arango.

map), the members decided to persevere. They adopted the name Artesanías Guayacán, derived from the Atrato tree 'Guayacán', valued for its resistant wood and used to construct the houses and boats characteristic of the area.

The tapestry bears the embroidered names of the victims of the massacre perpetrated on 2 May 2002 in Bellavista,[10] accompanied by flowers, animals, boats and crafts typical of the region. The tapestry is exhibited every year in commemoration of the massacre to remember and denounce those responsible. In the process of exhuming the dead, the list of names has served as a document for the memory of the relatives, as the first record of the victims. It measures 6 by 2.5 metres high. After the list of names is inscribed:

> Por ríos y por selvas que guardan la memoria de tantos pueblos negros que aquí hacemos historia.
>
> Through rivers and jungles that preserve the memory of so many black communities, we make history here.

The tapestry comprises 14 horizontal lines of fabric, each embroidered with six names. The lines are yellow, red, white, green and blue. The arrangement of the lines is reminiscent of banners on the side of the road, which advertise meals in restaurants and invite people to stop. There are 84 embroidered names in total.

The tapestry documents the loss of these lives and, at the same time, the connection they had with the river, fish, birds, musical instruments, *champas* (canoes), plants and their work. It is present in the ritual spaces where relatives bid farewell to or commemorate their dead (Figure 8.4).[11] The remains of the dead were buried in November 2019. The tapestry sets the scene for the Eucharist, the novena and the ritual farewell to the dead at this event. In subsequent years, the women of Artesanías Guayacán have taken the piece to many cities in Colombia and the world to continue denouncing the violence in Chocó, past and present, and to show their desire for Memory and reparation.

Constant collective work led to the careful design and creation of the tapestry. The final product resulted from the women's collective participation in its production, as is characteristic of the textimonios production process. We read about the cooperative process that led to the tapestry in the Archivo Digital de Textiles Testimoniales:

> The process took place over four months both in collective spaces for reflection and discussion about the pain experienced, and in private spaces by each woman in her home. Each woman from *Artesanías Guayacán* embroidered the names of close relatives, friends or neighbours she had lost in the massacre, thus beginning the first exercise of 'collective mourning'; the women from Artesanías Choibá embroidered names chosen at random. Once the embroidery was finished, the sewers of the group, with the help of the Augustinian missionary sisters and Ursula Holzapfel (COVIJUPA), were responsible for assembling the strips, adding the backing fabric and sewing the details so that the tapestry could be hung in the church and the various exhibition spaces (para. 1).[12]

Before considering further the specific tapestry of *Our Victims* (Figures 8.3 and 8.4), it is important to consider the insights of women engaged in textimonial work as part of other group experiences. These

Figure 8.4 Relatives gathered to commemorate their dead
Source: Photograph taken by Natalia Quiceno, 2019. Courtesy of Isabel González Arango.

insights help identify and highlight the therapeutic value the women ascribe to collective work. An example can be found in the voice of those belonging to one of the pioneering and best-known sewing groups in Colombia, *Mujeres Tejiendo Sueños y Sabores de Paz* [*Women Weaving Dreams and Flavours of Peace*], which began to meet in 2004, following the forced displacement of their community. The tapestry they mention is entitled *Desplazamiento* [*Displacement*] (2009). It was the first tapestry made by the Collective.

> Proponiendo que las mujeres nos organizáramos y trabajáramos unas telas al principio nos pareció una pérdida de tiempo, pero en la medida en que le cogimos el hilo comenzábamos a coser y hablar sobre el tema descubríamos que teníamos muchas heridas. En ese momento ya empezábamos a trabajar, nos dimos cuenta que era bueno porque iba quedando como bonito, ya a medida que hablábamos y sacábamos cosas, íbamos recibiendo la sanidad, poco a poco y cuando quisimos terminar el tapiz nos dimos cuenta que ya nos reíamos, cuando nos tocaba recordar una historia de alguno pues, nos causaba mucho sentimiento pero ya después nos causaba risa y de hecho hoy nos reímos no porque la cosa de risa, sino que de pronto creemos que ya está sana. (Entrevista a mujeres, anónimas en el texto original. Belalcázar-Valencia & Molina-Valencia, 2017: 68)
>
> They proposed that we women should organise ourselves and work on fabrics. At first, it seemed like a waste of time, but as we got the hang of it and began to sew and talk about it, we discovered we had many wounds. At that moment, we began to work. We realised it was good because it was becoming beautiful, and as we talked and took things out, we were healing, little by little. When we wanted to finish the tapestry, we realised that we were already laughing when we had to remember someone's story. It caused us many feelings, but later, it caused us to laugh; today, we laugh not because it is a laughing matter but because we suddenly believe it has already been healed. (Interview with women, anonymous in the original text. Belalcázar-Valencia & Molina-Valencia, 2017: 68)

Additionally, for Doris, Óscar's mother, whom I have already introduced, and for Claudia Girón, a psychologist and human rights defender, one of the founders of *Costurero de la Memoria Kilómetros de Vida y Memoria* [*Sewing Workshop of Memory: Kilometres of Life and Memory*] (Bello-Tocancipá, 2018), the healing effect provided by textile work is deeply rooted in the creation of bonds and 'spaces of trust' (Bello-Tocancipá & Aranguren-Romero, 2020) in which individuals can feel safe and share their experiences and narratives. According to Doris:

> La recompensa por toda esta lucha es estar con las compañeras, compartir sus dolores con los míos y hacer los míos llevaderos: aprender a
>
> The reward for all this struggle is to be with the partners, to share their pain with mine and make mine bearable: to learn to under-

entenderlas, respetarlas y quererlas y a compartir con ellas las buenas y las malas. (Entrevista a Doris. Bello-Tocancipá & Aranguren-Romero 2020: 189)	stand, respect and love them and to share with them the good and the bad. (Interview with Doris. Bello-Tocancipá & Aranguren-Romero 2020: 189)

As Claudia Girón says, 'It is necessary to create communities of support where a common history is woven; it is not about being spectators of the drama of others' (Bello-Tocancipá & Aranguren-Romero, 2020: 190).

Proximity makes testimonio possible: it generates dialogue, exchange, circulation and the expression of emotions. It transforms solitude into solidarity. It concretises the practice of 'maternal knowledge' (Muraro, 2006) as knowledge of the intersubjective relationship that promotes another symbolic order for culture, antithetical to that of violence. This is a symbolic order based on lack and not on potency; on the relational nature of human beings, which is permanently recognised as 'part of'; on the ethics of care and desire. In her conceptualisation, Muraro, an Italian philosopher owes much to the thought and militancy of the Mothers of the Plaza de Mayo, the embroidering mothers, with their white handkerchiefs (which had been nappies) on which the names of their disappeared children were inscribed forever. Their politics of resistance was based precisely on the socialisation of pain, transforming it from singular to plural, politicising mourning and the domestic space.

Textualities/Textilities

The cooperative and semiotic process of collective work fuses multiple levels of experience, different subjectivities, a diverse range of memories and the juxtaposition of different cultural layers.

If we look at the *Nuestras Víctimas* [*Our Victims*] (Figures 8.3 and 8.4), tapestry figuratively, the enumeration of names stands out. This trope is typical of the funerary rhetoric established by the Christian epigraphic tradition, a tradition that inscribes, by carving names on monumental tombstones (steles, columns, slabs), memories of the dead that are the community's heritage, destined for eternal remembrance. In contrast to the rigidity of stone, the enumeration of names on the tapestry is represented by a fabric that allows for mobility. The materiality of the support allows it to move through various settings, including buildings (houses, churches, museums, institutional headquarters), pavements, cities and nations. It thus accompanies the expansive movement of a Memory that does not remain fixed but is ready for contact, circulation and transmission. Word or Memory 'walking the word', to use the epistemological repertoire of the Nasa (discussed in Chapter 4 of this book) is conceptualised by Vilma Almendra (2017).

This walking re-signifies the staticity of the commemorative tradition, revisiting it through contact with another, everyday, popular counter-memorial tradition, as mentioned: that of the banners that invite us to visit restaurants on the side of Colombian roads. Memory appeals to naturalisation in everyday life, preferring to install itself in a space not regulated by the institutional culture of remembrance. It favours its incorporation into the everyday gaze, not into the exceptionality of official calendars. It is a living Memory (Nora, 2008) that inhabits the social space as a sign of attention and an invitation to stop, to enter the socially familiar and every day.

Conversely, the trope of the enumeration of names provokes a rhetoric of accumulation that evidences horror. To enumerate is to decompose the whole into its parts, to make possible its analytical perception (Mortara-Garavelli, 1997: 216). Indexing the person in their uniqueness, an essential attribute of the definition of the subject, the lost proper name is a sign of the radical loss of the same subject. The return of the name, as with the return of autobiography, is the nucleus of a poetics of the reinstallation of the subject that opposes the negation that is programmed by violence.

The tapestry functions as documentary proof of events and as a commemorative act that historicises, restores identity and recognises the presence of the absent. Collective work determines the shaping of a plural enunciation, negotiating multiple subjective instances. Textile work is not merely an abstract exercise in democratic space-building; it is also 'demo-practical' (Naldini, 2012), a concrete manifestation of politics organised by civil society. This politics is centred on integration and relationship, woven by the threads of a will for peace that repairs what is broken and gives new meaning to the future.

The *Nuestras Víctimas* [*Our Victims*] (Figures 8.3 and 8.4), tapestry can be considered one of the foundational pieces opening the testimonial narrative cycle of the armed conflict in Colombia. It can be likened to an epitaph in homage to the martyrs, occupying the sacred space of the church of Bellavista Nuevo and being present in the ritual spaces of commemoration through which it moves. The tapestry represents the dead and absent as a tangible representation of the new historical community that the textile collectives reimagine. The tapestry thus contains a promise of the future, the fulfilment of which belongs to the survivors. The principle of hope is rooted in the principle of collective responsibility.

In my opinion, the tapestry *Nuestras Víctimas* [*Our Victims*] finds its emblematic correlate among the many that could be chosen in the *Recomenzar* [*Begin Again*] tapestry, made in 2015 (Figure 8.5) by the *Sewing Workshop Fabric, Memory and Mental Health of Medellín*.

The Costurero [Sewing Workshop] is a project of the Red Nacional de Tejedoras por la Memoria y la Vida [National Network of Weavers for Memory and Life]. Its objectives include generating meeting spaces to reconstruct family and social ties in communities affected by the armed conflict and to promote the exchange of experiences between textile collectives. It comprises women from different generations, the majority of

Figure 8.5 *Begin Again* tapestry
Source: *Costurero Tejido, Memoria y Salud Mental de Medellín* [Sewing Workshop, Memory and Mental Health of Medellín] (2015). Medellín. See http://www.textilestestimoniales.org/creadores/18. Courtesy of Isabel Arango and Diosa Caren García.

whom are victims of the armed conflict. Diosa García, and her fellow women, created *Recomenzar* to bear witness, remember and reinstall daily life and hope.

A red heart marked by wounds and stitches in black stands out in the scene's centre. In the background on the left is a picture of a massacre in a house, the dead, the blood, the horror. The colours maintain the vividness of the memory of what happened. Moving towards the centre of this background, imposing black silhouettes, which intentionally do not respect the proportions of the perspective, indicate the indelible, irreducible presence of the absent, as indescribable as pain. The absence of physiognomy differs from the general tone of the tapestry, full of expressive and carefully portrayed figurines, ghosting the black bodies. Their colour dialogues with that of the wounds in the central heart.

The silhouettes are part of the landscape that encompasses them and is used as a vanishing point of the perspective, whose line fixes the horizon and structures the surrounding space. The gaze is directed towards the silhouettes as the first call for attention. Gradually and meticulously, the scene expands and saturates the tapestry's plan. The community is shown, through the joy of the colours, the harmonious order of its territorial arrangement, the relationships between the figures, the neatness of the houses and the games being played. In the foreground, under the heart, is a dreamcatcher to ward off evil spirits and express the hope of living in peace after mending the broken.

The woven story unfolds in two temporal dimensions, the past and the future, both intertwined and coexisting. We also saw this characteristic of temporal convergence in the *testimonios* in fragments in Chapter 3 of this book. The community rewrites its story to inaugurate it actively, from its dreams, in the tapestry. This process of restarting and establishing a new beginning is, according to Hannah Arendt in *What Is Politics?* (1997: 20), a fundamental aspect of political action; 'action as *initium* is not the beginning of something, but of someone: with words and action we insert ourselves into the human world'. *Initium,* or beginning, is as an insertion, a return to life after having crossed death.

The words of one of the seamstresses, Diosa García, summarises perfectly the meaning of the title and the concept of the tapestry:

Recomenzar, tener la firme convicción de que siempre podré reinventarme, que siempre habrá otros panoramas y que, aunque las tormentas se lleven todas mis hojas, brotarán otras nuevas, frescas, coloradas, hermosas, que hablarán por mi solas de mi esencia. Es por eso que sigo aquí y si caigo me levanto; así sea llorando. (Diosa García, 2015)	To start again, to have the firm conviction that I will always be able to reinvent myself, that there will always be other panoramas, and that, even if the storms carry away all my leaves, new ones will sprout, fresh, colourful, beautiful, that will speak for themselves of my essence. That is why I am still here, and if I fall, I get up, even if I cry. (Diosa García, 2015)[13]

In exploring the Colombian and Latin American textimonial universe, we enter an extraordinarily dynamic space woven by the contacts, exchanges and connections of women who join together in collectives that combine into networks that weave themselves into transnational communities. In fact, like a wave that grows stronger as it advances, amassing distant objects in its giddiness, textile practices applied to the struggle for the defence of human rights have gradually become one of the great discursive fields of our century, with precursor and foundational experiences such as those of the British Suffragettes in the first decades of the 20th century (Parker, 2010) and the Chilean *arpilleristas* in the 1970s (Agosín, 2008; Larrere-Salort, 2019; Museo de la Memoria y Derechos Humanos, 2019).

However, its contemporary trajectory cannot be considered without the contributions of feminist and decolonial agencies, without the thought and experiences of resistance in contexts of political violence, and without the processes of elaboration of trauma and construction of Memory against the disappearing power of dictatorships. In the face of the discourse of catastrophe, textile work (has) provides(ded) a vast symbolic repertoire, both figurative and conceptual, to rearticulate the loss of meaning caused by the occurrence of violence.

All textile arts are founded upon thread: thread that weaves, embroiders, sews, joins, transforms and repairs. Metaphorically and literally, thread represents another mode of narration and a distinct experience of doing so. It is a material that bridges separated or dispersed parts, connects elements, transforms the given and regenerates the (ab)used and the broken. The thread used for weaving, embroidering, sewing and mending prompts the creation of a relational grammar that practises union, (re) eneration and care. It also enables tracing an unlimited atlas of signs that transmit meanings and arrange graphics, icons and symbols to form another alphabet and other textualities. What can be described as the *material turn* of contemporary cultural and literary criticism has led to a renewed interest in objects. One of its emblematic variants is undoubtedly the *textile turn,* theorised by philosophers such as Paul Leclercq (2016) and Tim Ingold (2010) (Roussillon-Constanty & Dickinson, 2018: 5). The 'turn' is a constant: the overflowing history of a never-ending narrative practice such as textile, which runs parallel to the history of women and native peoples, shaping textualities – or better textilities – that organise other relations between text and body; knowledge and making; subject (who writes) and object (on which it is written); community and State.

Notes

(1) *Doktoro Esperanto* (Doctor Hopeful or The One Who Hopes) was the name used by its creator to sign the booklet published in 1887 in which he explained the rules of this language (Menaszek, 2012). In this context, it is used metaphorically to represent the universality of a shared language, in this case that of textiles, and the collective hope of the weavers and seamstresses to mend what has been broken by violence.
(2) The short film, based on a true story, is produced by the animation studio ¡EnPánico! In the story, the names of the characters are replaced by colours. See https://www.youtube.com/watch?v=IL_7uUw7CFI&t=361s
(3) Fragment of the idea 'To Embroider is to Unite, because society has been dismembered. It is also therapeutic, the relatives of the dead get closer to them and to their inner peace' by Libertad García Sanabria, member of the Mexican collective 'Bordando por la Paz'[Embroidering for Peace] (Gargallo, 2014: 57).
(4) The digital open-access volume *Remendar lo nuevo: Compartiendo aprendizajes* [Mending the new: Sharing learning] (a compilation of the project's trajectory written by many hands) provides a comprehensive description of the initiative. See https://bibliotecadigital.udea.edu.co/bitstream/10495/21041/1/VillamizarAdriana_2020_RemendarNuevoCompartiendo.pdf. The book also contains the 'textile biographies' of the members of the collectives.
(5) See https://artishockrevista.com/2020/09/27/textil-sonoro-colombia-artesanal-tecnologica/.
(6) See https://artishockrevista.com/2020/09/27/textil-sonoro-colombia-artesanal-tecnologica/.
The Artesanal Tecnológica website also contains a rich collection of videos on projects, images and academic texts written by leading researchers on these subjects. The repository contains an essential textile library. See https://www.artesanaltecnologica.org/proyectos/.

(7) The Archive is in dialogue with other repositories such as: Story Cloth DataBase.
See http://www.storyclothdatabase.org/
Conflict Textiles Website, associated with CAIN (Conflict Archive on the Internet) of Ulster University, Northern Ireland.
See https://cain.ulster.ac.uk/conflicttextiles/
Archivo Digital de Fondos y Colecciones del Museo de la Memoria y Derechos Humanos de Chile.
See http://archivomuseodelamemoria.cl/index.php/330303;term/browseTerm
Costurero viajero. See https://www.artesanaltecnologica.org/cost_viajero/
El Ojo de la aguja. See https://www.artesanaltecnologica.org/el-ojo-de-la-aguja/All these repositories together give an idea of the sheer consistency of textimonial practices in the world.
(8) See http://www.textilestestimoniales.org/acerca-de
(9) It is a small group of Christians, generally laypeople, who regularly meet to read the Bible, pray, reflect on their faith, and address social issues from a Christian perspective. Their aim is to live and practice their faith in a communal way, committed to social justice and solidarity. These communities are usually rooted in Liberation Theology and are common in Latin America (Costadoat, 2021).
(10) See http://www.textilestestimoniales.org/piezas/4
(11) See http://www.textilestestimoniales.org/piezas/4
(12) *How was the piece made?* See http://www.textilestestimoniales.org/piezas/4
(13) *What does the piece tell us?* See http://www.textilestestimoniales.org/piezas/18

References

Agamben, G. (1998) *Quel che resta di Auschwitz. L'archivio e il testimone*. Bollati Boringhieri.
Agosín, M. (2008) *Tapestries of Hope, Threads of Love: The Arpillera Movement in Chile*. Rowman and Littlefield Publishers.
Almendra, V. (2017) *Entre la emancipación y la captura. Memorias y caminos desde la lucha Nasa en Colombia*. Grietas Editores.
Arendt, H. (1997) *¿Qué es la política?* Paidós.
Arendt, H. (2015) *Vita activa. La condizione umana*. Bompiani.
Arias, B. (2018) Subjects suffering in resistance: An approach to the subjectivities of the Colombian armed conflict. *Social Medicine* 12 (12), 1–7.
Augé, M. (1998) *Dios como objeto. Símbolos – cuerpos – materias – palabras*. Gedisa.
Belalcázar-Valencia, J.G. and Molina-Valencia, N. (2017) Los tejidos de las mujeres de Mampuján: Prácticas estético-artísticas de memoria situada en el marco del conflicto armado colombiano. *Andamios* 14 (34), 59–85.
Bello-Tocancipá, A.C. (2018) Cuando las palabras faltan, las manos hablan: Prácticas textiles en el conflicto armado colombiano. Tesis de grado inédita, Universidad de Los Andes.
Bello-Tocancipá, A.C. and Aranguren-Romero, J. (2020) Voces de hilo y aguja: Construcciones de sentido y gestión emocional por medio de prácticas textiles en el conflicto armado colombiano. *H-ART* 6, 181–204.
CNMH. (2016) Hasta encontrarlos. Víctimas y resistentes en el Caribe colombiano. See https://centrodememoriahistorica.gov.co/micrositios/hasta-encontrarlos/(accessed November 2023).
Costadoat, J. (2021) Comunidades eclesiales de base reflexión teológica a partir de un caso. *Revista latinoamericana de teología* 113, 183–205.
Costurero de la Memoria Kilómetros de Vida y de Memoria (2022) *Textimoniando: Trayectorias y quehaceres textiles*. See https://read.bookcreator.com/u7OzRDgcfmhd

NaATpqgDUBUc4062/joZ8DPE4TEyUE6gCCTeUnQ/UweIWYYLT3eI91LjvV9CEw (accessed January 2024).

Gargallo, F. (2014) (ed.) *Bordados de paz, memoria y justicia: un proceso de visibilización*, Ediciones Colectivos Bordados por la Paz, Bordamos por la Paz y Bordando por la Paz. See https://ia800900.us.archive.org/22/items/BordadosDePaz/BordadosDePazMemoriaYJusticia.pdf (accessed February 2024).

González-Arango, I.C. (2019) Repositorio digital para la documentación de textiles testimoniales del conflicto armado en Colombia. Tesis de maestría inédita, Universidad de Antioquia. See https://bibliotecadigital.udea.edu.co/bitstream/10495/16377/1/Gonz%c3%a1lezIsabel_2019_RepositorioTextilesTestimoniales.pdf (accessed January 2024).

González-Arango, I.C., Villamizar-Gelves, A.M., Chocontá-Piraquive, A. and Quinceno-Toro, N. (2022) Pedagogías textiles sobre el conflicto armado en Colombia: Activismos, trayectorias y transmisión de saberes desde la experiencia de cuatro colectivos de mujeres en Quibdó, Bojayá, Sonsón y María La Baja. *Revista de Estudios Sociales* 79 (01). See http://journals.openedition.org/revestudsoc/51511 (accessed January 2024).

Ingold, T. (2010) The textuality of making. *Cambridge Journal of Economics* 34 (1), 91–102.

Larrere-Salort, C. (2019) *Arpilleras: Hilván de memorias: El colectivo memorarte Arpilleras Urbanas, un legado de lucha social*. Pie de texto.

Leclercq, J. (2016) Interview with Jean-Paul Leclercq by Remi Labrusse (trans. Trista Selous). *Perspective: Actualité en histoire de l'art* 1, 61–74. See https://journals.openedition.org/perspective/6303 (accessed February 2024).

Menaszek, E. (2012) *Esperanto: Un intento de crear una voz uniforme para los pueblos de Europa y del mundo*. Universidad Jaguelónica.

Mortara-Garavelli, B. (1997) *Manuale di retorica*. Bompiani.

Muraro, L. (2006) *L'ordine simbolico della madre*. Editori Riuniti.

Museo de la Memoria y Derechos Humanos (2019) *Arpilleras. Colección del Museo de la Memoria y Derechos Humanos*. Ocho Libros Editores.

Naldini, P. (2012) *L'arte della demopraxia*. Cittàdell'arte edizioni.

Noguera-Montoya, S. (2018) Las mujeres de Mampuján llegan por primera vez a Expoartesanías. *A-A Agencia Anadolu*. See https://www.aa.com.tr/es/mundo/las-tejedoras-de-mampuj%C3%A1n-llegan-por-primera-vez-a-expoartesan%C3%ADas/1332364 (accessed February 2024).

Ochoa, M. (2017) La memoria envuelve la justicia. *Dissolve. Cartographies* 5, 1–16. See www.dissolvesf.org/issue-5/la-memoria-envuelve-la-justicia?rq=Ochoa (accessed February 2024).

Parker, R. (2010) *The Subversive Stitch. Embroidery and the Making of the Feminine*. Bloomsbury.

Ramírez-Gómez, L. (2021) Oropéndolas: Artes y literatura en la Colombia de los siglos XX y XXI. *Colección Noventa Ideas*. Universidad Javeriana. See issuu.com/pujaveriana/docs/978-958-781-654-9 (accessed February 2024).

Ramírez, Y. (2021) George Lavarca, hilar el alma. *The Wynwoodtimes*. See https://www.thewynwoodtimes.com/george-lavarca-artista-entrevista/ (accessed February 2021).

Rangel-Barragán, M.C. (2016) El tejido: El papel de las prácticas artísticas en la construcción de memoria histórica. El caso de las víctimas de Sonsón. Tesis de grado inédita, Universidad Colegio Mayor Nuestra Señora del Rosario.

Raye-Garlock, L. (2016) Stories in the cloth: Art therapy and narrative textiles. *Art Therapy. Journal of the American Art Therapy Association* 33 (2), 58–66.

Rocha-Vivas, M. (2018) *Mingas de la palabra. Textualidades oralitegráficas y visiones de cabeza en las oralituras y literaturas indígenas contemporáneas.* Universidad de Los Andes – Pontificia Universidad Javeriana.

Roussillon-Constanty, L. and Dickinson, R. (2018) Converging lines: Needlework in English literature and visual arts. *E-rea* 16 (1). See https://journals.openedition.org/erea/6586 (accessed February 2024).

Violi, M.P. (2014) *Paesaggi della memoria, il trauma, lo spazio, la storia.* Bompiani.

Part 3
Reflections

9 Voicing Experiences of Conflict and Violence: Placed, Dis-placed and Re-placed Resources

Theresa Lillis

I've been taught bloodstones can cure a snakebite,
Can stop the bleeding – most people forgot this
when the war ended. The war ended depending on which war you mean: those we started,
before those, millennia ago and onward, those which started me, which I lost and won –
these ever-blooming wounds.

(Natalie Díaz, *Postcolonial Love Poem*. English original.)

Me han enseñado que las piedras de sangre pueden curar una mordedura de serpiente,
Pueden detener la hemorragia – la mayoría de la gente olvidó esto cuando terminó la guerra. La guerra terminó
dependiendo de a qué guerra te refieras: las que nosotros empezamos, las anteriores, las de hace milenios en adelante,
las que me empezaron a mí, que perdí y gané -
estas heridas siempre florecientes

(Natalie Díaz, *Postcolonial Love Poem*. Translation by T. Lillis)

When I was invited to offer reflections on the chapters in this book I was reluctant to do so. Me: 'What could someone so distant from the lived experiences and knowledges expressed in the book meaningfully offer?' Blanca: 'It's important to show the value and potential connections with readers from many different geopolitical and academic locations.' Here I offer some thoughts as an outsider, and speaking primarily from my working life in social linguistics.

The work undertaken in this edited collection is the recuperation and representation of the lived experiences of some of the many thousands of people who have suffered as a result of the violent conflicts in Colombia over the past 80 years. The representation of their memories in this book is important for individual survivors and a crucial step towards building a collective and sustained peace. The public recuperation of Memory through different media – books, film, theatre, art, textiles – is important in the specific context of Colombia but for all peoples around the world who live on 'the other side of history' (Introduction), the side which is often invisibilised in State, codified and/or academically legitimised versions of wars and routinised violence. The narratives in this book contest hegemonic accounts of the nature and impact of conflict, together constituting a written *testimonio/textimonio* (Emilia Perassi, Chapter 8) of the unheard experiences of pain, and violence, but also of hopes and possible futures. From our different personal, historical-social positionalities in many different parts of the world, we are asked to bear witness to such experiences: through our acts of reading and new ways of knowing, we may contribute towards fulfilling the fundamental goal of the book, that of *No Repetición* (Luis Eduardo Celis, Chapter 1) and an end to violence, *Basta Ya*! (Blanca Yaneth González Pinzón, Chapters 2 and 3).

In conceptualising this complex book which is produced and published in two languages, Spanish and English, and available open access, it seems to me that two important decisions were made by the lead editor, Blanca Yaneth González Pinzón and the contributing authors. The first decision was to prioritise the inclusion of accounts and analyses of contributors who, over many years, have been actively working with adults and children in community-based projects in the recuperation of individual and Collective Memory, rather than to impose any single *a priori* rigid academic or disciplinary framework. The contributors therefore come from, and draw on, a range of practices and discourses – journalism, academia, art and film, philology and linguistics, education, literature, human rights, sociology, urban geography, cosmogony and grassroots activism. The primary aim of the contributors is to articulate the feelings, meanings and subjectivities of people who have experienced violence in different ways and from different positionalities: children forced into guerilla fighting, combatants taking violent and non-violent action, indigenous communities attacked by one or more factions, hired killers *(sicarios)* acting for different interests, citizens in urban and rural areas suffering violence. In seeking to represent the complex and previously often unheard narratives, contributors draw on what they consider to be both valuable insider (emic) and outsider (etic) categories, ranging from the more conventionally established academic etic categories such as *narrative, discourse, hegemony* to local emic categories such as *land, Tierra Madre, the strength of the umbilical cord* which are grounded in indigenous cosmovision perspectives of the strong but vulnerable interrelationship between land and peoples, body and spirit, people and the universe. Readers approaching this book from within a monologic academic disciplinary space will be challenged to rethink core presuppositions founded solely on Northern/Western categories.

The second important decision that all of us involved in the creation of the book had to make centres on the amount and level of macro-contextual detail essential for a multidisciplinary and transnational readership, with greater and lesser familiarity of Colombian history and politics. The decision to offer detailed layers of context, drawing on sociology, politics and history (particularly in the Introduction and Chapter 1) enables readers from our different understandings to begin to grapple with and come to recognise (rather than misrecognise; Bourdieu, 1990) the specific narratives presented. For while at one level, we do not need to know the details of every war to be able to hear and understand human pain, it is important that we to come to know more about specific geohistorical conflicts to deepen our understanding, to look beyond our immediate borders towards building a shared social imaginary (Castoriadis, 1987; Pérez, 1999) of the world we inhabit and create.

The collection calls us to engage intellectually and emotionally with people's lived experience of coming to know their past, present and future and the significance of the relationship between these different timescapes. Intellectually – thinking here of academic disciplinary spaces – we will each no doubt draw on categories and frameworks familiar to us to connect with the experiences and lives touched on in the book. As a reader coming from the broad fields of social linguistics and literacy studies, for me the chapters connect powerfully with works within these fields which centre on the problematics of language, power and social transformation. Here, I highlight four dimensions which are of concern to me and which I think intersect powerfully in this collection.

- **Voice.** Voice is central to this book at the levels of *ideology* – foregrounding issues of power and the need to actively seek out the voices of those socially/historically marginalised – *epistemology* foregrounding the significance of multiple perspectives and sources of data types in generating knowledge – *methodology* foregrounding the need to develop methodologies which value insider or 'emic' perspectives. This book works at these different layers of voice, making clear the *processes* (workshops, interviews, reflection, film and artefact creation) through which memory becomes instantiated in the *textual representation* of voices, verbal extracts, images, film and textiles. The chapters also repeatedly underscore the significance of voice as 'uptake' (Blommaert, 2005) that is, to exist, voices need to be heard and acknowledged. The importance of being heard is underlined by those sharing their narratives, *Saber que alguien lo escucha, sin juzgarlo/ To know that someone is listening, without judging you* (a woman giving *testimonio*, Chapter 3). Different linguistic and semiotic resources are shown as potentially enabling the 'sayability/'decibilidad' of what often remains unsaid/unsayable (Violi, as discussed in Chapter 8).

- **The body and symbolic violence.** The way violence is experienced physically and inscribed symbolically – through language(s), discourses, image(ination) – is central to the narratives in this book, echoing the significance of *habitus* (Bourdieu, 1977) for understanding the constraints and possibilities for meaning making, and fundamentally challenging any straightforward masculinist Western/Northern dichotomies such as mind/body, lived experience/discourse, people/place, society/natural universe (Anzaldúa, 2021; Cabnal, 2019). The importance of adopting a cosmogonic orientation to understand people's narratives is emphasised in particular in relation to the indigenous Nasa People, which includes the importance of accepting the impossibility of ever reaching full expression or representation of meaning in words (Chapter 4). As reflected in this book, the body cannot be separated from symbolic expression and meaning. The body experiences and witnesses violence and at the same time is part of reconfiguring and reimagining bodily social spaces: an example is that of the women 'reincorporadas', reincorporated combatants, challenging patriarchal norms in 'everyday' civil society (Chapter 7.)
- **(Dis/re) placed resources and subjectivities.** The notion of 'placed resources' (Blommaert, 2005; Scollon & Scollon, 2003) which signals the ways in which all semiotic resources including language are tied to places in complex and problematic ways is at the heart of many narratives in this book. *Si hubiéramos estado en otro lugar, nuestras palabras habrían sido diferentes/If we had been in another place, our words would have been different* (Mujeres Ave Fénix, quoted in the Introduction). The specific semiotic resources that people use for articulating Memory and truth – spoken and written languages and discourses, film, weaving – are tied to specific places and the local meanings attached to such places, often in contradistinction to hegemonic discourses about wars and conflict. However, what the book foregrounds in particular is the notion of *dis*placed resources, that is the impact of the enforced displacing of peoples – Colombia has one of the largest displaced populations in the world (ACNUR 2016) – on the fracturing of semiotic, discoursal and symbolic resources, with consequences for the ways in which Memory and truth can be articulated (particularly evident in Chapters 4 and 7). This spatial fracturing also involves a complex temporal displacement, a sociopolitical dynamic which is underlined in decolonial works (e.g. Grosfoguel, 2007; Mignolo, 2013), and which makes people's articulation of memories (different moments and places in the past) in relation to the present (what it is and what it could become) often a painful and deeply troubling experience. Furthermore, this fragmentation of displaced resources mirrors the complex subjectivities of the many people who – across time and place – have lived experiences of being both perpetrators and survivors of violence. A key focus throughout the book is

how dis-placed resources can be re-placed with meanings and possibilities for a transformed future.
- **Semiotic resources towards** *No Repeticion* **and transformation.** The book foregrounds the different ways in which clusters of semiotic and symbolic resources can be harnessed to the goal of *No Repetición* of future violence. Absence or forgetting/letting go may be as important a part of this process as explicitly recuperating some memories (Chapter 2). Many chapters in the book illustrate the ways in which creative interventions – verbal narratives, film making, weaving – mediated by teachers, participants, artists, journalists, comrades and family members can enable the expression of Memory but also the invention of future hopes. The collapsing of the relationship between 'the critical' (often construed as rational) and 'the creative/poetic' (often construed as emotional) echoes a concern in social linguistics and literacy studies (e.g. Aboelezz, 2014; López-Gopar *et al.*, 2024) to move beyond such binary frames to enact transformed subjectivities and agency for the future. Similarly, the personal, social and symbolic significance of the labour of creating critical-creative material artefacts as part of this process is underscored (in particular, Chapters 6 and 8).

Emotionally, the book is a necessarily troubling read. It is painful to witness pain. Different parts of the book may also speak to our different personal narratives of pain, conflict and grief, and our attempts to come to terms with these and move into new ways of being and knowing.

The chapters encourage us to draw on the range of semiotic and aesthetic resources available to us – in addition to any theorisations or disciplinary abstractions we have become familiar with – to help in such attempts.

Como volver a nacer	Like being born again
después de años turbulentos	after turbulent years
esquivando silencios	dodging silences
ahuyentando espinas	scaring thorns away
¿Cómo volver a nacer?	How to be born again?
calculando cada paso	calculating each step
conteniendo cada emoción	holding still each emotion
para sobrevivir cada día	to survive each day
¿Cómo volver a nacer?	How to be born again?
en una jauría de ecos	amidst a howl of furious echoes
perseguido por fantasmas pasados	haunted by past ghosts
asediado por trampas ajenas	besieged by others' traps

Como volver a nacer	Like being born again
buscando ritmos distantes	seeking distant rhythms
cultivando sendas ocultas	cultivating hidden paths
parando el tiempo	stopping time
(Guillermo Garcia Maza, Extracts, Spanish original, Unpublished)	(Guillermo Garcia Maza, Extracts, Spanish original, Trans. G.G. Maza, Unpublished)

The chapters in this book require us, as readers from our different specific positionalities (geopolitical, academic, experiential), to dig deep into our intellectual and emotional resources to grasp what it is we are listening to and are coming to know. A central goal in the chapters, and the projects underlying these, is to explore the possibilities for coming to know differently, to build and sustain a world edging towards peace. Everyday knowing is prioritised over codified, institutionally legitimised knowledge in this book, which, while drawing explicitly on both Western/Northern and Southern/decolonial research and theory, foregrounds local knowing – of individuals, peoples, communities, political and human rights activists – as the key resource for personal, social and epistemological transformation.

This book instantiates people's narratives of knowing and being in Colombia yet it speaks to the lives of peoples and societies in many parts of the world where violence has long been a daily organising thread to existence. Whatever our positionalities, we are all implicated, through our acts of reading/listening and in our daily lives in working towards unravelling that thread. The authors and peoples represented in this book invite us to 'caminar la palabra'/walk the word (Chapter 4) alongside them.

References

Aboelezz, M. (2014) The geosemiotics of Tahrir Square: A study of the relationship between discourse and space. *Journal of Language and Politics* 13 (4), 599–622.

ACNUR (2016) Colombian situation. See https://reporting.unhcr.org/operational/situations/colombia-situation#:~:text=2024%20situation%20overview,the%20Peace%20Agreement%20in%202016 (accessed March 2024).

Anzaldúa, G. (2021) *Borderlands/La frontera: La nueva mestiza* (2nd edn). Capitán Swing Libros.

Blommaert, J. (2005) *Discourse: A Critical Introduction*. Cambridge University Press.

Bourdieu, P. (1977) *Outline of a Theory of Practice* (trans. R. Nice). Cambridge University Press.

Bourdieu, P. (1990) *The Logic of Practice* (trans. R. Nice). Polity Press.

Cabnal, L. (2019) El relato de las violencias desde mi territorio cuerpo-tierra. *En tiempos de muerte: Cuerpos, rebeldías, resistencias* 4, 113–126.

Castoriadis, C. (1987) *The Imaginary Institution of Society*. Polity Press.

Grosfoguel, R. (2007) The epistemic decolonial turn: Beyond political-economy paradigms. *Cultural Studies* 21 (2–3), 211–223.

López-Gopar, M., Córdova-Hernandez, L. and Valtierra Zamudio, J. (2024) (De)colonial multilingual/multiomodal practices. In C. McKinney, P. Makoe and V. Zavala (eds) *The Routledge Handbook of Multilingualism* (2nd edn, pp. 31–46). Routledge.
Mignolo, W. (2013) *De la hermenéutica y la semiosis colonial al pensar descolonial*. Abya-Yala.
Nora, P. (2008) Entre memoria e historia. La problemática de los lugares. In *Los lugares de la memoria*. Trilce.
Pérez, E. (1999) *The Decolonial Imaginary*. Indiana University Press.
Scollon, R. and Scollon, S. (2003) *Discourses in Place. Language in the Material World*. Routledge.

10 *Chronos* and *Kairos*: A Time to Resist and a Time to Speak Out

José Vicente Arizmendi Correa

> There is only one history – the history of man [sic].
> All national histories are merely chapters in the larger one.
> Rabindranath Tagore, 1917

As I turned the pages of this book, I thought of the Greeks and their concept of time. *Chronos* was the giant god who devoured his offspring and embodied the empirical passage of time, divided into past, present and future. It was difficult to escape this idea while reading the chapters in this book, as it seems to permeate the issues of narrative and, of course, the very fact of living.

Chronos inspired famous painters such as Francisco de Goya and Peter Paul Rubens, who depicted the god devouring his children, and Pierre Mignard, who depicted him clipping Cupid's wings. *Chronos* is also the material with which historians and journalists work. Journalism is the 'second hand of history', according to Schopenhauer. Pierre Nora (2008), for his part, linked history to temporal continuities, evolutions and relationships between things.

Since narrative is at the heart of this book, as a form of Memory and knowledge, placing the stories in a chronological perspective and in parallel with Colombian history makes them more meaningful to the reader. Celis's temporal trajectory in Chapter 1 is fundamental to understanding the weight of the *testimonios*, which, although collected at different times, together present a single face of the conflict. The temporal map serves as a backdrop to contextualise the fragments and reflections in the second part of the book, placing them in specific moments of the eight decades that describe the Colombian wars. In Celis's words, 'the narratives that the authors reflect on in this book are correlates of that other great narrative called Colombia'. Hence the idea of Tagore, which serves as a call in the epigraph.

Celis proposes an order in linear time, a tracing of events that helps us to understand a logic based on succession. This particular chronological gaze has the function of helping us to locate in certain stages what has happened and, why not, to risk forwarding some ideas about the future. The stories themselves make the scenario more complex, they give voice to what official history may ignore and, as the book reiterates, they are the great witnesses that ratify the events.

Let us look at some of the events that make up this convulsive timeline, and at the time periods in which the fragments are set.

This book centres on a collection of narratives that emerged from fieldwork carried out between 1985 and 2022. The earliest *testimonio* that appears in these pages was collected in the first quarter of 1985, for the journalistic chronicles published by José Navia (Chapter 4), based on his interaction with the inhabitants of three *resguardos* in the municipality of Toribío, Cauca (number 10 on the map). It is a declaration of intent by one of the first commanders of the recently formed armed movement Quintín Lame, in which echoes of the violence of the 'pájaros', the rural assassins of the 1950s, can be heard, a few months before the most important guerrilla group of the time, the M-19, reached a turning point whose decline was marked with the seizure of the Palace of Justice in Bogotá.

Navia then jumps to 1991, when the Quintín Lame, the M-19 and other armed groups had disappeared and a new constitution was being discussed. In Cauca, however, the FARC moved in to occupy the territory. His ethnographic work lasted until 2019, although to describe the Nasa People's coexistence with the war, Navia's chapter alludes to events from 1965, when the first guerrillas appeared in the indigenous territories, to later document the (re)emergence and development of the indigenous guard in 1971 and the creation of the ONIC. These deliberate jumps in time, however, help to maintain a narrative thread, as the same chronotope comes and goes.

The narratives reviewed by Blanca González (Chapter 3) cover the years 2006–2018 and are set in different parts of the country. In these two decades of the 21st century, as Celis tells us, powerful military structures were dismantled and illusions of peace arose, but a new cycle of violence also emerged. The *testimonios* from this period reflect the spaces opened up by the Law on Victims and Land Restitution (2011) and the five years of peace dialogues between the FARC guerrillas and the government between 2012 and 2016. The first stories of victims whose visibility has been recognised by the State and society and who have been offered support programmes appear, as well as *testimonios* from ex-combatants of paramilitary groups, feminist movements, different ethnic groups, retired soldiers and victims' organisations, among others.

For her part, Claudia Bungard (Chapter 6) has worked with *testimonios* collected between 2006 and 2010, which Celis shows was part of a decade in which the guerrillas' strength doubled as a result of frustrated attempts at dialogue and the coming to power of so-called democratic security, supported by the mafia and paramilitarism and accepted by the population thanks to its rejection of the FARC. Similarly, the control of large productive areas by politicians and the AUC was consolidated, and the resulting dispossession, which, as we see in the stories, is one of the evils that has most affected Colombia, leaving almost seven million internally displaced people. It was the time of the parapolitical investigations, resulting from the denunciations of the opposition and the left-wing sectors against the government. According to Bungard, it was during this period that the first reparation and Memory workshops were promoted in Medellín, as a result of the cascading effect of the Law of Justice and Peace and the Law on Victims and Land Restitution.

The stories that Cecilia Traslaviña works from (Chapter 5), and which were recognised by the Truth Commission as a document of Memory, serve as an indelible record of the fact that children have suffered the war, not only as victims, but also in many cases as perpetrators, forcibly involved in events that they could hardly understand. These stories were collected between 2019 and 2020. Some children were demobilised from the guerrilla groups, as concerted in the Peace Agreement. Because the events took place at the end of the previous decade and the beginning of the current one, the stories do not signal any mitigation of the effects of the war; on the contrary, they reveal the intensification of forms of pain and torture. When a society shamelessly involves children in conflict, moral ruin is at its height, a fact evident not only nationally but globally.

From 2018 to 2020, Colombia 'debuted' the Havana Agreement, and Mario Ramírez-Orozco (Chapter 7), with a group of colleagues from the Universidad de La Salle, spoke to nine former FARC excombatants living in the ETCR of Tierra Grata, Department of Cesar (number 11 on the map). Through their interviews, they sought to identify the imaginaries of peace being constructed by recently reincorporated men and women. We read in the fragments concerns about the uncertainty of an unprecedented event, the demobilisation of the largest number of combatants ever recorded in the country.

Weaving (Chapter 8), another form of symbolic expression centres on the events that took place from the 1990s until the end of the 2010s. From Emilia Perassi's description of the way in which various collectives organised themselves to make weaving and embroidery their form of protest, we conclude that although the war intensified perpetuating the horror, people have found complex forms of resistance that are more powerful in their message, as Navia showed us with the Nasa People.

The chapters in this book show how individuals from villages, hamlets, small towns and large cities were brought together by the conflict. Our greater Colombian history is nothing more than the confluence of these stories, told and collected over the years, now finding a place in Memory and History. As summarised in Celis's chapter, which also belongs to the realm of *Chronos*, the periods between the 1990s and the 2020s find in the chapters first-hand evidence of the Memory recovered, to contribute to history with a capital 'H' what history with a small 'h' would not record.

In my role as a journalist and current director of a university radio station, I directed the collection of 213 interviews (from 2020 to 2023, for 78 of which I was personally responsible) to produce and broadcast four radio series that made public the *testimonios* of people affected by the armed conflict in many parts of Colombia. As I read this book, I thought about how some of these *testimonios* came to complement Celis's map, while contributing to the objective of the primary aim of all this work, the collection of Memory. We have seen how the *testimonios* collected in the different chapters give a detailed account of the events that took place before, during and very close to the Agreement between the Colombian State and the FARC. In the *testimonios* collected between 2020 and 2023, this *Chronos* is completed to insist, on the one hand, that the conflict in Colombia has not yet ended and, on the other hand, that we cannot allow ourselves to forget it. The traditional media, with its narrative full of immediacy and entertainment, can distract us from an essential objective as a nation, which is to recover what we have been and what we continue to be in these turbulent times. Alternative media, such as a university radio station, continues to participate in that purpose.

Ricoeur (2000), referred to in Chapter 2, argues that everything can be narrated because it happens in time. But the time to narrate may not be time itself, nor the present. It is also the work of the Greeks, the *Kairos*, that other temporal dimension related to the 'right moment', a concept without much plastic embodiment, which does not seem to have excited any significant artist at any time. There are few images of *Kairos* in Western culture, perhaps because its meaning has to be extracted from the context in which it is used. *Kairos*, as a time when the circumstances are perfect for the realisation of a meaningful action, helped me to realise that the narratives collected here are also the product of the specific moment in which they were produced and sufficiently processed by a person to acquire their status of sayability (chapters by Perassi and Lillis).

The oral *testimonios* I present below, collected in 2021 and 2022, are the most recent in this timeline; however, what the interviewees recount refers to their past and their current balance in the present time. Perhaps at the time, for whatever reason, it would not have been possible for people to elaborate their experiences. Now, years later, they find this the 'favourable or right time' along with the conditions to produce them, but above all, the will, in this case of an alternative communicative university project, to collect them and rescue them from oblivion and indifference.

A woman interviewee points to the significance of the right time for her *testimonio*:

> Si su sumercé me hubiera hecho esta entrevista hace diez años atrás yo hubiera llorado, llorado, llorado. En este momento no es que no me duela saber que hoy no tengo mi hermana, pero me da un alivio muy grande saber que ese dolor tan grande se me transformó fue en amor y en servicio a la comunidad. (Entrevista a mujer de 48 años de Algeciras, Huila (número 17 en el mapa) para la serie radial *50 vidas*, 4 de octubre de 2022)
>
> If *su sumercé* [you] had done this interview with me ten years ago, I would have cried, cried, cried. At this moment it doesn't mean that it doesn't hurt me to know that today I don't have my sister, but it gives me great relief to know that that great pain was transformed into love and service to the community. (Interview with 48-year-old woman from Algeciras, Huila (number 17 on the map) for the radio series *50 lives*, 4 October 2022)

Specifically, at the time of the events she refers to, it was not the right time for her to speak out.

For another citizen, silence and indecision were determined by the closeness of danger, which prevented him and his people from talking about what had happened. Now, after the demobilisations, he feels that there is a reasonable distance to tell what happened.

> Nosotros demoramos once años en silencio. Cuando los paramilitares se empezaron a desmovilizar, nosotros [dijimos]: 'ah, una masacre', 'esta masacre, esta masacre, esta masacre¡ Le empezó a aparecer dueño a las masacres! Pero a Los Guáimaros, que era la tercera más grande de Bolívar, no le aparecía dueño. Es más, hasta la presente van 20 años y todavía no tiene dueño, ni intelectual ni material, y puedes preguntar en el pueblo y la mayoría, todo el mundo sabe quiénes son y quiénes fueron y todo, pero para la Fiscalía todavía no hay responsable, ni intelectual ni material. ¿Por qué? Porque falta voluntad. (Entrevista a hombre de 40 años de San Juan Nepomuceno, Cesar (número 11 en el mapa) para la serie radial *50 vidas*, 5 de septiembre de 2022)
>
> We spent eleven years in silence. When the paramilitaries began to demobilise, we [said]: 'ah, a massacre', 'this massacre, this massacre, this massacre! But Los Guáimaros, which was the third largest massacre in Bolívar, had no one taking responsibility. What's more, it's been 20 years and it still has no owner, neither intellectual nor material, and you can ask in the village and the majority, everyone knows who they are and who they were and everything, but for the Prosecutor's Office there is still no one responsible, neither intellectual nor material. Why? Because there is a lack of will. (Interview with 40-year-old man from San Juan Nepomuceno, Cesar (number 11 on the map) for the radio series *50 lives*, 5 September 2022)

Other *testimonios* come from the desire to keep the Memory alive, not only to honour their loved ones, but also to ensure that justice is done and measures are taken to prevent a repetition of the crimes. For all of those speaking out, an invitation, questions or proposals for activities came at the right time, and they agreed to respond, to participate, to make themselves visible. In some cases, such as the cases of former child combatants mentioned in Chapter 5, acceptance was not immediate; it required a process.

For a resident of Apartadó, Antioquia (number 2 on the map), whom we interviewed for one of the station's documentary series, speaking out at this moment is a way of moving out of invisibility and from the periphery of indifference to the centre of recognition, not only individually but collectively (Arroyave, 2013; Fernández, 2000; López, 2012; Rueda, 2013).

> Bueno, yo soy una viuda de las que tanto ha rechazado la guerra, que en el momento ando pensando y mirando, y buscando que haya una oportunidad para cada una de aquellas personas secretas, que tienen la verdad, que no se atreven a decirla por miedo, por temor. Yo soy una de tantas de esas. Pero yo digo que para que esto no quede oculto, quiero que esto salga al aire, que todas seamos capaces de decir la verdad, mostrar todo aquello que nos hizo sufrir. (Entrevista a mujer de Apartadó, Antioquia (número 2 en el mapa) para la serie radial *Tiempo de restaurar*, 17 de octubre de 2021)
>
> Well, I am one of those widows who have rejected war so much, that at the moment I am thinking and looking, and looking for an opportunity for each of those secret people, who have the truth, who do not dare to tell it out of fear, out of fear. I am one of those people. But I say that in order for this not to remain hidden, I want this to be aired, for all of us to be able to tell the truth, to show everything that made us suffer. (Interview with woman from Apartadó, Antioquia (number 2 on the map) for the radio series *Time to restore*, 17 October 2021)

These decisions to participate, to make themselves visible at a certain moment, were based not only on the macro dimension of what was happening in the country and in their region, but above all on their vital moment, on what they considered important or urgent and according to their emotional and mental states. The decision to speak or not to speak, I believe, was also an act of ethics, understood as the individual and collective dictate of 'what should be done'. Those of us who have carried out preliminary research for interviews or face-to-face dynamics with victims or ex-victims know the ethical considerations that emerge when people are answering certain questions or participating in an activity, even if there are expectations of healing or reparation. It is not just a matter of shyness but of concerns about fundamental ethical issues.

One consideration is of course, suspicion. Who is behind the project? Who will be asking the questions or driving the momentum? What will they do with what I say or do? Will there be video and photos or just sound? Should I use my real name? These are some of the questions that make visible the precautions of people who are at risk and have to judge whether they are in the right *Kairos* to speak. Ethics is also present in the narrative thread of many of the *testimonios*. In the lives of many of those affected by violence, there have been decisive moments that were ultimately ethical dilemmas: whether to join the guerrillas, the legal armed forces or the paramilitary groups; whether to take revenge on those who killed one's father, sister or children; whether to stay where one lives, to go elsewhere, to put down roots in a new destination or to return.

A second consideration is that of addressivity. Each *testimonio* has an addressee (Beverley, 2005; Rivara-Kamiji, 2007; Yúdice, 2002), and it is in this ethical dimension that the greatest receptivity could be achieved on the part of the readers or viewers of the stories. The *testimonio* of a mother of five children in the southeast of Antioquia, who lost two of her children, one to the guerrillas and the other to the paramilitaries, will certainly resonate in the mind and heart of any sensitive person. But the fact that she decided to lead a crusade with all of the residents of her village to 'get the men out of the war', in which she ended up working side by side with those who recruited her sons, makes her a much more powerful and challenging figure.

A third consideration on which I felt the need to reflect as a journalist, and which also has to do with the ethical dimension of asking for, receiving, collecting or listening to a *testimonio*, is the role of the person who mediates and makes its production possible, whether that person is a researcher, journalist or historian. Experience has taught me that the 'right moment' for a *testimonio* to flow depends on specific circumstances. Simple examples are: Will the interview with the interviewer take place in the interviewee's home, in a 'neutral' place such as an NGO headquarters, a school or a hotel? In what specific place: the kitchen, the living room, an empty hall? Will other people be present? How long will the conversation be? Will video or photos be taken in addition to the voice?

The professional radio or television journalist also takes into account the circumstances that may affect the quality of the material: the ambient noise, the type of light available, the time of day, the way they identify themself to the interviewer, previous conversations. During the interview, a responsible journalist will often begin to think about the headline, the editing sequence, any additional material that would be needed to help the audience understand what is being said, in what context and with what possible impact. And, of course, he or she will make every effort to ensure that what is broadcast accurately reflects what the interviewee has said verbatim, avoiding manipulation, voluntary or otherwise.

We are the contemporary survivors of this conflict. Our absences and omissions would only deepen the wounds if our way of being were not one of solidarity. *Chronos* comes to our aid to say, with Octavio Paz (1962), that 'everything is present and all the centuries are this present'; in each Colombian there are the ideas and feelings of his or her previous generations. If we consider that a generation is about 20 or 25 years, we can estimate that at least three generations have lived the direct or indirect consequences of the conflict. So we have a responsibility. We now have several channels to enact it: this book, the many workshops that the chapters report on, and the documentary series by an alternative cultural and university radio station.

Throughout this work, authors of chapters have reiterated their/our intention to make the survivors visible, to restore some of their violated dignity, and to recover the Memory of what happened, which is buried under so many layers of violence concealed by the official accounts. But there are also two fundamental objectives without which any attempt at visibility would be useless: the 'non-repetition' of the events and the collective healing of a nation that, as Mario Ramírez points out in Chapter 7, has not been given the opportunity to recognise its ingrained evils and has lacked the pedagogy to accept a reality in which people of different ideological persuasions coexist and are obliged to think about reconciliation, despite their differences.

References

Beverley, J. (2005) Testimonio, subalternity, and narrative authority. In N.K. Denzin and Y.S. Lincoln (eds) *The Sage Handbook of Qualitative Research* (3rd edn, pp. 547–558). Sage Publications.

Fernández, J.W. (2000) Peripheral wisdom. In A. Cohen (ed.) *Signifying Identities. Anthropological Perspectives on Boundaries and Contested Values* (pp. 117–135). Routledge.

López, C. (2012) *Trauma, memoria y cuerpo: El testimonio femenino en Colombia (1985–2000)*. Asociación Internacional de Literatura y Cultura Femenina Hispánica.

Nora, P. (2008) Entre memoria e historia. La problemática de los lugares. In *Los lugares de la memoria*. Trilce.

Paz, O. (1962) *Blanco*. Poemario.

Ricoeur, P. (2000) Narratividad, fenomenología y hermenéutica. *Anàlisi: Quaderns de comunicació i cultura* 25, 189–207.

Rivara-Kamaji, G. (2007) El testimonio: Una forma de relato. *Revista Bajo Palabra* 2, 111–118.

Rueda, A.J. (2013) Reasoned historical memory. A proposal to include victims of Colombian internal armed conflict. *Revista de Historia Regional y Local* 5 (10), 17–51.

Yúdice, G. (1996) Testimonio and postmodernism. In G. Gugelberger (ed.) *The Real Thing: Testimonial Discourse and Latin America* (pp. 42–57). Duke University Press.

11 Closing Thoughts

Blanca Yaneth González Pinzón

Beyond gathering fragments from different voices to bring readers closer to the Colombian armed conflict, the panoramic view through which this book has been structured represents a genuine attempt to abandon an abstract and isolated notion of peace, and instead fill it with specific content, with new or recovered knowledge (Garzón, 2014; Muñoz-González, 2012; Muñoz, 2013; Reyes-Aparicio, 2013). The *testimonios* included throughout this book, show how the girls, boys, young people and adults not only returned to the past to recover part of their personal memories, but in so doing contribute both to the building of a collective Colombian Memory, and also, the imagining of a transformed Colombian future.

Despite the fact that their stories took them through different emotional and existential moments, the survivors who participated in these oral, pictorial, material and written narratives also reworked them, rationalized them, and became aware of what had happened, in order to give new meaning to their lives. In no case was this process of re-signification a straightforward, linear path; rather, it was a tortuous journey.

Why does Narrative appear as a central and general concept in the title of this book, and Testimony as a particular form of its materialization? Chase (2005: 667) poses a series of questions that not only reinforce the value of the *testimonios* collected but also highlights their importance for others and for the societies in which we are immersed: What kinds of narratives disrupt oppressive social processes? How and when do researchers' analyses and representations of others' stories promote social justice and democratic processes? Moreover, for whom are these social processes disrupted and facilitated? Which audiences need to hear which researchers' and narrators' stories? The chapters in the second part of the book explore these and other questions about survivors' lives and how these were affected, how survivors have made sense of what has happened, and how they face the future as a possibility for survival.

Narratives are structures capable of holding information that encompasses and transcends the intellectual; they integrate intersubjective, perceptual and emotional dimensions to human lived experience. Approaching traumatic and painful stories requires a great deal of effort, because logic and understanding of facts alone are not enough for citizens to be able to relate to the complex world in which they/we have (had) to live. It is therefore essential that listeners, readers, and observers possess a narrative imagination that enables them/you/us to empathize with the experiences of others, which can be achieved by adopting what Nussbaum (2015) refers to as 'an intelligent reading of another's story'.

For the fundamental question posed by the CEV in Colombia, 'How did people's lives, the conflict, its dynamics, and the contexts that explain them come together?'. Narrative and, of course, listening to narratives were part of the methodological approach towards clarifying and documenting the truth. From 5 April 2017 to 28 June 2022, the Commission collected *testimonios* in multiple listening spaces, from more than 1900 public and private events. In these spaces, the Commission listened to people individually and collectively: to peasant and ethnic communities, neighbourhood organisations, women and LGTBIQ+ people, children and young people, business people, traders, students, ex-combatants of the former FARC guerrillas, teachers, religious figures, journalists, members of the security forces and, in general, anyone who wanted to give a *testimonio*. Generating narrative thus functioned as part of a methodological design (Chase, 2005; Cohen *et al.*, 2000) and, as expressed in the Commission's reports (2022: 99), the collection of narratives 'is an attempt to question society in ethical and political terms, based on a narrative that articulates the factors, contexts, patterns and cases derived from the process of listening and contrasting'.

Clifford Geertz (1973, cited in Denzin & Lincoln, 2005: 17) highlights the transformative power of narrative in research approaches: 'The old, functional, positivist, behaviorist, totalising approaches to the human disciplines gave way to a more pluralistic, interpretive and open perspective'. In this way, narrative expands the possibilities not only for gathering information but also of interpreting it. Ultimately, the use of narratives in social research is justified by the possibility of describing, deepening and revealing meanings, unravelling subjectivities and explaining reasons for events produced in a specific space-time, and their impact on society and culture. Narrative research has contributed to the social sciences enabling creativity, elucidating the complexity and variability of subjective constructions, and by revealing the power of context and the multiple circumstances involved in the configuration of an identity and reality, permeated by spatial-temporal aspects. Both subjectivity and objectivity, imagination and reality are evident in the *testimonios* represented in the book.

As Feliu argues (2007: 269, based on Richardson, 2000) in order for narratives to fulfil essential social functions, they must provide elements such as:

(a) **Substantive contribution**: if the narrative contributes to the understanding of social life;
(b) **Aesthetic merit**: if the experience is interesting in its production, the descriptions contribute to understanding and invite further reading;

(c) **Reflexivity**: if the subjectivities, the conscious ethical-political positions of the producer and the decision-making processes can be identified to contribute to the value offered by the author;
(d) **Impact**: if the narrative raises new questions, challenges emotionally and intellectually, and stimulates further writing, action and research;
(e) **Realism**: if the story is plausible and leaves the impression of being in front of a lived experience.

As has been seen, the complex, profound, and painful *testimonios* collected in this book provide clear examples of these five elements.

As Jara and Vidal (1986) state, every narrativized image carries traces of the real; when the narratives of many people confront us with situations of resistance and demands for social justice and truth, we are no longer merely dealing with a simple story but with a *testimonio*. In these fragments of stories, we can observe the transformation of the concept of Testimony, which goes beyond resistance literature, where it has its roots, to become a means of denouncing community struggles for survival (Yúdice, 2002). The *testimonios* illustrated in this book, through the particularization of what was narrated, reveal material and real traces of people who have suffered human rights violations, making explicit the subjective and objective conditions of 'what' happened, 'where,' 'how,' to 'whom,' and a possible 'why.'

Narrating is a way of breaking the wall of silence and oblivion that separates us from the present, says Pablo Montoya (2022). Memory, Historical Memory, and Collective Memory – core concepts in this book – share a teleological condition by becoming the goal of what was narrated. Therefore, throughout this book, discussions revolve around the definition of the concept of Memory itself, how it enters the social arena, how much of what is narrated in the *testimonios* – by reconstructing what happened and contrasting various voices – contributes to people remembering their past, and, finally, the validity of the *testimonios* in terms of Historical Memory. In the words of Riaño (2006: 62), narratives form a 'bridge memory that connects past, present, and future'; for this reason, they constitute a fundamental part of Historical Memory and are necessary so that those prone to 'forgetting' cannot ignore so much ignominy and so that we can build a counter-hegemonic Memory in the search for long-term peace.

Given that they are an exercise in Memory, the *testimonios* necessarily involve a process of reinterpretation. This is because, in a public and social sense, what is narrated does not remain in the past but is consciously transformed into a political resource for demands and vindication (Garzón, 2014; Jelin, 2001; Muñoz-González, 2012). Memory is not only what happened, it is its interpretation and significance (Reyes-Aparicio, 2013). Even that which is unconsciously forgotten, and sometimes consciously set aside, is a constituent part of the will to remember (Halbwachs,

2004; Muñoz, 2013; Reyes-Aparicio, 2013; Rieff, 2012; Vélez-Rendón, 2003), as well as the will to silences (Garzón, 2014). It is for these reasons that the *testimonios* illustrated in this book, in the period of transition towards peace that Colombia is currently going through, are significant for the recovery of Memory.

Far from warranting a single history, which is the tendency of official history, these *testimonios* create universes of reference and existential territories that highlight singularity, exception, and rarity, even in their very interrelationship with others (Bruner, 1986; Chase, 2005; Muñoz-González, 2012; Reyes-Aparicio 2013). Individual *testimonios* are polyphonies that are distinct and absent from other possible experiences. The use of the first-person singular does not limit accounts to one person: rather each *testimonio* is imbued with the events experienced and the histories of many other survivors (Beverley, 1989: 548–549).

This book is built from oral, written, material and pictorial narratives that give voice to subjects who are generally anonymous and marginalized. They not only offer proposals for social justice but also unleash a liberating power. De Salvo (1999), Halbwachs (2004), Jensen (2005) and Reyes-Aparicio (2013) recognize the therapeutic value of such narratives, resulting from the dignity and visibility that the subjects acquire; overcoming the condition of being a cipher involves readers and listeners recognizing that these stories are worthwhile and meaningful.

The *testimonios* and analyses in this book run parallel to that other great story called Colombia. Just as the country has gone through tortuous events, incessantly searching for moments of calm, and is now projecting itself forward with hope towards a different future, the *testimonios* in this book have followed a similar path. A just end for them is the possibility of a life in total peace. This involves all of us acting as one single, united social body which rejects violence and works to recuperate Memory to ensure that there will be 'non repetition'.

This multidisciplinary book has brought together several conversations. Writers and researchers have sought to address the thorny issue of the audience of this book, considering who might 'benefit' from their analyses and research and who might need to know them (Chase, 2005). The range of perspectives, drawn from fields as diverse as education, the arts, journalism, literature, politics and social work, offers scholars in the human and social sciences a comprehensive understanding of Narrative, Testimony, Memory and Knowledge. The book also provides methodological guidance on how to implement initiatives without revictimization but rather ensuring the dignity of survivors, crucial in any initiative, for example by NGOs and any organizations that design and develop support and symbolic reparation strategies for people who have suffered traumatic situations.

In my opinion, this is one of the essential strengths of the book: to express, from different theoretical positions, what a society needs to do to recognize itself. Placing men, women, boys, girls and adolescents at the center of such recognition surely represents the most refined goal of the human sciences gathered here.

The book's content and discussions have relevance beyond Colombia's borders and serve as a reference point for other countries in similar situations. Colombia is not the only country to have experienced post-conflict crises. However, it is the most recent to have signed a peace agreement and to be moving towards a life of harmony, overcoming countless obstacles. This makes the country a point of reference for understanding conflict and its aftermath, as what has been achieved and what has not indicate and illustrate what can be accomplished when efforts are focused on finding reparations. Gamson (2002: 189) states that storytelling 'fosters empathy across different social occasions'. Because of the honesty offered in these chapters and how the experiences are narrated, I am sure that readers in different parts of the world will have found in these fragments of *testimonios* possibilities for identification, for understanding the pain of others, and for understanding the position of all actors involved in a war, including those who belong to no side.

This book has insisted on a call to the collective: we are all part of a social apparatus and are all involved in the tragedies of Colombians. Tolstoi (2013 [1899]) an expert on war and its catastrophes, said: 'If all are not saved, what is the use of some being saved'. Today we are all witnesses to the ravages of war in many parts of the world, and no one can escape its effects. Juan Gabriel Vásquez (2021) says that the inescapable reality is that we are all here together and no one can escape. He asks: Wouldn't it be a good idea to try to understand who the others are?

References

Beverley, J. (1989) *Testimonio: Sobre la política de la verdad*. Bonilla Artigas Editores.
Bruner, J. (1986) *Actual Minds, Possible Worlds*. Cambridge.
Chase, S. (2005) Narrative inquiry: Multiple lenses, approaches, voices. In N.K. Denzin and Y.S. Lincoln (eds) *The Sage Handbook of Qualitative Research* (3rd edn, pp. 651–679). Sage Publications.
Cohen, L., Manion, L. and Morrison, K. (2000) *Research Methods in Education*. Routledge.
Comisión para el Esclarecimiento de la Verdad, la Convivencia y la No Repetición (2022) Hay futuro si hay verdad: Informe Final de la Comisión para el Esclarecimiento de la Verdad, la Convivencia y la No Repetición. See https://www.comisiondelaverdad.co/hay-futuro-si-hay-verdad (accessed February 2023).
De Salvo, L. (1999) *Writing as a Way of Healing. How Telling Our Stories Transform Our Lives*. HarperCollins.
Denzin, N. and Lincoln, Y. (eds) (2005) *The Sage Handbook of Qualitative Research* (3rd edn). Sage Publications.
Gamson, W. (2002) How storytelling can be empowering. In K.A. Cerulo (ed.) *Culture in Mind: Toward a Sociology of Culture and Cognition* (pp. 187–198). Routledge.
Halbwachs, M. (2004) El sueño y las imágenes-recuerdos. *Los marcos sociales de la memoria* 39, 13–56.

Jara, R. and Vidal, H. (1986) *Testimonio y literatura*. Sociedad para el Estudio de las Literaturas Revolucionarias Hispánicas y Lusófonas Contemporáneas.
Jelin, E. (2001) *Los trabajos de la memoria*. Siglo XXI Editores.
Jensen, S. (2005) Del viaje no deseado al viaje de retorno. Representaciones del exilio en Libro de Navíos y Borrascas y Tangos. El exilio de Gardel. In E. Jelin and A. Longoni (comps.) *Escrituras, imágenes y escenarios ante la represión* (pp. 167–202). Siglo XXI Editores.
Montoya, P. (2022) *Una patria universal*. Editorial Universidad de Antioquia.
Muñoz, C.A. (2013) Acercamiento al concepto de memoria desde la visión crítica de la democracia. In A. Castillejo and F. Reyes (eds) *Violencia, memoria y sociedad: Debates y agendas en la Colombia actual* (pp. 375–387). Universidad Santo Tomás.
Muñoz-González, G. (2012) El alcance metodológico de las narrativas. In S. Soler Castillo (Comp.) *Lenguaje y Educación: Perspectivas metodológicas y teóricas para su estudio* (pp. 161–182). Universidad Distrital Francisco José de Caldas.
Nussbaum, M. (2015) Discurso de recibimiento del doctorado honoris causa de la Universidad de Antioquia. See https://redfilosofia.es/atheneblog/2015/12/25/discurso-de-martha-nussbaum-en-antioquia-con-ocasion-de-su-honoris-causa/ (accessed November 2023).
Reyes-Aparicio, P. (2013) Narrativa, violencia y memoria: Rupturas y secuencias. In A. Castillejo and F. Reyes (eds) *Violencia, memoria y sociedad: Debates y agendas en la Colombia actual* (pp. 237–256). Ediciones USTA.
Riaño, P. (2006) *Jóvenes, memoria y violencia en Medellín: Una antropología del recuerdo y el olvido*. Universidad de Antioquia.
Richardson, L. (2000) Writing: A method of inquiry. In N.K. Denzin and Y.S. Lincoln (eds) *Handbook of Qualitative Research*. (2nd edn, pp. 923–48). Sage.
Rieff, D. (2012) *Contra la memoria*. Random House Mondadori.
Tolstoi, L. (2013) *Resurrección*. Alianza Editorial.
Vásquez, J.G. (2021) Prólogo. In C. Ngozi Adichie (auth) *Todos deberíamos ser feministas* (pp. 5–8). Random House.
Yúdice, G. (2002) Testimonio y concientización. In J. Beverley and H. Achugar (eds) *La voz del otro: Testimonio, subalternidad y verdad narrativa* (pp. 221–242). Papiro.

Index

Note: References in *italics* are to figures, those in **bold** to tables.

Acedo 17 31, 151, 159, 173
ACIN (Association of Indigenous *Cabildos* of Northern Cauca) 104
Acosta, Luis 98, 103, 104
ACR (High Council for Social and Economic Reintegration of Armed Groups and Individuals) **47**
acronyms xvii–xx
active life 185
adaptation 58–59
addressivity 220
Adichie, Chimamanda Ngozi 67
ADM-19 (M-19 Democratic Alliance) 6–7, 8, 83
ADTTC *see* Digital Archive of Testimonial Textiles
Agamben, G. 121, 184
Agreement signed between Colombian state and FARC-EP guerrillas in 2016 158–159, 169–170
   context of agreement 159–160
   difficulties of transition 161–167
Almendra, Vilma 196
AMARÚ (Association of Women Defenders of Water and Life) 191
Amazon 7
analogue animation 123
ANAPO (National Popular Alliance) 5–6
Andes 7
Animated Documentary (2013) 114, 124
animation workshop with ex-guerrilla children 108–113
   evocation 114
   expressive and technical possibilities of animation 114–116
   meeting to create collectively 116–125
   mimetic/non-mimetic substitution 114
   possibilities of animation to expand imaginaries around violence 125–131
   techniques 123
Antioquia 30
ANUC (National Association of Peasant Users) 5
April 19 Movement (M-19) 6–7, 8, 83
Arango, Horacio 156
Aranguren-Romero, J. 187, 188, 195
Arendt, Hannah 185
   What Is Politics? 199
Arias, B. 185, 186
Arizmendi, José Vicente xxv
ARN *see* Governmental Agency for Reincorporation and Normalisation, 2022
Arroyave, Iván Darío 143–144, 145, 147, 150, 152
Arroyave, José Luis 143
Arroyave, M. 25
Artesanal Tecnológica xxvi, 191
Artesanías Choibá [Choiba Handicrafts] 191
Asociación Minga 189
Association for Women and Work **188**
Association of Indigenous *Cabildos* of Northern Cauca (ACIN) 104
Association of Women Defenders of Water and Life (AMARÚ) 191
Association of Women Victims, Craftswomen and Innovators of Today for Tomorrow (ASVIMARIN) 191
Aterciopelados 104
AUC (United Self-Defence Forces of Colombia) 9
Augé, M. 188

Autonomous Indigenous Intercultural University (UAIIN) 104
Ave Fénix collective 66
  narratives structure/progression **68**
  The Phoenix Refuge: The End of a Night of Agony 74
Ayala, Julio César Turbay 7

Bacic, Roberta 190
Barco, President Virgilio 7, 8
Bautista, Cristina 94, 95
Begin Again tapestry 197–199, *198*
Bellavista massacre 193
Bellavista Nuevo 197
Bello-Tocancipá, A. et al. 20 186, 187, 188, 189, 195
Benposta Foundation 108, 109, 113, 118, 121, 131
Betancur, Belisario 7
Betancur, Marden 94
Beverley, John 61, 63, 151, 159
Bhabha, Homi 170
Blandón Uribe, Helly Johana 145, 150, 152
Blommaert, J. 209, 210
Bloque Sur (South Bloc) 90
body and symbolic violence, the 210
Bogotá 7, 12, 71, 75, 83, 114, 122, 186
  Palace of Justice 186
  Sewing Workshop of Memory: Kilometres of Life and Memory project 189–190, 195
Bogota Philharmonic Orchestra 104
Bonanomi, Antonio 101
Borrero, Misael Pastrana 5, 6
Bourdieu, P. 208
British Suffragettes 199
Bruner, J. 17
Buchan, Suzanne 114, 118, 131
Buenaventura 131
Bungard, Claudia xxii, xxiv, 15–34, 133–156, 215–216
Bustamante, Francisco 189
Bustamante, Gabriel 135, 156
Bustos, G. 172

cabildos xxiii
Caguán 9
Cali 86
Camargo, Alberto Lleras 5
cambuches 173

Camilo, Cristian 139
Caribbean 7
Castillejo, A. 24–25, 121
Castoriadis, Cornelius 161
catharsis 130
Cauca xxiii, xxvii, 30, 80–81
  CRIC (Regional Indigenous Council of Cauca) 93–101
  La Susana village 80–81, *81*, 93
  multiple forms of resistance 93–101
  a social laboratory for other struggles in the country 102–104, *103*
Celis, Luis Eduardo xxii, 3–14, 134, 214, 215–217
Center for Human Rights and International Litigation (CEDHUL) 180
Centre of Memory, Peace and Reconciliation (CMPR) 45
CEV *see* Commission for the Clarification of Truth, Coexistence and Non-Repetition
Chará, Virgelina 188–189
Charles, Mathew 108, 120, 132n1
Chase, Susan 16, 225
Chilean *arpilleras* 190
Chilean *arpilleristas* 199
chivas 89, *89*, 91, 92
Chocó 30
Chocué, Eibar Fernández 86
Chocué, Yermi 94
Choiba Handicrafts [Artesanías Choibá] 191
Chronos and *Kairos*: a time to resist and a time to speak out xxv, 214–221
CIDH (Inter-American Commission on Human Rights) 7
CIRC (International Committee of the Red Cross) 22, 164
Ciudad de los Muchachos 108
Civic Guard *see* Guardians of the land, The (*Kiwe Thegnas*)
closing thoughts 222–226
Club el Nogal 75
CMPR (Centre of Memory, Peace and Reconciliation) 45
CNMH *see* National Centre of Historical Memory
CNTI (National Commission of Indigenous Territories) 85

Coca business, The 122, 130
coexisting with war 90–93
Collective Memory 151, 156, 171–176, 222, 224
collective reparation 44
Colombia, eight decades in search of peace and democracy xxii, 3
  1940s: a violence that takes root 3–4
  1950s: decade of horror and deep wounds 4–5
  1960s: exclusions and new rebel identities 5
  1970s: growing mistrust and rebellion 5–6
  1980s: early peace dialogues and intersecting violence 6–8
  1990s: political peace and expansion of violence 8–9
  consequences of conflict 28
  displaced populations 210
  National Centre for Historical Memory (CNMH) 15, 24, 28, 29, 45, 182
  new millennium: war and the dismantling of powerful military structures 9–10
  second decade: illusions of peace and new cycle of violence 11–12
  third decade: transformation and 'total peace' with democratic transition 12, 134
  notes 13–14
  see also Commission for the Clarification of Truth (CEV); weaving memory and unweaving trauma: textile narratives on conflict in Colombia
Colombian Federation of Special Sports (FEDES) *Sewing Workshop of Memory* 189
Colombian State 22, 158–167, 169–170
  see also Agreement signed between Colombian state and FARC-EP guerrillas in 2016
Colombian Virtual Archive of Human Rights 151
Combatant Dolls Fighting for Peace and Life 191
Commission for the Clarification of Truth, Coexistence and Non-Repetition (CEV) 24, 29, 35n2, 108, 134, 216, 223
  Basta Ya! [Enough already] Report xxvi, 13n3, 26, 57, 208
  Final Report 85
  Hay futuro si hay verdad 26
  La verdad de las mujeres 26
Communist Party 5, 7
CONADEP (National Commission for the Disappearance of Persons (Argentina)) 76
Connerton, P. 30, 54, 152
Conquest of America 95
Correa, José Vicente Arizmendi 214–221
COVIJUPA 194
CRIC (Regional Indigenous Council of Cauca) 93–104
Cuban Revolution 5
Cundinamarca 30
cut-out animation 116
Cxhab Wala Kiwe (ACIN) 104

data analysis and organisation **47–50, 51–52**
Day I saw the light, The 120
Day of the Dead 93
de Roux, Francisco xxi, 28
De Salvo, L. 225
Denzin, N. 223
Department of Vaupés 109
Diario de Paz xxiv, 151–152
Díaz, Blanca Nubia 188
Díaz, Natalie: *Postcolonial Love Poem* 207
Digital Archive of Testimonial Textiles (ADTTC) xxvi, 191–192, 194
DIH (International Humanitarian Law) 140
Dindicué, Benjamín 94
'direct *testimonios*' 134
Displacement 195, 210–211
Doris (mother) 187, 195–196
drug-trafficking 8
Duque, Ivan 161–162

ecotourism 174–175
education 174
Elkin, Jhon 139
ELN (National Liberation Army) 5, 9
embassy takeover 6–7
'embroidery is to unite' 189–192
emotional *receta* 55
empowerment 15

Enough already [Basta Ya!] Report xxvi, 13n3, 26, 57, 208
Enrique, Luis 142
EPL (People's Liberation Army) 5, 7
Erll, Astrid 131
ESAP (Graduate School of Public Administration) 174
Escobar, Pablo 8
Estrada, F. 169, 170
ETCR *see* Tierra Grata Territorial Training and Reincorporation Space
Eternal conflicts in the Nasa territory, The 90
'ex-combatants' 161
'exemplary memory' 152
exploratory research 45–46

Fals-Borda, O. 32–33
FARC-EP guerrillas 22, 215
 see also Agreement signed between Colombian state and FARC-EP guerrillas in 2016
FARC (Revolutionary Armed Forces of Colombia—People's Army) 7, 8, 9–10, 11, 29, 83, 92, 99, 101, 103, 158–159, 216
Father Antonio got tired of burying the dead 101
FEDES *see* Colombian Federation of Special Sports
Feliu, J. 32, 33, 223–224
Fernández, J.W. 33
FESCOL (Friedrich-Ebert-Stiftung Foundation in Colombia) 81
fetish object 188
FIV (International Victims Forum) **49**
Foley 117
Folman, Ari 114
forgetting 27, 59
freedom 180
Friedrich-Ebert-Stiftung Foundation in Colombia (FESCOL) 81

Gaitán, Jorge Eliécer 4
Gamson, W. 225
García, Diosa 198, 199
García-González 11 33–34
García Márquez, Gabriel 6, 22, 27
Garzón, M.A. 17, 31, 58, 60
Geertz, Clifford 223
Giraldo, Alejandro 148–149
Giraldo, Felip Hernando Restrepo 147
Giraldo, María Theresa 139, 148–149, 150
Girón, Claudia 189, 195, 196
Global Challenges Research Fund 108
Global Fund for Women 180
GMH *see* Historical Memory Group
González, Cecilia Traslaviña xxiii–xxiv, 24, 108–132
González Arango, Isabel xxvi, 190, 191–192
González Pinzón, Blanca Yaneth xxii–xxiii, xxv, 15–34, 208, 215, 222–226
Governmental Agency for Reincorporation and Normalisation, 2022 (ARN) 158, 161–167
Goya, Francisco de 214
Graduate School of Public Administration (ESAP) 174
Guardia de Toribío 101, 103
Guardians of the land, The (Kiwe Thegnas) xxiii, 88–89, 95–97, 96, 97, 99, 104
Guarín Morales, Orlando de Jesús 146–147
Guatemala Commission for Historical Clarification (1999) 153
Guayacan Handicrafts [Artesanías Guayacán] 191, 192
Guzmán, Laura 145, 148, 150, 153
Guzmán Pérez, Cristina and Yuri 139

habitus 210
Halbwachs, Maurice 27, 29, 114, 117, 172, 225
Han, Byung-Chul 169, 171
Havana Agreement 216
Heaven does not abandon me 138, 139
Hernández, Dr. Esperanza 159
Hernández, F. 54
High Council for Social and Economic Reintegration of Armed Groups and Individuals (ACR) **47**
historical context of Colombian armed conflict and theoretical approaches to analysing its narratives 1, 25
 Colombia, eight decades in search of peace and democracy 3–14
 map vii
Historical Memory 224

contributions of *Testimonios* 23–25
resistance, survival and knowledge 28–34
role of subjectivity in 25–28
see also National Centre of Historical Memory (CNMH)
Historical Memory Group (GMH) 54, 57, 58, 62
Hobsbawm, E. 159
Holzapfel, Ursula (COVIJUPA) 194
homicides of indigenous people 85, *85*
Hope of the Úsuga brothers, The 141–142
Human Rights 140
Hurtado, Álvaro, Gómez 8

I was leaving behind my life as I knew it 120, 122, 124, *125*
I will never forget your name 47, 138
'imaginary' 161
Imbachí, Oswaldo 101
'import substitution policy' 4
In their own handwriting 154–156, *155*
incorporation 84
INDEPAZ (Institute of Development and Peace Studies) 170
Indigenous Guard xxiii, 80, 93, 95–100, *96*, *97*, *99*, 103, 104
industrialisation 4
Information System on Sociopolitical Violence Against Indigenous Peoples (SIVOSPI) 85
Inglis, J.T. 32
Ingold, Tim 200
inscription 30
Institute of Development and Peace Studies (INDEPAZ) 170
integral reparation 44
intellectual colonialism 32
Inter-American Commission on Human Rights (CIDH) 7
internal displacement 56
International Committee of the Red Cross (CIRC) 22, 164
International Day of Indigenous Peoples 85
International Humanitarian Law (DIH) 140
International Organisation for Migration (OIM) **49**
International Victims Forum (FIV) **49**

introduction xxi–xxvi
Inzá 90

Jambaló 91–92
Jara, R. 224
Jelin, E. 152, 167–168, 171
Jensen, S. 225
JEP (Special Jurisdiction for Peace) 11
journalism 82–84, 214
Juan Tama 86

Kairos 217
Kentridge, William 124
Kiwe Thegnas see Guardians of the land, The
knowledge *see* resistance, survival and knowledge
Kolawole 01 32
Kueke neehnwee'sx xxiii

La Dorada 182
La Fuerza del Ombligo see 'Walking the Word' with the Nasa people: perspective from narrative of *The Strength of the Umbilical Cord*
La Gaitana 95
La Lagua Siberia 94
La Quintinada 83
La Salle University 158–159
La Susana village 80–81, *81*, 93
Labov, W. 16–17
Lame, José Navia xxiii, 80–107
Lame, Quintín 95, 215
land and subsistence allowances 161–167
language 169
Lara, Patricia xxi, 28
Lavarca, Jorge 180
Law 975 of 2005 (*Law of Justice and Peace*) 44
Law 1448 of 2011 (*Law on Victims and Land Restitution*) 44–45, 64, 138, 140, 153, 215, 216
Leal, Jaime Pardo 7
Leclercq, Paul 200
Legislative Act 1 of 2017 25
Leiva, Camilo 182
Leongómez, Carlos Pizarro 8
Lesbian, Gay, Bisexual, Trans, Intersex, Queer and Other Identities (LGBTIQ+) 66, 93

Letters from the jungle 109
Liberal Party 4, 5
Lillis, Theresa xxi–xxvi, 207–212
Lincoln, Y. 223
'literal memory' 152
literature 18, 21, 22, 156
local knowledge 32
Lopera, G. 31
López, Beatriz Elena Arias 190
López, C. 134
López, Gledys 186
López, Jorge Iván 153
López-Moreno, L. 165

M-19 Democratic Alliance (ADM-19) 6–7, 8, 83
MAFAPO (*Mothers of False Positives from Soacha and Bogotá*) 186
Manuel Cepeda Vargas Foundation 189
map vii
MAQL (Quintín Lame Armed Movement) 82–83, 215
Márquez, Francia 12
'*matacho*' [poorly drawn picture] 123
material turn 200
Maza, Guillermo Garcia 212
McCay, Winsor: *Sinking on the Lusitania* (1918) 114
Medellín 138
Medellín cartel 9
media 122–123
Mejía, Juan Luis 156
memory xxiv–xxv, 15, 31, 131, 134, 224
  acts of memory 172
  Collective Memory 151, 156, 171–176, 222, 224
  as a connection 128, 168
  contributions of *Testimonios* to Historical Memory 23–25
  defined xxi
  as the future 171–176
  role of subjectivity in Historical Memory 25–28
  selective memory 27
  workshops 134–135, 138, 145, 216
  see also weaving memory and unweaving trauma: textile narratives on conflict in Colombia
memory as the future *see* voices of FARC-EP reincorporated combatants in the construction of peace imaginaries

Memory of silence 153
Méndez, Gloria Astrid 185
Mending the new 191
Mendoza, J. 30
Meneses, Blanca Nieves 182–185, *183*, 186–187, 189
Meneses, Nancy 182, 183
mental health 185
Menza, Luis Alberto 99
Mesa, Salomón Chavarría 142
Mi historia: la niñez que peleó la guerra en Colombia 108–109
Mignard, Pierre 214
Ministry of Science and Technology (Minciencias) 190
Missing Persons Search Unit (UBPD) 11
Montoya, Pablo 19, 54, 224
moral reparation 44
Mothers of False Positives from Soacha and Bogotá (MAFAPO) 186
Movimiento Armado Quintín Lame (MAQL) 82–83, 215
Muñoz, C.A. 28
Muñoz-González, G. 17, 24, 173
Muraro, L. 196
Museo Casa de la Memoria de Medellín 190
My Story: the children who fought war in Colombia 108–109

Naldini, P. 197
narrative as emotional resource for empowerment of survivors of the Colombian armed conflict
  concept of 'Symbolic Reparation' 44–45
  consequences of war as engine of transformation and elaboration of imaginaries of the future 67–75, **68**
  data analysis and organisation 46–53, **47–50, 51–52**
  exploratory research 45–46
  'I' and 'We' in narratives as a contribution to memory and search for truth and justice 61–66
  intelligibility 17
  narrative as a liberating and healing action 53–61
  notes 76
narratives of the Colombian armed conflict 102–104

Walking the Word' with the Nasa people: perspective from narrative of *The strength of the umbilical cord* 80–107
narratives to transform war imaginaries in Colombia *see* animation workshop with ex-guerrilla children
Narváez, J. 159
Nasa Cshacsha 104
Nasa (Paez) People 29, 80–81, 85, 196, 210
  anthem 99
  coexisting with war 90–93, 215
  history 95
  magical-political 86–90
  multiple forms of resistance 15, 93–101, 216
  survivors of the conflict xxv–xxvi, 85, 85–86, 92–93
  Thê Walas xxiii, 86–87, 88, 89, 89–90, 100–101, 104
  transformations of 104, *105*
  women 93–94, 129, 166–167
Nasa Yuwe language 93
National Apprenticeship Service (SENA) 163
National Association of Peasant Users (ANUC) 5
National Centre of Historical Memory (CNMH) 15, 24, 28, 29, 45, 182
  Oropéndola project 182
National Commission for the Disappearance of Persons (Argentina) (CONADEP) 76
National Commission of Indigenous Territories (CNTI) 85
National Constituent Assembly 8
National Front 5
National Indigenous Organisation of Colombia (ONIC) 102, 104, 215
National Liberation Army (ELN) 5, 9
National Network of Weavers for Memory and Life 198–199
National Open and Distance University (UNAD) 162
National Popular Alliance (ANAPO) 5–6
national security 8
National University 191
Native American cultures 34
Navia, José 91–92

Navia-Lame, J. 100
Neehnwee'sx xxiii
Nejwes'x 95
Network of Weavers for Memory and Life 190
new millennium: war and dismantling of powerful mlitary structures 9–10
Newton Fund 190
Ngozi-Adichie, Chimamanda 15, 29
Nieto, Patricia 54, 135, 137, 138–139, 151
Non-Governmental Organisations (ONG) 23, 45, 169
'non-repetition' 25, 208
Nora, Pierre 23–24, 26, 27, 214
Nussbaum, M. 223

Observatory on Memory and Conflict (OMC) 85
Ochoa, Manuela 182, 189, 190
Office of the High Commissioner for Peace 158
OIM (International Organisation for Migration) 49
OMC (Observatory on Memory and Conflict) 85
One gets used to violence 117–118, 119, 126, *127*
ONG *see* Non-Governmental Organisations
ONIC *see* National Indigenous Organisation of Colombia
ONU (United Nations) 86
oral history 24
Orinoco 7
Orinoquia 6
Oropéndola project 182
Orozco, Mario Ramírez xxiv
Osorio, Luz Dary 182
Our Victims tapestry 192–196, *193*, *194*, 197

Pablo Montoya22 54
Pacific 7–8, 129
Paez people *see* Nasa (Paez) people
Pagés, J. 24
Palace of Justice, Bogotá 189, 192
paramilitarism 7
Parranderos del Cauca 4 + 3 104
Pastrana, President Andrés 9
Pastrana, President Misael 9
Patiño, Carlos 84
Patrick, E. 114

Patriotic Union (UP) 7, 8, 186
Paz, Octavio 220
Peña, Sandra 94
People's Liberation Army (EPL) 5, 7
Perassi, Emilia xxiv–xxv, xxvi, 179–201
Persepolis 114–115
Petro, Gustavo 12
Phoenix Refuge: The End of a Night of Agony, The 74
Phoenix Women 53, 210
Pinilla, General Gustavo Rojas 5, 6
Pinilla, General Rojas 4
Pinochet, Augusto 190
placed resources 210
political action 199
political system 4
political violence 185
Pontificia Universidad Javeriana 109
positional narratives 34
possibilities of animation to expand imaginaries around violence 125–131
post-traumatic stress disorder 185
Programme of Attention to the Victims of the Armed Confliect in Medellín 135
psychological support 113
Pulecio, Ingrid Betancourt 10

Quilcué, Aída 94
quilt of remembrances *183*, 189–192
Quintín Lame Armed Movement (MAQL) 82–83, 215

Rajasekaran, B. *et al.* 32
Ramírez, Ana María 189
Ramírez, Y. 180
Ramírez-Gómez, L. 183, 184, 216
Ramírez-Orozco, Mario 158–177, 216, 221
Ramos, Dagoberto 84
Raye-Garlock, L. 188
'Reasoned Historical Memory' 155–156
Recomenzar [Begin Again] tapestry 197–199, *198*
reconciliation 27–28
Red and Black 122
Regional Indigenous Council of Cauca (CRIC) 93–104
regions 3, 13n1
Regreso a casa 95

'reincorporated' individuals 160–161
remembering, purpose of 152
resistance *181*
  forms of 15, 93–101, *96*, *97*, 216
  of women 180–182, *181*
resistance, survival and knowledge
  future expectations 30–31
  survivor empowerment 28–30
  transforming knowledge and adopting new ways of knowing 31–34
respect 109, 113
Restrepo, Camilo Torres 5
Restrepo, Carlos Lleras 5
return 58–59
Return Home 84, 88–89
Revolutionary Armed Forces of Colombia – People's Army *see* FARC
Reyes-Aparicio, P. 17, 27, 59, 225
Riaño, P. 31, 224
Ricardo Franco group 83
Richardson, L. 223
Ricoeur, P. 16, 17, 217
Rieff, D. 27
rights 3, 13n2
Riochiquito, Cauca 90
Rivara-Kamaji, G. 63, 129
Roa-Mendoza, C.P. 170
Rocha, Angélica 159
Rocha-Vivas, M. 184
Rodríguez Orejuela brothers 9
Roe, Anabelle 114
Roehelp 115
Rojaz, Bibiana 124
Romir 83
Rosario University 108
Rosmira 142
rotoscoping 116
Rubens, Peter Paul 214
Rueda, A.J. 155
Rueda, E. 28, 33
Ruiz, Luz Adriana 146

Said, E.W. 32
Salazar, A. 91
Salazar-Henao, M. 165
San Francisco 81
San José de Oriente, Tierra Grata, Cesar Department 29, 158
Santos, Juan Manuel 11
Satrapi, Marjane 114

Saviours, The 115, *115*, 120, 126, *127*, 127–128
Schopenhauer, Arthur 214
Scollon, R. and Scollon, S. 210
second decade of 21st century: illusions of peace and new cycle of violence 11–12
Secue, Cristóbal 94
selective memory 27
Semana Magazaine 101
SENA (National Apprenticeship Service) 163
Serpa, Horacio 8
Sewing Workshop, Memory and Mental Health of Medellín 198
Sewing Workshop of Memory: Kilometres of Life and Memory project 189–190, 195
Sewing Workshop Weavers for Memory 191
Shamans *see Thê Walas*
SIVOSPI (Information System on Sociopolitical Violence Against Indigenous Peoples) 85
Social Memory 151
social ties 28
Sousa Santos 31
South Bloc (Bloque Sur) 90
Spanish language xxvi
Special Jurisdiction for Peace (JEP) 11
stop-motion animation 116
storyboarding 123–124, *124*
Strejilevich, N. 29
Strength of the umbilical cord, The 80–107
subaltern testimonios 18, 19, 21, 134
subjectivity 25–28
'suffering-resisting subjects' 186
survivor empowerment 28–30
survivors xxv–xxvi, 85, 85–86, 92–93
  see also narrative as emotional resource for empowerment of survivors of the Colombian armed conflict; resistance, survival and knowledge
Symbolic Reparation xxiii, 43, 44–45, 46, 55

Tacueyó 81, 91, 94
Tagore, Rabindranath 214
testimonial textiles 190, 191, 192

testimonios xxi, xxii, xxiii–xxiv, xxv–xxvi, xxvii, 13n3, 15, 25, 27, 214, 222, 224–226
  analogue animation 123
  and Historical Memory 23–25
  narrative value of 54
  themes developed for the animations 109, **110–112**
testimonios of armed conflict survivors: participants in narrative workshops in Medellín xxi, 134–135
  diverse effects of writing *testimonios* 145–151
  inscription, importance and contributions to sociopolitical transformation 151–154
  'Interview' 138
  methodology of research **137**, 137–138
  organisation of original workshops (2006—2010) 135–136, **136**
  reflections on being a 'victim'/'victimisation' 138–145
  '*Testimonio*' 138
  conclusion: value of *In their own handwriting* and contributions to other experiences 154–156
  notes 156
Testimony 16, 31, 222
  contributions to Historical Memory 23–25
textile turn 200
Textimoning and textile work 189
The coco business 130
Thê Walas (Shamans) xxiii, 86–87, 88, 89, 89–90, 100–101, 104
theoretical approaches to analysing conflict narratives xxii, 15
  Memory 23–28
  modalities for collecting *testimonios*/contributions to social justice in post-conflict contexts 19–20
  notes 35
  resistance, survival and knowledge 28–34
  topics of convergence between Narrative and Testimony 16–23
  notes 35
third decade of 21st century: transformation and 'total peace' with democratic transition 12, 134

Tierra Grata Territorial Training and Reincorporation Space (ETCR) xxiv, 22, 29, 159, 162–163, 169, 216
Tierradentro 104
Times of listening 191
Tinker Foundation 137
Tocafondo, Gianluigi 124
Toconás, Rosa Elena 99
Todorov, T. 152
topics of convergence between Narrative and Testimony 16–19
   development of testimony in Colombia 20–23
   modalities for collecting *testimonios* and contributions to social justice in post-conflict contexts 19–20
Toribío 80, 81–82, 86, 91, 92, 101
translations xxvi
Traslaviña, Cecilia 216
trauma 185
trusting relationship 123
Truth Commission *see* Commission for the Clarification of Truth, Coexistence and Non-Repetition (CEV)

UAIIN (Autonomous Indigenous Intercultural University) 104
UBPD (Missing Persons Search Unit) 11
UK Arts and Humanities Research Council 108
Ulcué, Álvaro 94
Ulcué, José María 94
UNAD (National Open and Distance University) 162
Union of Bogotá Sewing Workshops 188–189
United Nations (ONU) 86
United Self-Defence Forces of Colombia (AUC) 9
Universidad de La Salle 216
Universidad del Rosario, Bogotá 108
University of Antioquia 190, 191
University of Leeds 108
University of Los Andes 191
UP *see* Patriotic Union
Uribe, Horacio Serpa 10
Uribe, María Teresa 156
Úsuga, Octavio 141–142, 145, 152

Valencia, Feliciano 93
Valencia, Sofía 94, 98
Vásquez Astudillo, María Efigenia 94–95
Vélez, Álvaro Uribe 10
Vélez-Rendón, J.C. 59, 151
'victim' 140
Victim Assistance Programme (2005-2010) 155–156
'victimisation' 140, 185
Victims and Land Restitution Law (Law 1448 of 2011) 138
Vidal, H. 224
Vignolo, Paolo 128
violence 3–9, 11–12, 208
   second decade: illusions of peace and new cycle of violence 224
   symbolic violence 210
Violeta (film) 180–182, *181*
Violi, M.P. 182
Vitonás, Arquímedes 97, 98
Vives-Riera 11 34
voice 209
voices of FARC-EP reincorporated combatants in the construction of peace imaginaries 158–159
   context of agreement signed between Colombian state and FARC-EP guerrillas in 2016 159–161
   difficulties of transition from combatants armed with rifles to combatants armed with discourse 161–167
   memory as the future 171–176
   obstacles to construction of new social imaginaries 167–171
   final considerations 176–177
   notes 177
voicing experiences of conflict and violence: placed, dis-placed and re-placed resources xxv, 207–09
   the body and symbolic violence 210
   (dis/re) placed resources and subjectivities 210–211
   semiotic resources towards *No Repetición* and transformation 211–212
   voice 209

'Walking the Word' with the Nasa people: perspective from narrative of *The strength of the umbilical cord* 80–107

Cauca, a social laboratory for other struggles in the country 102–104, *103*
coexisting with war 90–93
the journalist: returning to my roots 82–84
to keep on living *105*, 105–106
La Susana village 80–81, *81*, 93
the magical-political 86–90
multiple forms of resistance 93–101, *96*, *97*
Nasa people, survivors of the conflict xxv–xxvi, *85*, 85–86, 92–93
San Francisco 81
Tacueyó 81, 91, 94
Toribío 80, 81–82, 86, 91, 92, 101
'walking the word' 81–82
where it all happens *80*, 80–81
notes 106–107
Waltz with Bashir (2008) 114–115
war
coexisting with war 90–93
as engine of transformation and elaboration of imaginaries of the future 67–68, **68**
new millennium: war and the dismantling of powerful military structures 182
Ward, P. 114
We all knew they would come back for me 122, 131
We were the children of El Jordán 142–143

weaving memory and unweaving trauma: textile narratives on conflict in Colombia 29–30, 93, 216
blankets that do not let people sleep 179–180
'embroidery is to unite' 189–192
materialising absence 182–189
ontology of the textile 184
textualities/textilities 196–200
Violeta (film) 180–182, *181*
weaving a common history 192–196
notes 200–201
Where I stepped, the grass still grows 138, 141–142
witnessing 185–186
Wolff, Antonio Navarro 8
women 93–94, 129, 166–167
Association of Women Defenders of Water and Life (AMARÚ) 191
dehumanisation of 169
resistance 180–182, *181*
Women Weaving Dreams and Flavours of Peace 186, 191, *194*
workshop: a meeting to create collectively 116–117
classical animation 116–117
cut-out animation 116
rotoscoping 116
stop-motion 116
Woven life, The 190

Yaya, Lilia 186

For Product Safety Concerns and Information please contact our EU Authorised Representative:

Easy Access System Europe

Mustamäe tee 50

10621 Tallinn

Estonia

gpsr.requests@easproject.com

www.ingramcontent.com/pod-product-compliance
Lightning Source LLC
Chambersburg PA
CBHW070027010526
44117CB00011B/1734